Before They Were
Belly Dancers

Before They Were Belly Dancers

European Accounts of Female Entertainers in Egypt, 1760–1870

KATHLEEN W. FRASER

McFarland & Company, Inc., Publishers
Jefferson, North Carolina

ISBN 978-0-7864-9433-0 (softcover : acid free paper) ∞
ISBN 978-1-4766-1916-3 (ebook)

BRITISH LIBRARY CATALOGUING DATA ARE AVAILABLE

© 2015 Kathleen W. Fraser. All rights reserved

No part of this book may be reproduced or transmitted in any form or by any means, electronic or mechanical, including photocopying or recording, or by any information storage and retrieval system, without permission in writing from the publisher.

On the cover: *Egyptian Dancer in a Tent* by Willem de Famars Testas, 1863 (Rijksmuseum, Amsterdam)

Printed in the United States of America

McFarland & Company, Inc., Publishers
Box 611, Jefferson, North Carolina 28640
www.mcfarlandpub.com

To Jenny,
Laura, Miriam
and Hannah

Not chaste, they are by no means common.
—William George Browne
Travels in Africa, Egypt and Syria from the year 1792 to 1798

Table of Contents

List of Illustrations — xi
Preface — 1

Section One: Background

1. On Writing This Book — 9
2. Selected Egyptian History—the Study Period — 15
3. Writers and Painters in Egypt from 1760 to 1870 — 18

Section Two: Setting the Stage

4. A Name for the Dance and a Name for the Dancer — 33
5. The Low Reputation of Female Entertainers — 43
6. The Geography of Going to the Show — 48

Section Three: Going to the Show— Professionals at Work

7. The Corporation of Female Singers—the Chanteuses — 59
8. Identifying the Raqqâsin, Corporation 200 — 64
9. Identifying the Ghawâzî, Corporation 192 — 72
10. Male Performers—Dancers and Musicians — 81

Section Four: The Lives of Female Entertainers

11. Relationships with Various Groups in Egyptian Society — 89

12. Professional Relationships with the Audience	99
13. Training	105
14. Economic Position of Female Entertainers	108

Section Five: Biographies

15. Thirty-One Female Dancers and One Male	125

Section Six: Gossip, Hearsay, Rumors and Myths

16. The Missing 'Awâlim	147
17. The Massacre of "The Four Hundred"	151
18. Banning the Dance in Muhammad Ali's Egypt	158
19. Myths of Origins of Female Dancers and Singers	167

Section Seven: Building the Aesthetic of Performance

20. A Costume Benchmark Set by Edward Lane	177
21. The Musicianship of Dancers	200
22. The Aesthetic of Dance Movements	205

Section Eight: Choreography and Performance

23. Six Choreographic Elements Basic to the Dance	215
24. Extending the Definition of Choreography	219
25. Three Identifiable Dances	223
26. Accessory Dances	236

Epilogue	241
Appendix One: Biographical Facts About Selected 18th- and Early 19th-Century Travel Writers and Artists	253
Appendix Two: Travelers' Terms for Female Entertainers: Selected Passages by Date of Travel	260
Chapter Notes	265
Bibliography	281
Index	291

List of Illustrations

Fig. 1.	Richard Pococke. *Dancing Women of Egypt*. c. 1738.	13
Fig. 2.	Wilhelm Baurenseind. *Représentation des Danseuses et de Leur Musiciens à Kahira* (Representation of Dancers and Their Musicians at Cairo). c. 1761 (From Baurenfeind, dessinateur, *Illustrations de Voyage en Arabie* [Amsterdam-Utrecht: S.J. Baalde-J. Van Schoonhoven, 1776]).	19
Fig. 3.	Luigi Mayer. *An Egyptian Ball, at Ned Sili*. c. 1798 (From Luigi Mayer, *Views in Egypt* [London: R. Boyer, 1813]. Reproduction by permission of the Buffalo and Erie County Public Library, Buffalo, New York).	20
Fig. 4.	J.J. Rifaud. *Danse d' Almées et leur musique* (Dance of the Almées and Their Music). c. 1825 (With permission of the Société Royal d'Archéologie, d'Histoire et de Folklore de Nivelles et du Brabant Wallon).	21
Fig. 5.	Vivant Denon. *Almée*. c. 1800 (With permission of the Royal Ontario Museum © ROM).	51
Fig. 6.	Egyptian Copt (unidentified). *Almés*. c. 1800 (From Commission des sciences et arts d'Egypte. *Description de l'Egypte* [Paris: Imprimerie imp., 1809–1822]. Courtesy of the Thomas Fisher Rare Book Library, University of Toronto).	70
Fig. 7.	J. Riudavets. *Feria de Tanta* (Tanta Fair). c. 1880 (From Eduardo Toda y Güell, *A Través del Egipto* [Madrid: El Progresso Editorial, 1889]).	73
Fig. 8.	Heinrich von Mayr. *Kostueme von Oberaegypten* (Costume from Upper Egypt). c. 1838 (From Maximilian Duke of Bavaria, Herzogs. *Wanderung nach dem Orient im Jahre 1838* [Munich: Verlag W. Ludwig, 1978, repr.]. Image reprinted here courtesy of the publisher).	77
Fig. 9.	André Dutertre. *Almés ou danseuses publiques* (Almés or public dancers). c. 1800 (From Commission des sciences et arts d'Egypte. *Description de l'Egypte* [Paris: Imprimerie imp., 1809–1822]. Courtesy of the Thomas Fisher Rare Book Library, University of Toronto).	97
Fig. 10.	W.H. Bartlett. Untitled. 1845 (From W.H. Bartlett, *The Nile boat; or glimpses of the land of Egypt* [London: Arthur Hall, Virtue, 1849]).	100
Fig. 11.	J.J. Rifaud. *Repas de noces d'un chaik el beled (de Thebaïde)* (Wedding Breakfast of a Village Shaik of Luxor). c. 1825 (With permission of the Société Royal d'Archéologie, d'Histoire et de Folklore de Nivelles et du Brabant Wallon).	102

List of Illustrations

Fig. 12.	Frank and Frances Carpenter Collection. *Egypt: Dancing Girl.* c. 1890 (Library of Congress, Prints & Photographs Division [LC-USZ62–87592]).	119
Fig. 13.	Jean-Léon Gérôme. *Almée.* c. 1868 (From Paul Lenoir, *Le Fayoum, le Sinai et Petra: expedition dans la moyenne Egype et l'Arabie petrée, sous la direction de J.L. Gérôme* [Paris: H. Plon, 1872]).	139
Fig. 14.	Willem de Famars Testas. *Egyptische danseres in een tent* (Egyptian Dancer in a Tent). 1863 (Rijksmuseum, Amsterdam).	141
Fig. 15.	Jean-Léon Gérôme. *Danse du Sabre, from the painting by Jean Leon Gérôme* (partial) (Saber Dance). c. 1875 (From *Photograuves After Paintings by Jean-Léon Gérôme* [New York: D. Appleton & Co., 187- or later]).	142
Fig. 16.	David Roberts. *Dancing Girls at Cairo.* c. 1839 (From David Roberts, *Egypt and Nubia* [London: F.G. Moon, 1849]. Courtesy of the Thomas Fisher Rare Book Library, University of Toronto).	162
Fig. 17.	Edward Lane. *Dancing Girls (Ghawa'zee or Gha'zee'yahs).* c. 1840 (From E.W. Lane, *An Account of the Manners and Customs of the Modern Egyptians* [London: A.M. Nattali, 1846]).	178
Fig. 18.	Émile Prisse d'Avennes. *Ghawazi or Dancing Girls.* c. 1835.	180
Fig. 19.	Eugène Fromentin. *Danse d'Almées, à Sihout, d'après un croquis de M. Stop* (Dance of the Almées at Asyût, After a Sketch by Mr. Stop). c. 1869 (From Djamila Henni-Chebra and Christian Poché, *Les danses dans le monde arabe* [Paris: L'Harmattan, 1996]. Image reprinted here courtesy of the publisher).	185
Fig. 20.	Thomas Gold Appleton. *A Ghawazee.* c. 1875 (From Thomas Gold Appleton, *A Nile Journey by T.G. Appleton* [London: MacMillan, 1876]).	186
Fig. 21a.	Alexandre Bida. *Danseuse Almé* (Dancing Almé). c. 1855 (© Victoria and Albert Museum, London).	188
Fig. 21b.	Alexandre Bida. *Joueuse de Tarabouka* (Girl Performing on the Darabukka). c. 1855 (© Victoria and Albert Museum, London).	189
Fig. 22.	Brandin. *Almée, danseuse au Caire* (Almée, Dancer at Cairo) (Garnier Frères Edit., Paris. Imp. Dufrénoy, Paris).	191
Fig. 23.	Gustav Richter. *Egyptian Dancing Women—after Gustav Richter.* c. 1861 (From *The Aldine, the Art Journal of America* vol. 9 [1879]).	192
Fig. 24.	Louis Forbin. *La danse de l'Almée à Beni Souëf* (Dance of the Almée at Beni Suef). c. 1818 (From Louis Forbin, *Voyage dans le Levant en 1817 et 1818* [Paris: Imprimerie royale, 1819]. Courtesy of the Thomas Fisher Rare Book Library, University of Toronto).	194
Fig. 25.	Jean-Léon Gérôme (1824–1904) French, *Dance of the Almeh*, 1863. Oil on wood panel. 19 ¾ × 32 inches (The Dayton Art Institute. Gift of Robert Badenhop, 1951.15).	198
Fig. 26.	George Montbard. *Ghâwazi dansant la danse de "la guêpe"* (Ghâwazi Dancing the Dance of *The Bee*). c. 1880 (From Georges Montbard [Charles A. Loyes], *En Egypte: notes et croquis d'un artiste* [Paris: Monde illustrée, [18—]).	210
Fig. 27.	Alfred-Henri Darjou. *La Danse de la Gargoulette* (Pot Dance). 1869 (From Florian Pharaon, *Le Caire et la Haute Egypte* [Paris: E. Dentu, 1872]. Princeton University Library).	239

Preface

In 1896, my paternal great-grandmother and her only child, my grandmother, set out from Peoria, Illinois, on their Grand Tour of Europe, an extended vacation that eventually included a Cook's cruise of Egypt's Nile. At the dock in Asyût, under a bright February sun, my great-grandmother wrote in her diary:

> Boats were drawn up along the shore; camels with huge loads went by and altogether it was a strange and lively scene. Today just before the steamer started it was still more so. Many freight dahabeahs [boats] were unloaded onto the camels and men with pig- and goat-skin water bags were filling them from the river. A great gaunt, pink-legged ostrich strode by. A dancing girl with her face tattooed danced on the sand to the music of a coconut fiddle.

On reading this, I first came to know that my grandmothers had seen one of the famous dancing girls of Egypt in performance. I was thrilled to find this long-neglected diary while I was well into the research for this book, for at that point I realized that my own family had taken part in the story I was trying to reconstruct, that is, an account of the professional female entertainers of 18th- and 19th-century Egypt.

As its primary goal, then, this book begins to fill in the historical blanks for a Middle Eastern dance form often known today in the Middle East as *raqs sharki*, or *raqs baladi*, and in Western countries as belly dance. To this end I focus on one country, Egypt, and one time period, 1760 to 1870. Eye-witness accounts written by European travelers, the major source of primary data still remaining to us as modern researchers, have provided most of my material. A great deal of the travel literature on Egypt is in French—if I have used a French source then all translations are my own, unless I am working with an English edition of a French original.

The specific aims of the book were several. I wanted to shape the almost-inexhaustible travel accounts into a coherent whole, one that would begin to provide a meaningful picture of Egyptian female entertainers and their lives. I wanted to be able to see Egyptian female entertainers of the period as professionals in the arts, not just as unnamed "ethnic" dancers plus one or two identified women of dubious reputation. I wanted to create an analysis of the contexts of this dance, the many times when and places where it took place legitimately within the context of Egyptian society for a wide variety of audiences. I particularly wanted to focus on actual performances—was it possible after all this time to recreate choreography?

The need to evaluate many primary sources, both texts and illustrations, as acceptable sources for this dance history resulted in my appreciation of the travelers included here as fascinating in their own right. The many men and the few women authors who appear in this book seem to evoke the extraordinary spirit of the period under study. They were daring, inquisitive, competent, and opinionated, and open to a world whose political and cultural boundaries were rapidly shifting immediately before and after the Napoleonic order. And they knew their experiences would be eagerly shared by a broad reading public. As witnesses and recorders of this dance, they have become embedded in this dance's history. I wanted to make sure that my readers appreciated them as people integral to the story.

Karin van Nieuwkerk's (1995) *A Trade Like Any Other: Female Singers and Dancers in Egypt* stands as a unique sociological study of modern Egyptian dancers who perform on the modest wedding circuits. Nieuwkerk began her book with two chapters devoted to accounts of earlier female performers in 19th- and early 20th-century Egypt (using Europeans' travel accounts), and she highlighted many significant topics for future historical research in this field. My own work owes much to hers, particularly to the dignity she accorded her female respondents' lives. As a sociologist, Nieuwkerk was primarily interested in the field of occupations, however, and for this reason did not attempt to deal with the topic of the dance and actual performances as I do.

Djamila Henni-Chebra and Christian Poché's (1996) *Les danses dans le monde arabe ou l'héritage des almées* (*Dances in the Arab World or the Patrimony of the Almées*) also used travel writings. Two of the historical essays in this anthology cover dance in Egypt in the 19th century (and later) and discuss the place of dance in early Islam. I have found the material and insights particularly important in writing my own book—for example, performance is discussed—but I have gone beyond these essays in producing a full-length work.

Sherifa Zuhur's (1998, 2001) two important anthologies on the visual and performing arts of the Middle East, *Images of Enchantment: Visual and Perform-*

ing Arts of the Middle East, and *Colors of Enchantment: Theater, Dance, Music, and the Visual Arts of the Middle East,* contain seven essays on dance. Three of these deal with Egypt, but only one with the past (by Nieuwkerk, in a synopsis of the material in her earlier book). Other essays cover present practices in Yemen, Saudi Arabia and the Gulf, and the Sudan. A seventh essay deals with Orientalism in North America in the nineteenth century. A search of Zuhur's exhaustive bibliography reveals that the topic of dance in the Middle East does not compare in popularity with the topics of music, theater, and film, for example, and shows the need for far more attention by researchers. Zuhur's scholarship in the creation of these anthologies is impressive, particularly shown in her introductions to both books. As resources for the writing of my own work these excellent anthologies made only a limited contribution, unfortunately.

Anthony Shay and Barbara Sellers-Young's (2005) anthology *Belly Dance: Orientalism, Transnationalism and Harem Fantasy* is a recent entrant into this field. As editors Shay and Sellers-Young assembled an interesting set of essays on topics ranging from dance and Islamic jurisprudence, night clubs in the United States, and the transformation of belly dance in North America. Two articles of interest here, by Najwa Adra and by Roberta L. Dougherty, deal, respectively, with belly dance performed within the modern Egyptian family setting, and research into the belly dancer as seen through contemporary Egyptian films. These two studies show the modern attitudes to belly dance within Egyptian society as similar to those revealed in my university thesis and in my work on the nineteenth century. This is an interesting continuity. This anthology as a whole, however, does not tackle the issue of research into past centuries.

Wendy Buonaventura's (1990) *Serpent of the Nile: Women and Dance in the Arab World* was a seminal attempt to capture the history and present attraction of belly dance in a book intended for the popular market. She concentrated on Egypt and used European travel accounts for some of her material on the nineteenth century. Her particular strength lay in the many historical dance images she brought to a wide reading public for the first time. Buonaventura devoted much of her book to topics as diverse as dance in Polynesia, Hollywood, the American dancer Ruth St. Denis, and prehistoric dance. In this way she covered topics that seem unrelated to the title of her work. Despite this, Buonaventura wrote an important book. She is an early dance history pioneer in this field without whose work I could not possibly have imagined my own.

My book goes beyond this existing literature in the field, I believe, through an extended attention to female entertainers of the time (1760 to 1870). Because of the depth of this research into the primary data, I have been able to take themes and topics these other writers have dealt with only in short articles or in chapters within books and expand them considerably. The new and the different in this book include: a series of short biographies of a number of named dancers to begin to answer the question, "Who was dancing?," a first attempt to describe types of choreography, along with the corpus of body movements used by dancers; a short history of Egyptian dance costumes—a topic not previously addressed in the literature; the geographical extent of performance within Egypt itself, the locations where professional dance was economically viable—again, a topic scarcely addressed.

With its focus on a time and a place, this book begins to fill a serious gap in dance history literature on the Middle East. It speaks directly to dance historians on subjects in which they are interested. I also hope that my methodology will encourage others to do likewise for other areas of the Middle East where the indigenous historical record is scant but where the travel literature can still give important insights. Since I began this research, the exponential potential of the internet makes it possible now for readers to take off from my material into vast new riches available on virtually any aspect covered in this book.

This book will also be important, I hope, for those many women worldwide—in Europe, North and South America, in Japan and in other parts of the Far East—who now practice belly dancing as a hobby and as a profession. Many have been taught this dance without acquiring either a sense of its original culture or knowledge of its history. Nieuwkerk's book certainly exposed the severe reality of dancers' lives in present-day Egypt; nevertheless, today exported belly dance all too often exhibits a fantasy Orientalism. Further, it has developed a tendency to evolve into strange hybrids. I hope my book will help provide a more realistic and recognizable link to the past. I realize that there are a great many endnotes in this book, and two highly detailed appendices, but they are not essential to the basic story. They are intended for the specialist—giving extra examples to bolster my arguments—and providing intriguing facts for those interested in the minutiae of dance history.

I myself became involved in the practice of belly dance after a serious illness, when physicality seemed the only way back to health. As with many North American women, my interest grew until it became engrossing. A graduate degree in dance history appealed to me as a further way to enrich my experience and I enrolled at York University, Toronto, Canada. Local dancers had told me that Egyptian Canadian audiences were extraordinarily well-informed critics of belly dance. I therefore decided to use this group to explore the underlying aesthetics of its performance practices. I wanted to know what constituted a truly excellent performance and a fine dancer from the Egyptian perspective.

I interviewed Egyptian Canadians, born in Egypt but living in Canada, about their views on contemporary professional Egyptian belly dance. I used the film elicitation technique, with video clips of the well-known Egyptian stars

Samia Gamal, Nagwa Fouad, Suhair Zaki, and Fifi Abdou as spring boards for what inevitably became intense two- or three-hour discussions. It was obvious from the very first that Egyptians loved this dance; they loved their famous dancers; they loved to talk about this dance and its practitioners—and they knew their stuff as dance critics. It was a joy to talk to them. It also became quite evident that they really didn't grant this dance (and even its most talented practitioners) much respect.

As part of the final thesis I needed to produce a background history of belly dance in Egypt, and was dismayed to discover how little material was available. Dance history is not, and has not been, a topic of real scholarly interest in the Middle East, and in the conclusion of my thesis I therefore remarked, "The entire field of the immediate antecedents of the *baladi* [belly dance] in Egypt during the nineteenth and twentieth centuries (and earlier, if possible) must be clarified if one wishes to say anything of historical significance about belly dance." At that time I certainly had no intention of doing this work myself, and was expecting others eventually to take up this line of research. Soon after I found I was much too intrigued to extricate myself from this field of study. I had begun to read the travel literature on Egypt and was finding it utterly compelling.

I did the research for this book mainly from Toronto, Canada, within the excellent collections of the Thomas Fisher Rare Book Library, and the University of Toronto's Robarts Library, the latter with a most helpful inter-library loan department. Two extended trips to Egypt gave me a marvelous feel for the country and its people—and its modern professional belly dance. There, I was able to wander among the locales spoken of so often in the travel literature. Magda Saleh (1979), who had produced a dissertation on the ethnic dance tradition of her native Egypt, with an accompanying full-length film, kindly met with me to discuss my work. As well, in the Cairo shops, I began my collection of original eighteenth- and nineteenth-century dance prints; I was able to add to them later in Beirut, Lebanon, and, surprisingly, some also turned up in Toronto.

Various libraries and museums helped significantly in facilitating work on the images in this book. The photographic services of the Robarts Library at the University of Toronto made numerous digital reproductions for me, as did that of the Thomas Fisher Rare Book Library. The Robarts Library staff also researched and clarified issues of copyright for visual materials they held in their collection. The Buffalo and Erie County Public Library encouraged me to visit in person, to good advantage, to choose between two versions of the Luigi Mayer print they owned. The Princeton University Library went beyond its mandate to provide me with a copy of Alfred-Henri Darjou's *Danse de la Gargoulette*. I am most appreciative. The Société Royal d'Archéologie, d'Histoire et de Folklore de Nivelles et du Brabant Wallon, the Dayton Art Institute, the Royal Ontario

Museum, and the Rijksmuseum gave permission to reproduce images. When I was unable to find original sources for two images I knew of, two publishers kindly allowed me to reproduce from their books—L'Harmattan, and Verlag W. Ludwig. I thank them very much.

Certain people have been central to this book: dance teachers Eddie Manneh and Dahlia Obadia, who started me on this path in the first place; George Sawa, a peerless music teacher whose knowledge of Middle Eastern music history is acknowledged as world-class; Selma Odom and Mary Jane Warner of York University, who exemplify the best in dance history research; Jasmina Ramzy, who, in creating the International Bellydance Conference of Canada series with an academic component, enabled me to share my research with others of like mind. I thank Samantha Mehra Donaldson for her hard work in preparing the bibliography. Finally, I am deeply grateful to Libby Smigel, executive director, Dance Heritage Coalition, Inc. When my manuscript seemed to be in limbo, she was able to point out an ultimately fruitful future direction.

Belly dance seems to have a quality that makes it difficult to forget, ignore, or dismiss. Despite their ambivalence toward this dance, western travelers went out of their way to watch performances and found it all but impossible not to write about them. Switching to the present, in a similar fashion those Egyptians I interviewed found it rewarding to talk about this dance and to express their satisfaction with it as part of their culture—all the while showing a certain discomfort toward both practice and practitioners. Like it or loathe it, or like it *and* loathe it, belly dance has a long and persistent history, and shows absolutely no sign of fading away in the 21st century.

Section One
Background

1

On Writing This Book

Martin R. Kalfatovic's (1992) annotated bibliography *Nile Notes of a Howadji: A Bibliography of Travelers' Tales from Egypt, from the Earliest Time to 1918* makes it abundantly clear that for thousands of years Egypt attracted and fascinated travelers, many of them leaving memorable accounts of their voyage. Herodotus and Julius Caesar are two notable early examples. From its beginnings, the spread of Christianity throughout the Mediterranean and Europe induced Christian pilgrimages to travel to Palestine, often with an added visit to northern Egypt. Later, from the 13th century onward, a European trade presence developed in Alexandria, Egypt. Early in the 17th century the amount of literature focused specifically on Egypt grew exponentially as European nations took an increasing interest in the eastern Mediterranean within the context of its relationship to India and the Far East, with the promise of trade and conquest.

The professional female entertainer, both as singer and dancer, provided a highly visible part of the Egyptian scene, and European travel documents of later periods often included descriptions of her performance, sometimes with great detail, sometimes in a bare mention, inevitably with editorial commentaries. This book assembles and analyzes a wide selection of these so-called travel materials dealing with the professional female dancers of Egypt, and, to some extent, the female singers and male dancers, over roughly a century, from 1760 to 1870.

Creating such a detailed historical review of Egyptian entertainers had long been my wish ever since I researched the aesthetics of modern Egyptian belly dance through interviews with Egyptians living in Canada.[1] At that time I was disappointed to discover that research literature on the dance traditions of the Middle East was virtually non-existent. I was also frustrated by the lack of answers to my many questions about this particular dance form in its Egyptian manifestation. I wanted to meet its earlier professional dancers as real human beings, to imagine them in performance, to gain some sense of their lives—both on and off the stage—as members of a Middle Eastern culture. Since the commonly used term belly dance (also the French equivalent *danse du ventre*) is a Western construct, I wanted to know what this dance was called in previous centuries.

Among those Westerners who devote themselves to the broad field of Middle Eastern dance, both as dancers and historians, a sense of the need to develop a scholarly background against which intelligent discussions can take place is increasingly evident. Andrea Deagon states that[2]

> we need to take our own histories [of Middle Eastern dance] more seriously, both to preserve our self-respect and to do justice to the people whose past we have appropriated. Exploring the real past, with every tool available to us, will give us insights into the dance that we could never get by simply projecting our own concerns backward. It is possible to adopt research strategies that will clarify the real dances of the past [2003, 33].

Karin van Nieuwkerk's (1995) seminal book on present-day Egyptian female performers, *A Trade Like Any Other: Female Singers and Dancers in Egypt,* had been a major inspiration, for she had demonstrated how a judicious review of travel literature might result in scholarly dance history. The first two chapters of her book are devoted to accounts of female performers in the 19th and early–20th centuries. Djamila Henni-Chebra and Christian Poché's (1996) *Les danses dans le monde arabe ou l'héritage des almées* (*Dances in the Arab World or the Patrimony of the Almées*) also used travel writings in a rich and creative manner, and included materials on Egypt in the 19th century. The challenge for me was to go further, to use the travel literature to produce a full-length history with in-depth studies of topics of particular interest to dance scholars. For such a result it seemed obligatory to bring to light many more forgotten and previously unexamined travel accounts that dealt with this dance in Egypt, as Zarifa Aradoon (1979) had done so ably in *The Oldest Dance.* It also seemed important to discover more of the pictorial record of this Egyptian dance that Wendy Buonaventura (1990) began so well in her beautiful *Serpent of the Nile: Women and Dance in the Arab World.*

The research tools and insights from the fields of dance ethnology also proved invaluable. Dance ethnologists believe that no dance gives up its secrets easily, for, beyond what the observer can see and hear, any dance always includes elements of its social, political, and historical contexts (Kaeppler 2000, 117). Accordingly, the performer may be skilled in the dance, but the viewer is just as important in the creation of meaning and must also be able to understand fully the movement messages arising from the social context (ibid., 121). In his *Choreophobia,* a study of Iranian dance and modern Iranians' attitudes to their own dance traditions, Anthony Shay (1999) has taken these research ideas to considerable length. He stresses the important cultural skill used by modern Iranians to interpret their dances from an insider's point of view (1999, 5–6). He warns that the interpretation of cultural artifacts from earlier periods, such as miniature paintings, requires such an eye, that their meanings are not obvious to outsiders to the culture (60–65).

The guidelines of dance ethnology are clear, then, but pose serious challenges for those working to create histories of dance in the Middle East. Since most dance ethnologists work in the present, they can avail themselves of the insights of native participants (I myself had used Egyptian Canadian views in creating my thesis on present Egyptian practices). Historians recreating the distant past, however, must work with what data has survived, however flawed, or abandon the effort entirely.[3] European travel writers certainly have not, nor ever could have, provided a fully authentic picture of the Egyptian dancers of that period, the history I wanted so much to discover. For such authenticity one would need contemporary accounts from Egyptian observers or, better still, first-hand accounts from dancers themselves. Such indigenous documents for this particular period, unfortunately, scarcely exist.

In her PhD dissertation, "A Documentation of the Ethnic Dance Traditions of the Arab Republic of Egypt," wherein she accords belly dance, or *raqs baladi* as she calls it, a legitimate place within this folk dance tradition, Magda Ahmed Abdel Saleh (1979) describes the paradox of dance research in Egypt. She explains that despite the fact that Egypt is known as a nation with a rich folk dance tradition,[4] both its historical records of the past and the research interests of the present pay little or no attention to its ethnic dancing (1979, 3–4). Saleh attributes this situation to "a prevailing negative attitude towards indigenous dance in Egypt as an art form or even as a human activity" (459).

At this point, then, the dance researcher needs to ask some key questions. Are foreign authors credible at all as dance observers and dance critics? Are they reliable and trustworthy to any extent? Can one even use such material to create a dance history tied to time and place? Present attitudes towards such materials more often than not hold them in disrespect. For example, in his wide-ranging and lucid dance memoir, *Dancing Fear and Desire: Race, Sexuality, and Imperial Politics in Middle Eastern Dance,* Stavros Stavrou Karayanni writes:

> In its initial conception, I intended this project to investigate and interrogate various travel narratives where Middle Eastern dancers appeared and danced only to vanish behind a curtain of ideological conceits and (mostly male) censuring remarks. Now I realize that such a project, though promising, would have to struggle against tedium since many of the narratives repeat the same images so that the dance is buried beneath a growing mound of tautological signifiers [2004, xii].

Certainly the writings of those European men and women I consulted for the most part contain opinions that jar modern sensibilities. Not surprisingly, these materials often reflect not only the cultural bias of these authors, but also their lack of willingness to appreciate in any way the new experiences available. The travel literature also presents, however, much that is positive.

But for the historian the personality of each of her sources is hardly the point. The key question is whether her sources could be keen and objective viewers of the dance scene in Egypt. In other words, the researcher has a relationship not only with the traveler but also with the text (and often with a picture), and has the task of unlocking the secrets it conceals. In my re-creation of the past I was particularly inspired by remarks by Lynn Matluck Brooks (2001, 5) who speaks of her 20 years of archival work attempting to "hear" the "meaning embodied in texts." She writes:

> I have found in the work of Hans Georg Gadamer, whose "philosophical hermeneutics" addresses the nature of "alienation" in our encounters with art and with history—appropriate encounters for the dance historian. Gadamer's stress on "dialogue" between text and researcher provides a useful context for reconsidering the role of the historian as a translator or mediator of the past into the present [ibid., 5].[5]

Based on these principles of translation and mediation, I saw that I had two responsibilities. As a historian it was important for me not only to "read" the travel materials but also to explore beneath them, asking what reality lay behind the written word or the illustration. As a dance researcher writing about another culture, I had to remain mindful that it was not possible for me to write "the" history of these Egyptian performers, but rather that I was creating "a" history, inevitably a personal one defined within the limits of my skills of cultural awareness. The challenge, for me, became a careful assembling and assessing of the available data.

Since both texts and illustrations for this book had been selected to include only work by travelers actually present at performances, each account and pictorial record became, for me, a real person who had watched a dance event. I discovered that Europeans came to Egypt for widely differing reasons, and their accounts varied according to their professional interests. A constant reading and rereading of this material yielded more depths of meaning, more cross connections, far more possibilities. As I worked with the historical records, their very richness took over production. Time and time again I returned to the same accounts and illustrations, each time finding something new and exciting.

It is obvious that each travel writer or artist consulted could miss the mark in varying degrees, yet in the center of all these disparate gazes more and more clearly a real dance took shape for me. In sum, any weaknesses in the travel literature turned out to be primarily individual, while the collective impact of the data had enormous value. The bits of worthwhile evidence from many authors, even when not identical, seem to fit together coherently. Ironically, the most negatively biased observer was not necessarily the least useful. Even from deep disapproval of a dance event, if carefully described, I could discover or infer extraordinarily valuable facts. One might identify what was going on during a dance performance, sort the objective from the subjective, and discarding the latter, emerge with something resembling reality.[6]

At first there seemed no clear idea of a range of topics the book might address or the period to cover. The format of the book eventually arose organically from the travel literature itself, what westerners were saying about the performance and the performers. While not every writer spoke on every topic equally, most touched on each to some extent. It seemed natural to use their interests as a framework of the book.

Why choose the period 1760 to 1870 and the messy concept of 110 years? It would have been instructive to go back further in time in the travel literature, to search somewhat earlier roots of the dance, but there were no identifiable sources with sufficient detail on the dancing itself. I decided, therefore, to begin with the first adequate European record available of the dance in Egypt along with an accompanying illustration, that is Carsten Niebuhr's (n.d.) account from his 1761 passage through Lower Egypt on a voyage sponsored by the king of Denmark.[7] I chose an ending in 1869, a date for the opening of the Suez Canal.

Fig.1. Richard Pococke. *Dancing Women of Egypt*. c. 1738.

At that time Egypt opened up to substantial routine tourist travel, with Cook's steamship tours a regular feature. Travel literature then became qualitatively different, reflecting perhaps an entirely differently motivated group of visitors.[8]

As research and writing progressed, the century-and-a-decade framework proved problematic at times. For example, I discovered that Richard Pococke (1743–45), British author of *Description of the East and Some Other Countries,* had produced a print (fig. 1) of a dancer and her female drummer. Since Pococke traveled in 1737, his valuable illustration did not lie within the chosen period but seemed important enough to include. Also, certain materials from after the chosen ending date, accounts too evocative or substantive, or even amusing, to ignore, kept turning up. To enrich my account, therefore, I incorporated particularly useful bits of data from before and after the official period of the book. In this way the century-and-a-decade mostly maintains its clear focus but, at times, has decidedly blurry edges.

After working for almost a decade with this particular body of so-called travel materials as the almost-exclusive primary materials for my work I no longer apologize for these European sources. I have concluded that its creators must be accorded a respectable place within the history of professional female entertainers in Egypt. When we dismiss these authors as unworthy keys to unlocking this dance's past, we ignore certain facts out of hand. They themselves are inextricably woven into the fabric of this dance's history, their very presence as audience makes them part of this equation. However questionable certain aspects of their records, western observers existed as a unique group of primary recorders of real performances. They bore witness to the existence of this dance, and have kept its memory alive. Collectively, what they have said provides a complex and rich picture. It would be foolish to wish away their existence and their testimony.

2

Selected Egyptian History— the Study Period

This account of the entertainment arts of Egypt cannot be truly understood without a sense of the complex history of the period 1760 to 1870. These decades saw great political and cultural changes in Egypt, tumultuous ones even for a country subject to many foreign invasions over thousands of years. Such changes had consequences for the performing arts.

Having conquered Egypt in 1517, the Ottoman Turks who ruled their vast empire from Istanbul were still nominally lords of Egypt in the middle of the 18th century, and the Turkish sultan continued to send his governor to Cairo for a yearly tenure. On conquering Egypt, however, Istanbul had merely laid another layer of rule upon an earlier one. The real local power still lay in the hands of the Mamluks, a holdover from previous conquests of Egypt by outsiders. A loose federation of Muslim military regiments, they perpetuated a system in which they were the elites under whom local Egyptians formed three major classes. First came the 'ulamâ,[1] financiers, upper bureaucrats, and the wealthy merchants; next came the artisans, rural affluent peasants and village heads; and, finally, came most Egyptians, that is, the poorer segments of urban and rural society. Local political power, however, rested effectively in the hands of the Mamluks.

The Mamluk military system, based on slavery, had entrenched itself across the Middle East from the 9th century onward. In Egypt, Mamluk soldiers had overthrown the previous dynasty in the 13th century and formed a military oligarchy of enfranchised former slaves. The new rulers perpetuated themselves through continued purchase of non–Muslim slave children.[2] Elite households trained these children in the military arts, then freed them to serve as fighters for their former master. Members of the same household treated each other as brothers and regarded their master as a father.³ Just as frequently, Mamluk brothers fought one another and even challenged their master when the temptation to seize power grew too great. In ruling the country and extracting the bulk of wealth for itself, the Mamluk system held together through alliances and delicate balances of power among elite households.

By the middle of the 18th century, the system began to break down. Two households established themselves as a duumvirate, ruling over the country; on their death their followers constantly battled among themselves, ushering in a period of instability from 1754 until the end of the century, manifested in famines, plagues, depopulation, and economic distress. This weak and unstable Egypt increasingly presented a tempting target to European monarchs in a continent now vigorously expanding its influence around the world.

As part of his strategy for a campaign rapidly becoming a European war on three continents, the French general Napoleon Bonaparte and his divisions entered Egypt in 1798. Landing at Alexandria, he fought his way to Cairo, then engaged the combined Mamluk armies at the Battle of the Pyramids, ending with a major French victory. The Mamluk leaders and their many followers fled south to Upper Egypt to continue battling the French for the next three years. Meanwhile, Napoleon found himself stranded in Egypt when the English naval hero Horatio Nelson shortly afterward sank his entire fleet moored off the northern Egyptian coast.⁴ Eventually, the Ottoman Turks formed an alliance with the British; both successfully invaded Egypt in 1801, sending the defeated French troops back to France.

After the expulsion of the French, Egypt plunged into self-imposed unrest, as the Mamluks began a comeback. In alliance with the Egyptian religious authorities, Muhammad Ali, an Albanian Muslim officer who had entered Egypt with the Ottoman troops, took advantage of the situation. Promising stability not known for a generation, he managed to have himself proclaimed governor of Egypt in 1805, under the Ottoman Turks. He then began to consolidate his power among local Egyptian elites, eventually massacring all the remaining senior Mamluks in a coup in 1811. From then on, Egypt effectively belonged to him, and eventually to his family dynasty.⁵

As the "last Mamluk," Muhammad Ali emphasized Europe and modernization as the source of new methods of enriching Egypt and entered more and more into the European sphere of influence. He began to employ expatriate Frenchmen as senior members of his administration, and gave increasing privileges to resident Europeans, a practice that often distressed his Muslim subjects. He routinely granted personal audiences to European visitors, and ensured their travel to remote places by issuing special permits under his name. The Mediterranean Sea was not safe for general European travel during the Napoleonic wars, however, and from 1801 to 1815 travelers seldom went to Egypt. From the 1820s onward, Egypt increasingly became the temporary home of foreigners, and data on the dance becomes increasingly available for the period 1820 to 1870. Ironically, while information on the dance increased during Muhammad Ali's reign, dancers seem to have suffered greatly under him. Around 1834, certain female dancers were prohibited from dancing in public places.

3

Writers and Painters in Egypt from 1760 to 1870

Overview

The French played an important role in Egypt in the 19th century, first as conquerors then as employees of the state in many capacities, culminating in constructing the Suez Canal under Ismail, Muhammad Ali's descendant. The Egypt of Muhammad Ali provided a comfortable atmosphere for the French, and they went there in numbers. As a consequence, the French literature on Egypt is extensive.[1] During the same period, the British came primarily as visitors, not as employees; still, their literature on Egypt is also rich.[2]

Some of these European narratives included information about the women who served as public entertainers, information most usually found scattered throughout the text, and often associated with eye-witness descriptions of an unplanned encounter. In the early stages of this particular travel writing (and travel art), Europeans wrote about or depicted female professional dancers because they wished to record certain experiences more or less accurately, less because they wanted to impose their fantasies upon these dance events. In other words, the Orientalism or romanticism stressing sentiment and wishful imagination that clouded so much later European writing and painting was not a phenomenon found throughout the entire period of this particular study. This earlier practice changed after the middle of the 19th century when the idiom of European travel writing became more established, and artists actively sought particular areas of the Middle East as a source of inspiration. Some 19th-century European artists even painted "The Orient" entirely from their imagination without leaving home, unlike travel writers who were certainly expected to have gone abroad.

European Artists and Egyptian Dance, 1760 to 1870: Selected Examples

Artists represented one important trend of European travel to Egypt, as several examples illustrate. The growing political interest of 18th-century European rulers in the eastern Mediterranean region and the Middle East motivated them to send representatives to Egypt to serve as their eyes and ears in the region. Artists might serve as a member of such a group. Georg Wilhelm Baurenseind, for example, took part in a 1761 scientific expedition mounted by Frederick V of Denmark and led by Niebuhr. The group spent several months in Lower Egypt, and then descended the Red Sea, heading for Bombay. It was Baurenseind (fig. 2) who drew, in a simple manner, the ordinary public dancers described by Niebuhr as dancing in the dry canal in front of their lodgings.[3] Luigi [Ludwig] Mayer accompanied Sir Robert Ainslie, British ambassador to Istanbul, on his

Fig. 2. Wilhelm Baurenseind. *Représentation des Danseuses et de Leur Musiciens à Kahira* (Representation of Dancers and Their Musicians at Cairo). c. 1761 (from Baurenfeind, dessinateur, *Illustrations de Voyage en Arabie* [Amsterdam-Utrecht: S.J. Baalde-J. Van Schoonhoven, 1776]).

Fig. 3. Luigi Mayer. *An Egyptian Ball, at Ned Sili.* c. 1798 (from Luigi Mayer, *Views in Egypt* [London: R. Boyer, 1813]. Reproduction by permission of the Buffalo and Erie County Public Library, Buffalo, New York).

trips throughout the Ottoman Empire from 1792 to 1796 and produced several books of illustrations of the countries they saw. He illustrated about 100 scenes from Egypt alone, remarkable for their details and keen observations, among them two dance images. One (fig. 3) depicts a full troupe of well-dressed female dancers and musicians, a picture almost unique as a quasi-ethnographic record.

The most extraordinary tie of politics to pictorial records of dancers, though, lies in the Napoleonic invasion of Egypt in 1798. Not only did Napoleon bring troops, he also brought a body of French scholars to study and record both ancient and contemporary Egypt. Known as the Savants, these dedicated men managed to carry out their work under war conditions, and eventually published the monumental multi-volume *Description de l'Égypte* (France, Commission des sciences et arts de l'Égypte 1809–28). This document serves as a virtual encyclopedia of the antiquities, contemporary life, and natural history of the country. Four important late–18th–century images of dance and dancers appear in it, three attributed to a certain André Dutertre (fig. 9) and a fourth (fig. 6) attributed to "a Copt," that is a native Christian Egyptian. These four beautiful images arise out of the French spirit of scientific research so alive at the time of the French Revolution.

Some travelers had both writing and artistic talents, using personal drawings to augment their texts. For example, the already-mentioned Pococke (later, Bishop of Meath), who traveled widely in Egypt from 1737 to 1738, wrote and illustrated his *Observations on Egypt: Description of the East and Some Other Countries*. He made only a slight passing reference to dancers but did include his simple line drawing of a dancer with her female drummer (fig. 1), the first known pictorial record by a European. Louis Nicolas Phillippe Auguste comte de Forbin had been an officer under Napoleon and survived the Republic to become director of the Louvre museum in Paris. His book (1819), describing his 1818 trip to Egypt, includes a magnificent leaping dancer with a tambourine (fig. 24) in a style reminiscent of the French artist Jacques Louis David, whose pupil Forbin had been. William Henry Bartlett (1849), a British topographical artist and world traveler, is well known in Canada for his pictures of the towns and landscapes of the country. His trip to Egypt in 1845 resulted in a small but fascinating quick sketch of an outdoor public performance before a crowd of native Egyptians (fig. 10), and he included this in his travel book *The Nile Boat* (1849). Later, Thomas Gold Appleton (traveled in 1874) and Georges Montbard (traveled around 1880) included their own illustrations of dancers (figs. 20, 26) in their books, recorded in a journalistic style useful for the future dance record.

Other Europeans made Egypt their home over extended periods of time, their interests ranging widely over Egyptian history, art, archeology, and natural

Fig. 4. J.J. Rifaud. *Danse d' Almées et leur musique* (Dance of the Almées and Their Music). c. 1825 (with permission of the Société Royal d'Archéologie, d'Histoire et de Folklore de Nivelles et du Brabant Wallon).

history. Two examples, one French and one British, Jean-Jacques Rifaud (Société Royal d'Archéologie, d'Histoire et de Folklore de Nivelles et du Brabant Wallon 1998), and Edward Lane (1978, 1984), left illustrations of the dance. The young Rifaud worked in Egypt from 1814 to 1827 with the French consul Bernadino Drovetti, collecting antiques intended for the Louvre. He also studied and recorded, in hundreds of illustrations, Egypt's botany, zoology, mineralogy, and ethnography.[4] Two lithographs (figs. 4, 11) show a pair of female dancers with their musicians, and a wedding with both groups of male musicians and female dancers and musicians. Both illustrations arise out of Rifaud's longstanding passion for recording accurately the Egypt he knew and loved. Edward William Lane is discussed later—more properly as a writer—but it is important to note that he included a small line sketch of two dancers and their musicians (fig. 17) in his chapter on the public dancers of Egypt, in his *Manners and Customs of the Modern Egyptians*, first appearing in 1836. To his wide reading audience this particular image would have served as the template for imagining Egyptian dancers of the time. Like Rifaud's, Lane's image is informational, as are his many other drawings, with no element of fantasy, nor attempts to record an imaginary world.[5]

In the same period, artists went to Egypt for the sole purpose of recording scenes of that country. For example, David Roberts (1846–49), a talented Scottish draftsman, traveled widely in Egypt in 1838 and 1839, making sketches of architecture and scenery for his books of lithographs. His now well-known illustration of a private Cairo dance performance (fig. 16) came about by accident. An acquaintance staying briefly in the city invited him to a private party and he brought his skills as a conscientious draftsman to the recording of an actual event. He obviously found the event worth his attention as an artist, although the picture is not typical of the remainder of his work on Egypt.

The artist as romantic appears around the year 1850 (as represented among the illustrations in this book) and accuracy of depiction changes; one sees more personal interpretations. It is difficult to know which traveling artist or artists originally initiated the imposition of sentimentality, exoticism, and eroticism into their visions of the dancers of Egypt, but Alexandre Bida (1851) would be a good candidate for the element of sentimentality. A French artist famous for his elegant black-and-white illustrations for literary texts, Bida made four trips to the Middle East and included visits to Egypt in two of them (1850 and 1861). He published *Souvenirs d'Egypte* with a number of lithographs, one of a female drummer (fig. 21b) and one of a female dancer (fig. 21a).[6] One might describe these pictures as sweet or charming.

The Frenchman Émile Prisse d'Avennes (J. St. James 1851) published a major book of plates in England, depicting Egyptian costumes and people of that country. His lithograph of two dancers from that book (fig. 18) also manifests the same sentimentality as Bida's though here drawn despite long practical experience, since Prisse d'Avennes lived in Egypt from 1829 to 1844 and later from 1858 to 1860.[7] A draftsman, he served in the Egyptian army, and then embarked on a career as an archaeologist. He sought to popularize Middle Eastern culture in Europe through his many drawings and publications on the Islamic arts. While the beautiful and elaborate costumes of his dancers are probably accurate, the dancers' faces show a European-style prettiness and the dance positions seem an attempt to please the viewer.

With the showing of his *Dance of the Almeh* (fig. 25) at the Paris Salon in 1863, the French artist Jean-Léon Gérôme introduced the elements of sensuality and exoticism into the pictorial record of Egyptian dance. Gérôme traveled extensively in Egypt,[8] looking for sources of artistic inspiration, later to be used as elements in the painting of semi-imaginary worlds. While his dance canvases may lack authenticity as actual events, each of the various components can be taken as an accurate source of information, since he sketched from observation. For example, the dance stance in *Dance of the Almeh* with feet disturbing the carpet, and finger cymbals accurately placed on the correct fingers, all show Gérôme perfectly capable of journalistic artwork.

European Writers on Egyptian Dance, 1760 to 1870: Selected Examples

Far more western authors wrote about Egyptian dance practices than artists recorded them pictorially. These writers comprise four types, categories that represent the original forces that sent them to Egypt in the first place, that is, politics, adventure, scholarship, and tourism.

It is extraordinary how politics influenced the literature, for throughout the period many writers found their political affiliations drove them to Egypt rather than their love of travel. At the time when France began to take a serious interest in Egypt, Claude Etienne Savary lived there from around 1775 to 1779, charged with communicating directly with the royal family in Paris about aspects of Egyptian society. His book (1785) assembles a series of entertaining letters written as the spirit moved him, though probably he also sent secret dispatches on sensitive political issues. Well connected, well read, and reasonably fluent in Arabic, Savary mixed with the upper echelons of Egyptian society. He knew firsthand those female entertainers who charmed the wealthy, and his descriptions merit serious scholarly attention. Unfortunately, they are too brief.

Napoleon's occupation (1798 to 1801) generated an enormous amount of literature on Egypt. Individual military officers wrote personal accounts (e.g.,

Belliard, Denon, Larrey). The Savants (e.g., Chabrol, Coutelle, Du Bois-Aymé, Galland, Jollois, Jomard, Redouté, Villoteau) contributed separate essays to the great *Description de l'Égypte*, published by the French government over a 15-year period. One can find throughout these texts numerous but brief references to Egyptian dance and dancers. In the *Description*, however, the musicologist Guillaume Villoteau (1809a, 1809b) wrote several hundred pages about Egyptian music, musical instruments, and song texts. Importantly, he also devoted many pages to dance and its practitioners, including a unique description of dancers' skills with their brass finger cymbals.

During the early 19th century, the French began to appear in Egypt on more friendly diplomatic missions, and wrote about their travels. For example, Isidore Justin Severin Taylor (1856) visited Egypt in 1828 and then in 1830, on a mission from Charles X of France to negotiate and oversee the transport of an obelisk from Luxor to the Place de la Concorde in Paris, the gift of Muhammad Ali. The landscape artist Adrien Dauzats (Dumas [and Dauzats] 1846) accompanied Baron Taylor on the 1830 trip. Both wrote books about this visit. As important personages, they were entertained officially with a dinner party including dance and music, which Dauzats describes in excellent detail, his artist's eye capturing in print many nuances of the choreography.[9] A few years later, in 1834, Auguste Frédéric Louis Viesse de Marmont, Duke of Raguse (1837–38), arrived in Egypt on a diplomatic mission. Entertained officially on a lavish scale with a dinner and dance performance, he includes a short but fascinating description in his materials.

The working-class feminist Suzanne Voilquin (1978) can also be described as motivated, first, by politics and, second, by travel. She lived in Egypt from 1834 to 1836, a member of the newly arrived Saint Simoneon group dedicated to altruistic work in the name of the French social philosopher Claude Saint-Simon. Disguised as a male Voilquin worked as a medical assistant to an expatriate French doctor, even throughout the great plague of 1835. Voilquin is a good example of someone who loathed the dance yet contributed significantly to its history. As a guest at a Muslim wedding, among the female family members at the window of the harem, she witnessed and described a dance entertainment presented in front of the male guests, a unique account in western dance literature.[10]

Interestingly, one could also include the French author Gustave Flaubert (1965, 1991) among politically motivated travelers, for indeed he went to Egypt in 1849 primarily to accompany his friend Maxime Du Camp, who had accepted a French government contract.[11] Flaubert is noted and discussed today in dance circles for his frank personal details on two visits to a famous dancer, Kutchuk Hanem.[12] It should be stressed, however, that Flaubert did not see himself as a travel writer; he did not publish any of his Egyptian materials during his lifetime.

The German states also took an interest in Egypt, and politically connected travelers toured the country and wrote about their experiences. For example, Wolfradine von Watzdorf freiherrn von Minutoli (1827) traveled extensively with her husband in Egypt from 1820 to 1822, meeting with all the intelligentsia. Her rather disparaging account of a dance entertainment in a (Christian) harem is one of only a few such descriptions in the literature, and useful in that regard. The 1838 tour to Egypt of Herzogs Maximilian, duke of Bavaria (1978), undoubtedly also had political underpinnings since his royal nephew had only recently become king of a Greece liberated from the Ottoman Empire by the European Powers. Egypt had served on the losing side and merited some close on-the-spot observations. The duke made only passing remarks about the public dancers, but the court painter in his entourage, Heinrich von Mayr, captured their image at a small café along the Nile (fig. 8).

Finally, the Egyptian government of Ismail entertained hundreds of royal and other important foreign guests from numerous European countries in a kind of political theater celebrating the Suez Canal opening in the fall of 1869. French journalists and artists were also guests of the government. Among them, Louise Colet (1879), Charles Blanc (1876), and Eugène Fromentin (1881) left their professional comments on three dance entertainments organized by the Egyptian government. Colet is remembered today less as a journalist and more as the unfortunate and angry ex-mistress of Flaubert. She did not write a distinguished book about her trip to Egypt but did include an excellent and full description of the famous Badawiyya of Qena, an artist she praised for her extraordinary talent. As an art critic, Blanc turned a practiced and reasoned eye on dancers and their dance, again giving good material on Badawiyya. The well-known Orientalist artist Fromentin recorded short, insightful travel notes on these three official dance events of 1869.

The second type of authors found themselves in Egypt for extended periods of time, motivated by the search for employment abroad. Their writings reflect extensive experience with Egypt and, despite their inevitably European perspectives, usually a reasonably honest involvement with its culture and history. Two authors represent those Frenchmen employed by Muhammad Ali in his modernization of Egypt: Antoine-Barthélemy Clot (1840), often known as Clot Bey, and P.N. Hamont (1845). As Muhammad Ali's surgeon in chief, Clot Bey lived in Egypt from 1823 to 1860. His two-volume work covers extensive topics about Egypt's economics, history, and culture. Modern authors have rediscovered this work. His material is probably reasonably reliable in most respects concerning dance and dancers, but he writes generally rather than specifically in the section of the book devoted to this topic. Less known among dance historians, P. N. Hamont[13] served directly under Muhammad Ali as a veterinary surgeon from 1828 to 1842, traveling throughout Egypt dealing with problems in the field. Unlike Clot Bey, who wrote flatteringly about Muhammad Ali's attempts to force Egypt to modernize, Hamont often made harsh remarks about the administration's impact on the ordinary people. In that respect these authors represent two poles among all the European travel literature, those enthusiastic about Muhammad Ali's goals and methods and those strongly opposed. Hamont had interesting things to say about dance and dancers, but he scattered this information throughout his work. It seems reasonably reliable but is limited at times by an unfortunate tendency to confuse terms when speaking of dancers and prostitutes.

Other writers, obviously financially independent, chose to live in Egypt for various reasons. For example, the Swiss explorer John Lewis Burkhardt (1984) arrived in Egypt in 1812 intending eventually to seek the source of the river Niger. He traveled to many parts of Africa and the Middle East, from 1812 to 1817, then settled in Egypt, during which time he worked on excavations carried out by another expatriate Henry Salt, British consul in Egypt. Burkhardt died in Cairo, and was buried as a Muslim, Ibrahim ibn Abdalla. He possessed a personal magnetism that allegedly influenced many Europeans associated with Egypt. His reprinted work on Arabic proverbs quotes some idiosyncratic information on dance and dancers.

The British writer Bayle St. John is best known today for his *Village Life in Egypt* (1973), a modern reprint of his 1852 edition. This work is a standard traveler's book, however. His earlier *Two Years in a Levantine Family* (1850) remains obscure, unfortunately. Here, St. John recounts how as a 20-something daredevil he lived in Alexandria from 1846 to 1847, boarding with a Christian family of Syrian origin. St. John plunged into his experience, learned Arabic, and associated with the young men of the family in their daily rounds. His accounts of their dance encounters are full of life, fun, and rich social commentaries.

Lady Lucie Duff Gordon (1983), a British author already famous for her *Letters from the Cape* [Of Good Hope in South Africa] moved to Luxor in southern Egypt in 1862 because of her rapidly declining health. She eventually died there, in 1869. Duff Gordon immersed herself in the local community, learned Arabic, and took a caring interest in the people of Egypt at all levels. She seems to have been a patron of sorts for the dancers of the area, and speaks warmly of them in a number of vignettes. Written as a series of letters home to England, her book still generates interest and exists today in reprints.

The British author Edward William Lane (1973, 1978, 2000) provides a final example of those whose long sojourn and total involvement in Egypt provides solidity for their writings. Lane lived in Egypt during three periods, from 1825 to 1828, from 1833 to 1835, and from 1842 to 1849. He first went to Egypt for his health, but soon found his life's direction there. His soon-to-be-famous

Manners and Customs of the Modern Egyptians appeared first in 1836, and its focus on "modern" Egypt rather than its antiquities was unusual at the time. Lane wrote an entire chapter of this work on the public dancers of Egypt. Lane's translation of *The Thousand and One Nights* next appeared in 1839–41. He then embarked on what he considered his major work, his classical *Arabic-English Lexicon*, for which he returned to Egypt in 1842. He died in England in 1876 before completing this work. His *Manners and Customs* continued to be reprinted, the classic edition being the fifth, printed in 1860. It was widely read by his European contemporaries, and often plagiarized when they wanted to make remarks about the dance and dancers of Egypt. It is difficult to rehabilitate Lane today after the devastating attack on *Manners and Customs* by the modern scholar Edward Said (1978) in his *Orientalism*. Yet one must protest that Said is reading Lane with the sensibility of a century and a half later. Whatever European ideas colored his work, Lane himself was motivated in preserving a record of an Egyptian culture that he found valuable and could see was rapidly passing away under Muhammad Ali's steely direction.

A third type of writer traveled to Egypt motivated by scholarship. Two examples illustrate this considerably smaller group. The French scientist Charles Nicolas Sigisbert Sonnini (1799) traveled throughout Egypt from 1777 to 1778, reaching even as far south as Aswan. His primary interests lay in the fauna and flora of the country. Throughout the three-volume account of his visit, however, he made numerous short remarks about the public dancers, recording how and when he saw them. Generally, in his distaste, he described them as diseased and depraved, yet his scientific observational skills made him an excellent recorder of several dance steps. The brilliant French scholar Jean-François Champollion (1986) had already published, in 1821, his work with the Rosetta stone, one key to ancient Egypt's past, when he made a first trip to Egypt in 1828. His account describes a private party with a renowned female singer, and three dance parties, two with female and one with male performers. The young artist Nestor L'Hôte (1993) accompanied him, and his account includes two of these dance events in detail.

The fourth and final identified group of writers constitutes those most commonly considered today as the authentic travel writers, that is, those who went to Egypt specifically for the experiences of the temporary voyage, recording these in a work intended to entertain a western audience interested in faraway places. In a sense, this group of workers in print corresponds reasonably closely to those artists who traveled to Egypt to find materials to create their own imaginary worlds. These writers were more inclined to seek out dance and dancers as colorful elements almost obligatory to the narrative on Egypt. Still they have provided excellent descriptions in many instances. Several examples illustrate these points and the range of types of materials.

Prior to this present research, contemporary dance historians eager to discover traces of the dance in Egypt had already rescued certain authors from oblivion, for example, James St. John (1834, 1845, 1851), father of Bayle St. John discussed earlier. A British writer, he explored Egypt widely during the fall, winter and spring of 1832 and 1833, and managed to use this same material three times. His first book contains major polemics against the rule of Muhammad Ali and much evidence of the sad state of Egypt. Like Hamont, he disliked what he saw. He rehashed his first book in a later edition (1845) into a more traditional book of travel, and included considerable material from other authors. Importantly, he reproduced an account by the German writer S.W. Hackländer, who went to Cairo in 1840 and wrote an account unique for its detail of an entire evening's entertainment with a set of four choreographies. St. John also wrote all the plate captions for Prisse d'Avennes's lithographs in the 1851 *Oriental Album* that included the latter's well-known dance image (discussed earlier). St. John's major encounter with public dancers took place at a large coffee house just outside Cairo; each book contains a different version of this event.[14] St. John provides much useful information about dancers and the dance, but his material needs careful sifting.

The American George William Curtis (1856), an editor at *Harper's Magazine* and Harper and Brothers publishing house, went to Egypt over the winter of 1849–50, exactly the same year and months as Flaubert. His work continues to be quoted today for its important account of a visit to Kutchuk Hanem, but he is disparaged for his extraordinarily Orientalist and sentimental writing style.[15] Curtis seems to have truly appreciated Kutchuk Hanem's artistry, however, and underneath the verbosity one finds a sensitive and carefully detailed description of Egyptian artists at a small private party. Curtis is a good example of a travel writer whose personal reputation might usefully be rehabilitated. One cannot say the same for Charles Leland (1874), the British author of the *Egyptian Sketchbook*. By November 1872, when he went to Egypt, an unfortunate tone was becoming established in the travel literature, and throughout his book he sneers, sees himself as the modern viewer from a superior world, and generally presents Egypt as a decayed culture. When he turns to the dance, however, his eye is objective, and the details on choreography too fine to discard. One uses his material with reluctance, as if giving credibility to someone one would rather not. Leland turns up regularly in present-day bibliographies.[16]

Certain still-obscure authors served well the writing of this book, for example Charles Didier (1858, 1860), a Swiss by nationality.[17] He spent the fall, winter, and spring of 1853 and 1854 visiting Cairo, the Red Sea, the Arabian Peninsula, and Nubia, returning north along the Nile from Khartoum. Didier wrote three books about this one trip, two of them dealing with Egypt. Although a mediocre travel writer, he took a genuine interest in people, and throughout his works shine excellent vignettes on real human beings. He includes unique accounts of singers and dancers, their music, and their lives, and accords them the dignity of mentioning them by name. The story of his rescue of the dancer Safiyya in Aswan, for example, is illuminating as well as heartbreaking.

The forgotten writer Joseph Estourmel (1844) presents a far less attractive personality. His contribution to dance history consists of an account of a private party with dance performance at the home of a well-to-do Christian Cairo family. Estourmel is repulsed by the entire evening, as he is by Egypt in general. One is grateful for the dance materials, however, for he provided excellent details on audience reaction (female guests and female members of the family were present in numbers), a unique choreography, and dancers' physiques.

While it seemed important to give a female perspective on Egyptian dance history, women travel writers presented a problem in the writing of this book. For one thing, during this period there were far fewer women than men writing about their experiences in Egypt, so only a small body of works exists. Those few titles turned up in the local libraries far less than those of their male colleagues, and attempts to locate them by inter-library loans met with inadequate success. It appears that today books by women writers of the 19th century have become a rare commodity in North American libraries. From the minute sample available, though, certain trends tentatively present themselves but need to be more fully researched—that European women disparaged the dance more than their male colleagues, and a stronger vein of unease runs through their accounts.[18]

Sophia Lane-Poole (1846, 1851) went to Egypt in 1842 with her brother Edward Lane, the now-noted author of *Manners and Customs of the Modern Egyptians*, who had returned in order to carry out research for his new Arabic lexicon. Lane-Poole had agreed to do her own study on the women of Egypt, and under her brother's supervision wrote several books consisting of letters about her three-year experiences in Cairo. Her material is often trite and disapproving, but her lengthy account as a guest in the royal harem during eight days of wedding festivities yields rich information, including descriptions of the strong role of professional dance and music at such events. The British professional travel writer Isabella Frances Romer (1846) appeared in Egypt during the same period as Lane-Poole, that is 1845 to 1846, carrying heavy cultural baggage that saturates her book. For example, she felt it obligatory to set up her own private performance with a famous dancer of Isna, but sent ahead to warn her not to include anything in the presentation style that might be construed as immoral. In spite of Romer's attitude, one still gains objective information from her several encounters with dancers.

Summary Remarks on European Travel Materials

The representative examples drawn from the body of European art and literature on the entertainment arts of Egypt make two important points. First of all, use of the word *travel* to describe the materials may easily end in a misleading misnomer. The word suggests an unfortunate stereotype where one imagines an uninformed casual visitor describing something beyond his or her understanding. Yet as has been shown, these resource materials spring from writers and artists of highly varied motives, experience, and abilities. Second, certainly most so-called travelers came to Egypt imbued with European belief systems, but these did not necessarily destroy objectivity when describing aspects of the dance. For these reasons, throughout this book, a sustained effort has been made always to evaluate the evidence in the light of individual writers' and artists' skills and backgrounds, and to give the reader an assessment of the research value of each bit of information used in creation of this particular story of dance in Egypt.

Section Two
Setting the Stage

4

A Name for the Dance and a Name for the Dancer

A Name for the Dance

Modern scholars have interested themselves with both past and current names for the professional dance performed by the female dancers of Egypt. Today there are several native terms according to Sherifa Zuhur, who writes:

> A historical dispute has ensued over the origins of solo dance performance, identified in Egypt as raqs baladi (dance of the country) and converted through a long process into the cabaret forms of raqs sharki (Eastern, or Oriental dance) or raqs baladi as observed today in Arab cities and nightclubs in and outside the Middle East [1998, 6].

In her dissertation, Saleh (1979, 128) says that the terms employed by Egyptians to identify what westerners call "belly dance" are: *raqs masri* (Egyptian dance); *raqs baladi* (native dance); *raqs sharqi* (oriental dance); *raqs Arabi* (Arabian dance). Unlike Zuhur, she does not differentiate among these terms.

Said, however, acknowledges the controversial term "belly dance" as a more universal one. He writes of Tahia Carioca as "the most stunning and long-lived of the Arab world's Eastern dancers (belly dancers, as they are called today)" (2001, 228). The modern researcher Poché writes of the French equivalent, *danse du ventre* (belly dance), "Even though it is difficult to be precise about this nomenclature it appeared in the second half of the nineteenth century" (1966, 55). Anne Décoret-Ahiha believes that the term *danse du ventre* originated with French troops in French North African colonies, later becoming a generic identifier for all female dance of the "Orient" (2004, 28).

None of these now-current local or western terms appeared in the travel literature on Egypt from 1760 to 1870. All writers of that period referred to the dances they witnessed as being of the dancers themselves, such as the "dance of the ghawâzî" or the *"danse des almées"* (dance of the almées). As such, the travel literature of the study period has contributed negative evidence on this topic.[1]

A Name for Female Entertainers

Two terms associated with 18th- and 19th-century Egyptian female dancers and singers frequently appear today in both popular and scholarly western dance literature, the words *ghawâzî* (used as both singular and plural) and *'alma/'awâlim,* both reasonably close transcriptions from the Arabic.[2] As used in these modern contexts, the two terms usually refer to late 18th- and 19th-century Egyptian female dancers and Egyptian female singers, respectively. It is often assumed today that the words came from local Egyptian usage picked up by European travelers of all nationalities and then made popular in the West. A careful review of the travel literature, however, shows that these same terms (in many variations and transcriptions from the Arabic) did appear widely, but demonstrates that, in this literature, there was no consensus as to how the terms related to female professionals practicing singing and dancing.

Appendix two lists how travelers over 110 years (primarily British and French) named and defined the female Egyptian dancers and singers they encountered. In the appendix one can see that during this 110-year period European travelers did not necessarily choose to use Arabic terms for the performers they met. Savary, whose letters date sequentially from his first arrival in Egypt in 1775, did not use an approximated Arabic word for female performer until after he arrived in Cairo. Pococke never did use either term in his 1743 writing on "dancing women of Egypt," nor did Sonnini, traveling from 1777 to 1778. Maximilian used the generic term "dancing girls" even as late as 1838. William George Browne, who arrived in 1772, made the first known identified use of the term *ghawzee* in the British travel literature. Two Frenchmen, Savary and Constantin François Volney, traveling in 1777 and 1783, were the first European writers to use an approximation of another Arabic term, speaking of an *almah*.[3]

There was a clear national preference, with writers in French generally choosing variations of their newly created word *almée* to describe all female performers, both singers and dancers. They used *almées* (with numerous variations) for the plural.[4] On the whole, British writers discontinued the use of alma by the middle of the 19th century, concentrating on the term ghawâzî.[5] Normally, they preferred to use the term as both a singular and a plural. As a good example of the existing nationalist preferences, the British author Romer called the dancer Safiyya by the term Ghawazee (1846, 1:272) while the French author Edmund

Combes called her "la reine des almés" (queen of the almés) (1846, 1:220). The American author Curtis called the dancer Kutchuk Hanem a Ghazeeyah (1856, 130) while Flaubert called her an almée (1965, 244).

Throughout the entire period of the study, few authors used both terms—'alma and ghawâzî—much less felt they needed to make clear distinctions between them when referring to either dancers or singers.⁶ The issue of clarity did have some advocates, for example Taylor: "Most travelers confound the ghawazy with the almées; according to others, the almées are uniquely singers. We who have visited the Orient twice are convinced that the almées sing and dance" (1856, 263).⁷ Even in choosing only knowledgeable authors on this issue, that is, those with awareness of both terms and the implications, fluent Arabic, longtime residence, interest in dance and music, and sensitivity to local customs,⁸ the evidence is inconclusive. The modern researcher, therefore, cannot rely on travelers' remarks as evidence that they were using the term almées to identify singers of Egypt and ghawâzî as dancers during the period of the study.

On the other hand, appendix two, listing a sampling of travelers' use of terms for singer and dancer, does shed light on one important cultural fact of performance, the status of various classes of dancers and singers. Over and over, European travelers identified two classes of performer: one more esteemed and attached to high society; the other of low esteem, entertaining the lower classes, generally in public places. They might use only one term (selecting either 'alma or ghawâzî) with qualifying adjectives such as *more decent* or *lesser*. Europeans sought to explain this social division in ways that were meaningful to them according to their own norms, and used various criteria such as skills of performance, decency of performance, place of performance, or ethnicity of audience.⁹

The early French traveler Volney criticized all female entertainers strongly, but did claim a gulf between two groups based on skill of performance: "Those who make this their profession [dancing] are called raouazi, those who excel take on the title of almé, or savants in the art" (1959, 392). Savary (1785, 1:149) suggested the same by saying the 'awâlim formed a celebrated society that admitted only performers with extensive skills of singing, knowledge of poetry, and the Arabic language.

Other authors believed that vulgarity was the defining feature between the two groups. "The a'oualem have two kinds: one decent and thus esteemed by honest people, the other, those who treat all conventions with disdain, despised for their shamelessness" (Villoteau 1809a, 694). Taylor (1856, 265) also suggested that the street dancers needed vulgarity to make up for their lack of training and skills.¹⁰

Other authors developed the explanation that place of performance defined the dancer, ghawâzî found in the public outdoor places of cities and towns and 'awâlim in upper-class homes and the palaces of the nobility.[11] Galland (1804, 2:23) said the "alméhs of the first order" entertained only within the home, leaving "an inferior class" to play in public in the streets.[12] Clot Bey also placed his discussion into this framework of place of performance, introducing the further refinement of ethnicity: "It is rare that Muslims have the gaouasys come to their homes. The Jews and the Europeans are almost the only ones who give themselves this license" (Clot Bey 1840, 2:90).[13]

As argued by these European writers, huge differentiations in skills, style, and places of performance may have helped define the two classes of performers, but these European writers were looking primarily for explanations in innate qualities within the performers themselves, in a sense blaming the lower-class dancers for their own misfortunes. Those writers who argued for performance locale as a defining feature did, however, approximate a possible explanation for the status of the two groups. With a basis in medieval Egyptian Mamluk society, these distinctions among female entertainers appear to have had a long tradition.

In a work on women in medieval Egypt, the modern author Ahmad 'Abd ar-Raziq (1973, 66) writes that singers of two kinds lived in 14th-century Egypt. One group included costly, specially purchased slaves, normally of foreign birth, owned by the nobility and upper class. The other group constituted free "popular" singers (presumably Egyptians) who entertained the masses (ibid., 67). 'Abd ar-Râziq further says:

> There existed still in the Mamluk period, as in all the previous periods, slave singers.... Each sovereign and each emir owned at that time a whole orchestra that consisted of female slave singers and dancers [ibid., 55].

He also identifies (ibid., 66) teachers instructing female slaves to both sing and dance, then presenting them to the nobility as gifts. One might assume dancers and dancing also were subject to the same status dichotomy mentioned by 'Abd ar-Raziq, resulting in both slave dancers owned by the wealthy and free dancers of the people. 'Abd ar-Raziq's work shows clearly how this two-group split in performing groups in medieval times related to the social status of their audience.[14]

One needs then to turn the European argument on its head. In the medieval period, performers did not dance for the wealthy because they were high class. They were considered high class because they danced for the wealthy. This rigid distinction continued of major relevance during subsequent centuries, traces existing even up to the period of this study when such slave-orchestras hardly existed as a practice among the nobility, and free women (presumably of native origin) had almost entirely replaced them. Unaware of the long tradition, travelers sought to explain what they saw in Egyptian society according to their own

European notions of performance. In effect, they largely tried to blame the lower-status performers for their own situation through inherent qualities they constantly, but unsuccessfully, tried to identify. On the other hand, Europeans' discussion of social-status differentials among female professional performers identified an important topic, one explored more fully in the later discussion of guilds.

Dictionaries and Modern Research on Performance Terms

Since European travelers of the time did not shed adequate light on the words 'alma and ghawâzî as defining performance practices between 1760 and 1870, it seems useful to turn to Arabic dictionaries. The two terms certainly have an authentic place in modern Arabic usage. In Hans Wehr's (1994) *Arabic-English Dictionary*, the verb root for the noun 'alma is '-l-m, meaning "to know, be cognizant be informed," a root word in classical Arabic with many words derived from it, including science, learning, teacher, theologian (ibid., 743). One can see how the term might include talented female singers, poets, and dancers. Indeed, Wehr's modern meanings for the noun 'alma include "woman of learning, woman scholar; singer, chanteuse and belly dancer."[15] Wehr lists the term ghâziya (pl. ghâwâzin) with the translation "woman dancer; *danseuse*" (ibid., 788). He lists this noun under the verb-stem gh-z-w, meaning "to strive, aspire, mean, intend, carry out military expedition, raid." This stem root has no relevance to any performance activities, however, unlike the stem root for 'alma.

Significantly, even though Lane (1978, 372) writes of the public dancers as *ghawâzee* in his *Manners and Customs of the Modern Egyptians*, the term does not appear in his *Arabic-English Lexicon*, a standard for earlier classical Arabic (as opposed to modern Arabic). In the *Lexicon*, as in Wehr's modern dictionary, there are no connotations of dancing or singing associated with the verb-stem gh-z-w.[16] It is possible that in the travelers' day the term ghawâzî (or its approximation) was only an informal colloquial Turkish-Egyptian term for public performers, nomenclature that eventually became well established in that country.

Several pieces of modern research on medieval and early Ottoman Egypt do contain scattered references to dancers and singers, along with three other terms used at that time in Egypt for these professions. One medieval term for female singer was *mughaniyya*, with the suggestion that the term might also indicate a singer-dancer ('Abd ar-Raziq 1973, 66). This word is simply the Arabic for "female singer." In the 17th century, Ottoman-Egyptian usage included a second term for a dancer, *jankiyya* (al–Sayyid Marsot 1995, 119; Raymond 1973–74, 2:650).

Afaf Lutfi al–Sayyid Marsot (1995, 119) does identify two female dancers of that period by name, Janash al–Jankiyya and Amna al–Jankiyya. Their very names contain the information that they were dancers by trade. The term *jankiyya* still echoed down to the time of the Savants in Egypt, for Villoteau (1809a, 700) speaks in 1800 of the *genk* or *djenk,* a Jewish woman who taught dancing, and followed the wedding procession playing on a drum. The memory of the term connected to female performers continued even into the middle of the 19th century, for Didier learned from a female dancer he encountered in 1854 that "once they called themselves cenghi, from the Turkish word cenghe, a kind of harp on which they once accompanied themselves, but which they now no longer use" (quoted in Aradoon 1979, 132).[17] According to Lane's *Lexicon* (1984, 472), the word *jank* refers to a type of Persian harp, the word itself passing into Arabic from Persian.[18]

The same cross connection of a Persian word providing an Arabic word for a female entertainer might also be inferred in the case of the term ghawâzî. The oldest-written version of this word thus far located in European travel literature on Egypt dates from Niebuhr's 1761 voyage, and, interestingly, he used a shorter version of the word, that is, "ghasie" (n.d., 139). Both Sulayman Hayyim's *New Persian-English Dictionary* and Francis Joseph Steingass's *Comprehensive Persian-English Dictionary* list the Persian word *ghaazi,* meaning specifically "rope dancer; courtesan; and sheep's gut stuffed with spices" (Hayyim 1968, 405–06; Steingass 1984, 878). The coincidence is striking.[19]

An example of a third, and important, term used for female entertainers can be found in the Egyptian literature in the late 18th century. The modern researcher André Raymond (1956–57, 160n8) points out that the Egyptian chronicler 'Abd al-Rahman al-Jabarti used the word *raqqâsin* in his writings. Al-Jabarti used the term in referring to a guild of performers appearing at a royal wedding.

One concludes that the various Egyptian-Arabic terms for female entertainers varied and changed over the centuries. This brief examination of terms for dancer, singer, and musician found in dictionaries and selected modern research has opened some interesting avenues for future specialized investigations. It has proved as elusive as the writings of European travelers in defining definitively various groups of female performers in Egypt in the period 1760 to 1870, both as to performance practices and to category of performer.

Guilds and Guild Lists as Evidence for Dancers and Singers

Modern research on Egyptian guilds of the period makes clear, however, that in late 18th- and early 19th-century Egypt, not two but three clearly recognized groups of female entertainers existed, known administratively as the singers, the raqqâsin, and a third called simply the dancers.

By 1801, with empty pockets, the stranded French army that had temporarily conquered Egypt determined to identify all existing Cairo corporations, intending to tax them for the continuing occupation of the country. Staff under General Auguste Daniel Belliard compiled a list of the Cairo guilds. The original of this document has survived, discovered by Raymond (1956–57, 150–163) in the French military archives. The guild list was drawn up in French, with occasional transcriptions of Arabic.[20] Fortunately, the French language of the original list (also in Raymond's French-language journal article) clearly identifies those corporations pertaining only to females and only to males. Of the 278 guilds identified, five are key to this study, three for female entertainers and two for male entertainers.

The three women's guilds are listed here, first with the French wording for the guild on the 1801 guild list as provided in Raymond's article, then in my English translation, then with the number assigned to the corporation on the original list of 1801. Significantly, neither term ghawâzî nor ʿawâlim appears on this guild list. Used instead for one group of dancers is the generic Arabic *rakassin*, or female dancers. A more correct transcription would be *raqqâsin*, used from here on. The three guilds are the following:

- *Chanteuses du Caire*—[female] singers of Cairo (Corporation 137)
- *Danseuses et musiciens qui les accompagnent qui sont au Caire*—[female] dancers and [male] musicians[21] who accompany them who are in Cairo (Corporation 192)
- *Danseuses qui sont au Caire dites Rakassin*—[female] dancers of Cairo, called *rakassin* (Corporation 200)

Raymond also identifies one guild for male dancers of Cairo (Corporation 139), and another for male singers and male musicians of Cairo (Corporation 126), the latter clearly distinct and separate from those of Corporation 192, consisting of musicians attached professionally to one group of female dancers. It is important to note that two types of male dancers (known locally as *ginks* and *khawals*), were grouped into one guild, and both male singers and male musicians had only one guild among them. On the other hand, the differentials among female entertainers necessitated three separate guilds. Female dancers had two guilds, which were distinct from the one for female singers.

Why the need to have two dance groups so clearly separated, one with affiliated male musicians? Corporation 137, female singers, clearly relates to those who make singing an exclusive career and does not pose problems of definition. On the other hand, Corporation 192 describes a guild of dancers with their own musicians, the two types of performers forming a "package deal." Since Egyptian guilds normally were segregated by gender, this association is significant. Several writers over the first quarter of the 19th century had spoken of dancers who performed in open public places as having their own musicians. In Asyût, there "are almées who run in the streets accompanied by [male] musicians" (Boustany 1971, 1:112). The French traveler Combes said of dancers generally that "they gather in small troupes, each with its own orchestra" (1846, 1:222).[22]

The Napoleonic Savant Villoteau alone identifies a local Arabic word for the musicians who accompanied these ghawâzî: "The ghaouâzy are often accompanied by certain minstrels called ghazouâty" (1809a, 695).[23] The term *ghazouâty* (roughly translated as "those who are of the ghawâzî") differs from the word travelers usually used then for musician, *alâtya*.[24] Villoteau's choice of *ménétrier* (minstrel) rather than *musicien* (musician) to describe those musicians working with the ghawâzî, is also significant. The former term would certainly have had a relatively negative connotation for the French Savant, again suggesting a lower status position consistent with the public dancers. The term *ghazouâty*, and the fact of a guild of female dancers with musicians suggest that Corporation 192 relates to a guild of dancers known in local parlance as *ghawâzî*.

Since Corporation 200, the raqqâsin provides one clear instance where a type of female entertainer is definitively associated with an Arabic term meaning female dancers, one must acknowledge its significance in dance studies.[25] As noted earlier, the same term for female dancers existed in literary Arabic at the turn of the 19th century, for al-Jabarti wrote that the *raqqâsin* appeared as a guild at the marriage of the daughter of Isma'il Bey.[26] His use of this term to describe a corporation of dancers associated with a wedding of the nobility of Egypt implies the raqqâsin had some social status. They would not be the lowly street dancers, now equated with Corporation 192, but another clearly differentiated group of female entertainers who not only practiced dancing but derived their professional name specifically from this activity.

Needed obviously is a tri-part classification of female entertainers that not only makes sense of the 1801 guild list, which must have had a solid basis in reality, but also clarifies all the travel literature with its confusion about the classification of dancers and singers. If one reads his early 19th-century comments carefully, Lane had already provided evidence about such a three-way split consistent with the 1801 guild list. He says:

> There are also female professional singers. These are called "Awalim": literally signifying a learned female.... Some of them are also instrumental performers.... There are also many of an *inferior class* [emphasis mine] who sometimes dance in the hareem; hence travellers have often misapplied the name of "almé," meaning "'ál'meh," to the *common dancing-girls* [emphasis mine] of whom an account will be given in another chapter of this work [1978, 354, 355].

He also said, "Some of these women [ghawâzî] add to their other allurements the art of singing and equal the *ordinary* [emphasis mine] 'Awâlim" (1978, 376).

Leaving aside his terminology, one finds in Lane the same three bundles of tasks of the 1801 guild list. The guild list's "chanteuses" are Lane's "female professional singers." The guild list's "danseuses ... dites rakkassin" are Lane's "many of an inferior class, who sometimes dance in the harem." The guild list's "danseuses et musiciens" are Lane's "common dancing girls." The exact parallels seem quite clear. Lane chose to use such words as "inferior class" and "ordinary 'Awâlim" to refer to the group known administratively as raqqâsîn, whom he obviously felt had less prestige than the professional singers, and used the terms "common dancing girls" to refer to the ghawâzî, who had less prestige still. It is clear he implied an important ranking of the three guilds in descending order, according to social status. In her research, Nieuwkerk (1995, 27) also identifies three distinct groups of female entertainers: "There was also a category of female entertainers between the 'awâlim and the ghawâzî. This group consisted of lower-class singers and dancers." She does not tie a full discussion to the 1801 guild list, however.

Analysis of the 1801 guild list prepared by the French army establishes solid evidence of distinctions between three corporations of female entertainers. Clearly, the tri-part guild division and the two-part terminology of ghawâzî and 'awâlim that permeates most of the travel literature, cannot easily be reconciled except through a careful reading of each writer's account. One can usually locate the guild of female singers of the 1801 list in the literature, and understand their exclusiveness as a separate corporation, but it has been often difficult for me to identify and separate with any assurance the ghawâzî and raqqâsin at work, for many historical reasons to be explored at greater length in the next two chapters. One reason, of course, may be that, in practice, as the century progressed the differentiation among the guilds began to lose its clarity.

Although it has been gratifying to identify a second separate corporation of dancers/singers, future use in this book of the term for their guild, raqqâsin, presents difficulties. Since this word does not appear anywhere in the travel literature of the period, and has not validated itself in modern research literature, it would be pedantic to insist on the practice here. It seems easier to allow that the well-established word 'awâlim may be thought of generally as a generic term often usefully covering both raqqâsin and singers, with the specific term ghawâzî kept for Corporation 192, both as a singular and a plural, in keeping with most modern literature today. The term raqqâsin, then, will appear later in section three only, with examples that illustrate this class of entertainer. From this point onwards in the text use of the term *singer* usually refers specifically to members of Corporation 197 (unless the context clearly indicates otherwise). I use "female entertainers" as a generic expression to include all guilds together or to refer to only one guild, particularly in cases when it is not clear from the travel account which guild members were present (which, unfortunately, is often). I use the term *dancers* for either of the two guilds of female dancers in similarly vague instances. In direct quotations, of course, the terms used in the original documents are retained, sometimes with my commentary as to whether they probably do or do not relate to the guild identified by the travel writer.

5

The Low Reputation of Female Entertainers

Although certain female singers might gain money and esteem through their talents, on the whole female entertainers had a low reputation within Egyptian society. This situation becomes clear through a reading of Egyptian proverbs of the time. An Egyptian leader of standing, al–Jabarti chose a dance proverb when he ruefully judged what he saw as the increasing corruption of Egyptian morals during the Napoleonic occupation—"When the master of the house starts to beat the tambourine, the members of the household have only to dance" (1888–96, 6:151). Other early Egyptian proverbs reveal society's feelings about female entertainers. These proverbs express a picture of self-serving flattery, false faces, and lack of morals generally. "The fly knows the face of the milk-seller" (Burkhardt 1984, 21).[1] "To the good luck of my wedding festivities the night was short and the female singers became penitents" (ibid., 133).[2] "If the harlot repents, she becomes a procuress" (ibid., 35). Such proverbs imply a poor reputation for dance and its female practitioners among Egyptians of the period.

Many foreign writers also took similar positions on dance and female dancers. Minutoli called the dance "a sight destitute of taste and sense, which offends modesty, and frightens away the graces" (1827, 200). Although they did not attack entertainers' characters as did the proverbs, travelers often took for granted their sexual immorality. "They are prepared and accustomed to a trade still more dishonorable than that of performing lascivious dance in public" (Sonnini 1799, 1:321). "Song and dance are not their only industry, although one hides their commerce" (Didier 1858, 52). Others, however, were able to take a more nuanced approach. Hamont (1845, 1:315), although not particularly a champion of female entertainers, pointed out that though lacking social status, dancers participated in all the important Egyptian festivities, and in fact were the very "soul" and "active principle" of these events. They enchanted all classes of society; Muslims, Jews and Christians alike welcomed them into their homes. Others made similar remarks on dancers' limited but accepted place in Egyptian society.[3]

Because of the ambivalence within society regarding the dance and the dancer, the route to a purely private party might involve some self-justification. Bayle St. John writes in considerable detail of such a situation in the Alexandrian (Christian) household where he boarded in 1847. The matriarch of the household, Sitt Madoula, knew very well that he and her son were most eager to see the dancers, and was willing to help them. She felt she had found the required reason for her son had just been excused from military service.[4] But because it was "only on rare occasions that a Levantine, or indeed any Eastern family, indulges in the kind of dissipation I have described" (B. St. John 1850, 151) she "inflexibly condemned anything that resembled a defiance to public opinion" (ibid., 145). Besides, she was still in mourning for her third husband. She made the young men wait for almost a year, but then, "not long after the few days' grace which she allowed herself ... she announced her readiness to give a regular Levantine soiree—of which 'the Awalim' were to form the principal attractions" (ibid., 146).

The travel writing also points out that, despite standing somewhat outside respectable society, dancers might become reintegrated on marriage. "If a dancing girl repents, the most respectable man may and does marry her, and no one blames or laughs at him" (Duff Gordon 1983, 136). Hamont (1845, 1:320) provides an anecdote about such repentance. Entertainers would enter a mosque and present themselves before a *santon* [holy fool] pronouncing aloud, "I convert to God and I return to him." Then, upon tearing her shirt, she became an honest woman.[5]

Only rarely could Europeans give a picture of real female entertainers with a sense of the complexity of their position. Almost uniquely, Duff Gordon attempts to give a balanced reading of the relationship of dancers and society in 1860s Luxor:

> I think you would enjoy, as I do, the peculiar sort of social equality which prevails here; ... There are the great and powerful people, much honoured (outwardly, at all events), but nobody has inferiors.... He is not my inferior, he is my poor brother.... Even the dancing-girl is not an outcast; she is free to talk to me, and it is highly irreligious to show any contempt or aversion. The rules of politeness are the same for all [1983, 141].

The travel literature gives useful hints, but one turns to modern research on Egyptian music and dance and its practitioners for a more reasoned understanding of the status of performers and explanations for their ambivalent reputations. Poché and Nieuwkerk have both addressed the important topic of the Islamic context for music and dance. Poché (1996, 21–30) writes that *dance* is not mentioned in the Qur'an, but may appear in two hadiths.[6] He puts forth in some detail the various arguments given by Muslim scholars over the centuries as to whether the actual Arabic verbs used in the hadiths show dance was occurring, who was dancing, what kind of body movements were involved, and whether, as a result, certain kinds of dancing would be acceptable in Islam. He finds examples of early types of dance in the Middle East. He also cites (ibid., 35) a 16th-century Egyptian jurist who clearly identified dance (using the verb *raqs* of the Arabic vocabulary) as only applicable to a female practice.

Drawing on a wide review of literature, Nieuwkerk (1995, 10–12) writes that serious discussions by religious leaders about the legality of dance, music, and singing within Islam began shortly after the Prophet Muhammad's death and continue to this day. Of particular concern have always been the issues of context of the performance, with certain situations (such as family celebrations) lending legitimacy, and others (such as those with consumption of alcohol) off limits. Nieuwkerk also presents the factors of type of music, length of time devoted to these pleasures, and people present, as keys to determining religious acceptability. She argues that, based on her reading of certain Islamic authorities, gender becomes a crucial factor, as "female dancing is accordingly considered the most shameful form of entertainment" (ibid., 13). Nieuwkerk however, also points out that religious doctrines may not necessarily produce absolutely congruent observances. Based on the examples to be discussed fully in section three, it appears Egyptians of the period were prepared to avail themselves fully of legitimate opportunities for entertainments, such as weddings and public festivals, and even to stretch the definition of appropriate circumstances to coffee house performances.

Besides the disfavor of religious authorities, there were other reasons for the poor reputations of female entertainers. The modern writer Judith Tucker (Nashat and Tucker 1999, 95) suggests that dancers would "enter a social netherworld" because they performed in public in front of men, but some further refinement here might be useful. Certainly the public dancers were freely available to the indigenous male population, in particular transient males such as merchants, soldiers, and sailors. Without being explicit, travelers' tales show a certain tension existing between female entertainers and their male public, a tension coming from the Islamic context in which, as women, they worked beyond the normal boundaries separating male and female. For example, John Carne (1826, 125) reports that, around 1822 at Qena, he saw "women of pleasure of various nations" and heard the sound of music and dancing coming from houses where they were passing the evening with Albanian merchants. Champollion (c. 1986, 54) complained that his 1828 expedition was forced to wait for the boat's captain, who had profited from the stop in Fuwa to "pass time with the Almeh." It was the intimacy of these face-to-face situations that placed female entertainers outside the range of normally acceptable occasions for entertainment, and general public disapproval would fall most heavily on the women, with cumulative results to their reputations.

The travel literature does contain hints about the factor of place as a determinant of status, a concept involved in women's issues worldwide.[7] Local Egyptian thinking held that female entertainers frequented questionable places and thereby became both contaminated and contaminating. The travel literature mentions the set-aside areas in which they lived, often at the edges of cities and towns. Edmé François Jomard (1822, 771) relates information about the area around Cairo's Zouaila gate. Its dilapidated site in Napoleonic times lay on the way to the bazaar where musical instruments were sold. An entrance there allegedly ruined any future enterprise planned by those who passed through it. The reputation of the area continued, with some Egyptians saying it arose from the ancient curse, while others maintaining the presence of musical instruments, and various categories of entertainers who normally thronged there gave rise to the toxic effects. Al-Jabarti (1888–96, 6:101) said that authorities used this already-disreputable gate as the site for executions.

Modern writers have examined two other reasons for the low status of female performers, unveiling and a roving lifestyle. Some argue that dancers were not respected because they appeared unveiled in public, specifically they did not observe the normal dress codes expected of decent women outside their homes.[8] "Dancers were the only women who transgressed this law and appeared unveiled in public" (Buonaventura 1990, 50). Al-Sayyid Marsot (1995, 89–90), however, gives important insights into veiling among the Egyptian female population of the 18th and 19th centuries. She discusses a short invasion of Egypt by Turkey in 1786 when the troops behaved aggressively towards many segments of the female population, bothering them in the streets and perhaps even removing them from the public baths. They excused themselves by accusing the Egyptian women of asking for these attentions through their own licentious behavior. The Ottoman invaders then tried to keep all women at home, but found it impossible to restrict business women from going about Cairo. Finally, they decreed that these tradeswomen were not to wear a headdress called the *qazdaghliyya*. Al-Sayyid Marsot argues this must have been a scarf that left the face and much hair uncovered, one sexually alluring to the foreign Ottomans and the probable original cause of the troops' behavior. She also accepts (ibid., 117) Lane's comments that even respectable women of the lower classes did not hide their faces in his day (in the 1820s and 1830s); only women of the middle and upper classes followed that custom.

Egyptian female entertainers, then, did not transgress the dress code more than others of their lower class peers. While the question of "proper" dress for women is an important sociological concept across time and geographical location,[9] in this instance it cannot provide a significant rationale for dancers' reputations. Their unveiled faces, though, would proclaim their lower class origins, a factor contributing to their lack of status.

The issue of a roving lifestyle also carries weight as an explanatory concept. Al-Sayyid Marsot (1995, 100) argues that, in Egypt, trades such as itinerant peddlers, porters, donkey boys, and grooms were despised because they did not work from a fixed place.[10] They were less able to be controlled by the public official in charge of the markets, and were free to come and go. By implication, a peripatetic lifestyle must have increased entertainers' poor reputations, particularly for the ghawâzî. "They are constantly moving about ... attending the country fairs, or the camps of the troops" (Burkhardt 1984, 175). A wandering life served their trade well, but authorities obviously looked with suspicion on all professions with no fixed address. Dancers, with their supposed capacity to slip through the official net of control and taxation, or engage in questionable practices with impunity, would fall into this category. It should be pointed out, however, that these factors added to their low status but did not explain it in total since other professions were in the same position.

There seems no single variable to explain the low status of female entertainers within Egyptian society. Rather, the cumulative effects of their gender, peripatetic lifestyle, habiting of stigmatized places, lower class origin, willingness to transgress the usual male/female boundaries of association, their assumed immorality, and, finally, the ambivalent place of their professions within a Muslim society must all be taken into account. The fact that female entertainers could leave this netherworld and re-enter respectable society on marriage, however, shows a remarkable flexibility within Egyptian society towards this particular group.

6

The Geography of Going to the Show

Numbers

The travel literature cannot answer the question of how many professional female entertainers of the various guilds existed in 18th- and 19th-century Egypt. Only Burkhardt (1984, 177) hazards a guess at specific numbers, saying there might be between 6,000 to 8,000 female and male dancers in Egypt, with two areas of concentration—certain towns of the Delta, and Qena in Upper Egypt. There is no way to verify these numbers.

A few writers make impressionistic guesses as to their number in remarks such as: "The ghowazys have in every town or considerable village a small quarter assigned to them" (Burkhardt 1984, 175); "The almées of Cairo, those of Upper Egypt, those of the Delta and of all the banks of the Nile, flock every year [to Tanta] in the first weeks of April" (Michaud 1833–35, 7:219); "They were found in great numbers scattered over the whole of Egypt, enlivening ... not only the great towns and cities but even the smallest and humblest villages" (J. St. John 1851, 3). Of Cairo one reads, "One finds them everywhere. The public squares and promenades of Cairo are full of them" (Savary 1785, 1:155). While the travel literature is singularly uninformative on the issue of numbers, it does provide useful facts on geography.

Lower Egypt

In the Nile's Delta region, the decaying town of Fuwa and the larger Mutûbis (six miles apart on the Nile, just south of Rosetta) formed a kind of twin town area, both noted as places where female entertainers lived permanently. In the late 18th-century the authorities of Fuwa allowed female entertainers to live there in a "khan" and to pursue their profession actively (Savary 1785, 1:67). A dance performance for General Menou's invading French troops took place at Mutûbis in 1798 (Denon 1973, 230). Champollion (c. 1986, 54) complained that his 1828 expedition was forced to wait for the boat's captain who had profited from the stop in Fuwa to visit the entertainment quarter.[1]

Joseph F. Michaud relates an intriguing story involving European crusaders who invaded Egypt in 1249, and local female entertainers of Fuwa/Mutûbis. Citing the French chronicler Matthew Paris, Michaud (1833–35, 5:50) tells that the crusaders, having captured Damietta, made a foray southwest into the Delta and returned with much booty. They also brought back some Muslim women from a town along the route. Michaud is convinced the town was Fuwa or Mutûbis, and the women were entertainers. If Paris's account can be believed, the story indicates a very old connection of the region with female professionals.

A continuation of this history of the twin towns lies in Savary's (1785, 1:66) account. He remarks on Fuwa's earlier 15th-century glories when the city was second only to Cairo, and boasted a Venetian consulate. At that time Egypt's trade passed from Fuwa along a canal to Alexandria. With the later silting of the canal, Fuwa lost its trade, and Rosetta took its place. It seems that, despite the growing ruin of the town, female entertainers still continued their residence there into the early 19th century. Perhaps at that time, though, they were transferring their major operations to Mahalla el Kubra.

Mahalla el-Kubra, in mid–Delta, was another city known for its resident female entertainers. Just outside the city on the Damietta branch of the Nile, Savary (1785, 1:297) witnessed a young dancer performing in a coffee house in 1779. In their trip through the Delta in 1799, Jean-Marie Du Bois-Aymé and Jean-Beptiste Jollois (1812, 109) noted the high population of "public women" who apparently were fairly free to conduct business there. Indeed, the two Frenchmen claimed these women's leader worked out of this city, sending entertainers to all parts of the Delta. The two Frenchmen attended a society wedding in that city, with excellent singing and dancing. By Michaud's time (the 1830s) the city still had a large concentration of female entertainers. They lived within the walls in a segregated area. He writes (1833–35, 7:36) that their leader still directed members of the guild to assignments throughout the region.[2]

Although an important Mediterranean port, Alexandria was not a long-standing major center for female entertainers.[3] During Vivant-Dominique Denon's travels with Napoleon's troops, at Alexandria he saw only Greek dancing boys (1973, 202). Hume (1818, 400) says that "at Alexandria there were very few dancing girls," and saw only a transvestite dancer. Muhammad Ali favored Alexandria as a residence, and in his rule the city grew in importance, with many foreign residents and European consuls (Mengin 1839, 227–28). Female entertainers probably grew in numbers in response to these new opportunities, although this may have been a short-lived phenomenon. Referring to the year of his visit, 1833, James St. John (1845, 20) remarked that while dancers were no longer permitted to perform in the private homes of Alexandria's resident Europeans, it was still possible to watch them at the town's many coffee houses.

The ports of Rosetta and Damietta had their entertainers, but there were differences between the two towns. Rosetta seems to have boasted a considerable public presence. Sonnini (1799, 1:248) mentions a coffee house in Rosetta with entertainment available from dancing girls, buffoons and storytellers. The later Napoleonic writers also noted the presence of public dancers at Rosetta, performing for a few small coins at the coffee houses, along with musicians, clowns and storytellers (Jollois 1822, 350). Two illustrations also indicate the presence of dancers at Rosetta. Denon's 1802 work includes an illustration (fig. 5) of an *Almée of Egypt* that identifies Rosetta depicted in the background. Prisse d'Avennes' *Ghawazi or Dancing Girls* (fig. 18) also represents entertainers from Rosetta. The text for this plate indicates dancers might be seen "in the open spaces of those beautiful gardens which extend, like so many little paradises, along the left bank of the Nile" (J. St. John 1851, 4). Michaud (1833–35, 6:358) describes Damietta of the early 1830s as a quiet place, less turbulent than Cairo. There were fewer clowns and male dancers, and though there were female entertainers, they never appeared in public places, only at parties given by the rich. Both Carne (1826, 73) and Minutoli (1827, 198) had earlier described such private parties.

Apart from towns discussed above, in Lower Egypt only the isolated village of Nadir, considerably farther south on the Rosetta branch of the Nile, seems to have had connections with dance and music entertainment. The village was a natural revitalization stop. It also provided a good place to anchor for those who did not wish to travel by night, being halfway on the river trip, from Alexandria to Cairo. Both Champollion (1986, 67) and Michaud (1833–35, 5:87) mention modest performances they witnessed there.

After a general ban on performance around 1834, dancers probably still concentrated together in the Delta. Bayle St. John implies that there was considerable business-as-usual in the area, "They are supposed it is true, to be banished to Upper Egypt; but the edict was never effectually carried out" (1973, 1:28). Maximilian (1978, 56), for example, implies that somehow he saw dancers perform in Alexandria in 1838. He says these Alexandrian dancers were not as "shameless" as those in Upper Egypt. The Fuwa area probably continued to be important, but other references available imply that female entertainers normally withdrew from the mainstream. Bayle St. John (1973, 1:22) describes the village where he saw the school for young dancers and a colony of dancers as "probably

6. The Geography of Going to the Show

Fig. 5. Vivant Denon. *Almée*. c. 1800 (with permission of the Royal Ontario Museum © ROM).

seldom visited by Europeans." Called Kafr Mustana, it stood inland, several miles above Fuwa. From Frédéric Auguste Antoine Goupil-Fesquet's (1843, 69) account one learns about the reconstituted tourist entertainments offered along the Nile in the late 1830s. Docking at an obscure village he called "Kafr Raiak," he found a village inhabited by many female entertainers awaiting employment from the Nile boat traffic.

Cairo

The Cairo area had always boasted a large concentration of female entertainers, and many references to dancers and to dance performances in the travel literature relate to the capital. Only Burkhardt (1984, 178) implied they were not numerous in the capital but perhaps he only means they did not live within Cairo proper, for despite their ubiquitous presence dancers normally did not make their homes in the city but in the outskirts. Burkhardt comments that, in his day (1812–1817), they all lived together in a "khan" near the Mukattam Hills to the southeast of central Cairo, "under the citadel" (ibid., 178). As Cairo grew, dancers may have relocated their settlement across the Nile to the western shore, for Michaud (1833–35, 5:306–308) mentions dancers in the general vicinity of the pyramids of Giza. Bayle St. John's (1973, 1:25–26) remarks about the famous dancer Kutchuk Hanem implies her career took place at certain times in the Giza area.

In the period around 1830, dancers seem to have had permanent settlements also to the northeast of the city, near present-day Heliopolis. "I recall having seen, near Heliopolis, a village entirely populated by these women" (Prisse d'Avennes 1930, 63). When James St. John visited "Sha'arah"[4] to see a performance at a village inhabited by dancers, he first crossed the city, then went northeast across fields to "one of the most ruinous and unfrequented suburbs" (J. St. John 1834, 1:106). Marmont, too, locates a village of entertainers in that same general area around 1834: "The village of Matarieh is celebrated just now by the great number of public women who gather there and normally live there" (1837–38, 3:371).

Upper Egypt

While many female performers and prostitutes were exiled to Upper Egypt after a performance ban around 1834, they had always had a presence in that part of the country. Far to the south of Cairo, on the east bank of the Nile, Qena (along with nearby Qûs) lay strategically on the routes to the Red Sea, the Arabian peninsula with its key cities of Mecca and Medina, and, ultimately, India.

As well, its annual festival of the revered saint Said 'Abd al-Rachîm was an important national event. Qena was a hub of transit commerce, piety, and military movement.

Qena and surroundings obviously provided good professional opportunities for female entertainers of all kinds. Early in the 19th century, Burkhardt (1984, 177) identified Qena as an important dance center, numbering 300 dancers. In the early 1820s, Minutoli (1827, 119) saw many dancers there, attributing their presence to the annual Red Sea caravan stopping for a certain period. Carne (1826, 125) reports that around 1822 at Qena he saw "women of pleasure" and heard the sound of music and dancing coming from houses where they were passing the evening with Albanian merchants. Forbin (1819, 87) saw dancers at nearby Qûs in 1818. Romer (1846, 1:136) saw a dancer on the riverbank at Dishna, a small center slightly north of Qena, in 1846; there were many other entertainers in that same location. Flaubert (1965, 289) visited Qena twice in 1850, once to visit the talented dancer Hasna. Significantly, the great Badawiyya, who performed for the royal cruise for foreign visitors at the opening of the Suez Canal in 1869, lived in Qena. At that time there was an entire area of the city where female entertainers lived (Fromentin 1881, 290–91).

Asyût (and nearby Abu Tig and Manfalut) appears to be another important pre-ban center of dancers' settlement. Sonnini (1799, 3:282) remarks on personal encounters in 1778 with dancers in Abu Tig, just south of Asyût. During the Napoleonic period, a report indicated that "there are almées who run in the streets accompanied by musicians"; "there are 'public women' who stop those who pass by at the gates of Asiut" (Boustany 1971, 1:112). In the early 1820s, Carne (1826, 116) remarked that "the Almek [sic] girls abound in the towns of Upper Egypt" and noted many at Manfalut, just north of Asyût. After the ban, dancers were still available to tourists in the area. Maximilian (1978, 56) saw a dance performance behind closed doors in Asyût in 1838. Appleton (1876, 24) witnessed fine dancing there at a private Egyptian wedding in 1874. By the end of the century, regulations seem much more relaxed. Leland (1874, 135) mentions in passing seeing a dancer in Asyût around 1873, and V. Andreievsky (quoted in Volkoff 1972, 295) was able to arrange an officially sanctioned impromptu performance in Abu Tig around 1885. The Asyût area maintained itself as a dance center for over a hundred years. Significantly, it was one of three stops for official entertainments on the Nile cruise for the opening of the Suez Canal in 1869.

Travel accounts also mention events at Minya and Girga, towns located between Asyût and Qena. Combes (1846, 1:162) talks of some indifferently talented dancers at Minya in 1834. Some 13 months earlier, James St. John had explored Minya and commented that "in all these towns the coffee-houses, where dancing girls are invariably found, appear to be constantly open" (1834, 1:251).

L'Hôte, in 1828, and Leland, in 1873, held private dance parties at Girga (L'Hôte c. 1993, 129–31; Leland 1874, 133–37).

There is some data on the town of Luxor (Thebes) as a center of dance. Sonnini (1799, 3:207) commented on the presence of dancers and courtesans there during his trip up the Nile in 1777. Forbin saw "Arabes Ghaouazy" (1819, 93–94) dancing there during his 1818 return trip down river. In 1851, Bayle St. John moored there and remarked (1973, 2:69) that dancers had grown to be even more common in Luxor than in Isna. They were able to see the finest dancers of the town, the talented Hasna and seven other fine performers.

His experience suggests that many performers were there, but, by 1866, according to Duff Gordon (1983, 322), there were only three dancers in Luxor. There was still, however, an "almée's quarter" (Fromentin 1881, 293). Leland suggests that the young women he saw in Luxor around 1873 were not professionals, but only "mere peasant girls who work by day and dance by night; and others are low caste, and dance coarsely, with a male jester taking occasional part in the performances" (1874, 137). In 1876, Appleton (1876, 247–48) attended a dance entertainment there with four dancers given by the American consul. Appleton was disappointed with the quality of their dancing.

Luxor seems to have had only a brief period of dance importance; probably not-too-distant Qena normally provided much more professional opportunity. Hasna was working in Qena in the spring of 1850 when Flaubert met her, not in Luxor as she was when Bayle St. John watched her perform a year later. Perhaps Luxor's glory, as noted by Bayle St. John, may have coincided with Abbas' short reign from 1849 to 1854, with official pressure on dancers in Qena, and their subsequent short-lived removal, farther south to Luxor.[5]

Isna does not appear to have existed as a dance center prior to the dance ban around 1834; indeed, Isna lies a very long way up the Nile, far from civilization and commerce. For example, in the early 1820s Minutoli describes the town as a continuing refuge for the Mamluks during their wars with Istanbul and the viceroys of Egypt, for "its favourable position, and its distance from Cairo, secured their independence" (1827, 151). Certainly, Isna received a large influx of exiled entertainers from Cairo in the early 1830s, and an eye-witness description of the renowned Safiyya took place in 1834 (Combes 1846, 1:216–222). Significantly, however, Romer implies that, by the time of her visit to Safiyya in the 1840s, deportations there had ceased. She claims that "of the original Cairo-bred Ghawazee, only two now remain, and one of these, the celebrated Sofia" (1846, 1:272).

Did renewed actions against female entertainers under Abbas after 1849 result in more deportations at that time, and a second repopulation of Isna? In saying that dancers were numerous there early in 1854, and that most travelers treated themselves to dance entertainments there, Didier (1858, 296) leads us to believe this was the case.[6] Except for the presence of the great Safiyya, from 1833 to 1849, and the talented Kutchuk Hanem, temporarily around 1850, the general level of talent in Isna was probably not noteworthy. Blanc and Fromentin were not impressed with the performance there in 1869, and by 1882 Montbard spoke scathingly of the dancers of Isna, whom he said performed badly in disreputable locations, as "frightful sluts, ugly and old, with down-at-heel shoes, dressed in a sort of gaudy striped bath robe, stained with vermouth" (18—, 8).

Other Upper Egyptian centers where dancers performed include Beni Suef (considerably closer to Cairo than Asyût and Qena) mentioned by Forbin in 1818, James St. John in 1833, and Bartlett in 1845 (Forbin 1819, 82; J. St. John 1834, 265; Bartlett 1849, 112). Dance associated with the geographically important nearby Faiyûm area, southwest of Cairo, appears only in Paul Lenoir's (1872, 96–117) account of his 1868 travels. Both Flaubert (1991, 295, 353) and Didier (1858, 272–79) describe and name dancers as far south as the first cataract on the Nile, in Aswan.

Sudan

After the total ban on dancers he experienced in Cairo in 1854, six months later Didier (1858, 46–60) was astounded to discover a large dance community active in far-away Khartoum, at the confluence of the Blue Nile and the White Nile. As the capital of Egypt's recently conquered Sudan, with an Egyptian governor, Khartoum served as both the administrative center of the region and as a place of political exile. A small expatriate population of Turks, Egyptians, and Europeans that lived there seems to have reconstituted an earlier social life of Cairo, with its enthusiasm for professional music and dance. Here, female entertainers from both Egypt and Ethiopia had set up a thriving dance community, their arts patronized by the local elites. Didier describes them as free to live where they chose, to come and go at liberty, and to keep the money they earned. Such a relatively open society would obviously have offered attractions to young professionals, even though the voyage to distant Khartoum was long, difficult, and dangerous.

Section Three

*Going to the Show—
Professionals at Work*

7

The Corporation of Female Singers—the Chanteuses

Overview

Section three examines the three guilds of professional female entertainers, giving examples of specific performances of their art, and showing the settings in which they performed. Some attention is also given to male dancers and musicians. Egyptian dance of this period never took place except as an add-on to some other activity. The great annual religious events of Islam, the birthdays (*mawâlid*) of local Egyptian saints and a few festivals with pre–Islamic roots, provided the common Egyptian people with opportunities to see professional dance and hear music. Day to day, dance and music appeared at coffee houses throughout the country. Another entrée came through weddings, as dance entertainments would often be available both to guests and to those passing by. Finally, both male and female well-to-do Egyptians might take advantage of having visitors to their homes as a justification for a private party with professional entertainers.

Early Antecedents of Corporation 137, the Singers

As far back as medieval Mamluk society, female singers enjoyed enormous popularity with the noble houses. The modern writer 'Abd ar-Raziq's (1973, 68) material from the chronicles gives names and anecdotes about the lives of a number of celebrated singers, although sometimes it is not clear whether he is talking about slaves or free indigenous performers. In Mamluk Egypt there would have been no impediment in keeping greatly talented singers from wealth and societal approval. Similarly, slave women were well able to amass a fortune, and might be freed by their masters, then functioning as independent artists outside their original circle or household.[1] Ibn Ayas (1955–60, 1:6), an Egyptian chronicler of the 16th century, gives a clear idea about the status of a great singer, Aziza bint Sathi. Relating her death in 1501 at the age of 80, the author identifies her as one of the most celebrated singers of Egypt. She possessed enormous talents of voice and diction that elaborated the poetry of her songs. She was justly famous throughout the country, and was much appreciated by the great families. His account is instructive on several accounts: first, the use of the term *chanteuse* (in the French translation) to describe her profession; second, the idea that she was part of a recognized group of talented singers, respected for her skills even by the nobility; third, the fact of her evident literacy allied to her singing talent.

Late 18th-Century and 19th-Century Qualities of Singers

These same traditional abilities of voice, diction, and poetic language were still alive at the end of the 18th century, and there are several early accounts of the talents of female singers. Savary (1785, 1:149), in particular, devoted some paragraphs to complimenting the great performers he heard during his years in Egypt, calling them "improvisatrices" (improvisers). As to their abilities, he said they needed a beautiful voice, a large repertoire of all types of songs, an ability to memorize new material, and a good education in the Arabic language. He was particularly impressed with their ability to compose and sing couplets on the spot relating to the circumstances of the moment—this might include, for example, words of praise for a principal guest. He considered them among the best-educated women in Egypt.[2] The professional talents of the chanteuses seem to have declined only slightly during the next 50 years. Speaking particularly of the singers, Lane (1978, 354) personally found their talents far surpassed that of the male performers, and concurred one might give some individuals among the Cairo elite the title of "learned females" because of their literary abilities. In 1830, the thoughtful French writer Michaud (1833–35, 5:255) described the gifts still necessary for distinguished singers. They learned the rules of poetry, and how to improvise songs. Those who were most accomplished had a better social position than the others.

These singers accompanied themselves, and accounts name several instruments. Browne describes how chanteuses accompanied themselves on "an instrument touched like the guitar" (1806, 92). Villoteau (1809a, 695) says they used two kinds of drum. Eduard de Montulé adds that they used the "drum and the flute" (1821, 88). Didier (1860, 177, 286) explains that singers played the drum during the intervals between the verses of their songs. Oddly, only he (1860, 177) and Duff Gordon (1983, 20) a decade later, relate how a principal singer had the backing of a female choir. Didier (1860, 177) gives further details—the principal singer sang alone, with the choir singing the refrains to each verse.

Appearances of Singers

Most travel writing describes famous singers at private parties, making the point that they would not perform except before the wealthy and the noble, and only for extravagant fees. Minutoli includes an anecdote about the diva Nafissa. Even to entice her to perform, the hopeful host first had to send her a costly cashmere shawl, while after the performance, she "laid the whole company under contribution ... she had the art of stimulating the self-love of the audience by proclaiming aloud the value of each present which she received" (1827, 199n).

Clot Bey (1840, 2:74) suggests that distinguished female singers entertained during the great public feasts, giving voice to the latest offerings of the poets and passing them on to a wide, receptive public, even to the ordinary people, who quickly learned and repeated them. A detailed firsthand description of such an event has yet to appear in the travel literature, but Didier (1860, 288) has an interesting account of listening for two entire nights to singing at wedding festivities in his quarter in Cairo. Although the well-known singers performed indoors, in the harem of the adjacent house, the sound was powerful enough to be heard throughout the nearby streets, giving much pleasure to passersby, and to the inhabitants of the area who took pride in being part of this local event.

There is agreement in the literature that when such singers came to private houses they sang in the harem. Because of the design of upper-class homes, however, the singing was equally available to males of the household and male guests who would be situated elsewhere. Singers sang upstairs in the harem, and the master and guests placed themselves just below, in the court, for the performance (Clot Bey 1840, 2:86). Lane (1978, 354–55), as usual, gives many details. If the master is alone, he listens with his family in the harem, with the singer concealed behind a screen. If there are male guests, the men assemble below, in the court; the women in the upstairs harem; and the singer placed at a window of the harem, screened by the lattice.

Firsthand accounts of performances confirm the concealment of singers. In 1828, Champollion (1986, 78) says, specifically, that he only heard the most famous singer of Cairo, Nafissa; she sang hidden behind a curtain.[3] In 1853, during the particularly fundamentalist rule of Abbas,[4] Didier (1860, 174–77) attended a private party at the home of a wealthy Jewish-Egyptian banker on the occasion of the circumcision of his son. While the host willingly introduced Didier into his home to meet the female members of the family, Didier was not allowed to see the great diva of the day, since she sang hidden behind a curtained-off area in the harem. Ten years later, in 1862, Duff Gordon (1983, 18–20) describes hearing the same artist at an Armenian christening party; while she sang veiled, it seems that she sat among the mixed sex guests. Perhaps the protocol was more relaxed at this period.

Status of the Guild of Chanteuses

Villoteau (1809a, 694) makes some astonishing comments on the corporation of singers at the time of the French invasion. He and his colleagues spent many months working closely with Egyptian male musicians in Cairo in an attempt to understand their art firsthand, and Arabic music in general. Thus, the French scholars had many opportunities to gain a thorough knowledge of the local music scene and did hear remarks on the talents of female singers. But, he says, he and his colleagues had not been able to hear them for they refused to sing "in front of men, particularly Frenchmen" (ibid. 694). Villoteau also originates the notion that these artists left Cairo at the time of the French conquest, not to return until some time later, even then holding themselves aloof from associating with the invaders (ibid. 694). Considering that, at that time, the French were masters of Egypt, his statement is a particularly remarkable comment on certain singers' status and independence in Egyptian society. It also suggests they had riches enough to wait out the occupation. Villoteau's account contrasts powerfully with Denon's (1973, 229–34) story of General Menou, who forced local authorities to mount an impromptu dance performance for the amusement of his officers at Mutûbis in 1798, just after the invasion of Egypt and on the march to conquer Cairo. The same sense of the chanteuses' social standing seems to have continued 50 years after. Didier (1860, 331) believed that during Abbas' time, dancers and dancing were prohibited, but singers still maintained their favor in Cairo.

Names and Faces of Singers: An Evening with Sakna

Travelers left only a few names for these talented female performers with the rarest of voices. Giovanni Battista Belzoni, in 1818, Minutoli, in 1821, and Champollion, in 1828, talk of Nafissa of Cairo, normally called by Europeans the "Arabian Catalani," alluding to a famous contemporary European singer.

Didier gives three other names dating from 1854: Sakna, the most famous singer of the day (1860, 177); Saida, only slightly less talented (ibid., 285); and Jammala, a rival of Saida (ibid., 288).

Duff Gordon (1983, 145) speaks of Sakna a decade later, still a great Cairo singer, and of Almaz, her rival.[5] Reproduced in Buonaventura (1990, 49) is a portrait of Sakina-al-Maz by Lorie, dated around 1870; her face is unveiled. According to Duff Gordon's (1983, 20) dating, Sakna was 55 years old in 1862. According to this reckoning, her career would have been 40 years long at this point.[6] When Duff Gordon (1983, 20) heard the immortal Sakna, and also actually saw her and the eight female singers of her choir, she could not see her veiled face, but was told it was ugly. The "grace and beauty" of her vital and youthful body impressed Duff Gordon; she guessed she was 35, but knew she was 20 years older. She described her voice as "harsh and thrilling" and emphasized the "finesse and grace" of her improvised segments. The voices of the choir impressed her not at all.

Didier (1860, 174–83) devotes an entire chapter to the (already mentioned) performance by Sakna at a circumcision feast given by a wealthy Jewish-Egyptian banker. This was not a party for Europeans (only five were present) but geared to local tastes. At first unnerved by his first experience of Arabic singing, by the end of the performance in the early hours of the morning, Didier was totally moved by Sakna's artistry. The local Egyptians met her performance with "a fury of enthusiasm." To them she was the "pearl of pearls," "marvel of marvels," and "nightingale of nightingales" (ibid., 288).[7] (She was called also the "restorer of hearts" [Duff Gordon 1983, 18].) Didier explains that the host had given his guests the ultimate compliment by engaging her for the entire night. For those guests, Sakna was supreme; she epitomized the Cairo fantasia[8] and her name was whispered excitedly throughout the area in anticipation of her performance. She came late with her female chorus, her arrival announced from the harem where she was to sing. Male guests sat in another room, separated by a curtain.

Didier includes short French translations of verses from no less than 11 of the 30 or 40 songs she sang throughout the night. Between songs, she played on a tambourine. About 20 songs were followed by an intermission, during which Didier tried to spy upon the artists behind the curtain, but all he could see, fleetingly, was a group of women sitting on carpets and drinking spirits. After the intermission, Didier was astonished to hear Sakna's voice become even more powerful, increasing with each song. Generally singing slowly in a monotone, she interjected occasional outbursts of passion. Over the evening the repertoire was generally sad or tragic, but after a night of so many laments on painful subjects, she ended her concert with a joyful song of love.

8

Identifying the Raqqâsin, Corporation 200

While the corporation of chanteuses seems distinctly defined in the guild list of 1801, when one tries to identify first-hand examples of performance by the raqqâsin, there are difficulties. While the term may have been an official designation for members of this corporation, and the chronicler al–Jabarti illustrates that it appeared in classical Arabic, Egyptians apparently did not pass on this term to European travelers, for it does not appear in their writings. Finding the raqqâsin in the travel literature has involved, therefore, the author's personal selection criteria, with the assumption that wealthy Muslims, and other high officials of the government (including Europeans hired by Muhammad Ali) would normally employ only the most esteemed talent. As a consequence, any descriptions of dancing in their homes might be attributed to members of this higher status guild. Michaud makes this point clearly. He says the better entertainers "are admitted into the harems and into the houses of the rich; the others are reserved for the entertainment of the people" (1833–35, 5:255). According to his definition, one could conclude that the raqqâsin would only appear in front of elite audiences.

It should be noted that the guild list of 1801 identified only corporations existing in Cairo itself and may have had far less relevance to other parts of the country. The raqqâsin probably performed primarily in Cairo, where the wealthy families concentrated, with some, perhaps, in one or two major centers of Lower Egypt. After Muhammad Ali made Alexandria a more important place, some may have made that port city their home as well. There may also have been a presence in the important center of Qena in the south.

Significantly, these entertainers continued their work, despite the fact that the government of Muhammad Ali went out of its way to ban the other corporation of dancers, Corporation 192. Around 1834, the government of Muhammad Ali prohibited these female dancers from performing in public spaces, meaning that they were not free to dance at the annual public festivals, and saints' days, and day-to-day at the coffee houses. The ban seems to have been applied mainly to Cairo and to Alexandria, and to restrict these dancers also from appearing in the homes of Europeans. A full discussion of this ban and its implications appears in Chapter 18, but it is important to note here that the ban applied to female public dancers and not to public dance itself, since transvestite boys and men dancers still continued their trade lawfully. It is interesting, too, that one account mentions a female gypsy ropedancer performing outdoors as part of the public festivities at a royal wedding shortly after the ban (Lane-Poole 1846, 70). Obviously, then, the ban did not apply to all female public performers. This example further reinforces the point that the ban had Corporation 192 as its main target.

The raqqâsin seem to have continued freely in their profession. Dancers-singers to the influential still had an official blessing, although there may have been increasing government control over their audiences and their performance opportunities as the century progressed.[1] That wealthy Egyptians throughout the century had continued to use their services at their parties appears in the 1870s quotation discussing the continuing ban that still existed at that time:

> The result of the moral restriction [i.e., the ban] has been to confine familiarity with their feats to the wealthy, since it is still the fashion for the well-to-do, when they give "fantasias" in their houses, to send for Ghawâzi [for this read raqqâsin], who are invariably procured from somewhere [Leland 1874, 131].

Performances By the Corporation of Raqqâsin

Speaking of his time in Egypt (1828 to 1842), Hamont (1845, 1:316) says Egyptian officials used female entertainers to reinforce European opinion favorably towards Egypt's new institutions and Muhammad Ali's political aspirations. Scholars, artists, military men, authors, in fact all distinguished visitors of any influence, and many nationalities, were treated to a new experience, an evening of Egyptian dance. In the hands of local government functionaries, dance became a powerful propaganda tool. Hamont tells that "many a severe brow relaxed during one of these events" (ibid., 1:316). Surely, only the most elegant of entertainers would qualify as suitable for such important occurrences. No examples of such parties given by Egyptian officials of that period have turned up thus far in the travel literature. The Frenchman Clot-Bey, Muhammad Ali's chief medical officer, however, gave three parties for distinguished French visitors in the period around 1830. These can be taken as representative of the "official" party and the dancers most likely were raqqâsin.

It appears that Clot Bey was fond of entertaining his fellow Frenchmen lavishly in the local Egyptian style. Stationed at Abu Za'bal, just outside Cairo, where he had founded a teaching hospital, he held his parties there. The artist Dauzats (Dumas [and Dauzats] 1846, 1:218–229), visiting Egypt as part of a diplomatic mission in 1830, attended one such party, casting his practiced eye over the events.[2] From morning until two, the visitors toured the hospital. A formal bath came in the early evening, then an enormous dinner. After dinner the guests retired into another room for coffee and smokes. First making sure the guests were comfortable on their divans, Clot Bey then clapped his hands and the entertainers entered—four male musicians, a male clown, and four female dancers. Wearing hats of great value, the dancers were most elegantly, even lavishly, dressed.[3] Clot Bey was nonchalant but the Frenchmen were struck silent at this spectacle, while "the chibouks fell from our mouths, and we clapped our hands as in Paris one signals the entrance of a renowned actor" (ibid., 1:225). Dauzats comments on the cost of such an evening. Only "great seigneurs" could give such a party and then only rarely; for the same amount one could buy six or eight slaves (ibid., 1:229).

Clot Bey also entertained the visiting Frenchman Michaud at Abu Za'bal in 1831. Michaud gives only a few details of the event, but he does say that among the guests were the shaikh of Abu Za'bal and "the notables of the country who had come to compliment us and welcome us as the representatives of the country of light" (Michaud 1833–35, 6:85). The banquet came first, then "several companies of almées arrived" (ibid., 6:84). The evening passed with alternating performances, and serious conversation between the French visitors and the local professors about France and about Egypt. The distinguished Frenchman Marmont (1837–38, 3:314–316) visited Egypt in the fall of 1834 (after the ban on dancing in public) and he, too, enjoyed Clot Bey's hospitality at Abu Za'bal. He mentions the dancers who had come from Cairo to entertain them, all of great beauty and wearing jewelry of great price.

Similar to this diplomatic or official event might be an evening described by Hackländer (quoted in J. St. John 1845, 273–76), at the Cairo home of the Armenian-Egyptian director of the government mint around 1840. Hackländer had tried unsuccessfully to see dancing during his stay in the capital, but finally, through Egyptian connections, was invited to a stylish night of dance and music with the host's entire family and his guests, both male and female. Hackländer makes a great deal of the fact that the house was in a sequestered part of the town, implying the party was clandestine. Yet he also tells that when he left at two in the morning, light was streaming from the windows and the noisy revelry continued. This elaborate night-long party of both dancing and singing was obviously, therefore, not one held in secret, the high social position of the host obviously according it quasi-diplomatic status.

The tradition of co-opting raqqâsin for official entertainments seems to have continued. Much later, at the time of formal parties for the opening of the Suez Canal in 1869, the wealthy tax-farmer for fisheries, Enani Bey, invited many of the French delegation to an elaborate dinner and splendid dancing show (Blanc 1876, 50–55). Frédéric de Carcy (quoted in Aradoon 1979, 122), too, saw a performance of dance and music in a great house in Cairo around 1872.

The raqqâsin also may have entertained in other well-to-do but less exalted houses. Two of Napoleon's Savants (Du Bois-Aymé and Jollois 1812, 109–11) attended an elaborate wedding at the home of a citizen in the Delta town of Mahalla el–Kubra. The obvious wealth and status of the host suggest the inclusion of this dance event in this section on the raqqâsin. On the evening of the wedding a group of female performers sang apart in the downstairs *mandara*[4] for the women of the family and their female guests. Later, two of their number danced outside the mandara in the inner court of the house for the assembled local citizens and esteemed male guests. After the dancing the host and selected male guests joined the women for more singing, and music provided by male musicians.[5]

Based on his position in society, the two separate events taking place around 1820 in the Damietta household of the Christian consul, Basil Faker, would also probably have involved raqqâsin. Faker held a lavish wedding for his daughter, to which he invited European guests, including the traveling Carne. At the wedding, Carne (1826, 73) notes that the mixed-sex group of guests not only watched the dancers perform after dinner, but also joined with them. On a separate occasion, Faker's wife arranged a party in the harem especially for the visiting Minutoli. She watched a dance in the company of other invited guests, "Turkish and Arabian ladies" (Minutoli 1827, 198). She did not care at all for the dancing, but did manage to provide the information that it was executed "in this country by a privileged caste of females ... who enjoy perfect liberty, and support themselves by the public exhibition of their talents" (ibid., 198). One particularly valued individual among the performers danced, sang and "at intervals accompanying herself with a three-stringed instrument, resembling a Spanish mandolin" (ibid., 200).

Apart from government-sponsored dance events, and those held by high officials, there is some evidence that even after the ban on public dancers, dancers were performing openly for upper-middle-class Egyptian audiences in Cairo as well. These most likely were members of the raqqâsin. In 1836, Voilquin (1978, 376–77) witnessed dancing in Cairo at a Muslim wedding, that of a wealthy Turkish merchant. As a female invited guest, Voilquin watched the dancing from a large second-floor room in the harem of the bridegroom's home. Along with the bride and female family members she looked down through a grill upon the male members of the wedding party below. The dancing took place before the men after dinner.

Appearance of the Raqqâsin

While European visitors to Egypt might not appreciate the dancing, they usually presumed they could console themselves with the physical attractiveness of the dancers. This was not always the case, however, for performers were not all young, nor did their artistic talents depend on looks. At the May 1833 party attended by Estourmel in the Cairo home of the dragoman for the Austrian consulate, a Mr. Moktar, he looked forward to seeing dance by "the premier Almées of Cairo" (Estourmel 1844, 2:453). For Estourmel the promise of the evening did not live up to reality. Of the four dancers he says, three were "old and ugly" while the fourth was "younger without being prettier" (ibid., 2:454). Bayle St. John (1850, 184) had the same to say for Kala of Alexandria. As the performance went on, however, he was able to overcome his bias as he gradually acknowledged her undoubted singing and dancing talents.

The Raqqâsin at a Royal Wedding in 1845

It seems probable that as the raqqâsin entertained exclusively in the private homes of the great or at least well-to-do, usually Egyptians, they would never be found dancing in front of the lowest class of Egyptian citizens except under exceptional circumstances. An example of both types of audience combined in a major account of singing and dancing after the ban can be found in Lane-Poole's (1846, 78–138) 60-page record of a royal wedding in 1845. Her record is unique for its length, and detail. Actually living in the royal harem (a two-story separate building of the Citadel palace complex) for the eight days of celebrations, Lane-Poole kept a diary of the events available to an all-female assembly. The palace harem was thrown open to all female citizens during this period. Lane-Poole says that close to seven thousand women from all levels of Egyptian society daily mobbed the palace. The poorer women were obviously attracted by the rare chance to see wealth and power firsthand, witness the entertainments, and profit from the distribution of money and food.

Lane-Poole's account goes day-by-day and although the royal bride[6] had a sequence of ceremonial appearances over the week, the entertainments were similar each day and can be summarized. Those favored guests who had slept in the palace rose early to music and dance that were available all day in the great lower salon. Lane-Poole tells of a large hired orchestra of Egyptian women, "Arab females," who played a variety of local instruments (although she does not name them) and describes them as "beautifully picturesque in form, and daintily inlaid with mother-of-pearl and dark wood" (ibid., 106). The players seated themselves in a circle in the middle of the hall. Dressed simply, in contrast with the magnificence of the women of the royal family, the musicians wore white head-veils bound across their foreheads and under their chins, and falling down their backs. This circle of musicians remained all day, sometimes singing, sometimes playing, sometimes some of their members dancing. Obviously talented and versatile, they responded by playing and even singing Turkish music when Turkish and Georgian dance groups were performing.

Two women of this orchestra were preeminent in both singing and dancing. Lane-Poole says of the two stars, "The first Arab singers of Egypt ... they ... danced in the Arab manner, for which performance they are also celebrated as the first of their day" (ibid., 96). The two performed together, both dancing and singing. At other times three others from the group joined the dance. One afternoon a sixth performer, disguised as a clown with a fool's cap, imitated the other five and ridiculed their movements. Lane-Poole loved the singing, and found it enchanting: "The great saloon seemed filled with music ... yet their tones were so modulated that they fell sweetly on the ear" (ibid., 121). Lane-Poole also approved their attire as "tasteful," but found the dancing "extremely disgusting" (ibid., 96).

Lane-Poole tells of female troupes of Turkish and Georgian extraction, slaves of the royal household, who played tambourines and danced in the manner of their country. The several Turkish groups performed energetic, physical dances, tumbling, stepping, and hopping. They also danced with wooden swords and shields, hitting out at one another. Lane-Poole was dismayed to discover that they could also dance "in the manner of the Almeh" and found this took away their previous appearance of innocence. The young Georgian girls were lively and energetic, with flying hair.

Dinner was served at six and afterwards the same entertainments continued, in a somewhat more formal and exclusive manner than during the day, although still with hundreds of women watching. Muhammad Ali's eldest daughter presided over the affair, and the performers directed their efforts towards her and towards the important female guests, all seated on divans. The same Egyptian entertainers were present, as well as the harem slave troupes. Generally, the program stopped at 11 p.m. except for the last night when celebrations continued until two in the morning. Lane-Poole describes how each performer received a costly cashmere shawl, the one who had acted as a clown winding hers around her fool's cap.

Fig. 6. Egyptian Copt (unidentified). *Almés.* c. 1800 (from Commission des sciences et arts d'Egypte. *Description de l'Égypte* [Paris: Imprimerie imp., 1809–1822]. Courtesy of the Thomas Fisher Rare Book Library, University of Toronto).

These Egyptian entertainers who took part in the 1845 wedding, called by Lane-Poole both "Arab" and "almeh," were talented versatile artists who danced, sang, and played a variety of musical instruments in the style of both Arabic and Turkish musical traditions. Earlier, in 1836, Lane, her brother, had suggested that only "inferior" or "ordinary" 'awâlim would dance (as discussed in Chapter 4), but here two preeminent artists of the era, along with a large group of colleagues, performed for the Egyptian ruling house. These were no simple performers, but the most esteemed available. Certainly in them one sees the raqqâsin of Corporation 200, and becomes aware of the wide extent and elevated level of their skills in both dancing and singing.

Names and Faces of Raqqâsin

Unfortunately, Lane-Poole does not name the two star performers at the wedding. Since it would be extraordinary that 20 years after the ban talented ghawâzî would be practicing openly in Cairo and Alexandria, three dancers are good candidates for membership in the guild of raqqâsin. Bayle St. John writes of the dancer he met in 1847, Kala, a "Jewess, one of the finest singers and most audacious dancers in Alexandria" (B. St. John, 1850, 147). In her somewhat dismissive recounting of the ghawâzî myths about a Persian origin (in her conversation with St. John), Kala distances herself from this group; she probably is a member of the raqqâsin. Ghazal, the exceedingly well-appointed entertainer through whom Didier (1860, 328–41) attempted to arrange a failed fantasia in 1853, was most likely also a member. Didier (1858, 276) names another potential candidate, Safiyya, a talented performer whom he met in Aswan in 1854 after her recent banishment from Cairo.[7] Her refusal to become the mistress of a common soldier, despite her poverty, leads one to assume her past status.

It is impossible to identify raqqâsin for certain in any of the many illustrations of dancers by European artists. Perhaps the only verifiable example appears in the Napoleonic *Description de l'Égypte,* the central figure of a group of "types" of Egyptians (fig. 6), the original drawing attributed to an unknown Egyptian Copt who may have had access to this group of entertainers.[8]

9

Identifying the Ghawâzî, Corporation 192

As discussed in section two, the modern researcher 'Abd ar-Raziq (1973, 66, 67) identified how, during medieval times, a split existed among female performing groups, depending on whether they were owned or free. The second guild of dancers, Corporation 192, often known locally as the ghawâzî, might possibly be the artistic descendants of the free public performers of the Mamluk period. They formed the stuff of European legends, for throughout the period of this study they were exceedingly accessible to European travelers. Unlike members of the other two guilds, they were evident in Cairo's public places, even during the Napoleonic occupation (Belliard 1831, 4:69; Chabrol 1822, 418; Galland 1804, 2:23; Jomard 1822, 733; Villoteau 1809a, 694). They were also to be seen in the same period in the Delta area, for example in Alexandria, and Asyût (Du Bois-Aymé 1809, 109; Jollois 1822, 350; Boustany 1:112). Their corporation was the one banned by the government around 1834. After the dance ban, European travelers found these entertainers easily in Upper Egypt.

The ghawâzî found their traditional audiences among the ordinary Egyptian people. They performed outdoors in the streets, public squares, and byways of the country. Before the ban the ghawâzî traveled freely throughout Egypt, seeking employment (Burkhardt 1984, 175; Montulé 1821, 88; B. St. John 1973, 1:28). Their considerable presence was noted at fairs, such as that of Tanta in Lower Egypt (fig. 7), and at festivals where "they are to many persons, the chief attractions. Numerous tents of Gházeeyehs are seen on these occasions" (Lane 1978, 376.) Some of them accompanied the pilgrim caravans (ibid., 376). They seem to have entertained in some less respectable harems on the occasion of a marriage, or the birth of a child; they might also turn up in the street outside the

9. Identifying the Ghawâzî, Corporation 192

Fig. 7. J. Riudavets. *Feria de Tanta* (Tanta Fair). c. 1880 (from Eduardo Toda y Güell, *A Través del Egipto* [Madrid: El Progresso Editorial, 1889]).

door, seeking to perform, after the occasion of a wedding in a well-to-do household (ibid., 373). They haunted the coffee houses, seeking a living on a daily basis (Savary 1785, 1:297; Michaud 1833–35, 5:251; J. St. John 1834, 1:239). Some authors even claimed that they were particularly attractive to Egyptian men traveling within Egypt: "Few Arabs ever perform a journey to any large city without visiting the dancing girls" (J. St. John 1834, 2:374). They might be found at Egyptian bachelor parties "in the house of some rake" (Lane 1978, 373). They also appeared within certain Egyptian homes, particularly those of Jews (Clot Bey 1840, 2:90). They had their own group of musicians (Villoteau 1809a, 695; Combes 1846, 1:222), a variable group that might consist of only one male and an older woman (Niebuhr, n.d., 139; Browne 1806, 90). Although their corporation had the least status of the three guilds of female performers, some individuals were immensely talented performers, even recognized as such (Blanc 1876, 136).

Public Performances By Ghawâzî

First-hand 18th- and 19th-century descriptions of ghawâzî mostly indicate modest performance locales. Niebuhr (n.d., 140) first saw dancers accidentally at a public house within the city, then later was able to watch from the windows of his house when troupes of "Ghasie" came to entertain in the dried bed of the great canal of Cairo. Traveling in Upper Egypt in 1818, Forbin (1819, 82) saw "public dancers" performing dances of "a very lively expression" outdoors in front of a Nile-side coffee house in Beni Suef. He (ibid., 87) then saw another group in Qûs who performed for him there among the ancient ruins.

In 1830, Michaud (1833–35, 5:253) wandered throughout Cairo to see the sights at 'Id.[1] All the shops were closed, many people were seated outside their homes, streets were densely packed with pedestrians. After much meandering, Michaud left the city by one of its gates and found himself in a huge crowd of pleasure seekers. "Almées" danced in tents full of spectators, people amused themselves with ring games and swings, comedians put on their acts. Michaud noted spectators watching from the backs of camels as if in boxes in the theater. On one or more days of 'Id, families, in particular the women, visited the ancestors' graves. This cemetery north of the great Cairo gate of Bab al–Nasr was a popular spot for entertainment during 'Id. Lane gives a description of the same place[2] during this same festival:

> In a part next the city gate from which the burial-ground takes its name many swings and whirligigs [small Ferris-wheel] are erected, and several large tents, in some of which dancers, reciters of Aboo-Zeyd, and other performers, amuse a dense crowd of spectators; and throughout the burial-ground are seen numerous tents for the reception of the visitors of the tombs [1978, 475].[3]

Burkhardt (1984, 178) tells how, in his day, during this particular festival, dancers made the rounds of all the wealthy families in towns and villages, danced briefly in the courtyard of the house and received a gift.

At other public festivities dancers used the same area just outside the Cairo gates. During the annual departure of the caravan for Mecca, James St. John wandered beyond the Bab al-Nasr alongside the area's cemeteries. Here, many Egyptian men, women, and children were already assembled, watching trained monkeys, listening to drums or storytellers, and enjoying and applauding the dancing girls. "The more ordinary species of ghawazies had taken possession of the ruined tombs, and other old buildings, where they were at home to visitors of all descriptions" (J. St. John 1845, 217–18).

The Napoleonic Savant Gilbert-Joseph Chabrol (1822, 461) says that, in his day, wandering clowns, jugglers, "almeh," and sellers of sweetmeats crowded all the major public squares during celebrations for the birth of the Prophet Muhammad. Illuminations enabled secular entertainments to continue late into the night. Champollion (1986, 74–78) gives a graphic account during his visit a quarter-century later. Arriving in Cairo on the second day of the same event, he wandered through the Ezbekiyya area, then full of water. An enormous crowd filled the neighborhood, some mounted on horses, donkeys, or camels. He found fascinating the mix of sacred and profane, for groups of seated Muslims chanted the praises of the Prophet Muhammad, side by side with choirs of "awalim" singing erotic songs and dancing "with more than Bacchic liberty" (ibid., 75).

Ghawâzî also sought impromptu occasions to make money, and routinely met Nile boats carrying travelers of all nationalities. On the Damietta branch of the Nile in 1831:

> Our boat stopped in front of a village.... Several women ran onto the bank; they began to dance to the sound of castanets; they sang some obscene songs; then they threw themselves into our boat and we had considerable difficulty in getting them to leave [Michaud 1833–35, 6:322].

After the ban on public dance, ghawâzî performances still took place openly in Upper Egypt, in towns such as Beni Suef, Qena, and Luxor, and in the Faiyûm area of northwestern Egypt. Despite being unable to watch them easily in Cairo and Alexandria, Europeans routinely took advantage of opportunities outside of these two cities. In the early 1840s, the peripatetic illustrator Bartlett happened upon an outdoor performance in Beni Suef:

> The sound of music caught my ears, and I perceived an assemblage of people under the shade of a cluster of Sont trees near the river, and rising now and then over their heads, the braceleted arms and castanets of the famous "Ghawazee," or

dancing-girls, who, banished from the capital, were forced to carry their voluptuous allurements farther up the river [1849, 112].

With the Gérôme expedition in the Faiyûm in 1868, the French painter Lenoir (1872, 100–17) witnessed the locally esteemed dancer Hasna. She performed before the Frenchmen and invited local municipal dignitaries in the travelers' tent. Lenoir wrote glowingly about her person and her solo dancing.

The ghawâzî were still welcomed at festivals and saints' days in Upper Egypt in towns distant from Cairo, and they performed there routinely. At Said 'Abd al–Rachîm's saint's day in Qena in 1865:

> The whole way was lighted up and thronged with the most motley crowd, and the usual mixture of holy and profane, which we know at the Catholic fetes also; but more pronounced here. Dancing girls, glittering with gold brocade and coins, swaggered about among the brown-shirted fellaheen, and the profane singing of the Alateeyeh mingled with the songs in honour of the Arab prophet chanted by the Moosheeds and the deep tones of the "Allah, Allah" of the Zikeers [Duff Gordon 1983, 255].

Coffee Houses as Dance Performance Sites

During the early 16th century, coffee was introduced into the area near the al–Azhar mosque in Cairo as an aid to nightly devotions. This early association of coffee with religious practice soon broadened to include linking this beverage with conviviality. At that time the European Powers were beginning to round the Cape of Good Hope and reach the east. As a result, Cairo merchants lost control of the spice trade and promoted the local sale of coffee as an alternative economic strategy. Coffee then spread throughout Cairo to an entirely different clientele. The male urbanite found a new pleasure in the coffee house, spending an afternoon and early evening there away from home. By the late 18th century and early 19th century the coffee house constituted a major social institution throughout Egypt for the male population (Hattox 1985, 27–28). In Cairo, estimates of their numbers at that time ranged from one thousand (Chabrol 1822, 437) to twelve hundred (Lane 1978, 334).[4]

As urban coffee houses grew more numerous and competition increased, their managers added live entertainments. Sonnini gives a vivid sense of the range of entertainments available at small Egyptian coffee houses, while describing a specific one in Rosetta:

> It is a mere tobacco smoking rendezvous, totally destitute of decoration, and in which nothing absolutely is to be found, except coffee and a live-coal to light the pipes. Mats are spread for the company; these places of resort are frequented

by the men of all nations who reside in Egypt.... With the pipe in one hand, a cup of coffee in the other, they slowly wash down, every four or five whiffs of tobacco, with a gulp of coffee. Dancing girls, buffoons, extempore declaimers come to tender their services, and to earn a bit of money. There is scarcely one of those haunts but what attracts to it some story-teller by profession, who is never tired with talking, nor his auditors of listening to him [1799, 1:248].

The ghawâzî regularly used coffee houses as performance locales, both inside these establishments and in the streets just in front.[5] It seems that particular coffee houses even established a reputation as good places to see dance:

There is a café [in Cairo] where jugglers and almées *normally* [emphasis mine] gather; I wanted to see them.... We had chosen our time badly for Ramadan was just finishing and the principal cafés were deserted. There were two or three almées of mediocre beauty, some story-tellers ignored by the public, that's all we could see [Michaud 1833–35, 5:251].

Fig. 8. Heinrich von Mayr. *Kostueme von Oberaegypten* (Costume from Upper Egypt). c. 1838 (from Maximilian Duke of Bavaria, Herzogs. *Wanderung nach dem Orient im Jahre 1838* [Munich: Verlag W. Ludwig, 1978, repr.]. Image reprinted here courtesy of the publisher).

In the towns and smaller centers the connection of dance and coffee house was strong, both in Lower and Upper Egypt. Savary (1785, 1:297) met a talented Badawiyya in the Delta village of Samannûd, dancing in a small coffee house. At Nadir (Lower Egypt), Michaud's captain

> conducted us to a place that seemed devoted to joy; it was a café set up in a vast space and having only four walls. A lamp or kandil, set in a corner of the room replaced the light of the fading day; two musicians were playing.... Several young women were dancing [Michaud 1833–35, 5:87].

Sonnini relates that he passed a good deal of one day in Abu Tig (south of Asyût) at a coffee house and "according to custom, we were entertained with poets and female dancers, equally devoted to the worship of Venus" (1799, 3:282). Near Minya, in Upper Egypt, while walking along the Nile from one town to the next, James St. John found "coffee-houses, and almé of the most dissolute kind" (1834, 1:239). He eventually concluded that, in Upper Egypt, the coffee house was always open and dancing girls inevitably found there (ibid., 1:251).

After the ban on public performances, female dancers still congregated at the coffee houses outside the major centers. Maximilian (1978, 56) talks of a coffee house performance he saw by chance at Asyût in 1838. Here, the performance took place inside, so as not to break the law too openly, although the accompanying illustration (fig. 8) shows this performance as taking place on the banks of the Nile. Bayle St. John (1973, 1:22) describes a secluded coffee house near Fuwa (in Lower Egypt) as large and clean, and surrounded by small huts. Here, dancers had set up a place to train young female performers.

Social Status of Corporation 192

While membership in the corporation of ghawâzî gave members negligible social status, obviously there were some benefits. Performers insisted on their separate identity, and tried to keep it exclusive. Pococke, for example, tells of their claims to rectitude, if nothing else:

> There are other women who go barefaced about the streets, dancing, singing, and playing on some instruments.... These may not be supposed to be very virtuous; and yet they say they are so, in one respect, in which they might be most suspected [1743–45, 1:192].

Burkhardt also made the point that these dancers insisted on their superiority to common prostitutes, never "associating with other public women whom they regard as much inferior to themselves in rank" (1984, 175). Lane comments that other groups of female performers tried to borrow the reputations of the ghawâzî, indicating that such name borrowing would enhance their own reputation. This must have been low indeed. "There are some other dancing-girls and courtesans who call themselves Ghawázee, but who do not really belong to that tribe" (Lane 1978, 376). Ghawâzî also played the same name game in an attempt to increase their status, and avoid problems with authorities. "These girls themselves occasionally assume this appellation [raqqâsin?], and generally do so when (as has been often the case) the exercise of their art is prohibited by the government" (Lane 1973, 356).

An Ethnically Diverse Permeable Corporation

From personal names one identifies dancers' origins. For example, two dancers "Bedaoui" that is "the Bedouin" appear a century apart (Savary 1785, 1:298; Blanc 1876, 137). They were probably Egyptians of Arab extraction and, in fact, Burkhardt claimed that the ghawâzî boasted of their "true Bedouin blood" (1984, 174). A "*Maghribbiyyeh*," meaning "dancer from northwest Africa," appears in 1866 (Duff Gordon 1983, 168). Syrians also danced in Egypt. Burkhardt says, "There is another tribe of public women in Egypt called Halebye, they are fewer in number" (1984, 178). Burkhardt's term must surely derive from Halab, the Arabic form for Aleppo, Syria.[6] Abraham Norov gives the information that the ghawâzî were the "descendants of Syrian refugees" (quoted in Volkoff, 177); perhaps he means they were escaping from Muhammad Ali's wars in that country. The famous entertainer of Isna, Kutchuk Hanem, apparently came from Damascus, Syria (Flaubert 1991, 282).

Importantly, there was a considerable black presence in Egyptian dance, particularly in Upper Egypt. Aziza of Aswan danced for Flaubert and Du Camp in 1850 and made a great impression (Buonaventura 1990, 72; Flaubert 1991, 295). Kutchuk Hanem employed a black dancer during Flaubert's second visit to Isna (Flaubert 1991, 362). Didier (1858, 47) found both Egyptian girls and Ethiopian girls dancing in the Egyptian style for the expatriate Egyptian community in the Sudan in 1854. Duff Gordon (1983, 168) identifies a local black dancer, a "very pretty Abyssinian [Ethiopian]" in Upper Egypt in 1866. Fromentin (1881, 290, 303) mentions two black dancers, one about 12 and the other older, among the dancers at Qena in 1869.

Probably Corporation 192 had less control over its own activities and the lives of its members than the corporations of singers and raqqâsin. Because of the low power and prestige of this guild, perhaps anyone might join on paying a fee. Its ethnic diversity certainly suggests looseness in the corporation, one that might account for the confusing myths of foreign origins of the guild (discussed in Chapter 19), and suggestions about penetration of this guild at different times by outsiders, such as gypsies and other ethnic groups.

An Evening with Badawiyya at Qena in 1869

Despite treating the ghawâzî with contempt as artists and human beings, Egyptian authorities were quite prepared to exploit the talents of these banned entertainers. In 1869, the ruler of Egypt, Ismail, invited nine hundred important foreign guests to Egypt for the inauguration of the Suez Canal. He invited two hundred of these on an extended Nile cruise. Much of this description of the evening with Badawiyya comes from Blanc's (1876) account, with additional data from Colet (1879) and Fromentin (1881). The senior Egyptian official in charge of this expedition, Tonino Bey, ordered official entertainments in Asyût, Qena, and Isna, and charged local functionaries with arrangements. As the expedition approached Qena, Tonino Bey informed the Frenchman Blanc that he had arranged a magnificent surprise. They were to witness that evening "a dance that they had not seen yet," one that would certainly please them, by a performer Tonino Bey named "the first dancer of Egypt" (Blanc 1876, 136). Known as "Bedaoui" (the Bedouin), she would entertain with a sword dance, the centerpiece of the evening. Based on Blanc's unequivocal statements that the "almées" were found in Cairo and the "ghawazies" remained banned in Upper Egypt, Badawiyya would have been a member of the guild of ghawâzî.[7] She seems to have lived in Qena permanently.[8]

Bicharra, the host, received his many guests with traditional Egyptian hospitality. The party took place outdoors at his home beside the Nile, actually a small palace described as a fantastic house decorated in white and blue. Of the evening Fromentin (1881, 291) says it was "lovely ... and a great success." He was also impressed with the *rabab* (Egyptian violin) player and called him a "true artist." Badawiyya's sword dance captured the imagination of all three French writers. They described her as a celebrated artist whose "danse de caractère"[9] had captured their immense interest (Blanc 1881, 137). Unlike most European female spectators of Egyptian dance, Colet was even more enthusiastic than her male companions, saying, "The boldness and elegance of this incomparable dancer drew unanimous bravos from the crowd" (1879, 151). Obviously, Badawiyya deserved her reputation, for Fromentin (1881, 283, 295) and Blanc (1876, 112, 240) also describe the scheduled dance evenings at Asyût and at Isna. These were certainly the more normal level of ghawâzî performances of the period in Upper Egypt, and the two French visitors were not much impressed, finding them repetitive and mediocre.

10

Male Performers— Dancers and Musicians

General Comments on Male Dancers

The French guild list of 1801 identifies a guild for males who danced, "danseurs qui sont a Caire (male dancers who are in Cairo)," or Corporation 139. According to this list there was only one corporation for male dancers, unlike the two for females, suggesting that there was no hierarchy of male entertainers. According to 19th-century sources, however, male dancers were ethnically distinguishable into two groups: the indigenous Egyptian khawals; and dancers with other backgrounds, called ginks. Some of the latter were expatriates, some probably drawn from Egyptianized foreign groups.

Lane (1978, 376–77) describes both groups. The khawals were young males, Muslim and native to Egypt. They impersonated public female dancers, both in dress and in style of performance. Even before the ban on female public performances, they were employed in place of female dancers to perform at public festivals and for family occasions. The ginks were another class of young male transvestites, similar to the khawals, but ethnically Jews, Armenians, Greeks, and Turks.

Unlike local Egyptians both male and female who enjoyed their performances, European travelers almost universally found male dancers and their art highly distasteful. For example, Lane (1978, 377) points out the term describing them, *gink*, has a vulgar meaning. Since the word is only Persian for "harp" (as discussed in Chapter 4) obviously the attached vulgarity is an ascribed meaning, probably Lane's own discomfort with this class of performer. Foreign expatriates deplored the practice, and since male dancers were not affected by the ban on the ghawâzî, Europeans expressed dismay that Muhammad Ali continued to allow this disgraceful substitute. Unlike the abundance of descriptions of female dancers, there exist few for male dancers, and no European artist's rendering has yet come to light. The few accounts, unfortunately, do not often differentiate by ethnicity of dancer, and it is impossible in these instances to know whether performers are native khawals or ginks.

Khawals

Calling them "infamous beings," Hamont (1845, 1:319) says their number in Cairo increased after the ban on public female dancing. He was dismayed to see so many of them around the coffee houses and in the streets. Especially on Fridays, the day for Muslims to go to the mosque, and on holidays, he complains, students from Muhammad Ali's new schools would use their free time to watch the khawals' dancing and fraternize with them freely. Didier (1860, 239–40) saw such a Friday performance in 1853. He had spent a leisurely day at a café, near the Nile, gazing out over Roda Island and Gîza. It was Friday, a holy day and market day, too, and he says all day he had heard "fantasias"[1] passing in the nearby streets. Finally, one of these arrived in the garden where he sat, followed by a crowd of onlookers. The all-male group included dancers, singers, musicians, and clowns. Didier found the dancing not to his taste, and commented disapprovingly that such events took place on a religious Friday. He felt obliged, however, to give them a generous tip. Another day, he (ibid., 132–33) also saw the khawals, just outside the mosque of Touloun, dancing to the sound of brass cymbals. A circle of women was taking much pleasure from the dance, and Didier's servant also paused to admire them.

Bayle St. John (1850, 57–62) gives a vivid first-hand account of the nights of Ramadan he spent in the coffee houses of Alexandria in the company of two of his local male friends. He describes one covered bazaar packed with people where he watched shadow puppets and heard the best boy singer in Alexandria. In one shop the merchant invited him to sit, to smoke, and to watch the performance of a female impersonator dancing in the manner of the ghawâzî. The performer, a dwarf (a tailor by trade) had a great local reputation for his talents as dancer and clown. St. John describes the dance as a "miracle of agility and drollery, though highly indecent" (ibid., 57). The crowd in response "laughed with immense glee" (ibid., 57).

Flaubert (1991, 195, 236–37) is the only author who gives the name of a khawal, an Egyptian known as Hasan al-Bilbeissi, an adult male not a youth, whom he saw twice, once in a wedding procession and, later, performing in the Hôtel d'Orient in Cairo. Unlike the expressed dislike of male Egyptian dancing found in every other European writer consulted, Flaubert found Hasan's performance possessed high artistry.

Ginks

The term *gink* is an Egyptian pronunciation for the word jank, or jink. As explained in section two, this latter term (jankiyya) was applied to female dancers in the medieval period, and seems to have existed in some form at the time of the Napoleonic invasion. By Lane's day, the term seems to have been used exclusively for young male dancers.

While perhaps expatriate male dancers had been longstanding in Egypt, circumstances in Istanbul, Turkey, augmented their numbers. Dancing boys (ethnically Armenian, Jewish and Greek) were very popular with members of the Ottoman army who fraternized with them, and quarreled over them. These disputes allegedly caused so much disruption to discipline that the Sultan forbad dancers to appear in public, and many found greener pastures in Egypt. He eventually outlawed these boy dancers completely in 1857. The modern Turkish writer Metin And (1976, 140–41), the source for the above information on Turkey, gives no dates for the Sultan's earlier interventions, so exactly when these foreign boy dancers began to migrate into Egypt in numbers remains unclear.

As early as 1798, Denon (1973, 202–05) describes entertainments accorded the French by the chief city magistrate in Napoleonic Rosetta on the occasion of festivities for the Prophet. The street outside the magistrate's home formed the stage, with a carpeted alcove just in front of the house for distinguished guests. Fires, lamps, and tapers illuminated the scene. A band consisting of "hautboy, small kettle drums, and large Albanian drums stood on one side of the alcove; on the other side singers and violins." Attendants passed out sweetmeats, coffee, syrups, rosewater, and pipes. Here, Greek dancing boys provided the diversions. Male dancers seem also to have formed part of local notables' entourages. In 1828, Champollion's expedition attended a party in Upper Egypt, with musical and dance entertainment. The young Mamluk transvestites, members of the host's household, did Turkish and Greek dances, and also "imitated the almeh" (Champollion 1986, 148–49; L'Hôte 1993, 125).

After the ban on female public performance, female dancers could no longer use the coffee houses in Cairo, but boys continued to dance there. Voilquin (1978, 319) mentions with distaste boys from the Greek quarter singing and dancing at modest cafés around 1834. A description of such a scene comes from Lane:

> In one place were musicians; before a large coffee-shop were two Greek dancing-boys, or "gink," elegant but effeminate in appearance, with flowing hair, per-

forming to the accompaniment of mandolines played by two of their countrymen, and a crowd of admiring Turks, with a few Egyptians, surrounding them [1978, 453].

Ginks and Khawals at a Royal Wedding in 1834

As well as describing the women's entertainments in the harem at a royal wedding in 1845, Lane-Poole wished to make her accounts representative of similar entertainments available to the men of Cairo. She took unpublished notes, written in 1834 by her famous brother (Edward Lane) during an earlier visit to Cairo, and reproduced them in her own considerably later publication (Lane-Poole 1846, 61–77). Unique in their detail, they give an excellent glimpse of male dancing at a royal wedding when ghawâzî public performance was prohibited.[2]

In this instance, the bride was related to a nephew of Muhammad Ali, ruler of Egypt, and the groom an important Egyptian official. The nephew hosted the festivities at his palace situated beside the Ezbekiyya Garden, at that time full of water from the seasonal Nile flooding. Guns were periodically fired, and, at night, rockets were set off from a platform moored in the center of this temporary lake. Hired boats plied the water. On shore, swings and small Ferris wheels were set up. Onlookers sat on benches around the lake, drinking coffee and sweet beverages, and eating nuts and sweetmeats, all sold in temporary booths. Most of the palace was open to the male public, with one room set aside for European visitors. All the public rooms were crowded day and night. The host provided some refreshments and made entertainment available during the day in the main courtyard.

Major public performances took place during the eight evenings of the wedding celebrations, from just past sunset until midnight. Since entertainments were similar from one night to the next, they are summarized here. Every evening there were private parties for court notables (male) and important guests (male) in the few rooms kept closed for family use, and the royal family and their guests did not attend the public performances.

Ginks, here Armenian transvestite boys who performed in groups of six at a time, provided most of the dance entertainment. Lane describes the large ring of people around the dancers, so dense that he cannot get in to see them, forcing him to mount to an upper story and look down into the courtyard. The ginks danced in the manner of ghawâzî but with pirouettes and "other exercises." Ginks were present during each day and evening. One night, the sixth, an Egyptian khawal performed. Lane called this man's dance "mainly athletic" and described his jumping through hoops, standing on the shoulders of another man who walked about with him, next holding a boy aloft while still on the shoulders of the other. The dancer then supported five boys and men. As his final act, the khawal held a weight of 60 to 70 pounds with his teeth. His costume is not described. It is hard to imagine how he would have performed wearing women's dress.

The same ginks, along with their band, also participated in the elaborate procession of the bride to her groom's home on the morning after the week of celebrations; they marched, played their metal finger cymbals, and at times danced in the street. They seem to have been accompanied by a Turkish band. Also participating in the procession, but in a covered cart drawn by four horses, the "'awâlim" from the harem entertainments rode veiled, and sang periodically.

Male dancers provided only one of several kinds of entertainments at the wedding. During the eight days a military band played European music, and groups of Egyptian musicians both played and sang. Other acts included a buffoon (a servant of Muhammad Ali) dressed elaborately with a high pointed cap and bells, and castanets, who did amusing tricks; one night he impersonated a European. The crowds enjoyed a performer of sleight-of-hand tricks, men balancing long fire sticks, and two engaged in mock sword fights. One afternoon a rope was strung from the lake to the palace, 18 feet up and 12 feet long. Vast crowds watched rope dancing by two gypsies (more properly, Roma), a woman and a boy. Dancing consisted of walking the rope while holding a long balancing pole. Each evening a company of comedians presented popular farces. The plots of some included: a henpecked husband who ends by beating his wife; a husband with two wives and the ensuing miseries; one with little plot but much throwing about of fire crackers; and one dealing with setting up a marriage contract.

The Guild of Male Musicians and Singers

Male musicians and singers had their separate guild together, identified as Corporation 126 on the 1801 Napoleonic guild list, "musiciens du pays et chanteurs qui sont au Caire [male musicians of the country and male singers who are of Cairo]." As earlier noted, the guild of these artists was differentiated from that of those musicians closely associated with the ghawâzî. Villoteau (1809a, 678n) gave the local name for such artists as *alâtyeh*. Lane (1978, 354) called them *aláteeyeh* (sing. *alátee*). These musicians appeared separately, and also accompanied certain female and male dance performances. They emerge in contemporary accounts, along with the instruments they played, but most travel writers mention them very little and only as an adjunct to the dance. They had little status in Egyptian society, according to those who wrote about them. (Since this book deals with dance and female artists primarily, it cannot adequately portray these male artists in any detail.)

Lane, however, provides much information on early 19th-century Egyptian musicians and devotes far more attention to them than to female dancers. His chapter on music contains numerous illustrations of instruments and musicians, and transcribed songs. Lane's (1973; 1978) material is freely available in the modern reprints of his books. On the other hand, Villoteau's (1809a; 1809b) magnificent treatises on Arabic music, which constitute a major part of the first volume of the *Description de l'Égypte*, are available only in the original, usually part of a non-circulating rare book collection. Fortunately, with increasing attention to digitizing and making such types of materials available on the internet, this type of situation is rapidly remedying itself.

After the Napoleonic invasion, Villoteau and other Savants arranged to work closely with these local Egyptian musicians in Cairo in an attempt to further their knowledge of Arabic music. Villoteau had brought with him from Paris some Arabic treatises on musical theory, and was dismayed to discover his counterparts, the Egyptian musicians, were unable to read these. Their musical knowledge, he says, came from experience. The structure of their instruments, based on Arabic music systems, also contributed greatly to their practical artistic knowledge, he believed. Villoteau's detailed account of the confusions surrounding west meeting east, and the Savants' eventual discovery that Arabic music is improvised around a basic melody, make for fascinating examples of early ethnomusicology.

Section Four

The Lives of Female Entertainers

11

Relationships with Various Groups in Egyptian Society

A Capricious Administration

Al-Sayyid Marsot (1995, 132) points out that because of their lack of education, the rural and urban poor and often the middle classes found it virtually impossible to approach Egypt's rulers and their administration directly. They preferred to use intermediaries such as guild heads, religious leaders, or shaikhs of Sufi orders, villages, and tribes. Women tended to use other women as intermediaries, appealing for favors to elite women who would then communicate, through men of their families, with the grandees (ibid., 24).

As young females, with apparently little male family support, female entertainers would have been particularly vulnerable to the abuse and arbitrary rulings made by members of the administration. Even famous singers could be greatly exploited. Browne (1806, 95) recounts an anecdote about a group of singers who had earned a huge sum from performing at an aristocratic wedding, that of Ibrahim Bey's daughter in 1792. Summoned later by Ibrahim, their leader revealed that they had earned ten thousand half sequins. The Bey then demanded that she hand over eight thousand of these to him.

While traveling in Upper Egypt, Sonnini (1799, 3:131) claimed that women's associations there could not protect them from local Turkish authorities wishing to keep them out of their jurisdictions; some summarily banished entertainers from their district if complaints had been made against them. On the other hand, Lower Egypt seems to have been more tolerant. In the late 18th century the city of Mahalla el–Kubra in the Delta had the reputation as a refuge for female entertainers and those seeking to escape the attention of the police in other jurisdictions (Du Bois-Aymé and Jollois 1812, 109). Hamont (1845, 1:318) suggests that after the ban around 1834, shaikhs of their areas of Cairo protected some "public women" who continued to work in secret. Such protection probably had its down side. After the ban, certain governors in the Delta area allegedly extracted bribes and sexual favors from dancers as payments for overlooking their performances in their districts (ibid., 1:295).

The police seem always to have been a particular scourge for dancers. In Upper Egypt they allegedly paid a weekly sum to the local police officer who had unlimited powers to both punish and "protect" them (Sonnini 1799, 3:282). After the ban around 1834, dancers became even more fearful of the police. In Alexandria, Bayle St. John (1850, 148) tells of the initial impossibility in finding dancers for a party, one for the Levantine household in which he lived. Finally, a Jewess who "cared comparatively little for the police" agreed to come. Duff Gordon (1983, 322) speaks of the "caprices and extortions" of the police in connection with dancers performing legitimately in Luxor in the 1860s.

Finally, in any age Egyptian rulers found it difficult to forgo lucrative taxes during times of monetary crisis, yet they risked criticism from the religiously minded for taxing activities many considered vice. As a consequence, dancers and singers might find themselves subject to rapidly fluctuating policies. First, they might legitimately pay their fees, then find the tax repealed and they themselves under opprobrium, then the tax might be reinstated. The research literature tells of such situations in 1315, 1377, 1382 ('Abd ar-Raziq 1973, 80) and 1630 (Raymond 1974, 2:650). Other yet-unidentified instances must surely exist.

Administrative Officials and Consuls as Entertainment Providers

Despite often treating local entertainers callously, local administrators did provide important work for them in their districts. In the early days of the 19th century, when travel in Egypt still presented enormous difficulties, senior officials of the Egyptian administration, particularly in the provinces, entertained important accredited travelers and high officials arriving on state business. Such hospitality usually included an invitation to a dinner accompanied by music and often by dance. As additional guests, other local dignitaries would also attend.

In 1828, a senior official of a town in Upper Egypt gave a lavish entertainment for Champollion and his group, traveling under a special permit from Muhammad Ali. Before dinner, two Greek musicians of his household both sang and played Turkish and Arab music. After dinner, the singing continued, followed by male dancers performing in several styles—imitating female performers, then doing Turkish dances, then Greek (Champollion 1986, 146–149).¹ Bayle St. John (1973, 2:69–71) recounts a dinner party in Luxor in 1851, spent with the local military commander and his counterpart visiting from Isna. The company consisted of local officers, the mayor, other dignitaries of the village, and a crowd of lesser soldiers and servants. This was the occasion when St. John saw Hasna, the famous "Venus of the boatmen," along with other dancers brought in to entertain the Luxor commander.

Provincial consuls, local men representing European countries, seem also to have taken on a similar role, even later in the century, using their own establishments as places where entertainments might routinely be seen. Regional Egyptian consuls also made a practice of providing hospitality for more ordinary European travelers. Basil Faker served in Damietta in Lower Egypt as consul for several European countries in the 1820s, and seems to have been an obliging host to European visitors. Speaking of Isna in Upper Egypt, Appleton writes that he and his party had tried to arrange dance entertainment but found most unappealing the settings proposed by dancers themselves—their homes and a local dance hall. The travelers decided to wait until they had arrived back in Luxor: "We shall do better to postpone it all for the spacious and cleanly saloon of our consul at Luxor, who will gladly offer us *une nuit égyptienne*" (1876, 86). The financial arrangement for the service was understood and "for this and other civilities I was given to understand the worthy consul expected a backsheesh, I in return receiving antiquities" (ibid., 248).

The Military

Female entertainers had important ongoing relationships with the military, a clientele both highly available and often dangerous. Burkhardt gives the rather cryptic information that "in the time of the Mamelouks their [dancers'] influence in the open country was very considerable and the protection of a Ghazye was courted by many respectable persons" (1984, 177). His comments suggest that perhaps female entertainers and officers of the powerful Turkish regiments knew each other on a personal basis through contacts developed out of the taxation system, one controlled through the army and existing until the end of the 18th century. As a result, Egyptians of the middle and lower classes seeking to curry favor with the military might use these entertainers as intermediaries. Burkhardt's view fits well with the usual practice of using others to intercede on one's behalf with the rulers of Egypt. It also implies that some dancers and singers might indeed have enjoyed a kind of limited influence in Egyptian society at that time through their contacts with this important group.

Late in this century and particularly following upon the Napoleonic invasions, the military changed radically. Unlike the earlier enculturated Turkish Mamluk janissaries, many Albanian troops arrived in Egypt for the Ottoman conquest.[2] These had always served as mercenaries in the Turkish army where they had a reputation as being undisciplined, but Muhammad Ali relied on them in his rise to power. They soon became a constant source of trouble for they often rioted violently. He managed to disband some as early as 1806 (al–Sayyid Marsot 1984, 140) and after his wars in the Hijaz from 1812 to 1818 he dismissed even more (ibid., 200). He later sent many to the conquest of the Sudan during the 1820–22 invasions (ibid., 127). They seem to have manned the distant garrisons there throughout his reign.

There are early–19th-century references to local dancers and these essentially foreign troops. This uneasy relationship involved both a good source of income for dancers and also personal danger. Forbin (1819, 82), who arrived in Beni Suef in 1818, includes an anecdote about these mercenaries and the local dancers. He suggests many were the mistresses of local soldiers whom Muhammad Ali had removed south to the garrison there because of their unruliness in Cairo. In Beni Suef they "ran in the streets crying out like madmen, shooting as they went" (82). For fun they would chase the young dancers with bare swords. These Albanian *Arnauts* remained a feature of Egypt toward mid-century. Prisse d'Avennes (1930, 63) recalls that near Heliopolis (outside Cairo), around 1830, a settlement of dancers paid tribute to 50 Albanian soldiers who harassed their clients. James St. John tells that as he passed through Beni Suef in 1833 a division of the Egyptian army, moving back from Arabia, was "spreading themselves through the city, snatching in haste the coarse pleasures within their reach" (1834, 2:265). All the female dancers, singers, and musicians were busy with this "military rabble." The best lodgings were full, and St. John was obliged to spend the night in a common hostel.

Personal Relations with Elite Female Clients

Al-Sayyid Marsot (1995, 120–22) writes that while there were great social divisions between Egyptian classes there were also effective links between them, even with elite women theoretically isolated from outside society. In fact, they had constant visits from women of other classes, who might spend hours with them. Among these were tradeswomen, teachers, and those in the service industries. She also notes that middle class and lower class women used elite women as intermediaries on their behalf with the administration, and formed part of this large group of women coming and going in elite households. It seems that those who dealt professionally with elite women might equally approach them as petitioners in difficult times. Dancers may have petitioned wealthy women they knew to intercede for them with the administration when they were in trouble, as did other less fortunate women. They may have sought their help in other ways.

We do know that a wealthy woman of the exiled Tunisian ruling family took a dancer into her employ after the dance ban, and went nowhere in Cairo without her (Romer 1846, 2:127). Duff Gordon's relationships with the dancers of Upper Egypt give other clues as to possible close relationships between female entertainers and elite women. She relates an incident where the dancer who had come to entertain took it upon herself to lecture Duff Gordon's son about "evil ways," presumably his. Duff Gordon remarks, "She was an old friend of mine, and gave good and sound advice" (1983, 375). On another occasion, she says two dancers gave of their very best in performing for they felt themselves in the position of Duff Gordon's "own special ghawazee" (ibid., 380).

Lane paints a picture of women's freedom to experience professional dance and music within the harem, but does also contradict himself. He says that, in his day, the ghawâzî were introduced "not infrequently" into the harems of the wealthy "not merely to entertain the ladies with their dances, but to teach them their voluptuous arts" (1978, 299); he writes they "*often* [emphasis mine] perform in front of the house or in the court" (191). But Lane also says female entertainers are "very seldom admitted" to the harems (191) and never for "common occasions, in any respectable family, for this would be considered indecorous" (191). It is difficult to reconcile these statements.

Some evidence suggests that women would not normally contact dancers directly to arrange entertainments, but needed to work through a male intermediary. Even as a European, a woman alone, and completely in charge of her Luxor household, Duff Gordon felt herself constrained by this social custom: "It is not proper for a woman to send for the dancing-girls, and as I am the friend of the Maohn (police magistrate), the Kadee, and the respectable people here, I cannot do what is indecent in their eyes" (1983, 111).

Only three eye-witness accounts of harem entertainments for women only and involving professional dance exist in the travel literature of this period (thus far identified), those by Minutoli, Romer, and Lane-Poole. Minutoli (1827, 198–200) was invited expressly to watch the dance along with other local women of Damietta. Romer (2: 126–28), too, received such an invitation from a Levantine woman in Cairo, to meet the exiled daughter of the ruler of Tunis. Since the daughter always brought along her own dancer and singer, Romer participated, albeit unwillingly, at a performance. As described at length in Chapter 8, Lane-Poole (1846, 78–138) spent an entire week inside the royal harem on the occasion of the wedding of Muhammad Ali's daughter in 1845.

It is difficult to estimate any influence of the singers, 'awâlim, and ghawâzî on elite Egyptian women's lives. The three first-hand examples hardly begin to discuss the range of activities by female entertainers within the confines of the well-to-do harem, the types of programs they offered, and what they actually taught to women there on a regular basis. In the late 18th century allegedly the 'awâlim taught all the new songs, related amorous stories, recited poetry, "initiated them in the mysteries of their art," and instructed them in dancing. They also engaged in agreeable conversation (Savary 1785, 1:152). In the early 19th century female entertainers are described as instructing young girls of the harem in "agreeable arts" and, since versed in dancing, music, and singing, they constituted the "delight of the ladies of the East" (Minutoli 1827, 199).[3] By the 1830s the most elegant entertainers allegedly still served the Turkish harems (that is, the wealthy elites), teaching them singing, and storytelling, and relating Persian and Arabic stories (Voilquin 1978, 376). There is no presently available eye-witness confirmation of such types of instruction and varied repertoire in the travel literature.

Female Entertainers and the Banu Sasan

With *The Medieval Islamic Underworld: The Banu Sasan in Arabic Society and Literature,* Clifford Edmund Bosworth (1976) provides a definitive work about the ethnically diverse group of male vagabonds, beggars, and low-class entertainers called after their patron saint Sasan. The wandering nature of their lives and the nature of their occupations (often trickery and thievery in connection with other people's money) condemned them to the utmost social disapproval. It is important to note that Bosworth's list of the groups constituting the Banu Sasan does not include either male or female dancers and singers. At a certain earlier period in Egypt, female entertainers had been grouped occasionally with various Banu Sasan groups for administrative and taxation purposes. All dancers would probably have considered themselves above Banu Sasan groups in social status, however, and Egyptians in general may have thought the same.

There is little data about the professional relationship of public dancers and the Banu Sasan, but they often performed together, their appearance on the same "program" came about because public space was open to all. The travel literature provides examples of outdoor entertainments where public female dancers performed alongside tumblers, jugglers, buffoons, conjurors, rope dancers, comedians, monkey trainers, and, sometimes, storytellers.[4] For example, Michaud (1833–35, 5:251) identifies a Cairo coffee house when one might normally expect to find both female dancers and jugglers, and also discusses the outdoor aspects of a wedding in the Delta, where both female dancers and comedians performed (7:75). Lane (1978, 437) reports on the secular aspects of celebrations for the birth of the Prophet Muhammad, with storytellers, conjurers, buffoons, and rope dancers together with female dancers. Undoubtedly, some members of the ghawâzî would have known individuals of the Banu Sasan groups on a personal basis from these associations with them during performance events. The ghawâzî and the Banu Sasan may also have spent time together outside performance hours. For example, in the 13th century, the crumbling mosque of 'Amr in Old Cairo, no longer used for religious purposes, allegedly became a local hangout for musicians, ape trainers, conjurors, and ghawâzî.[5]

Female Entertainers and Prostitutes

It is important to examine a socially distinct group of women who were prostitutes, and separate their functions in Egyptian society from that of female entertainers. During the medieval period, the sources note professional female prostitutes taxed and administered as a distinct group ('Abd ar-Raziq 1973, 45). In the 18th century, European writers continued to identify prostitutes as administratively separate from female entertainers (Pococke 1743–45, 1:192; Browne 1806, 36; Chabrol 1822, 490). Describing prostitution during the first quarter of the 19th century, and distinguishing prostitutes clearly from female entertainers, Lane (1973, 381n) says that female prostitutes lived and worked in all the large urban centers in Egypt.[6] The ban proclaimed around 1834 applied equally to prostitutes and public dancers, and named them separately. "Public female dancing and prostitution have been prohibited by the government" (ibid., 377n). "The government has voluntarily renounced this branch of revenue. It has suppressed prostitution" (Clot Bey 1840, 1:336).

At the time of the Napoleonic invasion, Jomard (1822, 699) identified "public women" as having a "corporation," yet it should be noted that a corporation of prostitutes does not appear on the Napoleonic list of 1801, described in Chapter 4. This puts into question the idea that prostitutes formed a real guild, as opposed to being merely recognized as a distinct group for taxation. This absence from the corporation list also sets prostitutes apart from all female singers and dancers who do appear there. Despite the use of the term *corporation* by a few writers, professional prostitutes probably did not, and never did, have their own guild, with its rights and responsibilities, but simply constituted a pool of exploitable workers, particularly in the 19th century.

Lane (1973, 381n) notes that, in his time in Egypt, their number included women suddenly destitute, such as widows, divorcees, and women whose husbands were abroad for long periods of time. Muhammad Ali sent his army abroad in the early 1830s to fight for months at a time without paying their salary, and this policy was said to deprive wives, even of some officers, of any other way than prostitution to support their families (Prisse d'Avennes 1930, 58). Clot Bey (1840, 1:336) suggests that prostitutes were often repudiated wives with no other form of survival. Didier (1860, 328–30), on the other hand, claimed that, in his day, many of the Cairo prostitutes were foreign women from southern Europe and Malta.

Such evidence suggests that prostitution was then a highly elastic profession. The general poverty of the 1830s, however, seems to have driven many female entertainers to add regular prostitution to their other professions. "The almées [are] obliged today to prostitute themselves, to provide an existence that their dancing doesn't always given them" (Combes 1846, 1:222).

Female Entertainers' Relationships with Each Other

There is little information in the travel literature about dancers' and singers' connections with each other, yet one can imagine some particulars. Their lives offstage would be more extensive than onstage in terms of time and relationships. Many did live communally in their settlements outside the cities, and they would certainly have known each other, of their respective dancing talents, and about the progress of each other's careers.

Burkhardt spoke of dancers constantly moving throughout the country in the early years of the 19th century, both on business and on "visits to the sisterhood established in neighbouring places" (1984, 175). Certainly outstanding dancers' reputations were widely known throughout Egypt. During Du Camp and Flaubert's visit to Aswan, Aziza spoke gloatingly of her talent as being superior to Kutchuk Hanem's of down-river Isna (quoted in Buonaventura 1990, 76).

Dancers performed together, perhaps with compatible colleagues. A dancer who came to an untimely end in the Napoleonic period had performed nightly with "other women of her type" outside her own city district (al–Jabarti 1888–96, 6:102). Didier's (1860, 338) Gazal eagerly offered up her three friends Alima, Zarifa, and Nagafa, hidden throughout Cairo, for the illicit dance evening they were planning. As described in Flaubert's (1965; 1991) and Curtis's (1856) accounts, Kutchuk Hanem seems to have drawn on the local talent of Isna for her own uses; one does not know their relationship, but since the performances were at her home, she probably was in the role of employer or even sponsor of

Opposite: Fig. 9. André Dutertre. *Almés ou danseuses publiques* (Almés or public dancers). c. 1800 (from Commission des sciences et arts d'Egypte. *Description de l'Égypte* [Paris: Imprimerie imp., 1809–1822]. Courtesy of the Thomas Fisher Rare Book Library, University of Toronto).

11. Relationships with Various Groups in Egyptian Society

other dancers. Dancers would probably develop close relationships with the women who had trained them and perhaps had sponsored them in their careers.

Friendships were obviously possible in offstage relationships. The *Description de l'Égypte* (fig. 9) depicts two dancers seated solemnly side by side in a hut. They are related in some way, although we do not know whether they are sisters, professional colleagues, or simply friends. Duff Gordon writes that "some dancing girls came to the boat ... to ask after their friend el Maghribeeyeh, the good dancer at Luxor, whom they said was very ill. Omar did not know at all about her, and the girls seemed much distressed" (1983, 168). In Sinnûris, although she had danced alone the night before, Hasna arrived in the French camp at dawn with a number of her dancer friends to take advantage of the travelers' earlier generosity and to enjoy their company at leisure (Lenoir 1872, 107). Finally, Gérôme (Ackerman 1986, cat. no. 202) has painted a dancer and her female musician enjoying chess together in a café.[7]

Dancers spent time together in locales that might be described as hiring halls. James St. John (1834, 1:107) speaks of the many dancers assembled at a great coffee house just outside Cairo, and Lenoir (1872, 98–99) identifies the same phenomenon at the Café Anglais in Sinnûris. Goupil Fesquet (1843, 69–70) tells of a house near the Nile downstream from Cairo, from which, after the ban, travelers might employ dancers and singers to entertain them for a short while on their river trip. Many women were there awaiting employment. During such long waits women would certainly interact, forming friendships, enmities, and professional ties.

12

Professional Relationships with the Audience

Egyptian Women as Dance Consumers

The available European evidence about Egyptian women as consumers of dance entertainment is problematic—for two reasons. First, most of the European eye-witness information relates to Christian female residents of Egypt; that is, the Copts, Armenians, and Levantines. One can only presume that the majority—Muslim women—had the same attitudes toward the dance. Second, the majority of male and female European writers found it reprehensible that female audiences would enjoy this dancing, and devoted much ink to diatribes about what this pleasure implied about their basic morals. A careful reading of the material available, editing out the land mines of biased European criticism, can give some basic information, however.

Wealthy and middle-class women were far more confined to the home than lower class and peasant women. These latter, the majority in fact, had freer access to public dance in the out-of-doors, particularly on occasions of public festivities. At such events both men and women would watch the same performances together, within the same public space. In describing outdoor public festivals, writers usually fail to distinguish between male and female members of the crowds. Some accounts do, however, show that women participated in numbers.

The Mayer illustration (fig. 3) of a troupe dancing outdoors at Ned Sili shows both women and men among the audience. In Michaud's (1833–35, 5:253) account of 'Id, he notes the presence of women among the crowds watching female dancers outside the city gates. Bartlett happened upon an outdoor dance performance in a town south of Cairo in 1845 and describes in some detail both

Fig. 10. W.H. Bartlett. Untitled. 1845 (from W.H. Bartlett, *The Nile Boat; or Glimpses of the Land of Egypt* [London: Arthur Hall, Virtue, 1849]).

the seating arrangements and the audience assembled around an elevated platform where the dance was taking place.[1] Turkish civil and military officers occupied low seats on the platform, or squatted on the ground. Behind them, crowded together, "fellahs [peasant farmers] and boatmen, women and children of all ages, equally intent upon enjoying what may be considered the national dance" (1849, 113). In his illustration (fig. 10) of this performance, Bartlett shows unveiled peasant women in the background.[2] One might conclude that viewing of public dance would be a function of particular Egyptian women's abilities to come and go in communal spaces. Many women, specifically lower class women, apparently participated relatively freely in the outdoor events connected with diverse types of festivities; here they had access to public dancing more or less equally with their male counterparts.

One also asks whether Egyptian women enjoyed the arts of female performers. Some evidence shows that they did and participated willingly as dance audiences. The Napoleonic Savant Chabrol (1822, 463) witnessed young women so deeply moved by the songs and dances that they not only applauded with furor, but also joined their own voices to the singing, and imitated the movements of the dancers. On deciding whether to risk watching local dance for the first time, Estourmel (1844, 2:453) reassures himself that the "pretty and modest Mme. Moktar," wife of the Egyptian dragoman of the Austrian embassy, plans to host the event at her home. On arriving, he finds "the most honest women in the world, or at least in Cairo," prepared to give themselves the "innocent pleasure" of watching the dance. Personally appalled by the performance, Estourmel finds only "pleasure and approval" on every face (2:454). At a Muslim wedding, Voilquin (1978, 377) is stunned at the overwhelmingly positive reactions, of the young virgin bride and all her friends and family in the harem area, to the performance of the dance below. They laugh, and press her with questions. Did she enjoy the performance? they ask. Too polite to say what she really feels, and unwilling to jeopardize hospitality so generously given, she contents herself with the simple Arabic phrase, "It's very nice."[3]

In 1835, Voilquin's Coptic (Egyptian Christian) neighbors invited her to a women's party, held in their great salon. Her account (1978, 323) provides the most detailed description available of middle-class women's day-to-day self-entertainments and their enjoyment of them, and it merits some details. Here, women of the household and their female guests, 17 in all, drank coffee, smoked the *nargila* (water pipe), ate pastries and drank liqueurs. At first reserved towards her, soon they plied Voilquin with many questions about the lives of French women (Voilquin spoke Arabic well). Then the entertainments began, in this instance provided by those women present and some of the servants, not professional entertainers. One woman sang and accompanied herself on a stringed instrument, two servants enacted "grotesque farces" in travesti, that "made these women laugh a lot." Then "other Arabs" danced several dances "of the awalim," with "a great liberty of gestures and much effrontery of body movements. It was the least unequivocal intentions that had the most success in this assembly" (ibid., 323).[4] This account implies that by their replication of the professional dance form these local middle-class women both enjoyed and approved it.

Mixed Male and Female Audiences at Family Celebrations

Previous examples throughout this study have shown female entertainers with all-male audiences, with all-female audiences, and with mixed audiences at outdoor public festivals set before the common people. Within a family setting female entertainers were often obliged to observe the protocol of the separation of the sexes when they performed, and thus they created various ways of relating to their mixed-sex audiences. Belzoni describes an outdoor wedding in 1818, where both men and women were present though separated in space:

At night, the pole and all the place around it was illuminated. The people seated themselves in an orderly manner, in the form of an amphitheatre, the women forming a part of the circle, separated from the men ... the entertainment began with dancing, by two well-known and distinguished performers [1821, 18].[5]

An illustration by Rifaud (fig. 11) of an outdoor wedding at Luxor shows the seated male guests to one side, with the women guests standing on the flat roof of the home, looking down into the entertainment and dining space. Voilquin's account of a Muslim wedding gives a unique eye-witness account of watching a dance in such a setting, that is, from the screened quarters of the harem where women, the "invisible spectators, could participate in the rejoicing given in honour of the marriage" (1978, 375). She (ibid., 375–76) remarks on the protocol observed. No male guest glanced towards the upper screen nor gave by hint of a gesture that he knew what lay so close nearby; this act would have offended the host and groom. After dinner, with coffee, liqueurs, and pipes for the men, the dance took place, ostensibly for the men, but equally accessible to the women.

Fig. 11. J.J. Rifaud. *Repas de noces d'un chaik el beled (de Thebaïde)* (Wedding Breakfast of a Village Shaik of Luxor). c. 1825 (with permission of the Société Royal d'Archéologie, d'Histoire et de Folklore de Nivelles et du Brabant Wallon).

Sometimes women chose separation and seclusion even when other options were available. Bayle St. John (1850, 147–49) describes with some humor the problems he and his Christian landlady, Sitt Madoula, encountered in arranging a fantasia[6] to celebrate her son's escape from military service. St. John wished to invite some male English friends to this special event. Sitt Madoula, of course, had a guest list of locals and her own family, including some female members violently intolerant of Europeans. "At length it was determined that the prejudiced members of the family who were to be present should remain in ignorance that any strange heretics were expected" (1850, 147). The commodious room chosen had a high ceiling and an upper gallery on one end. Here the women sat, whispering and giggling, awaiting the performance. The men sat in the room proper, the young males of the family and guests consisting of five Englishmen, two Greek merchants, and three Levantines (here Christians of Syrian origin). This account shows a separation of males and females based on religious prejudice stemming from eastern and western forms of Christianity, rather than on social custom as in Muslim families.[7]

A separation by time, that is separate performances, would also allow men and women of respectable families to participate in the same dance event. The account of a Muslim wedding by Du Bois-Aymé and Jollois (1812, 109) describes such an arrangement. At first the performers sang among the women in a separate room for an hour and a half, but heard clearly by the host and his guests in the court, where the "ordinary people" were also assembled. Next, two of them went into the court to present a dance. A four-day party for some (not identified) family occasion, given by the Muslim Kurdish commander of the military post just north of Khartoum, employed dancers to perform for both men and women alternatively. "Sometimes, but rarely, they [dancers] functioned in the interior of the harem, and for the women only. One heard, then, the far-off sounds of the tambourines mingled with the tinkling of the castanets" (Didier 1858, 101). The entertainments for the host and his male guests took place in the open air in front of the commander's large stone house (ibid., 102).

Dance in the Provinces

It seems many hosts in 19th-century Egypt accepted the entertaining of visiting friends with food, drink, and dance as normal practice. Duff Gordon's account of her seven years in Egypt, from 1862 to 1869, provides a sense of just how much hospitality, and thus how much dance, might actually be taking place on a not-infrequent basis among well-to-do citizens in the provinces. During her years in Luxor, Duff Gordon traveled regularly to Cairo, stopping off to visit European and Egyptian friends at towns along the way. Qena was a favorite place, and she describes several occasions involving a fantasia with dancing there. "They all made me promise to see them again on my return and dine at their houses, and Wassef wanted to make a fantasia and have dancing girls" (1983, 35). On another occasion, "after dinner the French Consul, a Copt, one Jesus Buktor, sent to invite me to a fantasia at his house, where I found the Mouniers, the Moudir, and some other Turks, and a disagreeable Italian.... I was glad to see the dancing girls" (ibid., 99). At home in Luxor, through her Egyptian friends Duff Gordon would arrange to entertain foreign acquaintances, and family connections passing through on their Egyptian tour (1983, 111, 120, 188).

13

Training

A Guild Responsibility?

The constant training of new performers to replace those retiring is key to any continuity in the arts, but, unfortunately, the topic did not interest travelers, and information is almost non-existent. Villoteau (1809a, 610, 673) found that, in general, male Egyptian musicians were illiterate, and as such unable to read Arabic treatises about their own music, deriving their musical knowledge from experience and the structure of their instruments. Both the ghawâzî and the male musicians of their particular guild probably would also have been illiterate. In this corporation no educational gulf would exist between female dancer and male musician. Startling indeed is the educational gulf between male musicians and the higher classes of female entertainers, since, as already discussed, in the upper echelons of the female entertainment world, considerable literacy and other social accomplishments seem to have still existed into the 19th century. These skills need some kind of explanation as they would be as treasured and jealously guarded as the trade secrets of any other craft, handed down from generation to generation.

Medieval literature hints as to what procedures may have survived into later periods. Any female artist expecting to provide a witty presence at parties in wealthy homes needed an education far beyond the average. Wiebke Walther (1993, 101) quotes at length from a medieval reference to the special slave women who received a lengthy training in the arts and literature. This slave-buying guide of the early 11th century, written by a Christian doctor, identified the ideal female slave as a Berber from Morocco, purchased at the age of nine. She then spends three years in Mecca, three years in Medina, and then comes to Iraq for training in the fine arts. When she is sold, finally, at the age of 25 Walther says, "She combines the wit of the women of Medina with the mildness of the inhabitants of Mecca and the education of Mesopotamia" (101). Walther remarks that this training was "a piquant blend of wisdom and femininity that was greatly appreciated at the time" (101).

In the medieval period, female slave singers and dancers in the great houses of Egypt received an education that fitted them for participating "with charm, grace and spirit" in receptions given by their masters ('Abd ar-Raziq 1973, 55). Lane's (1865, 1:391) *The Thousand and One Nights* gives an excellent description of the type of education believed available to the most superior of slave women. The king of the story wishes a slave woman of unsurpassed beauty, one "endowed with all praiseworthy qualities." Finally, such a paragon is found. For the king, her price is ten thousand pieces of gold, but even this does not match the cost of her training, her present owner claims, as he lists her accomplishments:

> This sum does not equal the cost of the chickens which she hath eaten, nor the cost of the dresses which she hath bestowed upon her teachers; for she hath learnt writing and grammar and lexicology, and the interpretation of the Kuran, and the fundamentals of law and religion, and medicine, and the computation of the calendar, and the art of playing upon musical instruments [Lane 1865, 1:392].

Only traces of this sort of education and the tradition of learning persisted in descriptions of the singers and other female entertainers of 18th-century Egypt. Savary's (1785, 1:149–50) list of entry requirements for the class he calls "almées" shows the group still demanded high standards. He lists: skill in singing; excellent knowledge of Arabic and the rules of its poetry; ability to improvise on the spot both words and music suitable to the occasion; and possession of a vast repertoire of old and new songs. Fifty years after Savary's visit, Michaud's (1833–35, 5:255) informants told him dancers learned to dance and sing, acquired the rules of poetry, and could improvise songs.[1] Didier, who spent time in the company of expatriate Egyptian female entertainers he met in Khartoum, speaks of their literacy: "They are much more cultivated than other women in the Orient, know how to read and write and many are poets" (1858, 48).

Working-class Egyptian women learned Turkish in order to trade with their foreign-born elite female clients (al–Sayyid Marsot 1995, 121), and more than likely elite entertainers who dealt with this class would have added bilingualism to their list of talents. As already described, Turkish songs and music formed part of the repertoire for the royal harem's wedding entertainments of 1845 (Lane-Poole 1846, 106).

Traditionally Egyptian guilds provided the training for apprentices and usually drew future members from the families of existing members (al–Sayyid

Marsot 1995, 109). Senior members would carry out the training. How would dancers have been trained? The Napoleonic Savant Villoteau (1809a, 700) did provide the enigmatic information that there existed a class of Jewish women called "djenk" [jank] who taught dancing, but said nothing at all about how they practiced this profession.

It seems that some training might take place during an actual performance. On his third visit to Kutchuk Hanem, Flaubert (1991, 363) watched an older female drum player make signs to a young dancer, mark time, and indicate what steps she should take. Curtis noted that during her performance the young Zanuba danced "with her eyes fixed constantly upon the elder [Kutchuk Hanem]" (1856, 142).

There is a brief but important hint that the town of Fuwa, on the Nile in Lower Egypt, had been a long-time center for dance training:

> Foua, near which is supposed to have stood in ancient times the city of Metelis, celebrated for the female singers and dancers *educated* [emphasis mine] there, who made it their profession to travel about, and exhibit their skill at public festivals. Even in the present day [around 1790] most of the itinerants of this description in Egypt come from Foua [Mayer 1801, 45].

Bayle St. John (1973, 1:23) gives useful information about the training of young dancers, but this schooling bears little resemblance to the great training of the past, and, unfortunately, one cannot relate any aspects of his information definitely to any group of female entertainers. Around 1850 he visited a secluded village in Lower Egypt, where he found a group of "Ghawazees" who were training young peasant girls in the arts of dance and song in a coffee house, probably owned by one of them. The women informed St. John that they had purchased the two attractive children from local peasant families. He was disinclined to believe them. Such practices would make sense for guilds wishing to perpetuate themselves, since physical beauty and dance talents are not necessarily hereditary and outside recruitment may be necessary.

Reading here of dancers' use of a coffee house as a training center raises the interesting question of just where did entertainers first learn their craft. There were no studios, obviously, and most homes were far too modest. Perhaps the local coffee house served this capacity in many cities and towns. Earlier, in 1833, St. John's father had witnessed a dance performance at a grand coffee house at a village of "dancing girls" just outside Cairo, where he also saw a concentration of about a hundred other young potential performers that were "all young—none perhaps exceeding twenty; and the majority between ten and sixteen years old" (J. St. John 1845, 268). Perhaps this, too, served as their training center, but it is difficult to draw any conclusions from such sketchy evidence.

14

Economic Position of Female Entertainers

Guild Structures and Taxation Over the Centuries

Gabriel Baer (1964, 84) relates that after their victory over Egypt in 1517 the Ottoman Turks formalized existing loose associations of professionals and turned them into guild structures. The chief aim of the new Ottoman administration was taxation for the benefit of Istanbul, and with a large part of revenues obtained from the urban population, guilds became an important instrument in this process. The shaikhs of the guilds really represented authorities to the guilds, rather than acting primarily in the interests of their corporation, although they might do this to a limited degree. Michael Winter (1992, 250) explains that at first, after the Ottoman invasion, salaried functionaries extracted revenues. Later, tax farms were preferred, the sources of profits auctioned to the powerful and the wealthy. These men (and women) often sublet their tax farms to agents who would administer them for the original tax farmer.

How did female entertainers fit into this new Ottoman administrative organization? Did they, at that time, develop actual guilds? In terms of female entertainers forming guilds, based on some 18th-century information, Baer (1964, 32–33) certainly implies all groupings of male and female entertainers then constituted formal guilds, though he (ibid., 9) does suggest they were not considered worthy of comparison to the traditional hierarchy of ancient and honored guilds. Al-Sayyid Marsot (1995, 119) tends to agree that female entertainers formed guilds. She suggests the title *shaikha al-maghani* as applied to a famous 18th-century singer implies she was either the chief singer or the head of their guild. Raymond (1973–74, 2:509) is less inclined to this view. He points out that certain local Arabic documentation on corporations of that time does not even mention guilds of entertainers nor those of many poor and less respected groups. He believes (1973–74, 2:527) that many such corporations were on the margins of the normal guild structure, being perhaps only administrative groupings in the minds of the rulers of Egypt. Based on Raymond's (1956–57) own earlier work, however, as discussed at length in section two, we have seen that at the time of Napoleon's invasion three guilds were recognizable as including clearly distinct ranks of female entertainers.

Under Muhammad Ali and his family, Egypt increasingly had a more modern administration with less need of the intermediary guild structure. The rulers of Egypt never formally did away with the guild system nor deprived them of their functions, however most did cease to function by the end of the 19th century. The government retained some for purposes of control (Baer 1964, 144). There is some sketchy evidence in the travel literature for dancers' guild-like associations continuing into the 19th century, and hints of their functions. Around 1820 Burkhardt (1964, 178) suggested that where there were concentrations of entertainers they considered one the *ameer el-nezel* or "chief of the settlement"; this title would not place her in a position of authority over the others, however. Later, Prisse d'Avennes (1930, 63) speaks of the "queen" of the settlement of dancers near Heliopolis, just outside Cairo. In the 1830s Michaud (1833–35, 5:88) described a corporation of female entertainers in Lower Egypt with formal rules and an official shaikha who carried out administrative duties, such as sending entertainers as required throughout the Delta region. In the same period, Clot Bey (1840, 2:301) also suggested that, along with certain other types of entertainers, "female dancers" had their own shaikha who administered them, represented them before government, and defended their interests. Taken together, all this fragmentary information does suggest a sort of internal guild structure and hierarchy still existing into the century. It is inconclusive as to which specific guilds of female entertainers are being referenced.

While guilds could confer certain benefits to their members, they were conveniently grouped when the administration wanted easy access to more funds. This we have seen at the time of the Ottoman conquest in 1517, and at that of Napoleon in 1798 (section two). Interestingly enough, Egyptian women as a whole were not subject to these pressures.

In discussing 18th-century Egyptian women in general, al-Sayyid Marsot says women "were involved in the informal sector of the economy, which allowed them to earn a living but to pay no taxes at all, since their means of production was unrecognized by the state" (1995, 114). Tucker says much the same of Egyptian women of the early 19th century:

> Female economic and social ties were more likely to be formed in the context of associations of female design—in the streets and around the fountains of the quarter, in the public baths, in the small fruit and vegetable markets dominated by women traders. Lacking the formal organization and official recognition accorded other institutions, women's associations of the 19th century have left only occasional traces [1985, 110].

Al-Sayyid Marsot's and Tucker's statements about ordinary women are extraordinary in light of formal mechanisms for the taxation of female entertainers existing over many centuries under entirely separate Egyptian regimes, and continuing during the period of the study.

'Abd ar-Raziq's (1973) modern work on women's occupations in medieval Egypt contains important information regarding the taxation of female entertainers. In medieval Egypt the *dâmina al-maghânî*, he says, served as an important person who purchased, trained, and sold talented female entertainers (68n), and also undertook the payment of money to the state by means of a tax imposed upon non-slave entertainers (79). The government might make severe demands on her in times of fiscal crisis, these demands passed on to entertainers as higher levies (80). In normal times she took charge of a tax on weddings and parties (79). No female singer of the people could entertain at a wedding or circumcision without her authorization. As well, she could formally forbid entertainers from going to work without paying their fee, and chroniclers tell of her agents going from house to house checking to see who had gone out in the evenings, presumably to perform (79–80).

A reference to a dâmina al-maghânî in both Cairo and Bilbeis (ibid., 68n) suggests there might be women of this profession in other towns of Egypt. They were obviously powerful in the entertainment field, and probably able to amass a fortune. We do not know if the dâmina al-maghânî was appointed out of the professions she controlled, whether this was a real association with its head having at least some concerns for members' welfare. Based on 'Abd ar-Raziq's study, she appears to be acting primarily as an agent of the government, in charge of a highly controlled sphere of professional activity. Her position, however, would not preclude another person as head of the entertainers, one appointed by them or for them.

Facts on the taxing of entertainers in later centuries are sketchy, but some evidence remains. The Ottoman Turks continued to tax female entertainers as a group but the medieval position of dâmina al-maghânî did not survive. Early in the Ottoman administration a police officer (Baer 1964, 42) supervised "immoral" guilds, including entertainers, and collected taxes from them. By the middle of the 17th century a (male) official collected a levy on female entertainers (Raymond 1973–74, 2:650). In the 18th century a salaried official controlled and taxed all public spectacles in Egypt. He was in charge of all guilds of entertainers, and some others[1] (Baer 1964, 43).

Two sources list the tax revenues of Egypt during Muhammad Ali's reign, both compiled by the French expatriate Felix Mengin in 1822 and 1833.[2] Citing Mengin's "useful work," Jomard (1836, 8) lists the total revenue of Egypt in 1822 as 47,988,152 francs. Entertainers are the only professional grouping to be specifically identified, all other revenues being derived from products, customs duties, and so on. Their entry reads "droit sur les almées, etc. [tax on the almées, etc.]," and listed as 60,000 francs. It seems remarkable that a separate listing is made for such a small sum. Several items are listed here for comparison: the largest single item was the land tax (*miry*) at 28,125,000 francs, revenues from tax-farms produced 1,094,000 francs, taxes on cloth and industrial goods produced 6,186,000, taxes on rice and dates produced 4,742,900 francs.

Some time during the 1820s Muhammad Ali changed the taxation system, introducing a head tax (on adult males) that developed into a major item of Egyptian revenue. Mengin (quoted in Clot Bey 1840, 2:208–09) writes of taxation for the year 1833, saying the head tax is now listed as a major item of total revenue, being 8,750,000 francs. In the towns the corporations collected this tax, and the shaikhs became responsible for its transmission to the government (Baer 1964, 85). As in 1822, a separate listing of a tax on "danseuses, musiciens et les escamoteurs ([female] dancers, [male] musicians and magicians/jugglers)" appears in Mengin's statistics, though, again, this is a remarkable singling out of three professions. Again, the total is slight, given as 60,000 francs out of a total revenue of 62,778,750 francs.[3]

Difficulties arise in untangling the implications behind separate citations about "almées" and "danseuses" in the taxation records. Mengin does not make it entirely clear whether all three guilds of female entertainers, or just two, the 'awâlim and ghawâzî, are intended by this separate listing of 60,000 francs on the two tax records. The amounts cited are not very large in comparison with total revenues, inconsistent with popular notions that overall female entertainers contributed a great deal to the public purse.

Mengin's statistics seem to indicate that, under Muhammad Ali, certain female entertainers were taxed directly through the heads of their guilds by means of a "levy" or "droit," but the question remains whether they also constituted a suitable target for the tax farmer. We know that the tax farming of illicit, questionable, or pleasurable activities existed at the time of the French invasion in 1798, since a senior officer of police had a farm of coffee houses (Raymond 1973–74, 2:645), the janissary regiments controlled a farm on the production of wine and arak (ibid., 2:649), farms on houses of prostitution had been long established (ibid., 2:649). Anecdotal evidence does exist for tax farms on female dancers, later, in the early 19th century.

Referring to his first years in Egypt, in the 1820s, Lane (1978, 124) spoke of a tax-farm on "public women," one run by the military police. The individual in charge had a list and exacted a tax from each woman. James St. John adds that they were divided into three or four classes according to their beauty, and "pay a tax to the Pasha who ... farms out the vices of his subjects." Giving details highly reminiscent of procedures in the medieval system under the dâmina al-maghânî, he remarks that they were "under the superintendence of the ... Captain of the Courtesans; and when a party is sent for to perform in the evening at any private house, they must first repair to their chief, give in their names, and pay an extra sum" (1834 1: 115). Hamont (1845, 1:316–318) gives the most detailed account about the relationship of the government to certain female entertainers through the tax-farm system. "Public women"[4] formed a tax-farm, each paying according to her good looks. During the Syrian war that began in 1831, Muhammad Ali needed money for his war machine and listened sympathetically to an offer to increase the profit from the farm. The new administrator first doubled the tax on each woman, next sought ingenious ways of collecting even more money. As late as 1868, a tax-farm certainly is identified, at least in Luxor, Upper Egypt:

> I saw one of the poor dancing girls, the other day ... and she told me how cruel the new tax on them is. It is left to the discretion of the official who farms it to make each woman pay according to her presumed gains, i.e., her good looks, and thus the poor women are exposed to all the caprices and extortions of the police [Duff Gordon 1983, 322].

Unfortunately, none of the authors cited above made clear distinctions among the various classes of female entertainers.

Might one conclude that, under Muhammad Ali, Corporation 137 and Corporation 200 (singers and raqqâsîn) paid their taxes as the slightly more regularized "droit" or "levy" as indicated by the two rather skimpy 60,000 francs tax listings in the 1822 and 1833 revenue statements, and the ghawâzî tax-farmed as Lane, James St. John, Hamont, and Duff Gordon suggest? In this case, any revenues derived from the latter's activities (and perhaps the prostitutes') would have appeared subsumed under the huge amounts derived from all tax-farms taken together. While revenues from tax-farming are listed in the 1822 records, there is no such large item in the 1833 statement. Hopefully, future research will produce more clarification on this interesting aspect of female entertainers' lives.

Female Entertainers Making Money

Egyptian peasant women had a reputation for assertiveness. Duff Gordon commented that "the Pasha has ordered all the women of the lower classes to keep indoors while he [the Turkish Ottoman sultan] is here. Arab women are outspoken, and might shout out their grievances to the great Sultan" (1983, 52–53). Lower class in origin and self-employed business women, public female entertainers would have been forceful and assured, for they needed to attract an audience when performing in public. For example, Champollion (1986, 67–68) tells how female entertainers routinely solicited business directly from boats plying the Nile route in Lower Egypt. At celebrations for saints' days they were most conspicuous. "Nothing can exceed the audacious freedom with which they ply their trade [at Tanta]" (B. St. John 1973, 1:28). Others speak of dancers' forcefulness even becoming physical. They "assailed" passersby at Fuwa (Savary 1785, 1:66). "One of them [dancers] struggled hard with me to prevent my passing without giving them a present" (Lane 1978, 423–24). Dancers were not shy in seeking an increased remuneration. Dauzats (Dumas [and Dauzats] 1846, 1:228) tells of the intermission at Clot Bey's party, when the dancers threw themselves onto the laps of the men present, slithering "like serpents" among the folds of their robes.

Dancers freely expressed displeasure if cheated or abused. When Champollion and his companions did not provide generously for the party held at their riverside camp, the dance company returned in an uproar to Girga, proclaiming to the entire town that they had been robbed (L'Hôte 1993, 130). Bayle St. John (1973, 2:71) describes the best dancers of Luxor dancing indifferently and grudgingly because those who had engaged them would not be paying them for their efforts.[5]

An elaborate private party with fine dancers and musicians was costly. Dauzats (Dumas [and Dauzats] 1846, 1:228–29) says of the party given by Clot Bey to visiting French dignitaries that it was normally the privilege of a great lord who might expend as much as the price of six or eight black slaves. Lane (1978, 494) gives a detailed account of how dancers were paid. At a private party of Egyptians, guests normally assumed they would help defray the entertainment expenses, although a generous host might not permit this. Usually the fee for the evening would be decided beforehand, the host agreeing to subsidize any shortfall, or perhaps keeping any excess raised from a collection from his guests. At other times entertainers might agree to accept any money raised, whatever the sum might be. Pressure was on each guest to be generous.

One learns that dancers received extra tips directly onto their bodies. "It is a common custom for a man to wet with his tongue small gold coins, and stick them upon the forehead, cheeks, chin, and lips of a Gházeeyeh" (Lane 1978, 495). In Nadir, the jovial second-in-command of Champollion's boat repaid the singer by moistening coins and sticking them on her cheeks, then kissing her (1986, 68). At mixed-sex family parties dancers received payment in this manner, but only the male guests attached the coins. "Sometimes gold pieces were laid on the cheeks of the dancers, and between their lips, by the male guests" (Hackländer quoted in J. St. John 1845, 276).

Informal, impromptu public performances followed some of the same principles as private parties. Villoteau (1809a, 694) speaks of women throwing coins from the upper windows of the house into the streets as payment for the street dancers below. James St. John speaks of the performance at a great coffee house taking place in a separate room "where only those were admitted as spectators who contributed to defray the expense of the entertainment" (1851, 3).

Another type of payment existed. Minutoli passes on an anecdote about Nafissa, the celebrated Cairo singer of the 1820s: "To induce her to sing it was necessary to begin by sending her a Cashmere shawl worth a hundred Spanish piastres" (1827, 199n).[6] The shawl as payment was obviously a long-standing custom, one that continued on in the century. Lane-Poole (1846, 108) spoke of professional dancers in the harem at the royal wedding of 1845 receiving expensive cashmere shawls as gifts, but her account does not make it clear if the shawls were in addition to the fee or in lieu of it.

The travel literature explains how female entertainers valued the annual circuits of saints' day festivals. These events, which may be thought of as fairs as well as religious occasions, occurred particularly in Lower Egypt.[7] Since the inevitably recurring mawâlid often lasted for a full week, from one Friday to the next, they provided a stable source of income. Bayle St. John even suggested that dancers often had no permanent residence, but traveled throughout Egypt "according as the economists would say to the capricious fluctuations of demand" (1973, 1:28).

Michaud provides a sense of how certain female entertainers shaped their peripatetic lives to the mawâlid. Seeing dancers soliciting business at Nadir on the Rosetta branch of the Nile at the beginning of his tour in 1831, Michaud remarked that "these courtesans that we have seen at Nadir, will be going to the fair in Tanta which opens early in April" (1833–35, 5:88). Michaud (7:217) eventually arrived in Tanta that April, just too late to attend the famous fair in springtime, but describes the town as still full of life after the celebrations. First seeing the sights there, he then traveled toward the Nile, embarking on a boat full of passengers now bound for the fair at nearby Disûq (7:221). He described a city of three thousand people in preparation for the celebrations. The plain was filling up with stalls and some merchants had already set up shop in cafés. "Many almées, too, now were erecting tents; the authorities in charge of public order had established themselves in green tents" (7:223).

Even after the ban around 1834 female entertainers still appeared at Tanta for the festivities in search of gainful employment:

> They are supposed it is true, to be banished to Upper Egypt; but the edict was never effectually carried out, and when twice-a-year business and piety attract their votaries to Tanta, the Ghawazees, or substitutes strongly resembling them, are never absent [B. St. John 1973, 28].

Lane-Poole confirms this remark for, going by boat from Alexandria to Cairo in July of 1842, she saw many Egyptians on their way to Tanta, and remarked that "swarms of dancing-girls and singers contribute to their amusement" (1851, 1:56).

Performers exiled to Upper Egypt after the ban around 1834 often found themselves in a enforced state of semi-retirement and their economic situation deteriorated. The modern writer Auriant (1943, 16–17) contributes some pertinent facts about those exiles.[8] They worked from November until February, the high tourist season, both as dancers and as prostitutes, then were unemployed, in debt to the Coptic moneylenders. The arrival of the northern-bound caravans would bring temporary trade. The occasional arrival of troops bound south to the Sudan or east across the Red Sea, would also bring much-wanted business. Romer suggested their situation was not impossible, that the Egyptian government gave to each woman banished to Isna "house-rent free, and to each individual three loaves of bread and one piaster ten paras per diem (about twopence English) upon which, in this cheap country, they contrive to live very well" (1846, 1:272). Prisse d'Avennes (1930, 59) also suggested these ex-performers could exist on a government pension until they found husbands. Perhaps this solution sufficed in the 1830s. Writing later about the exiled dancers he had seen in Aswan in 1854, Didier says that they had "sold piece by piece, to satisfy their basic needs, their rivers of sequins that they had gained through the generosity of their admirers. One could see them, poorly dressed in the leftovers of their former magnificence" (1858, 273). Obviously these exiled semi-retired entertainers, their careers in jeopardy, lived precarious lives, not the relatively more secure ones of earlier times.

Evidence for the Making of Money

Al-Sayyid Marsot's (1995) *Women and Men in Late Eighteenth-Century Egypt* used archival materials on deeds, probate records, commercial transactions, and litigation from the Cairo archives, to achieve a fascinating analysis of the wealth of various strata of Egyptian women, and to clarify the extent of a woman's economic role within an Islamic culture in that period. She explains that Islam granted women certain economic rights, enabling them to inherit property, to administer it, and to be involved in the marketplace (11). She also points out that there were limitations on their complete freedom to manage their affairs (8).

In the 18th century, women from elite and wealthy middle-class families managed large estates, sued in court, and had many outlets for investments (ibid., 7). Women favored a house, or a part of a house, as a property investment. Next, they preferred a shop in a building or a story of a building, particularly a weaving establishment. Women also invested in tax farms, mills, slum accommodations, bakeries, coffee shops, and storage depots (ibid., 57). Some women invested in shops and tools in order to lease them to male guild members wishing to set themselves up in a trade (ibid., 109). Some dealt in slaves (ibid., 110).

Only scant anecdotal evidence exists for successful female entertainers' wealth. Lane (1978, 376) does comment on their economic activity, giving several examples. He writes that successful entertainers owned black slaves who acted as prostitutes for their mistresses. Such a corollary trade would be a normal outcome of dancers' knowledge concerning their male clients' tastes. Slave trading served as one investment outlet for affluent women (al–Sayyid Marsot 1995, 110), so obviously female entertainers did not act alone in this regard. Bayle St. John gives some information about a retired dancer: "A fat, frowzy dame accustomed no doubt, of old, herself to exhibit with the light fantastic hip was ... mistress of the coffee-house" (1973, 1:23). His remark suggests that she was the owner of this particular establishment, one identified above as an investment favored by well-to-do women. As discussed above, housing constituted the preferred investment for well-to-do women in general, for it was a secure investment at times of economic uncertainties. One can make certain deductions based on widespread remarks about successful dancers' housing. "Some of them settle themselves in large houses" (Lane 1978, 376). The famous Kutchuk Hanem and Safiyya both owned houses of quality in Isna,[9] and Safiyya also had a Cairo home, according to Didier (1860, 329). Dancers also owned camels, asses, and cows, and traded in livestock (Lane 1978, 376). If one invests where one has knowledge, such property implies an understanding of farming and the countryside, therefore a rural origin for certain female entertainers.

The average female entertainer—the majority, in fact—must be compared to others of her peers, that is, urban women working at the lowest economic echelons. Various sources give a sense of these types of female trades, and the realization that a surprising number of women were gainfully employed. Modern researchers believe that, at that period, Egyptian women in the modest trades might earn a respectable independent income (Nashat and Tucker 1999, 79).

14. Economic Position of Female Entertainers 117

These authors include female entertainers in this category for "women drummers, singers and dancers could be hired for festive occasions and earn modest livings as a result" (ibid., 95).

It would be informative here to give an overview of women's occupations of the time. Some Egyptian women followed itinerant trades involving servicing of the well-to-do harems: *munaqqisha* (woman who decorated the body with henna)[10]; *shaikha* (teacher); *ballâna* (beautician for the hair/bath attendant); sellers of cloth and articles of attire[11]; *alima* (here, meaning religious teacher)[12]; instructor on the lute, seller of perfumes cosmetics and jewelry, teacher of embroidery and needlework, dressmaker, maker of clarified butter[13]; marriage broker[14]; *dallâla* (general broker).[15] Other women followed occupations more permanently attached to the household, such as the wet nurse, and non-slave domestic servant.[16]

One also finds modest female occupations in the outside market: maker of dung fuel-cakes[17]; wool spinner[18]; jank (woman who teaches dancing)[19]; professional mourner, spinner of cotton yarn, seller of pigeons and other birds[20]; shopkeeper, seller of bread and vegetables[21]; cook attached to the male-dominated food guilds, maker of caps and handkerchiefs, embroiderer, nurse, midwife, slave dealer[22]; soothsayer, worker in weights and measures in the markets, female bath attendant[23]; seller of milk and pancakes[24]; woman who tattoos other women[25]; cook and baker.[26] This list of diverse female trades sets that of female entertainer in the broader context of ordinary Egyptian women's working lives.

Dancers were not normally well housed, living in what were usually described in the literature as huts or temporary shacks of wood or mud (or sometimes tents), built on the outskirts of towns and cities.[27] An illustration in the Napoleonic *Description de l'Égypte* (fig. 9), one of a series of portraits of Egyptian occupations and notables, shows "almées" in a tiny dwelling much as described verbally by many authors. The hut is dilapidated. The broken grill at the back of the room hangs in five pieces, reeds form the ceiling and the walls and floor consist of rough boards. There is no furniture other than a large box. The room is hardly more than a cupboard, the ceiling so low the women would not be able to stand.[28] Even the holy beggars depicted in another engraving on the same page of the *Description* (Taschen 1994, 720) seem much better housed. Such a dwelling indicates these two women had not achieved anything resembling the economic success of the likes of Kutchuk Hanem and Safiyya of Isna.

To understand most entertainers' real condition, however, one must compare their housing with much of the rest of the population. In Cairo,

> many of the lower level of workers lived in what we can only call slums on the outskirts of the cities ... there were also poorer people who had no fixed residence, not even a hut in a hawsh [open space in an open courtyard], who lived

in the streets, [and] slept in the mosques when they were not chased away [al-Sayyid Marsot 1995, 112].

Compared to these limited conditions, dancers seem less badly off. James St. John (1834, 106) described their small settlement just outside Cairo, as a collection of poor mud huts, but much cleaner than the rural villages he had passed through. This suggests a somewhat higher living standard. Too, people did not flaunt their wealth lest it be taxed (al-Sayyid Marsot 1995, 108), always a fear for highly visible entertainers.

Definite information about dancers' housing intermediate between the private house and the simple hut occurs only in early references. Savary (1785, 1:67) says that the town of Fuwa permitted "public women" to live there in a khan (often called a wikala). Burkhardt (1984, 178) says that during his Egyptian stay (1812 to 1817) female entertainers in Cairo lived under "the castle" in a large khan he called Hosh Bardak.[29] Khans normally served as a hotel for itinerant merchants, who stabled their mounts and stored their goods below, and lived in rooms upstairs above the central courtyard. The khan might also serve as temporary housing for other groups. If dancers lived under the same conditions, this suggests they traveled with asses or donkeys, and carried with them belongings of some worth.

As tools of the trade, dancers' costumes required an enormous financial investment. Early in the 19th century, their caps alone topped by an ornament of gold called a *kurs*, were of great price. Certainly over the entire period of the study some illustrations (included in this study) show simple outfits as well as more sumptuous ones. Still, one needs to contrast both these simple and elegant outfits with the level of dress among the poorer classes of the time. Dancers would need considerable money in order to dress to perform, raising the question of how a young dancer, drawn from the impoverished Egyptian stratum, acquired the capital to invest in her first costume? Did she rely on a loan from a guild, or from a retired dancer who held a contract with her? Did she rent a costume from a broker? Did dancers share costumes? Living under the conditions they did, and traveling as they did, how might they keep their precious dresses safe? Such speculations are raised here as ones of historical importance but cannot be answered.

Retirement of the Average Female Entertainer

What might the average entertainer look forward to at the end of her career? "The lowest echelons of urban artisans, both male and female, lived merely from day to day and left no estates" (al-Sayyid Marsot 1995, 120). One

Fig. 12. Frank and Frances Carpenter Collection. *Egypt: Dancing Girl.* c. 1890 (Library of Congress, Prints & Photographs Division [LC-USZ62–87592]).

can only speculate regarding the average female entertainer. Probably most of them, like the poorer professional women, did not accumulate wealth, and survived as best as they could after retirement. The career of a singer probably provided some longevity, and the great singer Sakna, for example, was still singing at 55 (Duff Gordon 1983, 20). Practicing dancers, however, were usually described in the travel literature as aged 15 to 25 (fig. 12), a short career indeed.

When dancers retired from active performance some still seem to have continued a professional involvement with dance and music. Such a gradual retirement, from dancer to accompanist or singer, might have progressed slowly. The ghawâzî did not normally operate as solo performers, but as part of a small group or even a troupe, depending on the circumstances. Such an arrangement allowed for divisions of labor. Within a troupe, the records suggest that the youngest and prettiest ones often danced, while the somewhat older ones sang or played the drum. "Most often their dance is accompanied by a tambourine ordinarily played by older dancers whose age has taken away the necessary agility to continue their trade" (Villoteau 1809a, 699). Dancers "are always attended by an old man and woman, who play on musical instruments" (Browne 1806, 90). Of 1818, Qûs, Forbin says, "The youngest almeh danced and brought us coffee" (1819, 87–88). The comte de Marcellus writes of an 1828 performance: "These dancers, seated on divans, sang.... At a signal, the orchestra ... remained seated; the youngest almées got up, and coming to the middle of the room displayed before me all the science of their expressive pantomime" (quoted in Carré 1956, 1:210). Describing the impromptu performance given for him in the late 1880s, Andreievsky says, "With a rustling of cloth, six almées appeared. Two of them, quite stout women, of a certain age, sat down with the [male] musicians.... The musicians began to play, the seated 'ghawazis' sang" (quoted in Volkoff 1972, 296).

Older women also seem to have served in other senior capacities, as artistic directors and guardians of the younger members of the groups. A senior woman may have chaperoned the younger members of the troupe, either by herself or with a man (Browne 1806, 90; Niebuhr, n.d., 139). Mayer's late–18th-century aquatint *An Egyptian Ball at Ned Sili* (fig. 3) of the dance troupe performing in the open is the only known pictorial record of a full performing group. It shows an older woman (perhaps the troupe director), six dancers, several veiled female musicians, a non-dancing troupe member, and a dwarf.

The earlier discussion of guilds dealt with the question of the shaikha, the head of the guild. While no concrete evidence or first-hand description of any actual person who held this post is known to exist, the data from other Egyptian guilds suggest that the position was probably held by a senior and respected member of the profession. In the dance field, the shaikha may have been a retired dancer.

Other retirement options are barely mentioned by western writers. Flaubert (1991, 353) fantasized that the women selling bread at the corners of the streets in Aswan were generally ex-dancers. Forbin (1819, pl.71) says the mother of the dancer he saw and drew in Upper Egypt in 1818 was a fortuneteller, a "zaggar." This suggests a gypsy ancestry for both. On the other hand, James St. John (1851, 4) states that although it was suggested to him that gypsies were related to the ghawâzî, he did not believe this, for he had never heard of retired dancers turning to fortune telling.

Many less-successful retired female entertainers may have resorted to full-time prostitution, particularly after a dance ban made their careers precarious. In 1833, Combes wrote, "The almés [are] obliged today to prostitute themselves to exist since their profession does not always let them do so" (1846, 1:222). Bayle St. John rather nastily implied even the same fate for the great Kutchuk Hanem: "No doubt she will one of these days be pushed from her stool by some more youthful competitor, and compelled to become a Magdalen in spite of herself" (1973, 25–26).

Marriage appears to have been a highly desirable option for a retired or retiring dancer, if such a course were possible.[30] Muhammad Ali obviously thought marriage a good solution to the problem of women banned to Upper Egypt around 1834, since he apparently disposed of some through marriage to his soldiers stationed there (J. St. John 1845, 273). Prisse d'Avennes (1930, 57) claimed many ex-dancers made excellent marriages. Bayle St. John (1973, 1:29) writes that any dancer who managed to save enough money could expect to marry favorably and retire into private life. Her past career, although well known, would not be held against her, and she could expect to live quietly and respectably.

Section Five
Biographies

15

Thirty-One Female Dancers and One Male

Overview

This section includes short biographies about Egyptian dancers, accounts that hopefully bear some resemblance to their actual lives. With few exceptions, like "ethnic" performers everywhere and in every period, those Egyptians who kept alive the arts of dance and music during the period 1760 to 1870 are generally nameless and faceless in the travel literature. This chapter does, however, contain a few surviving names (although travelers usually recorded names inaccurately) and restores to life individuals all the more important in being scant in number. The key lies in a name, for the act of naming gives each woman (and one man) a history and a dignity that descriptions of an unidentified "dancer" or anonymous pictures can never provide. While the accounts in the section are classified as biographies it is important to remember that most of the material consists of contemporary gossip, with little solid evidence.

Badawiyya of Samannûd

Badawiyya becomes the first identified dancer in the travel literature, her name implying she was of Bedouin origin. Savary saw her perform in a small coffee house in the Delta area, around 1779, and describes her as 14 years of age and "pretty as a picture" (1785, 1:297–98). She both danced and sang, with a repertoire of laments and joyful songs, and impressed Savary with her talent and spirit. She had come from Cairo, he says, and was setting out to seek her fortune. Believing that Savary might advance her career, she offered to accompany his party downriver to Damietta, but it is unclear from the account whether or not he took her with him. In any event, she does not figure in his subsequent material on Damietta, and so passes from the narrative.

Josephina, Hanka, and Zanuba of Mutûbis

Denon (1973, 229–35) and H. J. Redouté (quoted in Hermant 1895, 51) record the names (perhaps not exactly) of three of the five or six local performers commandeered to entertain the invading French troops in 1798 at Mutûbis. Even in 1798 many French citizens had heard of the dancers of Egypt and, in passing their famous center at Mutûbis, General Menou had decided to act on an impulse. Denon says the local shaikhs at first opposed the performance, arguing the women would lose their reputations by dancing before Christians, and therefore lose their livelihood. The presence of two hundred French soldiers, however, made the outcome inevitable. Denon says the women themselves did not appear at all reluctant to perform, only initially unwilling to unveil for the performance. Redouté, too, says they were timid and afraid to unveil. Brandy flowed freely, however, and eventually the dancers turned in a performance, but the two men found it disconcerting.

Despite affirming three of the women by providing their names, the two authors concentrate almost entirely on physical descriptions. Denon found them all good looking with a "soft and endearing voluptuousness" but "haggard and jaded," except for two (1973, 233). These, Josephina and Hanka, resembled two Parisian performers he knew in the gracious good manners they displayed after their dance. Redouté was not so impressed by the beauty of the young dancers, but describes one, Zanuba, as "less ugly" despite her olive complexion and the tattoos that "marred" her face (1895, 51). These three dancers impress us now with their poise and courage in meeting this extraordinary performance challenge. They were obviously clever enough to diffuse a potentially dangerous situation and leave their unexpected military audience generally satisfied with the encounter.

Nora and Fathma of Girga

L'Hôte (1993, 129–30) has a smattering of remarks about a party of young dancers who entertained the Champollion expedition in Upper Egypt at Girga in 1828. He concentrates mainly on physical traits, and is insulting about the dancers' motives for their post-performance attentions to their audience. Nora is a "young nymph" who flirts with L'Hôte, while "pretty" Fathma sits on Champollion's knees (130). This group had a male manager who arrived with them, and who haggled with the French for the evening's fee, which he eventually declared to be inadequate. The dancers, too, loudly voiced their disapproval.

This account is barely biographical, yet it does give a clear picture of particularly young dancers at work entertaining a party of male foreign travelers on the Nile. Probably because of their youth they do not seem as poised or as adept in a difficult social situation as were Josephina, Hanka, and Zanuba of Mutûbis, for the evening ended in a row that threatened to expand from the dance site to the town. Perhaps, too, as small-town girls, they lacked the sophistication of the performers of Lower Egypt.

Safiyya of Isna

The most written-about Egyptian dancer in the 19th century, Safiyya of Isna found herself in the contemporary memoirs of Combes, Didier, Flaubert, Hamont, Prisse d'Avennes, Romer, Eliot Warburton, and Bayle St. John. From their remarks it is possible to piece together a relatively extensive biography, hopefully with some resemblance to her true life. In her heyday her artistic reputation certainly far surpassed that of any other dancer. Although today the name of another dancer, Kutchuk Hanem, has eclipsed that of Safiyya, she may have been one of the best dancers ever to come out of Egypt. Safiyya likely had a long career, 20 years or more, possibly from around 1830 to 1850.[1] She was described as "still a young and pretty woman" in 1846 (Romer 1846, 1:276). She may have been born in 1815, started dancing at the age of 15, and concluded at the age of 35, sometime in 1850.

There are a few firm dates on which to pin a quick sketch of her life. Combes (1846, 1:216–22) saw her perform in Isna shortly after the New Year in 1834. She continued to live in that town, for Romer (1846, 1:272–77) visited her home in Isna in 1846 and saw her dance. Flaubert's account implies that she was still in Isna in March of 1850,[2] but Bayle St. John's (1973, 1:26) account says that she had "lately" retired to a respectable marriage, implying a date early in 1851 for this event. He comments that her wealth probably had much to do with her choice of husband, although her fame and long exposure to high society might also have attracted him. Although there are no further stories of her after that, her legend still existed in Cairo in 1853, for Didier mentions her early life briefly (1860, 329).

Her biography can be filled in with colorful anecdotal material. A young Abbas, Muhammad Ali's grandson, discovered her at the Tanta fair, where she was performing.[3] She became his mistress and received many costly gifts, including a "separate establishment in Cairo" (Romer 1846, 1:272). She fell from his favor, although the reasons seem in the realm of fantasy, and banished to Isna.[4]

She seems to have remained in Isna for the remainder of her career, but Isna evidently was good to Safiyya. The governor spoke well of her as a performer to Warburton (1846, 1:292) when he visited. Romer (1846, 1:274–75) described her sumptuous costume, and Bayle St. John (1973, 1:26) implied she had amassed a fortune. The rebuilding, in the 1840s, of a home belonging to her would also indicate her wealth, and, hence, some standing in the community.[5] Allegedly, she held a senior position in her guild. "Sophia is said to be the leader of this tribe, who have laws, finance regulations, and peculiar blood among themselves" (Warburton 1846, 1:295).

She was evidently a great dancer with a solid reputation. Combes describes her, in 1834, as "the most intrepid and most admirable of the dancers of Egypt" (1846, 1:217–18). He was enthralled with the artistry of her performance, calling her "the queen of the almés, at the same time dancer, singer and musician" (ibid., 1:220). He left a detailed description of her dancing, which concludes as follows:

> Everything the most supple and wavelike body can produce of wanton and provoking contortions, everything that the most impetuous and burning passion possesses of amorous and disordered convulsions, everything frantic of deranged delirium, and moreover all that Asiatic abandon has of voluptuous and inebriating poses, of captivating and irresistible seductions, all that Safia had, the dancer of Egypt, all that and something else more that one could not know how to describe nor imagine. Whoever has not seen these dances cannot imagine the absolute power and sovereignty of flesh [ibid., 1:220].

He then included a footnote apologizing for his choice of words, for he felt that the French language did not contain vocabulary adequate to describe this unique and powerful dance of high artistry.[6] Safiyya was obviously then at the height of her career. When Romer visited her in 1846 she described her as only "the celebrated Sofia ... considered *one* [emphasis mine] of the most accomplished Ghawazee in Egypt" (1846, 1:272).

As a performer, she possessed a charming presence, for Combes describes her as "joyful by nature, a true bacchante from antique times" (1846, 1:216–18). It seems that Safiyya loved to dance, and possessed great musicality. Combes describes how she chose to continue dancing, during the evening's break, to European violin music then being played by the French hosts. With her trained ear she could dance "with even more grace than before" to the great pleasure of the company (ibid., 1:221). By Romer's time, 12 years later, Safiyya had developed a grand manner, for she entered the dance room 20 minutes after her musicians, robed in a splendid coat, later removed for the performance (Romer 1846, 1:273).

What was Safiyya like as a person? It has been difficult to ascertain some personality from Combes's and Romer's first-hand accounts of her, and, to a great extent, she still remains enigmatic. She seems to have been a dancer first, to have relied on her great skills to carry her life's course, without actively directing affairs. While Isna provided her with a lucrative livelihood, she seems somewhat passive in accepting this banishment for her entire career, not seeking a return to the capital, nor even to the larger center of nearby Qena. She also appears acquiescent, for she accepted Romer's insulting dance commission with its orders to tone down the performance to suit a western woman's notion of decency. However, she possessed business acumen enough to become wealthy from her talents and clear-headed enough to know when to retire. Most probably it was the move to Isna of the younger and formidable Kutchuk Hanem, and the nearby presence of the beautiful and talented Hasna in Qena (both discussed shortly) that persuaded her to leave public life around 1850.

During her dancing years, despite her fame, certain negative qualities dogged Safiyya. She had a fondness for alcohol, a fact noted by both Combes and Romer. Also, her liaison and ultimate break with Abbas would have provided much gossip for public amusement. She could not escape her reputation and scandal would have followed her, for even being discussed in public was not acceptable in a society where respectable women were named only as the "wife of" their husband. Still, in the end, she married astutely, and removed herself from dance history, hopefully to a well-deserved anonymous and peaceful retirement.

Kala and Aisha of Alexandria

Kala, a Jewish dancer (B. St. John 1973, 27), appears in the pages of Bayle St. John's two books on Egypt. He first met her when he lived in Alexandria from 1846 to 1848; she was to give a clandestine performance for his Egyptian landlady's extended family and for certain invited European male guests. Thirty years of age, she was obviously self-possessed for she was prepared to defy the police ordinance against performance. St. John describes her as both a dancer and a singer. He admired the "vigour, the agility, the grace, the elegance" of her dancing. He found her very ugly, despite her tall, athletic body, but thought her voice powerful, and her singing very fine (1850, 147). St. John obviously met Kala more than once when he lived in Alexandria, and seems to have had intelligent conversations with her, for he records her version of the origin of the ghawâzî (1973, 1:27). He considers her opinions important enough to discuss in detail, and even gives her credit for them. Kala seems to have had an exceptionally strong personality and a powerful manner of performing. Her younger companion at the evening's performance, Aisha, was "delicate—even sickly" (1850, 148). She arrived with a baby she was nursing, a touching detail that reveals the vulnerability of dancers.

Both women were nervous that, unexpectedly, Europeans were among the audience. Kala became sullen, obviously angered at this extra danger sprung upon them. Despite these obstacles they rose to the occasion as professionals, gave an excellent, much-enjoyed performance (at least by the local Egyptians), then took shelter overnight in the room of the mistress of the house. Sadly, there is no more information about them.

Hadely of Cairo

Hadely (certainly an inaccurate spelling) worked in a Cairo brothel in the European quarter, in a small street behind the Hôtel d'Orient and near the French consulate, the business owned by an Italian woman. Flaubert suggests that the mistress was terrified of the police, while Didier states that they "religiously respected" her establishment. Flaubert (1991, 196) spent an evening there in December 1849, in his usual fashion, that is watching dance only as an unavoidable prelude to sex.

He tells that it was neither possible to see dance nor hear music because of the police, yet he did see dance of a sort. The owner of the establishment drummed on the table by hand quietly, while Hadely performed a "dance of Alexandria" and another with hip shimmies. He describes Hadely as having "large black eyes, regular nose, an indolent, fatigued air, perhaps the mistress of a European" (1991, 196). While Flaubert had sex with her, his dragoman Joseph translated from French to Arabic, "making love by interpreter" (1991, 198). This seems a pathetic dance performance seen by tourists during the Cairo of Abbas's rule, and Hadely, possibly an adequate dancer, completely debased by the situation in which she found herself.

Hasan al–Bilbeissi of Cairo

Hasan was a male transvestite dancer, allegedly in vogue in Cairo[7] after the ban on female public performers, but described only by Flaubert. Flaubert saw him twice, once in a wedding parade behind the Hôtel d'Orient on December 1 or 2, 1849 (1991, 195), and then in a two-hour performance in the Cairo Hôtel du Nil on December 29 (1991, 236–37). He records many excellent details of his dance but no biographical information. Still, from his name one knows he came from the Delta town of Bilbeis, and probably was a native Egyptian khawal. Flaubert enjoyed his ugliness, and considered it an important aesthetic element of his dance (1965, 185).[8] He was much impressed by his dance talent, which seems to have been extraordinary.

Kutchuk Hanem of Isna

Kutchuk Hanem[9] had an extensive reputation as a dancer and courtesan during her lifetime, and contemporary authors who mentioned her in their published materials include Du Camp, Curtis, Bayle St. John, and Didier. Friends and associates of Flaubert would have learned of her from his Egyptian letters and from his gossip after his Egyptian tour, but only with the 20th-century publication of his complete Egyptian travel material (1965; 1991) does the public have full access to his writings about her in March and April of 1850. Although Curtis (1856) devoted many pages of his Egyptian travelogue to his January 1850 visit with her, his work does not seem to have made much of splash at the time, nor (interestingly) even today. Today, most focus is on Flaubert's account of her. Yet the two assessments of her are completely different, and one would hardly imagine the two women to be one and the same.[10]

Kutchuk Hanem seems to have come from Damascus in Syria (Flaubert 1991, 282), so she was not an Egyptian but an outsider seeking the greater economic opportunities of a larger audience, therefore likely a member of the ghawâzî guild. She is first described in Curtis's account of her in Isna in January 1850, but she probably lived there only briefly (she was not living in Isna when Romer visited Safiyya in 1846). Didier's (1860) book described his tour of 1853 to 1854, when her return to Cairo was already local history. His book seems to confirm a Cairo-area career rather than one in Isna. He claimed that she, like Safiyya earlier, was Abbas's mistress, and was sent briefly to Isna as a punishment. She successfully petitioned him to return to Cairo, where she took up her career again (1860, 330). Bayle St. John, who traveled early in 1851, also implied she was working then in Giza, just outside of Cairo, and normally did so. "It is scarcely necessary to allude to the celebrated Kutchuk Hanem, who, for I know not how many seasons, has withstood the admiration of a whole procession of pilgrims to Gizeh" (1973, 25). When Didier passed through Isna in 1854 on his return to Cairo, he decided to skip the local dance scene there, explaining he was too blasé after the fine performances he had seen in Khartoum (1858, 296). I believe he would have made an exception for Kutchuk Hanem, but then he already knew she had returned to the Cairo area (1860, 330).

Buonaventura's modern account of Kutchuk Hanem's later years does lead to some misperceptions. She says that the French journalist Colet, who had been Flaubert's former mistress, avoided Isna (presumably where Kutchuk Hanem still lived) but asked about her when she visited Egypt in 1864, and found she was by then a "living mummy" (1990, 77). Colet traveled to Egypt in 1869 (not 1864) for the Suez Canal opening celebrations, an accredited member of the French delegation. As a matter of course she was present in Isna during the official stop for an evening's dance performance (although she did not attend because of sickness). There is no record in her account of her travels or any enquiries about Kutchuk Hanem, nor any written comment whatsoever on the dancer.[11] The "living mummy" quotation in Buonaventura comes perhaps from Auriant's (1943, 37) fanciful musings about what Colet might have been thinking and doing (or, as he believed, *ought* to have been thinking and doing) when she walked the streets of Isna.

When did Kutchuk Hanem arrive in Egypt, and how old was she in 1850? Flaubert described her then as "tall and splendid. Whiter than an Arab" (1991, 281). Curtis's description contains the comments—"large, laughing eyes, red pulpy lips, white teeth and arching nose, generous-featured, lazy, careless self-possessed ... a bud no longer yet a flower not too fully blown" (1856, 132). There is little here to give many clues.[12] Later, he says, she is 22 (ibid., 136), but she must have been older than that. Bayle St. John's 1851 remarked of her, who "for ... how many seasons, has withstood the admiration of a whole procession of pilgrims to Gizeh" and that "no doubt she will one of these days be pushed from her stool by some more youthful competitor" (1973, 25–26). These comments suggest she had been dancing in Egypt for some years already; in fact, she was in mid-career. Didier's (1869, 329) comment that she was Abbas's mistress before he became ruler indicates a Cairo career prior to 1849. Perhaps she arrived in the Cairo area after 1840, was sent to Isna in 1849, and returned late in 1850. She may have been born in 1823, come to Cairo at the age of 17, and been 27 or more when Curtis and Flaubert met her in 1850.

She almost certainly continued her successful career after 1850 to became a legend in her own time. There is an astonishing confirmation of this reputation in an incident that took place in 1884, 34 years after she so impressed both Curtis and Flaubert. The Russian traveler Andreievsky (quoted in Volkoff, 1972, 229) and his colleagues, visiting a small town not far from Asyût, watched a dance performance put on for their benefit, and attended by local officials of the town. One of these, the governor, pointed out the best dancer and called her "Koutchouk-Hanem." It could hardly be she but the incident shows the enduring force of her name.[13] Perhaps a local dancer had taken it on as good luck, perhaps the governor was saying the local dancer was as magnificent as the legend, perhaps he hoped to fool the travelers into believing they were watching the legend herself. The event has numerous possible interpretations, all witnesses to Kutchuk Hanem's enduring fame.

Whether her reputation came from her dancing is another matter. Bayle St. John, a knowledgeable critic of the Egyptian dance scene, admired Hasna of Qena and Luxor and described her dancing "as superior to Kutchuk as a pineapple to a potato" (1973, 71). Flaubert, later watching Aziza of Aswan, said,

"Her dance is more accomplished than that of Kuchiuk" (1991, 295). Certainly Aziza felt herself far superior as a performer (quoted in Buonaventura 1990, 72). Too, on reading both Curtis's and Flaubert's description of her performance, one does have the feeling that perhaps there was not much Egyptian-style dance going on, although both men were overwhelmed with their evenings with her. So where did her talents lie? One senses she was an excellent show woman with a strong business sense, able to sell herself (her product) in many guises. An astute judge of character, she could manipulate and flatter to her advantage. Highly intelligent and very ambitious, she rode unscathed above the usual turmoil of the professional dance scene of Egypt of her day. Many today seem to feel the need to take her side against the derogatory comments arising from 19th-century Orientalist thinking (e.g., Said 1979, 186–87), but, in real life, Kutchuk Hanem never needed to be rescued.

Perhaps it is possible to read into Kutchuk Hanem's chameleon-like character[14] (as seen by Flaubert and Curtis) a profound talent for understanding the needs of her clients, and responding skillfully to them. Flaubert was seeking another almost-brutal Oriental sexual experience, and she gave him an archetype for his future literary career. Curtis wanted sentiment and escape to an enchanted place. She became a beautiful sweet young thing, a tender memory for him to cherish. Even in Kutchuk Hanem's choice of other women she remains in character. For Flaubert she provides the sensual "Little" Safiyya,[15] with whom he can have sex, but for Curtis she provides the delicate, timid Zanuba, a real dancer. She saw Flaubert cared little for her arts, and gave an indifferent performance. She saw Curtis would respond well, and honored him with a memorable Egyptian evening (discussed at length in Chapter 21). She was also quite prepared to flatter and cajole. On Flaubert's return visit in April she gave many fulsome compliments. "She had thought much about them; they were like her children; she had never met such amiable travelers (Flaubert 1991, 362). Finally, it is important to remember that the great Safiyya never did return from exile during her career. Under Abbas's despotic rule, dancers were deported, and when they petitioned to return, he allegedly sent them even farther up the Nile (Didier 1860, 330). Not Kutchuk Hanem! Her adroit diplomacy, her understanding of power and influence, earned her a speedy forgiveness from Abbas and a return to the capital.

Bamba, "Little" Safiyya, and Zanuba of Isna

Kutchuk Hanem's household consisted of an Ethiopian slave, Zaynab, and one permanent dance assistant, Bamba, but she could call on local female and male performers when she needed to entertain in style. For example, during Flaubert's evening with her there, three other women played and sang. Bamba, previously a maid with an Italian family in Cairo, served as Kutchuk Hanem's messenger in Isna. She met tourists' boats to solicit business and ran errands. She also danced for Flaubert's group during the afternoon's performance, and played and sang that evening (Flaubert 1991, 279, 283, 285). She seems to have been sickly; Flaubert describes her as "thin" (1991, 179) and, on the second visit, her eye was bandaged (362). One suspects her dance talents were meager. Flaubert describes "Little" Safiyya, one of the three other female performers present on the evening of March 6, as a "small tigress, a petite woman with a large nose, dark lively eyes, and fierce and sensual" (284). There is no record of her actually dancing; she must have been one of the female singers or instrumentalists that evening. Curtis does not mention either Bamba or "Little" Safiyya. When he visited Kutchuk Hanem, she called on the dance talents of the young Zanuba (Xenobi), who danced both a solo and a duet with her. Curtis describes her thusly: "Younger and timid. Perhaps sixteen but a fully developed woman" (1856, 136). Curtis (146) says she danced gracefully and well but not with the skill of Kutchuk. Zanuba seems to have had potential talent; probably Kutchuk Hanem was helping her career. Both Flaubert and Curtis indicate other female performers worked with Kutchuk Hanem, but do not name them.

Hasna of Luxor and Qena

Hasna (known as Hasna "The Tall") seemingly enjoyed an enormous local reputation, and Bayle St. John went so far as to call her the "Venus of the boatmen" (1973, 2:69). On seeing her dance at a private party in Luxor in 1851 he described her as a "tall, elegantly-shaped, beautiful woman ... [who] would have attracted admiration and applause in any European ballroom." He continued in the following vein: "Her nose, her mouth, her chin—every feature—was exquisitely moulded; and nothing could exceed the beauty of her arms and hands. In this instance fame had fallen short of the truth" (1973, 2:70–71). He was much impressed with the "supple elegance" of her dancing, which he found far superior to that of her rival Kutchuk Hanem.

Hasna seems to have worked in both Luxor and Qena. A year earlier, in the spring of 1850, Flaubert had stopped at Qena on his return to Cairo, and found Hasna in residence there. He devotes only a few insulting lines to his meeting with her. "I had sex with a beautiful broad who found me very agreeable ... her name is Osneh Taouileh [Hasna "The Tall"] ... and with another large pig of a woman I enjoyed a lot" (1965, 289–90). If there was an artistic component, any dancing, to this meeting with the talented Hasna, Flaubert did not bother to mention it. On the other hand the event is significant if it shows even a notable dancer would be prepared to forego completely the artistic side of an encounter.

Was Hasna one of the unfortunates who petitioned Abbas to return to Cairo but sent even farther upstream (Didier 1860, 330). This fact might indicate that Hasna, normally, was a Cairo dancer, a member of Corporation 200 (the raqqâsin), caught in the renewed purge of professional dance under Abbas, and would account for her talents.

Aziza of Aswan

Aziza is known through the writings of both Flaubert and Du Camp, who visited her twice during their Nile trip in the spring of 1850, first after leaving Isna, and again on their return from the south. There are some discrepancies in their two accounts that do not impact, however, on the overall picture of Aziza. Flaubert (1991, 294) says they first saw her in a shop in the market, while Du Camp (quoted in Buonaventura 1990, 72) relates that she accosted them while they were seated in the bazaar and offered to dance for them. In the Du Camp version, Aziza returned to their boat that evening along with her two musicians to dance on the deck of their boat.[16] In Flaubert's version the performance on the boat took place on the return of the two Frenchmen downstream to Aswan. The mob of assembled sailors and Aswan public hoping for a free performance annoyed Flaubert and Du Camp. Consequently, Aziza, accompanied by another woman, performed in private for them (1991, 353).[17]

Flaubert (1991, 294) described her as tall, thin, and "black or rather greenish" of skin, with frizzy hair, and "droll tin-colored eyes." Her profile was "charming." In his letters he implies that he found her both beautiful as well as a fine dancer for he says he exempts her from his rule that "beautiful women dance badly" (1965, 243–44). Flaubert complimented her talent highly by saying, "Her dance is more accomplished[18] than Kuchiuk's" (1991, 295). He also described her style as, not authentically Egyptian, but "more ferocious, more abandoned, like a tiger and Negroid" (1965, 244). Flaubert, though, certainly thought it worthwhile to see her dance a second time.

Aziza seems a confident woman, able to present herself well and sell her skills to visiting travelers. She was certainly proud of her dancing and scornful of the talents of the famous Kutchuk Hanem. "*Cawadja,* what do you think of Kutchuk Hanem now?" she cried (quoted in Buonaventura 1990, 76). She had a young daughter of two or three years, present at her performances and taking part in them, and Flaubert mentions the girl twice. Aziza's earthen home suggests she was not wealthy like her Isna rival, even though popular locally with the people of Aswan, who flocked to see her when travelers arranged an opportunity. Aswan was far from the usual dance centers of Upper Egypt and one wonders how Aziza had settled in that town and how she managed to survive as a performer throughout her career.

Ghazal (and Alima, Zarifa and Nagafa) of Cairo

Didier, who traveled during the reign of Abbas and his renewed attack on dancers in Egypt, devoted an entire chapter of his book on Cairo to his two encounters with the dancer Ghazal (1860, chp. 45). He met her first quite by accident on the way to a luncheon in the Old Cairo area. Riding by a heavily veiled, elegantly dressed, well-mounted young woman, going into Cairo, Didier saw that "she pulled aside her veil as she passed near me, and gave me such an attractive look that, instantly turning my bridle, I followed her.... Adieu my luncheon" (1860, 334). Trailing discreetly behind her, he followed her into the Coptic quarter of Cairo, into a house of which he already had some knowledge. Presumably, it was one of the many houses of assignation he mentions earlier (1860, 330). Didier depicts her as very beautiful, and describes her talents as an expert comedian and mime. She sang for him, danced for him, and enchanted him completely with her company. He was obviously impressed with her skills and her charming personality.

Didier was not entirely satisfied, however, for he begged her to arrange an evening's entertainment, a full Egyptian fantasia. She knew the dangers and at first was apprehensive, finally admitting she knew three others who might make up the requisite foursome for an evening, provided Didier would recompense them adequately for the dangers run. The next day they met again. She had arranged the entertainment with her colleagues Alima, Zarifa, and Nagafa, and three male musicians (338). She wore her rich dance costume to give him a preview, even executing some of the intended dance steps for him. The event never did take place for Ghazal was apprehended when she left the Coptic quarter, was whipped and sent to Upper Egypt, as Didier discovered when he made discreet enquiries about her through his connection in the police.

Judging by her everyday clothing, her dance costume, her mount, and her black servant, Ghazal, was a successful professional, likely a member of the raqqâsin. She appears to have been a well-trained performer in both music and dance, indicating women had been able not only to keep these arts alive into the 1850s but also to renew them, since Ghazal would have been a second-generation dancer after the ban.[19] She seems to have been rather careless, almost heedless, in so openly addressing herself to a foreigner, but perhaps such liaisons were more commonplace than the literature leads one to believe; probably she placed too much trust in Didier's promise of police protection for the performance to come. Certainly she was tempted by the rich rewards for the upcoming fantasia, but she does not seem primarily mercenary. The modern writer Zarifa Aradoon (1979, 128) gives her writings on Ghazal the title "If I could have the Freedom to Dance—the story of Gazal" as if she sees Ghazal as a performer longing to express her art. One tends to agree with Aradoon. Ghazal comes across, through Didier's eyes, as genuinely excited about the upcoming evening, willing to take risks in order to dance and share her talent. Such love for the dance was ultimately her downfall.

Fathma, Cypris, Fregia, and Chama of Khartoum

After the repressions on dancers he had seen in Cairo in late 1853 and early 1854, Didier (1858, 20–60) was astounded six months later to discover a large dance community active in Khartoum. As the new capital of the recently conquered Sudan, faraway Khartoum was the administrative center of the region, with an Egyptian governor. A small but lively expatriate population of Turks, Egyptians, and Europeans lived there. They seem to have reconstituted the life of Cairo of an earlier era, with its enthusiasm for professional music and dance. Female dancers from Egypt and Ethiopia had set up a thriving dance community, even operating under the protection of the local elites. Here two dance traditions mingled, Sudanese and Egyptian, with Egyptian dancers able to imitate the Sudanese at will, and Ethiopian dancers learning the Egyptian style in order to please local expatriate elites.

Didier mentions some performers by name. Fathma, an Egyptian, was popular at that time. Another, Cypris, or "Gift of God," was a "very beautiful" Ethiopian.[20] He watched these two at several performances, public and private, where both impressed him with their grace and gentleness (1858, 53). A third dancer was Fregia, an Egyptian described simply as "pretty" and "gay"; her gold and green silk robe made her look like a cricket (102). Didier has the most words for a fourth dancer, a young Egyptian named Chama, for "after her one could look at nothing" (ibid., 105). Chama was far superior to the others, the "queen" with regular features in a dark complexion (102). Didier was impressed with the "perfect harmony" of her body and admired her dancing style greatly. Not even the slightest gesture was indecent; everything was reserved and yet still most seductive (102–03). In a moment of fun, she danced in imitation of the Sudanese dancers who had just performed on the program. Didier again was impressed with her extensive dance talents, for "she accredited herself well, as if she had been made to dance in this manner" (105).

Didier describes the three Egyptian dancers as having dark complexions and, therefore, they may have come from Upper Egypt. He makes a great deal of their presumed literacy in Arabic (48), their refined use of the language (53), and their good manners. These four enterprising and obviously talented young women (three Egyptian and one Ethiopian) had made their way by boat and overland to this remote city. For dancers prepared to undergo the risks of emigration, a good professional living existed here.

Safiyya of Aswan

When Didier (1858, 275–79) arrived in Aswan, traveling north from Khartoum in the summer of 1854, his party pitched their tents near two coffee houses on the river, a location well outside the town and set aside for many dancers deported from Cairo by Abbas. Albanian and Kurdish troops on their way south to the Sudan also camped nearby; they patronized the dancers and terrorized the town. Didier met a dancer as a result of such harassment, for on returning to his tent one day, he found a highly agitated woman hiding there. Through an interpreter, Didier learned her story. Named Safiyya,[21] she had been a successful dancer in Cairo, wealthy and popular, but recently rounded up and deported to Aswan. Now, to add to her troubles, she had caught the eye of one of the worst of the common soldiers, who threatened to kill her unless she accepted his attentions. Like other dancers who had recently fled from the visiting army, she wished to hide within the town but had no one to escort her safely. Would such a generous foreigner assist her? Didier agreed and accompanied her secretly to a Coptic couple's home, where she had arranged a refuge. Apparently she was welcome, for he describes how the Coptic wife received her warmly. Safiyya, overjoyed and grateful to Didier, expressed her thanks as she knelt and kissed his hands. On parting, he left her a small gift of money, an act that she much appreciated.

Two factors suggest that Safiyya must have been a member of the guild of raqqâsin in Cairo, as such having some status in the demi-monde. Despite her degraded state in exile, she rejected totally the attentions of a common soldier, preferring instead to flee. Secondly, a respectable Coptic family of Aswan not only willingly risked hiding her, but also seemed happy to do so. Their warmth in welcoming her suggests she entered their home, if not as an equal, then at least as a person of some status.

Didier's account puts a name and reality to the generalized accounts of Egyptian dancers and the military, both the rewards and the dangers of such an association. Importantly, it also shows how the local population sympathized with and extended protection to individual women known to be in danger. They were not left entirely without community support, for while dancers were forbidden normally to live within the boundaries of Aswan proper, even the local governor was prepared to turn a blind eye to the dancers escaping into temporary hiding within the city.[22] The account also personalizes the humiliation of what were, at one time, successful and independent professionals. In her exile in Aswan, Safiyya had reached the end of the line.

Hasna of Sinnûris

Besides the great Hasna "The Tall" of Luxor, there was another later Hasna, a dancer who impressed Gérôme and his party when the French artists visited the Faiyûm during an 1868 visit to Egypt. Lenoir's (1872, 96–117) travel memoirs recount the exceptional dance evening they arranged during their stop at Sinnûris, apparently a good locale for dance. When Gérôme's party visited the popular Café Anglais to arrange for a dance they found no less than a dozen women, presumably all entertainers, eating oranges and drinking with local dignitaries. With the formal permission of the municipal council, the dance evening took place in one of the travelers' large tents after the evening meal. In attendance were the council members (invited as a matter of diplomacy), the French and all their staff, and a few local residents who crowded in. Hasna was the only dancer mentioned; she performed a wild, brilliant solo that had the all-male crowd cheering her praises. She obviously was talented, and much appreciated locally.

Lenoir's account contains details about Hasna's offstage personality. She seems very young indeed, almost childish, kittenish in character, for she purloins Lenoir's precious talisman monkey puppet, retrieved only with difficulty. She appears almost pathetically eager to prolong this association with the foreigners who had praised her dance, as if the event were of the utmost importance to her. She insinuates

Fig. 13. Jean-Léon Gérôme. *Almée*. c. 1868 (from Paul Lenoir, *Le Fayoum, le Sinai et Petra: expedition dans la moyenne Egypte et l'Arabie petrée, sous la direction de J.L. Gérôme* [Paris: H. Plon, 1872]).

herself constantly into their daily chores, much to their chagrin. They cannot convince her they have work to do, and, finally, bribe her lavishly to let them work in peace. She is delighted with her parting gift: a pair of European gloves.

Since Gérôme was a great painter of Egyptian dancers, is it possible to find a portrait of Hasna among his works? It would be gratifying to believe, for once, there exists a name, a witnessed dance, and a likeness. Although identified as such by Aradoon (1979, 85), Gérôme's famous *Dance of the Almeh* cannot possibly depict Hasna, since this painting dates from 1863, and the visit to the Faiyûm took place in 1868. There is, though, some proof that the black-and-white sketch of an *Almée* (fig. 13) included with Lenoir's chapter on the sojourn at Sinnûris may be Hasna. On January 29, 1872, the famous French critic Théophile Gautier wrote a review of Lenoir's newly released book, in which he mentions the visit and the dancer Hasna. Gautier says:

> Gérôme made a sketch of her, engraved for the book, in which we can see the pure ancient Egyptian type. One would say a head raised on a canopic jar. Her immobile upright pose has a hieratic immobility. Her arms hang, her eyes are lowered, her half-open lips show her teeth. But do not rely on this deceptive calm [quoted in Lenoir 1872, 158].

In his book Lenoir describes Hasna as "striking, not by the regular beauty of her features, but by the savage character of her face and the extraordinary fire of her glance" (ibid., 100).

Gautier's verbal description of Hasna's pose in the 1872 book he reviewed is close enough to the sketch in the 1872 edition I examined to declare positively that one knows what Hasna looked like. The dancer in the sketch, however, has strongly African (or Ethiopian) features, a fact not mentioned by Lenoir. Perhaps, though, that is the reason behind Gautier's description of her as "the pure Egyptian type." Another likely portrait exists in Willem de Famars Testas's (fig. 14) watercolor of an Egyptian dancer in a tent. The Dutch artist was a member of the Gérôme expedition of 1868 and would have been present at this performance in Sinnûris.[23] If all of this information can be accepted, then for Hasna of Sinnûris, unique in the travel literature, there exists name, portrait, dance description, and performance image.

Latifa, al Maghibiyya, Zaynab and Hillaliyya of Upper Egypt

Latifa, al Maghibiyya, Zaynab and Hillaliyya, with professional careers in the cities of Qena, Luxor and Isna during the 1860s, are known today through

15. Thirty-One Female Dancers and One Male

Fig. 14. Willem de Famars Testas. *Egyptische danseres in een tent* (Egyptian Dancer in a Tent). 1863 (Rijksmuseum, Amsterdam).

Duff Gordon's (1983) published letters from Egypt, written during her residence in Luxor from 1862 to 1869. They seem to have been competent artists who never achieved legendary status.

Latifa of Qena is "ugly and clumsy-looking" until she rises to dance. Then

Fig. 15. Jean-Léon Gérôme. *Danse du Sabre, from the painting by Jean Leon Gérôme* (partial) (Saber Dance). c. 1875 (from *Photograuves After Paintings by Jean-Léon Gérôme* [New York: D. Appleton & Co., 187- or later]).

she overwhelms Duff Gordon with her talents as she performs a dance, which is compared to a "cobra about to strike" (1983, 100). At this point, January of 1864, Duff Gordon was traveling on the Nile and being entertained by Jesus Buktor, a Copt who acted as the local French consul. His guests at this particular party consisted of Egyptians, Turks, and Europeans. There were other female entertainers, but they did not impress Duff Gordon, nor did he identify them.

Obviously, Latifa was an excellent dancer, patronized by the elite of Qena, and widely known for her skills. It was the captain of Duff Gordon's boat who sought her out among the other female entertainers present to demonstrate for his employer an example of fine regional dance talent (ibid., 99–100).

Al-Maghibiyya had the reputation as the best dancer of the three in Luxor during the mid-1860s. Her name indicates that she was originally from the Morocco region, though no information exists as to the circumstances under which she immigrated to Egypt. Duff Gordon was much impressed with her as a person. She was highly intelligent, spoke an educated Arabic, and conducted herself off-stage with "perfect propriety" and "more like a man than a woman" (ibid., 136). Obviously she had the capacity to form loyal friendships; one incident describes how other dancers anxiously sought information about her as she lay very ill (ibid., 168).

Duff Gordon implies that better talent might be found in Isna than in Luxor, for in one letter she tells her husband that if he comes to see her she will bring "the best dancing girls down from Esneh for you" (ibid., 188). Zaynab and Hillaliyya were two of these dancers, who also seem to have had a close relationship with Duff Gordon, one going beyond the professional. They performed for her on her boat docked in Isna on a fine Christmas day in 1868. She describes them as the "ghawazee—the *real* dancing girls." These two claimed to be her "special Ghazawee" described as *"my Ballerine da camera"* and they danced for her that day with the utmost of their skills (ibid., 380). Perhaps they knew her life was slipping away, and sought to repay her years of kindness and concern.

Badawiyya of Qena

To date, the talented Badawiyya of Qena is known only through one performance, on the night of October 29, 1869. Three members of the French delegation to the Suez opening celebrations have left their recollections, Blanc (1876), Colet (1879), and Fromentin (1881). Oddly, Duff Gordon never mentioned this artist, though she traveled past Qena many times on her way to Cairo and back to her home in Luxor. Badawiyya's reputation as the finest dancer in Egypt at that time is advanced by one Tonino Bey, Egyptian commander of the Nile expedition of foreign guests, who says he has arranged for the local French consul to provide a surprise for the visitors, a "divertissement that will please you very much, a dance that you have not yet seen, performed by the first dancer of Egypt" (Blanc 1876, 136). Blanc states that the most renowned dancers and best musicians had been retained for this special evening, featuring the "celebrated Badawiyya" (ibid., 137).

The French travelers confirm this reputation after seeing her sword dance.

Fromentin calls her a "great talent" (1881, 291). Unusual in a 19th-century female critic, Colet (1879) goes to great lengths to dignify Badawiyya: she would never stoop to vulgarity in her art (149), she is the last descendant of the court dancers of the pharaohs, her art is noble (117). Colet also goes to great lengths to praise her, calling her a "famous artist," describing the unanimous bravos from the audience, even citing Shakespeare to make her point (151). In this admiring evaluation, Colet sounds positively 21st century, ahead of her time. Certainly one can conclude that Badawiyya was a great and exciting performer, but, even more important, she was an innovative and daring choreographer, with her dance of *The Bee* and sword dance (both described in Chapter 25).

Biographical material on Badawiyya is almost non-existent, though one learns that she was born in a village near "Siouk" (Colet 1879, 147n), perhaps Asyût. Her usual accompanist, a string player, came from this village as well (ibid., 151), suggesting the usual close professional association of dancer and musician in the guild of ghawâzî. Her name implies she was of Bedouin origin. Colet says she was 25 years of age (ibid., 146). Her permanent home appears to have been the major center of Qena, where she performed that night, for the travelers saw her again in Qena when they stopped there on their return trip down river. Despite her acknowledged artistic preeminence, one does not get the impression that she had achieved the financial success of a Safiyya of Isna or a Kutchuk Hanem. On the return to Cairo, stopping in Qena, Blanc saw her in public, idling in front of a café, smoking, and Fromentin remarked on "the great sad Bedauoia in her sordid shelter" (1881, 303).

Finally, did Badawiyya of Qena inspire the figure of the dancer in Gérôme's sword dance (fig. 15)? Since he returned to Egypt for a fourth trip in 1869, a distinguished member of the French delegation, one can assume that Gérôme witnessed her performance that night in Qena. In his two painted versions of a female sword dancer, Gérôme chose not to use the beautiful background of the actual performance, the nighttime setting and the Nile-side home of the French consul.[24] Instead, he created a café in one version, and a palace in the other (fig. 15). It seems reasonable to believe, however, that he did retain the figure of Badawiyya with her sword in a typical Egyptian dancing step, and captured the pride and strength of the real Badawiyya verified through the written accounts. Gérôme shows Badawiyya at the moment at which she has placed the sword on her head and is walking forward; she is on her toes, a position resembling Colet's remark that "she rose on her feet" (1879, 150). Unfortunately, unlike his practice for the *Dance of the Almeh* (fig. 25), here Gérôme seems to have used his French model's face, so only Badawiyya's dancer's body exists for us, and not a portrait.

Section Six

Gossip, Hearsay, Rumors and Myths

16

The Missing 'Awâlim

Overview

Living as they did in the public eye, the female entertainers of Egypt provided the raw stuff for much conjecture. Unlike the previous sections that try to create a reasoned dance history about these women, section six assembles materials that freely speculate about them. Here are accounts from the 18th century onward, ranging from possible fact, to gossip, and to fanciful musings, including those of the author. While acknowledging the lack of extensive proof behind the narratives included here, this section does honor these stories, not only for their importance to those who first recounted them, but also for their healthy longevity. Questions as to why such stories continue to intrigue and take on lives of their own reveal much about those who take an interest in them. The modern author William Irwin Thompson presents some intriguing arguments about the continuing necessity for myth in contemporary thinking. For him, myth "is a Platonic 'likely story' that helps us to remember spiritually who we are, where we come from, and where we are meant to go" (1989, 71). Obviously, both past and present western notions of Egyptian female entertainers often lie within this imaginary domain.

The section explores four mythological stories about Egyptian entertainers, accounts continuing to resonate within today's Western belly dance community, for all dance traditions have their associated stories that "everybody knows." These four lively myths have now probably escaped so widely across the western imagination that there is little hope of putting them back into the box. Still, the section attempts to sort what scant evidence remains from the accepted wisdom, and tries to give a balanced account of how each myth may have originated.

The first myth, a minor story of the Napoleonic period, still circulating today among the western belly dance community, states that elite female entertainers, refusing to perform for the invaders, left Cairo during most of the French occupation, only to reappear during its latter months.

The second, and "great" modern myth about the dancers of Egypt states that during Napoleon's invasion of Egypt four hundred public women (usually said to be dancers) were declared persona non grata by the French, and drowned in the Nile. The account has grown in strength since Napoleonic times, when the incident allegedly took place, and, in the Western imagination, now seems to have a secure place in the history of dance in Egypt. An examination of the myth, the "massacre of the four hundred" in all its various guises, reveals it to be a probable fabrication from several unrelated incidents that occurred during the year 1799.

The third myth deals with a ban on the common public dancers around the year 1834. The travel literature often tended to attribute reasons for the ban to the inherent immorality of the dance itself, or to the scandalous fraternizing of dancers with Western travelers. Today's belly dance community, while dismissing ideas regarding the dance's inherent immorality, does emphasize excessive liaisons between dancers and travelers. Yet a careful sifting of the evidence shows that there seems little difference between earlier bans mentioned in section four (1315, 1377, 1382, and 1637) and the banning of street dancers, the ghawâzî, in Muhammad Ali's reign. The ban around 1834 then seems based on reasons internal to the Egyptian community. Western imagination has embroidered the facts to suit its own fancy.

The fourth and final myth deals with a story already archaic, perhaps a thousand years old, when the Alexandrian dancer Kala related it to Bayle St. John in 1847. Not only Western travelers and modern belly dance aficionados, but also the 19th-century dancers of Egypt perpetuated the notion that they (and perhaps the dance) had a foreign source, originating in Persia. Many in the Western belly dance community also believe that gypsies (more properly called Roma) brought the dance to Egypt and developed it there. Others link the dance of ancient Egypt (however visualized) with present-day belly dance as if it were a direct descendant, conveniently forgetting two or three thousand years of blank dance history.

The question of origins is always tricky, particularly in a country with a culture as old as Egypt's. If it is still possible to untangle to some extent the "massacre of the four hundred" it is far too late to do the same with the myths of the origins of female public entertainers in Egypt. The section concludes with the author's wide-ranging speculations regarding the theme of the foreign dancer that runs through the various accounts.

The First Myth

The first myth, a minor story of the Napoleonic period, still circulating today among Western belly dance fanciers, states that the elite female entertainers left Cairo during most of the French occupation, only to reappear during the latter part of the occupation. "The *awalim* left Cairo during Napoleon's occupation of the city, refusing to entertain his troops. The *ghawazee,* on the other hand, fraternized with the French" (Buonaventura 1990, 60). The French musicologist Villoteau, who came to Egypt with Napoleon's troops, provides the unique source for this anecdote. He speaks of two kinds of "a'ouelem," one group who behaved "decently" and enjoyed the esteem of respectable people; the other, despised street performers:

> They praise greatly the songs of the first group, and the art of their performance, but we were not able to see them nor hear them. They removed themselves from Cairo, we were informed, as soon as the French made themselves the masters of it. It was not until toward the end of our residence in Egypt that they returned to the capital. Even then they held themselves in hiding, and it was not possible to overcome their aversion to sing before men, particularly Frenchmen [Villoteau 1809a, 694].

Can one believe this story in its entirety? Is it history or merely rumor? Villoteau is generally a reliable source, and he and his French colleagues had been working closely with male Egyptian musicians in an attempt to understand their music and its practices. Since those male Egyptian artists were the likely informants of the story, one concludes there may have been some truth in it. The implications for this story have already appeared in section two. For a group of performers to hold themselves apart from the temporary foreign rulers of Egypt would imply some power and influence, and wealth enough to refrain from performing for long periods of time. But there are other facets to the story. Did they actually leave the city, and when, and if so, where did they go?

Al-Jabarti's (1888–96, 6:18–22) chronicles reveal the mounting terror of the Egyptian residents of Cairo, Old Cairo, and Bulaq in 1798, while the invading French marched in force from the coast to the capital, and the Mamluk rulers massed their defenses. After Napoleon's defeat of the Mamluk army at the Battle of the Pyramids, rulers, officers, soldiers, and eminent and ordinary citizens alike fled from Cairo toward the south and east throughout the night and into the morning. Al-Jabarti says: "Most of the inhabitants of Cairo left.... There were only those who wanted to risk their lives or who stayed because they could not leave. They resigned themselves to the All-Powerful" (ibid., 6:19). Those who could fled on horseback, but the poor went on foot. When the fugitives reached the city gates, however, bands of marauding Bedouins and peasants fell upon rich and poor alike, stole their goods, stripped them, and killed all who resisted. Fleeing citizens hearing about the terrifying robberies outside the city returned to their homes to await their fate. In the morning, pathetic bands of almost-naked refugees crept back into Cairo. Several leading shaikhs finally sent a message to Napoleon to discover his demands. He professed the French to be enemies only of the Turkish Mamluk rulers, not of the Egyptian people. He then entered a more reassured Cairo with only a few of his troops, and began the three-year occupation.

Presumably, Villoteau's reference to the exodus of the "a'ouelem" does not refer to that night of terror, but one later when the city became calm. Where would they have gone? Upper Egypt was soon a dangerous battleground as French troops pursued the fleeing Mourad Bey and his army as far south as Aswan over the next year. Lower Egypt may have offered more attractive possibilities, especially dancers' headquarters in Mahalla el–Kubra in the Delta, where female entertainers lived quietly. They may also have lived in strict seclusion in Cairo, trying to avoid Napoleon's increasing need for money for his occupation.

Al-Jabarti (ibid., 6:27) talks of Napoleon's first act as a conqueror—the demand for an enormous loan from the Muslim merchants, the Copts, the Syrians, and the European residents. Napoleon also extracted money directly. Many fleeing Mamluks were allowed to return, on paying money into the French coffers. The wives of certain Turkish officers were also allowed to return to their Cairo homes on paying a ransom or revealing where their husbands' money was stashed.

The French eventually sought female company. After a revolt by the people of Cairo, the French "made off with the women and girls that pleased them ... [and] dressed them in the French fashion" (ibid., 6:305). Later in the occupation, the French asked to marry daughters of certain Muslim notables, who were unable to refuse (ibid., 6:305).

Even to avoid notice by the French invaders implies the "a'ouelem" were under some kind of protection that other women did not seem to have. Without primary sources other than Villoteau's to shed light on the "missing a'ouelem" (the account did not reappear later anywhere in the travel literature), it is impossible to do more than just speculate. Yet this story continues to fascinate even today.

17

The Massacre of "The Four Hundred"

Two Generations of Modern Western Authors and This Myth

Working usually from primary sources, but unfortunately often careless with his citations, Auriant seems to have been the first modern Western author to revive this myth for the 20th century. In 1943, he wrote:

> General Dugua ... complained to the general in chief and requested authorization to drown those [women] caught [near the barracks]. Bonaparte's reply said to put the aga in charge. The aga made a mass arrest. Four hundred ghawazies fell into his hands; he cut off their heads, sewed their bodies in sacks and threw them to the bottom of the Nile. This execution did not intimidate the survivors in the least; they gallivanted everywhere there were troops to debauch. Quarrels broke out among soldiers of which they were the cause and the object. Belliard wrote to the successor of Kleber, "It is a blight that must be destroyed," but Jacques-Abdallah Menou shrank from using such a barbarous method as the aga's, judging that it was a crime to take these girls' lives [1943, 13].

In Auriant, one finds a full-blown modern dance myth, complete with villains (Dugua, Napoleon, and the aga [Egyptian functionary] who actually carries out the executions), a horrible death of four hundred specifically ghawâzî dancers, defiant survivors, sexually starved soldiers who fight over the dancers, and a savior who ultimately brings mercy, General Menou.

J. Christopher Herold, another modern writer who could not resist this myth, produced a second revival of it in 1963. He does not seem to have been aware of Auriant's version, and bases his analysis on two French writers contemporary with the alleged event, Augustin Daniel Belliard and Clémont Étienne la Jonquière. In *Bonaparte in Egypt*, a serious history of the campaign, Herold wrote:

> There are no statistics on those classic hazards, syphilis and gonorrhoea, but all those who mention the matter at all agree that their incidence was high. To fight it, the French occasionally resorted to rather drastic means, borrowed from local practice. "The prostitutes are a plague in the [French] quarters," General Dugua, then governor of Cairo, wrote to Bonaparte in 1799. "To keep them away, it would be necessary to drown those caught in the barracks." Bonaparte's comment in the margin was: "Put the aga [of the Janissaries] in charge of this." An early history of the Egyptian campaign makes the assertion that 400 prostitutes were beheaded, sewn into sacks, and thrown into the Nile on the aga's order. The authors gloss over Bonaparte's responsibility for this atrocity; according to them he merely ordered the aga to have the women rounded up and treated in hospitals, and was incensed when he learned how his instructions had been interpreted. The documents flatly contradict this attempt to exonerate the General [1963, 161].

Herold's account differs slightly from Auriant's version, for Herold describes prostitutes, rather than dancers, who cause the disruptions. Rather than Auriant's general debauchery, here fear of syphilis and gonorrhea among the troops brings massive retaliation to the women involved. Herold states that Napoleon intended only to round up the women for treatment in his hospital, and is contrite after the event. Herold's other details are the same—the three villains, Dugua, Napoleon, and the aga, the cruel death of four hundred women, the women clamoring to enter the barracks, the French soldiers willing to receive them.

Jean-Marie Milleliri (1993) provides a third independent modern revival of the myth in a much less flamboyant version, and takes his information from Antoine Galland, one of the French Savants who accompanied the Napoleonic armies. Milleliri's book deals exclusively with medical matters related to Napoleon's Egyptian campaign. He wrote: "To believe Galland, certain measures taken to avoid venereal diseases were more radical: each public woman surprised with a Frenchman was shut in a sack and thrown into the Nile!" (1993, 198). In this account we have venereal disease; French soldiers; a cruel death of an unspecified number of women, identified only as "public women." No villains are named.

The next generation of modern writers on the "massacre of the four hundred" relied on secondary sources. Using only Auriant, Buonaventura (1983, 37–38; 1990, 60) writes of the myth in both her books, wherein she writes specifically that dancers were the victims of the French. Her first book makes much of the myth in all of Auriant's lurid details, but in the second she is more cautious. She mentions the event in only a few lines, and says that it took place "according to the French writer Auriant."

Writing in 1995, Nieuwkerk makes even more modest claims. She confines a truncated version of the story to an endnote, adding, "According to Auriant, four hundred public dancers and prostitutes were arrested and drowned in order to frighten others so they would not enter the barracks" (1995, 195n17). Nieuwkerk, though, has widened Auriant's story to include prostitutes as well as dancers, although Auriant spoke only of ghawâzî as victims.

Another relatively recent discussion of the myth can be found in Veronica Doubleday's 1999 article on women and the frame drum in the Middle East. She takes up Buonaventura's earlier 1983 material in order to suit her own hypothesis on outsider status. She argues that, even today, professional female dancers in the Middle East, who she claims are often gypsies as in Egypt, undergo stigmatization and frequent punishment. She repeats the story that four hundred dancers were decapitated for "causing trouble among the [Napoleonic] soldiers," and reaches the conclusion that this was "a barbaric incident which reveals their vulnerable status as outsiders" (1999, 121).

The Myth in 19th-Century French Travel Materials

This "myth of the four hundred" may have existed in Egypt as an accepted anecdote surrounding Egyptian–French relations a generation after the Napoleonic occupation, but only one account mentions it. The methodical French author Michaud, who traveled widely throughout Egypt during 1830 and 1831, included it in one of the letters that form his book.[1] He states:

> At the time of the French expedition, the general in chief complained about some women of ill-repute who were compromising the health of his soldiers; the Muslim authorities of Cairo soon caused four hundred of these unfortunate women to be drowned [1833–35, 7:426].

Michaud's version contains features similar to the six modern ones just discussed: the villains—being an unspecified French general and "Muslim authorities"— women of bad character; health risks (unspecified) to the French soldiers; and the cruel death of four hundred women.

Four Primary Sources for the Myth: la Jonquière, Belliard, Galland, and a Proclamation of 1799

Auriant, Herold and Milleliri, the early 20th-century authors who independently revived the myth, base their accounts on three primary French sources containing materials contemporary with the alleged massacre: works by la Jonquière, Galland, and Belliard.[2] A fourth source is a proclamation authorized by the French authorities in 1799. La Jonquière supervised the writing of the official history of the Napoleonic Egyptian campaign toward the end of the 19th century. As members of the Napoleonic expedition, Galland and Belliard remained in Egypt during the entire French campaign.

A proclamation of 1799, entitled "Proclamation from the Assembly of the General Diwan on Precautions against the Plague" appeared some time between April 6 and May 5, 1799. Addressed to all the inhabitants of Misr [Cairo], Bulaq, and Old Misr, it warned that

> the shortest and most auspicious means for alleviating or preventing the danger, viz. the ailment of the plague, is lack of association with women of ill-repute, for they are the primary vehicle for the above-mentioned ailment [Boustany 1971, 8:65].[3]

Obviously, the French were extremely fearful of the plague raging during the late spring of 1799.[4] They believed female prostitution to be a major contributing agent and warned that such women entering the three towns or the troop barracks faced the death penalty. Here are identified the crime, the likely perpetrators, and the punishment.

The multi-volume la Jonquière source appeared during the years 1899 to 1907, a definitive work reproducing authentic letters, orders, dispatches, and notes from Egypt, material deposited after the campaign with the military archives in France. At times, the account of the invasion and occupation seems to unroll hour by hour. Here are to be found two dated letters relevant to the "myth of the four hundred." A letter of June 20, 1799, from General Dugua to Napoleon, states:

> The commander of Boulak is complaining about the number of public women who are coming into Boulak and who endanger the soldiers' lives. He is asking what to do with those he is arresting. I will explore with the agha of public health means of reducing the number without resorting to the "Turkish expedient" [la Jonquière n.d., 5:231n].

A second letter from Dugua to Napoleon, dated June 23, 1799, contains numerous military questions and data. Among these, he includes "public women invade areas of the city; to make them stay away it is necessary to drown those taken in the barracks." Napoleon's note in the margin reads "in charge of the aga. B" (ibid., 5: 231). One gets the sense that, toward the end of June of 1799, General Dugua, who had days earlier declined to act, was becoming increasingly concerned on behalf of his troops, but there is no further information as to what the aga did with his charge. In this account there is danger to the soldiers' lives; the acquiescent French soldiers; and, in late spring of 1799, the possible execution of some scapegoated prostitutes.

Belliard, who was one of Napoleon's generals, remained in Egypt throughout the three-year occupation, and spent most of the first years subduing and occupying Upper Egypt. He returned to Cairo in March of 1800 to serve as governor of Cairo until August 1801. Belliard's recollections of the campaign are available in two sources. His personal memoirs, edited by an aide-de-camp and published in 1842, ten years after Belliard's death, contain nothing remotely related to the "massacre of the four hundred." There also exists, however, a six-volume *Scientific and Military History of the French Expedition to Egypt*, published in 1831; there is no specific author, but the listing indicates that the work came under the titular head of Belliard, though he may have had little to do with the actual production. These volumes are in no way first-hand accounts like those of the la Jonquière material; rather, they are a standard history, compiled 30 years after the events. Here, however, the massacre story appears in full-blown detail.

As the account goes (Belliard 1830–36, 4:113–15), Napoleon is holding one of his numerous conferences with the local Muslim authorities, insisting they take improved measures to prevent the spread of venereal diseases to the troops. The aga agrees, arresting four hundred Cairo women suspected of having sexual relations with the French. When "the French generals" inquire after them, they learn the women have been decapitated, put in sacks and thrown in the Nile. Not wishing to be thought an accomplice, Napoleon is furious and calls for the aga. Then follows a sentence-by-sentence record of an alleged conversation between the general and the aga, the latter explaining to Napoleon that the women had been executed for having sexual relations with non–Muslims, according to Muslim law. Napoleon then rounds up the surviving women, those infected with venereal diseases, and treats them at his specially setup hospital.

Here, the Belliard war history joins into one seamless action two disparate events quite separated in time: the alleged conversation about the massacre, dated here before Napoleon left for Syria (in February of 1799), and Napoleon's action bringing the surviving women into a hospital specifically for venereal diseases. In fact, this civilian hospital for infected Egyptian women was established toward the end of 1800 (Larrey 1809, 510–11), long after Napoleon's solo return to France in the summer of 1799.[5] For this reason, as a trustworthy record the Belliard material is highly suspect. Further, there is no identification of the person who recorded, word for word, this amazing conversation between Napoleon and the aga. One suspects the old retired general (Belliard) of having a laugh at the expense of his co-editors.

One can also suspect the neatness of exactly four hundred identified victims in Belliard's story, especially since Bosworth's modern research tells that "40 and 400 are favorite round numbers or vague expressions of large quantity all over the Middle East" (1976, 1:98).

It is also noteworthy that the contemporary Egyptian chronicler al–Jabarti did not mention such a horrible massacre, since he made much of the many executions and disasters under the French regime. Al-Jabarti (1888–96, 6:89) does record, however, the execution by drowning of two women towards the end of January 1799. The executions would have taken place just prior to Belliard's departure from Cairo for his extended campaigns in the south. Is this incident the real source of Belliard's so-called massacre of that period?

Besides al–Jabarti's account, more evidence exists concerning the execution of women who found themselves in trouble with the French military. In connection with his discussion of the plague, Galland, a classicist and a member of the Scientific Commission in Egypt, wrote of his experiences there:

> As some symptoms of that malady [plague] manifested themselves in the outskirts of Cairo, somewhat violent remedies were used to prevent us from catching it. All the public women caught in relationships with the French were put into sacks and thrown into the water [1804, 1:171–72].

Galland does not date his information, but continues almost immediately afterwards with the information that the French army was just returning from the Syrian campaign. As Galland wrote his account of events in a diary-like sequence, the incident to which he refers would have taken place before the army's return from its ill-fated expedition to Palestine, in the spring of 1799.[6] This was the exact period of the proclamation concerning measures against the plague. Galland's is a terse statement. There are no specific villains, the women are prostitutes,[7] the number punished is not given, the French (presumably the soldiers) are being protected, execution is by drowning but not beheading. Although some women's deaths seem to have occurred in the spring of 1799 (as well as the two deaths in January of that year), there is not much in Galland on which to base the lurid details of the myth of the "massacre of the four hundred."

There is one final piece of the puzzle, though, that might be enlightening. As governor of Cairo it was General Belliard's task to round up "public" women infected with venereal diseases for treatment in the new French hospital (Larrey

1809, 510–11). There may very well have been "four hundred" of them. Though the outcome was intended partly as benign rather than punitive, this coercive culling may still resonate within the story of the massacre.

So what does one make of these 20th-century versions of the original myth? Auriant's interest in Egyptian dance and Egyptian dancers caused him to turn all the alleged victims into female entertainers in a shamelessly exaggerated version of the myth. Even as a solid historian, Herold is unable to resist the myth. To create a titillating story of the Orient with its dangerous women he joins together two events that took place six months apart, without noticing the discrepancy. Milleliri, too, errs badly. Even when his entire book deals with medical matters of the Egypt campaign, in his version of the myth he mistakenly substitutes sexual diseases for the plague as identified by his primary source, Galland. Presumably, Milleliri—like Herold—was blinded by his vision of a sensual Orient.

Neither Herold nor Milleliri have any literary followers, but Auriant has created a family of dance historians who continue to repeat the story. Modern belly dance practitioners also seem particularly vulnerable to the attractions of the myth, and one suspects it is here to stay in the western dance community.

This unpicking of the myth of the massacre yields a case history of how myths are created. Because many facts are still identifiable one can even today read the history out of the myth. One can then see the separate elements entwine inexorably, embroidered step by step in numerous versions to create modern tales of wonder and imagination. The question remains, though, why are modern westerners so accepting of these versions? As it has come down to us, this dance myth now has many elements: illicit and destructive sex; retribution; pain, torture, and death; mass destruction; victims, villains, and saviors; female suffering and male triumph. Sometimes the East kills cruelly and the West deplores its evil. Sometimes the West triumphs over the dangerous East, killing those who threaten it but redeeming a few. It seems difficult to resist such alluring stuff.

18

Banning the Dance in Muhammad Ali's Egypt

Source of the Ban, Wording, and Target Groups

In any age Egyptian rulers found it difficult to forgo lucrative taxes during times of monetary crisis, yet they risked criticism from the religiously minded for taxing what many considered vice. Earlier, this book identified four repeals on the taxation of female entertainers found in the literature, in 1315, 1377, 1382 and 1637, and these repeals of taxation imply a ban on dancers themselves. There seems little difference between the earlier bans and the banning of street dancers, the ghawâzî, in Muhammad Ali's reign, by no means a unique event but part of a centuries' old pattern. There is no doubt that this ban did take place around 1834, but as derived from the travel literature the surrounding details that give historical meaning to the event are vague.

In examining evidence from European authors living in Egypt at the time of the event (our only sources to date), it has been difficult to ascertain precisely the purpose of the ban, the wording, the authority under which it was published, even the target groups. The first to come across information on a ban, Combes (1846, 1:129) identified an "order" against public women. Hamont, too, indicates that the ban was an official, rather than an unofficial, act, citing "an ordinance that excluded gallant women" (1845, 1:319) and "the decree that emanated from the cabinet of the vice-roy" (ibid., 1:320). Clot Bey (1840, 2:90) provides the detail that the ban appeared in the form of a police ordinance. In assigning ultimate responsibility for the ban, Combes (1846, 1:129) identifies Muhammad Ali by name. Others said the same (Hamont 1845, 1:318; Prisse d'Avennes 1930, 58).

No author gives much sense of its wording regarding both dancers and prostitutes. Clot Bey says, speaking specifically of dancers, that they could not "display themselves in the streets of Cairo and Alexandria" (1840, 2:90). Hamont, also speaking specifically of dancers, says they were not allowed to "be seen" (1845, 1:320). Combes (1846, 1:129) says that the ban simply "chased" female entertainers and prostitutes from Cairo. Lane talks of both public female dancing and prostitution being "prohibited" (1973, 337n).[1] Clot Bey (1840, 1:336) says the administration gave up both its revenue on prostitution and its official protection of that occupation.

James St. John, who traveled in the winter of 1832 and the spring of 1833, mentions a slightly earlier restriction on the freedom to perform in Alexandria: "Latterly the Pasha has affected extreme strictness on the subject of the ghawazi who are forbidden to visit professionally the houses of Europeans (1845, 20).[2] It would seem likely that this specific restriction against contact with Europeans would have been incorporated, too, into the next phase of the broader action against female performers.

Section two, in identifying the separate guilds of raqqâsin and ghawâzî, argued that only the ghawâzî were named in the ordinance, and the arguments are not repeated here. To sum up all information presently available, one concludes that a police ordinance, passed by the cabinet of the viceroy, stated that the female entertainers, known often as ghawâzî, were no longer allowed to use the public streets in Cairo and Alexandria as locales for practicing their profession. All prostitution was outlawed completely. It seems clear that the ban derived its authority from the secular and not the religious powers.

Punishments

The prohibition on public performance was in itself a severe punishment, one threatening the livelihood of dancers who probably led financially precarious lives. The modern belief holds that forced deportation to Isna also came inevitably for those caught breaking the performance ban, but the actual information is vague. Speaking of Isna, Combes says, "The most celebrated almés of Egypt had established their residences there" (1846, 1:216). He continues, giving some explanation for the destination. "Esneh ... is still a city for pleasure, if not for the governed, at least for its masters, rich merchants and travelers" (ibid., 1:216).

Combes's narrative also suggests that public dancers and prostitutes were obliged to leave the cities of Cairo and Alexandria if they wished to continue working, but that the move to places in Upper Egypt involved some freedom of choice. He mentions, for example, that many prostitutes had chosen to go south only to Beni Suef (ibid., 1:129). Wilkinson, too, implies some freedom of choice, for he says that many performers forbidden to dance in Cairo had gone to Qena (1843, 2:128), as well as Isna (ibid., 2:268). Later, in the 1850s, Didier implied that for dancers caught breaking the law in Abbas's reign there were still alternative destinations, if little freedom of choice on leaving Cairo. "They were strewn in passing into the cities of Upper Egypt, some at Kenné, some at Louqsor, many at Esné, ... all the way to Assouan" (1858, 276). As discussed in section one, there had been a longtime dance presence in Upper Egypt, particularly in Qena, so one wonders exactly what banishment there actually implied. Still, the addition of immigrant entertainers would have placed a strain on performance opportunities in the South. It would be interesting to know how such professional problems were dealt with, but the literature is silent on this topic.

For ghawâzî and prostitutes caught breaking the ban, whipping or imprisonment were two identified punishments under the legislation.[3] Lane states: "Women detected infringing this new law are to be punished with fifty stripes for the first offence, and for repeated offenses are to be also condemned to hard labour for one or more years" (1973, 377n).[4] Didier's Ghazal was probably whipped as well as deported for her association with him in Abbas's reign (Didier 1860, 341). Hamont's material suggests there was a prison for women in Isna, with his comment on the "prison of Isna where the prostitutes of Cairo are locked up" (1845, 1:404).

Date of the Ban of "1834"

Only Lane provides information on the exact month and the year of the ban that impacted Egyptian dance history for the rest of the century. A footnote in his 1860 edition, edited by his nephew Stanley Lane-Poole, reads: "Since this was written public female dancing and prostitution have been prohibited by the government in the beginning of June, in the year 1834" (1973, 377n). Lane, who had returned to Egypt in the late fall of 1833, presumably would have been a witness to the 1834 event. All subsequent writers have accepted his date, but other sources now suggest the ban came into force in 1833, not 1834.

Combes traveled on the Egyptian region of the Nile in late 1833 and the first months of 1834, and assigns quite specific dates to these travels.[5] He first mentions "public women" when he encounters many in Beni Suef. He says, "They told me that the public girls, chased from Alexandria and Cairo by order of Mehemet-Ali had taken refuge in the Said or Upper Egypt, and that they were to be found there in great number" (1846, 1:129).[6] Prisse d'Avennes (1930, 56) writes that "her lover" first spared Safiyya from the general ban then later sent her away to Isna to join the other banished women, and Combes saw her perform in Isna immediately after the New Year of 1834. Taken all together, the evidence shows that dancers and prostitutes must have left Cairo and Alexandria by mid-1833, to be already established in the South by January 1834.

Combes's account suggests the official prohibition probably occurred in the late summer of 1833, not 1834 as Lane's published account claimed. Unfortunately, no other precise account has been discovered to support Combes's version of events. Wilkinson indirectly suggests a date earlier than 1834 for the ban: "In 1832 the Pasha permitted them in public to exercise their vocation in Cairo ... [but after certain objections] their dancing was forbidden" (1843, 2:268). Bartlett also repeats the same date: "Up to a recent period, (as late as 1832) their performances constituted the principal excitement of the Cairenes" (1849, 115).[7]

Complicating the theory of an 1833 date, the modern writer Anthony Sattin, relying on Lane's diary entry[8] of February 12, 1834, describes Lane's visit to Burkhardt's tomb. "At the cemetery they had to force their way through a crowd of children playing on swings and adults watching conjurors and dancing girls" (1988, 72). The cemetery was Bab el–Nasr, outside a northern gate of Cairo, and the event was the festival of 'Id. One might argue that the performances were outside of Cairo proper and not on the streets of the city, and so did not contravene the letter of the law. Were authorities still prepared to accept this fine point early in the ban? In any event, what was once a seeming fixed point in the history of Egyptian dance, the ban of June 1834, now has become far less clear.

How Long the Ban Was in Force

Most modern historians and enthusiasts of this dance have accepted that the authorities eventually allowed all banished entertainers to return to Cairo (for example, Buonaventura 1990, 69; Nieuwkerk 1995, 36).[9] The only early source for this information, however, comes from Curtis, who traveled in the early months of 1850. His exact statement reads as follows:

> And so frailty was all boated up the Nile to Esne? Not quite, and even if it had been, Abbas Pacha, grandson of Mehemet Ali, and at the request of the old Pacha's daughter, has boated it all back again [1856, 124].

Curtis does not give any dates for such a repeal of the ban, but, presumably, he means it came previous to his visit. The evidence mostly indicates, however, that under Abbas's five-year reign female entertainers were rigorously regulated and deported. As described in section two, even as late as the official entertainments for the 1869 Suez festivities, the ban had never been repealed and the ghawâzî were still subject to its restrictions. For example, Blanc claimed, "Esneh is, like Qéneh, a residence assigned to the almées, or rather to *ghawasies,* by Méhémet-

Ali; they are interned there" (1876, 239). The American Leland, who traveled around 1870, said the same:

> The dancing-girls are obliged by law to remain at one or two places on the Nile.... The result of the moral restriction has been to confine familiarity with their feats to the wealthy, since it is still the fashion for the well-to-do, when they give "fantasias" in their houses to send for the Ghawâzi, who are invariably procured from somewhere [1874, 130–31].

Apparently, however, there were ways around the ban. It was theoretically possible for individual entertainers to petition for clemency. Hamont (1845, 1:320) explains that, in his day, some female entertainers petitioned the viceroy for permission to return to Cairo from Upper Egypt, but were refused. As already discussed, Kutchuk Hanem appealed and was allowed to return to the Cairo area. Others who did the same were ordered even farther away by a capricious government (Didier 1860, 330).

There were other options. Bribery was effective both in Cairo and in the Delta. Hamont (1845, 1:318, 319) tells that some "gallant women" in Cairo bribed local officials and operated freely, if not openly. Similarly, he says, entertainers bribed high officials in some of the Delta regions (ibid., 1:295). Even casual

Fig. 16. David Roberts. *Dancing Girls at Cairo*. c. 1839 (from David Roberts, *Egypt and Nubia* [London: F.G. Moon, 1849]. Courtesy of the Thomas Fisher Rare Book Library, University of Toronto).

tourists might see dance. Roberts's (fig. 16) famous illustration of a performance with two dancers and three musicians resulted from an invitation to attend a private party at the Cairo home of a touring Englishman, John Pell, in January 1839. Goupil-Fesquet (1843, 70) describes an arrangement in Lower Egypt, whereby dancers and singers came aboard travelers' boats well north of Cairo, entertained, then jumped ship to avoid the police at Bulaq, Cairo's port. Enforcement of the ban appears to have been uneven. Later, Bayle St. John (1850, 147; 1973, 1:28) suggests that the enforcement of the ban was often hot and cold, and that entertainers could still work in the Delta, particularly at the Tanta festival.

Contemporary Explanations for the Ban

The travel literature hardly explains specific reasons for the ban on dancers and prostitutes. Clot Bey (1840, 2:95) suggests that the ban's prohibition of public dance intended an increase in "morality" but points out that, in his opinion, it backfired since the resulting increase of boy dancers only made things worse. Such a simplistic explanation is not impressive.[10]

Hamont (1845, 1:316–18) provides the only helpful explanation contemporaneous with the event. He suggests that when Muhammad Ali handed over the tax farm on dance and prostitution to a new administrator, this individual became overzealous. He augmented the names of tax-paying "public women" by sending out spies to catch respectable women in questionable activities, such as talking to men in the street, then adding their names to the official register. Naturally, this caused consternation: women dared not go out of their houses; husbands were in an uproar; families cursed the tax farmer. Finally, the Muslim religious authorities intervened, pointing out the shame of such a system of taxation and begging Muhammad Ali to abolish this particular tax farm. Muhammad Ali finally agreed. The tax farm was done away with, and female entertainers and prostitutes either were encouraged to marry or were exiled to Upper Egypt. It should be noted that Hamont's explanation indicates that the ban resulted from causes purely internal to Egyptian society, not from reasons involving foreign interference or sensitivity to foreign wishes. Hamont's explanation, the perceived disgrace of an Islamic society profiting financially from vice, is certainly consistent with those bans already cited from the 14th and 17th centuries. Did other factors contribute to the decision to ban?

Other European writers seemed unable to accept that Egyptian authorities may simply have had the good of their society at stake (however defined), and sought explanations that made more sense to them as outsiders. One such explanation had to do with dancers' relationships with male European audiences; in other words, an explanation in which their own national groups featured. Bayle

St. John's explanations for troubles between dancers and the Alexandrian police in 1847 show this trend of thought:

> The police of late had been acting with renewed vigour ... and would have punished with severity the discovery that Muslim women had, in contravention of the Pasha's orders, employed their powers to kindle the imagination of infidels [1850, 147].

When St. John wrote these words he was a young man in his early twenties. His second and later book gives a more astute explanation for the ban. Paraphrased, his account (1973, 28–29) goes as follows. Muhammad Ali did not exile the dancers for any moral reasons but acted rather out of self-interest. Increasingly, he had given many extraordinary privileges to Europeans, ones bitterly resented by ordinary Egyptians. Allowing Europeans to have free access to the dancers, usually Muslim, was the last straw. Such relationships caused major inter-ethnic friction, and Muhammad Ali was forced to act.[11] The ban gave some satisfaction and eased local Muslim feelings, but did not accomplish what it had set out to do.

Reading carefully between the lines, one discovers insights in St. John's text, and his words reveal the following. Dance in itself was not a trigger for the ban, for, as part of the old Egyptian culture it was not immoral.[12] Muhammad Ali was courting the European Powers for his own dynastic purposes, and giving many privileges to those Europeans increasingly arriving in Egypt. The real issue involved threats to local power, attacks on old money, and the humiliation of indigenous Egyptians vis-à-vis previously despised Christian non-believers. There was a growing discontent coming from the Islamic "moral majority" with the modernization and Europeanization of Egypt, and grief for the passing of the old ways. A sign of this bitterness, the rallying point, came to be flagrant disregard for traditional female-male relations, symbolized by the professional public female entertainers.[13] The ban did not accomplish its original aims as the core question was, in truth, a struggle for Egypt itself. A deeper reading of St. John is not incompatible with Hamont, who also saw a moral cause behind the ban in a wish to return to Islamic principles, a deep sense of the loss of an earlier society.

Abbas and the Banning of Dancers

It is useful to note that while Muhammad Ali is cited as the ultimate authority for the ban, all the actual gossip circulating in Egypt surrounding the ban, including the persecution of dancers, and the naming of specific dancers, involve his grandson Abbas. These colorful and persistent stories in the travel literature (discussed particularly in section five) begin when he is a young man and continue through his life. He is said to have discovered Safiyya at the fair in Tanta.

He was not only her lover, but also the lover of Kutchuk Hanem, 15 or so years later. They both insult him, and he bans them to Isna. Flaubert and Didier identify Abbas as responsible for a renewed persecution of dancers during his five-year reign, a personal vendetta against them. Flaubert (1991, 196) repeats what must have been a local story, that because of his sexual orientation Abbas was not interested in the female entertainers, but only in males, hence had little to lose by the persecutions. Didier (1860, 329) repeats the common scuttlebutt that Abbas's religious fundamentalism caused his hatred of dance, and describes an exaggerated story of his continuing persecutions and deportation of five hundred dancers from Cairo. (Does this large even number seem familiar to the reader?) Curtis (1856, 124) says that it was Abbas who had "boated" all the dancers back to Lower Egypt.

Taken all together, these stories make little sense on the surface. The accounts may, however, correctly reflect strong links between Abbas and the original bans on public dancing and prostitution in his day. Historical facts about him allow this possibility. Abbas (1813–54) followed Muhammad Ali as ruler of Egypt.[14]

The heir apparent for many years had been Ibrahim, Muhammad Ali's oldest son, and both despaired of Abbas (al–Sayyid Marsot 1984, 87).[15] Abbas bore a grudge against his uncle Ibrahim and also hated his grandfather, though he managed to conceal this. "His resentment against his grandfather and his uncle was to surface when he headed a party of opposition to Ibrahim" (al–Sayyid Marsot 1984, 89). It is possible to imagine a link of this party with certain religious authorities (described by Hamont 1845, 1:318) responsible for mounting opposition to the "tax on vice" during the first years of the 1830s while Ibrahim was out of Egypt fighting the Syrian war. It would have been natural for Abbas to seek out reactionary forces in Egypt opposed to Ibrahim's tendency to look more towards Europe as the source of Egypt's future. Such a group would have been delighted to count on the support of a grandson of the ruler, now with some power of his own as an appointed governor. Abbas, too, may have been a convincing advocate before his grandfather for the return to "purity." In any event, the date of the first serious restriction on dancers in Alexandria[16] fits remarkably well with Abbas's return from Syria in 1832, after his army service. Perhaps the major ban of 1833 may be placed, too, at his door, not because he was its ultimate source, but because he manipulated its passing as part of his search for power within the Egyptian administration.[17]

Placing the Dance Ban in Context

While dance historians naturally emphasize bans on dancing, it is important to realize that throughout Egyptian Islamic history other aspects of popular culture have been subjected to intense official disapproval. The modern writer Boaz Shoshan (1993, 67) explores the relationships of Egyptian high culture and popular culture in the medieval period, suggesting that the expressions of popular culture often ran counter to elites' accepted religious beliefs and practices. For example, Shoshan (ibid., 43) identifies the feast of Nawruz (celebrated in Egypt with the maximum flood of the Nile in September), with its popular practices of violence, transvestite dressing, and sexual overtones, as particularly threatening to the social order. Nawruz was officially banned in 1385 (ibid., 49). Shoshan (ibid., 50–51) comments that popular festivals die hard, however, and that, despite disappearing from Cairo, certain basic aspects of Nawruz continued in the provinces, with evidence existing as late as 1914.

During the 19th century, expressions of popular culture certainly continued to offend elites. In the 1860s, Duff Gordon commented that "the Viceroy wages steady war against all festivals and customs. The Mahmal was burked this year, and the fair at Tantah forbidden.... It is only up country that the real things remain" (1983, 297). Such evidence reminds us not to make too much out of the banning of popular dance, that it was only one small part of a larger pattern. In the larger pattern, too, one can also see how the dance of the people continued to exist here and there, never to disappear completely during its years of official disapproval.

19

Myths of Origins of Female Dancers and Singers

Opinions of Modern Egyptians on Dance Origins

When I researched the aesthetics of modern belly dance for my master's thesis I hoped to discover information on the ancient origins of this dance, and supposed Egyptian Canadians could supply accurate facts. I put the question to them, "Do you know anything about the origin of this dance?" (Fraser 1991, 49–54). Without exception, they did not make any claims to having any other than speculative personal opinions. Despite believing that Egyptians today surpass all others in belly dance skills, the people I interviewed were not generally nationalistic in their ownership claims for the dance. Most vaguely imagined a foreign origin, with Turkey being mentioned particularly. One astute woman pointed out I would ultimately have to answer the question of why belly dance has strong similarities throughout the Middle East. A number suggested that the Egyptian rural areas had been a rich source for latter-day belly dance. Others felt that the dance was primarily an urban form. Two friends suggested an intriguing typology with four categories of Egyptian dance: belly dance, zar,[1] religious devotional dances, and folk dances continuing the ancient traditions of respect for the sun, moon, harvest, and particularly for the River Nile (Fraser 1991, 48). Here, belly dance is somehow seen as separate and distinctive from other types of dance in Egypt, but no reasons for this are provided.

Foreign Roots of Dancers

Modern Western writers and dance enthusiasts wishing to suggest a foreign origin for the public dancers most often quote Lane. He (1978, 374) says the ghawâzî (but evidently not the 'awâlim) claimed descent from the famous family called Barámikeh (or Barmek'ees), who first enjoyed the patronage of Harun al–Rashid, ruler in Baghdad, then his displeasure. A fuller account of such an origin appears in Bayle St. John, who agrees with Lane and adds details learned from Kala, the Alexandrian performer:

> The tribe, or rather corporation of dancing-girls, seem to have existed from the earliest times.... Kala, the Jewish Almeh, whom I knew in Alexandria, once told me a curious story of two daughters of a Barmekide, the virtuous family so celebrated in the "Arabian Nights," and in the history of Baghdad. One of them was invincibly impelled by fate to adopt a dissolute life, and became the mother of the Ghawazee; the other was virtuous, but eloping with a wandering stranger became the mother of the Gagarees, or gypsies [1973, 1:26–27].

Who were the Barámikeh [Barmacides] and what are the implications of such a claim? The now-derelict city of Balkh, the original home of the Barmacides, lay in what is now northern modern Afghanistan. Placed on the ancient East–West trade routes, over many centuries the city found itself within successive Persian empires, and that of Alexander the Great. The city also lay within range of the influences of the Buddhist empires of northern India. The Arabs conquered the city in 651 CE, during their eastward expansion. The *Encyclopedia of Islam* says the Barmacides, came from a Persian family of Balkh, and were perhaps Buddhist in origin. They served as governors, first ministers, and advisors to the Islamic rulers in what is now modern Iraq, becoming wealthy in the process, and noted for their generosity. They attended their new masters for three generations, from about 725 CE to 800 CE. At that time, they fell from favor, were disgraced, and never again regained their influence.

Because of their wide reputations, fabulous stories existed about them and continued to be related throughout many centuries. The modern writer Bosworth (1976, 1:16) says that Muslim writers often cited the fall of the Barmacides ministers as an example of immoderate pride reversed, the frailty of worldly power, and a reminder that no Muslim could be sure that he might not some day need the charity of others. In other words, the stories about them passed from the realm of history and entered the realm of Islamic moral instruction.

Today's Western thinking often insinuates that the claim to such an aristocratic Persian descent somehow ennobles the ghawâzî, or at least confers respectability. Lane implied that the ghawâzî did believe such a thing in his day.[2]

St. John's Kala seems more realistic in her appraisal. Her account states clearly a fall from greatness for both daughters, as a result of sin. One leads a dissolute life and therefore becomes the mother of the ghawâzî; the other elopes (presumably against the family's wishes) and becomes the mother of the despised gypsies. Kala's story seems a popular version of the literate condemnations of the too-proud Barmacides found in Bosworth. Her account suggests the following scenario: "See what happens when you are too proud; you are laid low! You are social nobodies! You are forced to earn your living in the streets!"

Bosworth (1976, 1:23) also quotes from an early chronicler who stated he heard the term *Barmaki* while in Egypt, and who suggested that, after the fall of that family, it came into use as a term of disparagement. In discussing the Banu Sasan, Bosworth compares their claims to be descended from the dispossessed pre–Islamic Persian Sassanian rulers, with the Egyptian ghawâzî's claims of descent from the Barmacides. Bosworth concludes that "one should bear in mind that a process whereby the name of a fallen dynasty is ironically or satirically applied ... seems psychologically possible" (ibid., 1:22). One tends to agree, therefore, that the alleged descent of the ghawâzî from the Persian Barmacides can hardly be taken seriously, either as an historical fact or even as a term implying social respectability.

Yet the hoary myth of descent, obviously believed by some Egyptian dancers themselves a thousand years after the fall of the great family, certainly grants a quasi legitimacy to the story. It does suggest once more the issue of certain possible foreign antecedents for both dancers and dance (first raised in section one) associated with the etymology of *jankiyya* and *ghazie*. Section two also found the guild of ghawâzî was not monolithic but ethnically permeable. Certainly words can travel internationally with greater ease than those who speak them, but perhaps a Persian or Mesopotamian origin for some elements of the medieval public dancers in Egypt is not unlikely. It is impossible, however, to determine just how early or how often dancers from these two areas might have migrated to Egypt (if they did). More importantly, one must disassociate the dancer from the dance, for there is no way of knowing what kinds of dances these performers would bring, or, once in Egypt, execute for their clients. One cannot thereby claim any foreign origin for the dance itself from such myths.

Gypsies

Many modern belly-dance enthusiasts believe that gypsies (more properly, Roma) from northern India were responsible for creating belly dance and, through their travels, disseminating it throughout the Islamic world, and that they constituted the entire corps of public dancers in Egypt for many centuries.

Buonaventura (1990, 39–52) finds these ideas attractive and devotes an entire chapter to the "Gypsy Trail."³ It is impossible to deal here with the global issue of Roma heritage and their possible influence on world dance, but some facts can be determined for Egypt. The Roma are generally said to have originated as tribes in northwestern India, leaving en masse in the 11th century CE. They settled for a long time in Persia, then, dividing into groups, emigrated slowly across Europe, from around 1500. In Persia, their skills as farriers made them particularly valuable for rulers' mounted cavalry, and they are said to have accompanied the armies of occupation moving throughout the Middle East. There is no question as to the foreignness of their origin; rather, the problem here centers on their contribution to the arts in Egypt.

Egyptian Roma had a range of occupations. Women among them practiced fortune telling, probably female circumcision, and sometimes rope dancing (Lane 1978, 383).⁴ They also sold amulets and medicines, particularly ones to counter infertility (Clot Bey 1840, 2:64). Men and boys worked as blacksmiths, braziers, tinkers, and merchants of brass trinkets (Lane 1978, 382–83). The men made ornaments, especially magic rings (B. St. John 1973, 1:27). As entertainers, men and boys were rope dancers, tumblers, and hoop jumpers (Lane 1978, 383). They displayed trained monkeys, dogs, and other animals (Clot Bey 1840, 2:100). Through this list of occupations one arrives at some positive correlations between Egyptian dance and the Roma. "Their [public dancers'] parents are commonly farriers by trade" (Neibuhr, n.d., 139). Forbin (1819, caption to pl. 71) described the mother of the ghawâzî he saw dance at Beni Suef as a *zaggar* or *fortune teller*. Obviously, he was equating ethnicity with a principal Roma female occupation. Bayle St. John used occupation-of-father to suggest some connection between the ghawâzî and the Roma. "I am inclined to think there is some affinity between them [public dancers] and the gypsies,—the men who profess to be their parents often following precisely the same occupations as these vagabonds" (1973, 1:27).

As well as practicing rope dancing, one can imagine certain female Roma in Egypt dancing in the manner of the ghawâzî. Evidence argues compellingly, however, against the entire ghawâzî population being Roma. Modern readers often take Niebuhr's (n.d., 139) comments on the public female dancers in Constantinople as "tschingane" or "gypsies" and "at Cairo ghazie" to mean all Egyptian dancers were Roma. Clot Bey also can be confusing when he says, "The almées form a caste, apart, as do the gypsies in Europe" (1840, 2:94). Clearly, neither Niebuhr nor Clot Bey necessarily mean by their remarks that all the dancers in Egypt were thereby Roma.

Contemporary enthusiasts also use the remarks of the modern Turkish researcher Metin And (1976, 138) to support their case for a Roma origin for all Egyptian public dancers, since many dancers in Turkey are indeed Roma. He provides two suggestions. First, in Turkey, the source for the Turkish word for dancer (*çengi*) arose from the Roma heritage of most dancers there (the *çingene*). Importantly, though, he also suggests an equally valid possibility, that dancers derived their name from the harp they played, the *çenk,* a word unrelated to any national origin. Eugenia Popescu-Judetz also notes that, in Turkey, the word *chenk* meant both a harp and cymbals. She argues, "Many writers have assumed that the name of çengi came from çingene (Turkish for 'Gypsy') and not from cymbals (çeng or çenk). This hypothesis seems less probable, though we do not categorically rule out this possibility" (1982, 54). Even in Turkey, with its high proportion of Roma dancers, modern research seemingly favors the notion that the musical instrument (harp or cymbals), rather than racial origins, gave rise to the term for dancer. The same process appears to have taken place in Egypt. As discussed in section one, the older word for dancer used in the Egyptian chronicles, *jankiyya*, came from its association with the harp they played, the Persian jank.[5] It would seem that in Egypt, too, one would choose not to argue Roma origins from the etymology.

There are other compelling reasons to reject the Roma origins of the entire corps of Egyptian public dancers. First, Lane (1978, 382) sets the Roma apart with a separate terminology for them, saying the term *ghagar* or *ghajar* was used for gypsies in Egypt. Too, the travel literature never used the term ghagar (or ghajar) to define the public ghawâzî, but used the word only when they referred specifically to Roma groups.[6] Second, compared to the allegedly great numbers of public entertainers, there were few Roma in Egypt. Burkhardt, who remarked that public dancers in Egypt in the second decade of the 19th century were many, also said, "Of the latter [Gypsies], which are called here Ghadjar ... very few families are found in Egypt; they are more numerous in Syria" (1984, 179). Lane says, "There are but few Gypsies in this country" (1978, 382). Thirdly, and importantly, the Roma, having a north–Indian heritage, were racially different and distinctive from the Egyptians and the Arabs. Clot Bey points this out: "The Bohemians of Egypt form a separate caste.... Their physiognomy is quite distinct; their colouring is darker than that of the Arabs" (1840, 2:64). Many writers, in contrast, spoke admiringly of the fair complexion of the public dancers, although they could indicate their complexions were darker in southern Egypt, as was that of the Egyptian population in general. To equate the entire population of public dancers with the Roma, then, does not jibe with word use, population numbers and physical appearance.

Finally, it seems the Roma themselves did not equate their persons with the ghawâzî. The traditional exclusiveness of the Roma formed an important aspect of their lives in Egypt. They kept themselves apart from others, wandering the country in family groups, and speaking a foreign language. The women wore a distinctive costume (Clot Bey 1840, 2:64). This feeling of separation is reflected even in the myth of their roots, for Lane says, "They profess themselves descendants of the Barámikeh, like the Ghawázee, but of a *different* [emphasis mine] branch" (1978, 382). Even here the Roma will not admit close relationships. More importantly, they personally consider themselves dissimilar from the ghawâzî of Egypt. Lane's remarks correlate well with those of Kala of Alexandria, speaking of the more virtuous of the two daughters of the Barmacides, who became the ancestress of the Roma. It is in this myth, accepted by both groups in question, that one can finally understand the clear separation of the two communities.

Speculations on Origins and the Arts

The foreign origin question seems to have run like a permanent thread through the discussions on the public dancers of Egypt, from popular Western thinking, through Egyptian Canadians musing on the dance of their own country, to the various myths just now explored, through the etymology of the words *jankiyya* and *ghazie*, even to the historically verifiable Persian stay of the Roma after their departure from northwest India. Perhaps the entire question of foreignness needs further exploration before this unsatisfactory section, based primarily on speculation, concludes.

As mentioned in section two, it is known that in the medieval period of 14th-century Egypt, the costly, specially purchased slave singers and dancers attached to aristocratic households included women of foreign birth ('Abd ar-Raziq 1973, 55, 66). No specific nationality is mentioned but female slaves were available from all areas of the Islamic world and beyond. It is also known that the Egyptian dâmina al-maghânî purchased and trained slaves as entertainers (ibid., 68n). Again, no details are given as to the nationality of these women. As already discussed in connection with training in section three, a slave-buying guide of the early 11th century stated that the ideal female entertainer would be a Berber girl with 16 years of training in Mecca, Medina and Iraq (Walther 1993, 101). In this instance, she would be ethnically Moroccan with the polish of the Middle East.

In conclusion, I offer my fanciful speculations about the foreign element in medieval Egyptian dance and beyond, but certainly only as themes for future research rather than established fact. The city of Baghdad, around 900 CE, was the great hub where the musical traditions of the Greeks, the Persians, and the Arabs fused to create the new music of the Islamic world. Foreign slave women were trained in the finest Arabic arts of their day, including music and dance. They themselves would symbolize the wealth and importance of their owners.

In later centuries the ideal (expressed in the quoted slave-buying guide) would grow into a social norm, spread throughout the Islamic world through the persons of these foreign slave women who exemplified it. Wherever they were sold into aristocratic households they took this highly sought-after ideal of music and dance performance. Imported into Egypt, these women would have sophisticated talents that were new, exciting, and compelling, while their foreign origins would lend a cachet of exoticism. They would set a standard that local Egyptian performers would feel compelled to emulate. Such standards and envied qualities would eventually influence even the levels of ordinary public performers.

Some of the ghawâzî of the 19th century and earlier may have descended from peoples who had come from elsewhere as we know some did migrate to Egypt. It was not these particular ethnic origins, however, that provided them with any status. Prestige came from the mythical link to the medieval past when foreign women set standards in the arts that still, after hundreds of years, dominated the notion of what was most admirable. Perhaps it was the "Persian" trait of these foreign slave entertainers that tempted certain public dancers eventually to capture a piece of the cherished exotic by means of their invented histories about the distinguished Persian Barmacides family who worked for the great rulers of Baghdad. At the same time, ironically, the Roma were despised everywhere in Egypt, their more authentic Persian national connections providing them with no social currency whatsoever.

Section Seven

Building the Aesthetic of Performance

20

A Costume Benchmark Set by Edward Lane

Costume in Lane's Day

The travel literature, together with selected illustrations by those artists who witnessed the dance firsthand, provide enough material to begin to answer such important questions as: What did dancers look like as they performed? What were the distinguishing characteristics essential to the dance aesthetic of the study period?

Costume provides an important aspect of this aesthetic, and a particularly attractive one. The illustrative materials are remarkably consistent within the various eras of the study, implying artists captured what they saw in a reasonably faithful manner across the century. Many written accounts add important details on dance costume, such as types of fabrics and their colors, elements not usually accurately available from the pictures.[1]

Lane (fig. 17) defines what many know today of Egyptian dancers' costumes, for his *Manners and Customs of the Modern Egyptians* has become widely available in modern reprints. Lane, however, was a mid-point in the evolution of Egyptian dance dress of the study period (that is, the early 1830s). There were significant differences before and after him, but his writings and illustrations can provide a familiar point to start the study of dance costume overall.

Lane illustrates a "typical" dance costume of his day, one he attributes to the ghawâzî (fig. 17). He described the normal performance outfit only briefly as "the dress in which they generally thus exhibit in public is similar to that which is worn by women of the middle classes in Egypt in private" and "most of them are richly dressed" (1978, 373). In his book, Lane had already dealt

Dancing Girls (Ghawa'zee, or Gha'zee'yehs).

Fig. 17. Edward Lane. *Dancing Girls (Ghawa'zee or Gha'zee'yahs)*. c. 1840 (from E.W. Lane, *An Account of the Manners and Customs of the Modern Egyptians* [London: A.M. Nattali, 1846]).

extensively with middle-class Egyptian women's dress, both in his text and in several illustrations, so could then identify dancers' outfits as a subset of the other. He (1978, 50–58; 549–60) included numerous beautiful illustrations of middle-class Egyptian women's indoor and outdoor outfits and accessories to illustrate their attire.

Lane's short comment here on dancers' costumes, taken together with his dance illustration, makes the important point that dancers dressed as middle-class women (i.e., their indoor wear), implying there was no dance costume, per se. On the other hand, writing in the same period, Clot Bey (1840, 2:91–92) remarked that the dancers' costume was actually "imprinted with a particular character" that differentiated them from other classes of women. He identified some of these details. Their clothes were form fitting, their arms bare, their breasts overly exposed, their jewelry abundant and showy.

The shirt, or *chemise,* wide, loose, and flowing, and reaching to just above the knees, was an important item of Lane's dancers' costume (Lane 1978, 49). Clot Bey (1840, 1:323) gives details about this article of clothing. It was made of fine muslin, crêpe, or other good-quality fabric. Colors might range from white, to pink, violet, bright yellow, sky blue, or black. Often there were gold thread embroidery or scattered paillettes. The lower part of this shirt masked underpants of toile or muslin. Egyptian women of the period, from the peasant women to the well to do,[2] exposed much cleavage through their chemise, and travelers often remarked on this practice.

Lane described the *shintiyan* as "a pair of very wide trousers of a coloured striped stuff of silk, and cotton, or of printed or worked or plain white muslin ... tied round the hips, under the shirt" (1978, 49). The shintiyan was excessively long. The lower lengths of the pant legs were looped up underneath and tied with a string just below the knees, the looped fabric then falling to the ground. Clot Bey (1840, 1:323) remarked that, in its fullness, the shintiyan resembled a skirt.

Over the shirt and shintiyan came a long vest, the *yelek,* often of the same material as the shintiyan. Middle-class women wore the yelek fitted tight to the body and arms, and buttoned down the front from below the breast area to a little below the hips. The breasts were then masked only by the shirt. The yelek was slit on both sides from the hips on down. It was a trailing garment. "According to the most approved fashion, it should be of sufficient length to reach to the ground, or should exceed that length by two or three inches or more" (Lane 1978, 49). Judging by some of the illustrations (figs. 3, 5, 6, 18), however, dancers favored a somewhat shorter yelek, just above the ground. Women, including dancers, also wore the *antari,* identical to the yelek except in reaching to just below the waist. Lane does not say so, but the very long sleeves of the yelek and antari provided an important part of the dance aesthetic. Slit from elbow to wrist, with the light fabric of the shirt hanging outside and loose along them, these long-sleeve extensions would rise and flow with all the arm movements of the dance. Prisse d'Avennes' (fig. 18) illustration of two dancers shows this important aspect of performance very clearly.

The square shawl and embroidered scarf were other distinctive dress items, usually doubled diagonally into a triangle, placed loosely around the hips, and tied in front with either a fancy knot or ribbon. In the hot season the belt tended to be silk or muslin, in the winter, wool or a shawl from Kashmir. There seems to have been another method of folding and attaching the scarf; first folded lengthwise then twisted over itself in front, and attached somehow in the back, presumably with the points loose. Lane (fig. 17) shows this second, more elegant, variation in his illustration of dancers, but only from the front.

Well-to-do women also wore the *gibba* and *salta*. The gibba was a loose, open, full-length coat of velvet or silk with long sleeves, worn over the entire above outfit. The salta, also worn over the entire outfit instead of the gibba, was a short jacket with long sleeves. Successful dancers might wear these garments to enter the performance space, removing them before dancing, and in a sense emphasizing their importance as first-class artists.[3]

An item not identified in the travel literature, hip padding, surely appears in some of the illustrative materials. A dress custom of Arab women, and one that persisted across North Africa until the middle of the 19th century, this cushioning exaggerated the dancers' hips so as to emphasize their ability to rapid swivel the pelvic area (Saleh 1979, 53). One plate of the Napoleonic *Description de l'Égypte* (Taschen 1994, 728) shows three almost identically dressed women, yet the dancer (fig. 6) alone has enormous hips under her shintiyan and yelek. Mayer (fig. 3) and Roberts (fig. 16) also show dancers with these exaggerated hips. Lane's dancers, however, seems to lack this dress item, as do others. In using this item of clothing, dancers enlarged themselves so as to occupy a wider performance space and exaggerate certain movements, important aspects of the aesthetic.

Simple Costume of Less Affluent Dancers in Lane's Day

Not all dancers could afford such an elaborate outfit as described above, and Lane describes the modest dress of the "lesser ghawazees" (1978, 376). He equates their attire, usually consisting of chemise, shintiyan, *tob* and *tarha*, to that of the street prostitutes. Their full-length loose tob was an open coat-like garment, shaped like the letter T, with enormous sleeves almost as wide as the gown was long, often pink, rose, or violet, and made of gauze, silk, or taffeta. The tarha was a headpiece resting on the back of the head and hanging down

Opposite: **Fig. 18. Émile Prisse d'Avennes.** *Ghawazi or Dancing Girls.* **c. 1835.**

almost to the ground. It was usually of white muslin, or colored crêpe, and embroidered in silk or gold thread.

Lane does not give an illustration of this simple costume, nor does any other artist of his period. In 1846, on the riverbank at "Dishna," Romer, however, did chance to meet a dancer whose basic costume fits Lane's description, though lacking even the outer-covering tob and head tarha:

> Her habiliments were exceedingly *light and loose* in every sense of the word— Turkish drawers, and over them a long robe of thin crimson silk, open at the bosom down to the "zone-less waist," and exhibiting no traces of any garment beneath [1846, 1:137].

If one accepts the premise that costume contributes to the performance aesthetic, one may well wonder how the simple dress of the common dancers affected the impact of their dance on their viewers. Did Egyptians on the whole value dancers' artistry the less because of their relative poverty as shown in their dress? Might street dancers, then, be seen as providing only a parody of the "real" dance?

Versions of Elegant Dance Dress Before Lane: 1760 to 1800

No illustrations or descriptions of elegant costumes prior to the Napoleonic era are known to exist in the travel material. Based on Napoleonic period illustrations by Mayer (fig. 3), from Denon (fig. 5), and the dancing figure with her drummer from the *Description de l'Égypte* (fig. 6), one concludes that the elegant dance costume showed some significant differences before Lane's time. The basic elements of chemise, shintiyan, yelek and shawl (or belt) existed, but with variations.

The shirt (chemise) was much longer in this earlier period, reaching over the shintiyan almost to the ankles. Coverage of the breast by the chemise varies widely in the three illustrative examples of Napoleonic costuming. The dancer in Figure 6 shows large breasts fully exposed by the costume.[4] Mayer's (fig. 3) dancers show the average cleavage of the period. Denon's (fig. 5) dancer modestly covers her breast area with a tight long yelek buttoned down to her ankles.

Completely different from those of Lane's day, the sleeves of the yelek in that period are tight and to the wrist in both Figure 3 and Figure 5. In the latter, the dancer's dress shows stiff ruffles at the wrists. Chabrol describes the yelek of the Napoleonic times as "placed over the shirt; it is open in front and has long *narrow* sleeves" [emphasis mine] (1822, 415). Mayer's (fig. 3) dancers wear yeleks with short sleeves reaching to just above the elbow, with no draping. These three sleeve variations would have impacted on the dance aesthetic, as dancers moved their arms during performance.

A feature of the Napoleonic period, an enormous and elaborate circular beret-like hat extending well beyond the head, appears in Figure 6. A veil hangs from the back. Such a hat obviously pleased the middle and upper classes of the time as it also appears on other women in the same plate (not shown on Figure 6). This head covering probably continued for a few decades as Forbin's (fig. 24) dancer of 1818 wears a similar hat with veil attached. It seems to have survived longer as a ceremonial item, for Lane-Poole describes an elaborate fantasy hat worn by the bride in the royal harem in 1845 (1846, 3:84).

Simple Costumes Pre-Lane

Although most travelers of Lane's day neither described nor illustrated his "simple" outfit, multiple examples exist from the Napoleonic and earlier periods. Jomard implied that dancers he knew in 1800 dressed like most poorer Egyptians, that "dancers' costumes do not amount to much as can be seen in the plates of the book" (1822, 733). Here he refers the reader to the two plates of the *Description de l'Égypte* showing three dancers and numerous separate renderings of their costumes and accessories (Taschen 1994, 740–41).[5] Three variations on dancers' modest outfits appear here. First, the tambourine dancer wears a costume resembling Lane's "simple" outfit; the full-length chemise and covering tob are evident, as is her head covering, but it is not clear if the dancer wears the shintiyan or long pants. The drawing gives a vivid idea of the flow of the tob and tarha during a dance performance. Second, the female drummer wears a garment that today we would call a kaftan; a separate rendering of the outfit appears on the same plate. This drummer's outfit possesses some elements of elegance, for the red silk dress has attached bands of probably appliquéd embroidery. On the back of her head trails a long *milaya*.[6] The third dancer stands with outstretched arms, showing the shape of her "common robe" as the artist calls it, a humble garment. The sleeves are huge, with three-foot-wide openings. It is split at the neck down to the waist. She wears the shintiyan, but narrow, not wide and billowing.

Two even earlier illustrations also show simple dance outfits. Pococke's (fig. 1) 18th-century dancer wears a long ankle-length robe, T-shaped with square inset sleeves, and resembling the kaftan-like dress of the drummer (see example two). The neck hole here is a single long slit, cut low to the breasts. The material has stripes on both sleeves and gown. On her head the dancer wears a tarha. It is impossible to see if she wears the long shintiyan underneath. Baurenseind's (fig. 2) two dancers, wear the period ankle-length shirt, with shintiyan, topped by a simple yelek with sleeves cut wide at the wrist. Wide loose belts with chunky ornaments encircle their hips. On their heads they wear the tarha flowing down their backs. These 18th-century outfits show ample cleavage.

After Lane: Modernization of Dance Dress

In 1830, Michaud described creeping changes in Egyptian dress of the middle and upper classes. "The new costumes have the appearance of being both European and Asiatic, and the stranger doesn't recognize finally either Europe or Asia" (1833–35, 5:237). Michaud (5:237, 5:247) had two explanations for the changes. First, many formerly wealthy landed proprietors had lost their money, and those few remaining wealthy families lived precariously. Second, a recent "reform" of dress had obliterated the older magnificence, a change that, he felt, had contributed to a healthy local industry and commerce. Clot Bey (1840, 1:326–27) describes changes in dress among the upper class of the same period as "modernizations" and, as such, improvements in good taste, but obviously he had his own bias. Among the changes he lists: large turbans embellished with jewels were no longer in fashion; women no longer plaited their hair and decorated it with gold coins but piled it on top of their heads; and they tucked their chemises into their shintiyan. The yelek changed extensively; it became less trailing, its sleeves now stopping at the wrist. The familiar generous cleft at the breast area disappeared, and women now modestly buttoned their yelek high or doubled over, in European fashion. Only women from the older generation wore the voluminous gibba over their outfits. Simpler fabrics, such as muslin, began to replace those decorated with gold threads. Unfortunately, neither Clot Bey nor Michaud gives further details on such changes, and one is left to speculate. One senses a growing European influence on middle-class and upper-class dress, as well as a reduced prosperity in general. These were rendering all dress less distinctively Egyptian, and at all levels of Egyptian society certainly less luxurious and less "Oriental."

Dance dress after Lane took several new directions, with less elaborate costumes becoming the norm, and probably showing some influences from both Europe and Turkey. Such changes could be slow. For example, in 1846 Romer (1846, 1:273) described the dancer Safiyya of Isna dressed like the great ladies of an earlier Cairo and detailed her outfit as consisting of white chemise with embroidery around the edges of the sleeves, crimson shintiyan, trailing crimson damask yelek embroidered in black braiding, cashmere shawl, and *salta* (jacket) of dark blue silk embroidered with gold and edged with gold braiding and buttons. Over her shawl she wore silver amulet cases. When she entered she also wore a large mantle. On the other hand, Safiyya lived in the provinces where modernization may have had less impact.[7]

Fig. 19. Eugène Fromentin. *Danse d'Almées, à Sihout, d'après un croquis de M. Stop* (Dance of the Almées at Asyût, After a Sketch by Mr. Stop). c. 1869 (from Djamila Henni-Chebra and Christian Poché, *Les danses dans le monde arabe* [Paris: L'Harmattan, 1996]. Image reprinted here courtesy of the publisher).

The costumes of other members of the dance community, however, manifested the new clothing trends. Head coverings became simple,[8] tucking shirt into shintiyan was adopted, and dancers mostly abandoned the yelek as a dress feature. Two illustrations from the 1840s, by Bartlett (fig. 10) and von Mayr (fig. 8), show pairs of public dancers whose outfits have chemise completely tucked into shintiyan, and hardly appear as a costume element. Here yeleks are gone as well, enabling leg movements to show through the thin silk shintiyan. On their heads dancers wear simple caps of two different styles. Dancers did retain certain aspects of the older fashion, particularly the elaborate hair dressing with gold coins (the *safa*). Most dance illustrations indicate that dancers did not generally follow the new modesty regarding cleavage.[9]

Some public dancers began to outfit themselves in European-style dresses.[10] As early as 1850, Flaubert (1991, 295) describes the dancer Aziza of Aswan preparing to dance by removing her regular large robe and replacing it with a dress of Indian material featuring a European-style bodice. In 1868, Hasna, of the Faiyûm, wore a long blue dress with fringes of silk at the waist (fig. 14; Lenoir 1872, 104). At the elegant Cairo party in 1869, Blanc (1876, 52) described a blue-green dress of the dancer who performed the egg dance, and who lifted this dress to bare her legs up to the knees. Such a dress needed not be plain, however, for the dance costumes at Blanc's party, with their gold, sequins, pearls, and gemstones, impressed him as elegant and opulent.

There exist both an illustration (fig. 19) of the official dance performance at Asyût in 1869 and Fromentin's (1881, 283) description of the event. In the picture, the dancers wear unusual outfits, European-style dresses form fitting to the hip, with lower skirt portion bulky over the hip area, then flaring wide at the hem. The dress has a wide V-shaped neckline. The sleeves are tight, two outfits with short and two with longer sleeves. Underneath these dresses the dancers wear shintiyan. Fromentin describes these dresses as being of damask and silk. The effect is totally unlike the two earlier styles existing for many years, both the elaborate style and the simple, and seems somehow less sumptuous.

The American Appleton captures well the mood of dancers' apparel then widespread in Upper Egypt. At a wedding of substance in Asyût, expecting to see the traditional shintiyan and sleeves, he is disappointed that the dancer wears a European-style dress and belt around her waist. He is pleased, however, with the traditional coins in her hair, and gold plaques hanging beside her cheeks and at her breast (1876, 26). Between Isna and Asyût he had a young woman come onto the boat (fig. 20). "This one could not dance much, but posed divinely. She wore a dark-blue dress, with a circlet of blue and white below her neck, and her dress had a chequerwork of crimson" (1876, 52). Things in Isna were also disappointing as the public dancers there wore "gaudy dresses of European calico" (85). One he found more appealing, however, for "round her neck was a circlet of gold horns, such as might have been worn by the Queen of Sheba" (86). Returning downriver to Cairo, Appleton was still offended by the Isna outfits; yet again, he described the costumes as "ugly

Fig. 20. Thomas Gold Appleton. *A Ghawazee.* c. 1875 (from Thomas Gold Appleton, *A Nile Journey by T.G. Appleton* [London: Macmillan, 1876]).

long striped calico dresses" (240). Since Lane's day, obviously much had changed in dance dress.

After Lane: Influence of Male Dance Costume?

Another major influence, the impact of male dance costuming, may also have proved irresistible. Professional competition from male dancers affected female dancers greatly in several ways. After the ban against female public dancers around 1833, the local dancing boys became more evident, and more came from Istanbul to seek these new economic opportunities. Lane had described the boy dancers' costumes of his day as consisting of a tight vest, girdle and kind of petticoat (1978, 377). They also wore gold caps and filmy muslin shirts (Nerval 1929, 1:64). Lane stressed the cross-dressing nature of the costume: "As if to prevent their being thought to be really females, their dress is suited to their unnatural profession, being partly male and partly female" (1978, 377). One might argue that under considerable professional pressure after the ban, many female dancers adopted features of male dance in order to maintain some of their popularity. About this time female dancers began to wear items of costuming normally worn by male dancers, the vest, small caps, and petticoats, and they abandoned the yelek, thus interpreting themselves along the lines of the same cross-dressing costuming style. The aesthetic then could be seen as a process of imitating males who were imitating females.[11]

The first mention of a vest as female attire occurs in Hackländer's 1841 description of a Cairo party.[12] Interestingly, it is worn here along with the older antari, instead of replacing it. The two dancers wore the usual chemise, shintiyan, antari, and shawl, but in addition, and *under* the antari, they sported "a kind of vest of yellow silk, open very low in front, and adorned on the breast with gold tassels" (quoted in J. St. John 1845, 274). In 1853, Ghazal gave Didier a preview of her dance costume prior to the fantasia to come. She, too, wore both close-fitting antari and vest together. Her complete outfit consisted of chemise, shintiyan, cashmere shawl, antari of violet satin, and the vest, in this case embroidered in gold, with considerable cleavage. Ghazal also sported a little cap of scarlet velvet, perhaps similar to boys' caps (Didier 1860, 339).

Later, the vest usually appeared alone, replacing the yelek or antari completely, and as a single item alone can be identified in numerous pictures of dancers (fig. 21a, fig. 21b). The most dramatic of these depictions is, of course, Gérôme's (fig. 25) 1863 *Dance of the Almeh,* in her untucked chemise and shintiyan, with tight skimpy yellow vest tight below the breasts.

Colet has left a good description of Badawiyya's costume when she danced for the Suez Canal visitors in 1869. She wore a chemise of light pink, not tucked

Fig. 21a. Alexandre Bida. *Danseuse Almé* (Dancing Almé). c. 1855 (© Victoria and Albert Museum, London).

Fig. 21b. Alexandre Bida. *Joueuse de Tarabouka* (Girl Performing on the Darabukka). c. 1855 (© Victoria and Albert Museum, London).

but "floating over her hips," and shintiyan decorated in silver. At her hips she wore a belt decorated with stones. She, too, chose to wear the vest, and hers was "short and embroidered in gold. It held up her bare breasts" (1879, 145).[13] During this official tour in 1869 this costume co-existed with the already-described dresses present at the party in Cairo and the dresses-over-shintiyan (fig. 19) at Asyût.[14]

While the male style in vests and caps was popular with female dance costuming, the few references to dancers adopting the petticoats that boys wore date from much later in the century. When Leland traveled to Girga around 1871, he found an intriguing female costume. He (1874, 134) describes the dancers as dressed in several skirts, one placed over the other. On their upper bodies they wore a tight dark-colored shirt with white stripes that he describes as tiger-like. Over this was a tight-fitting waist-length jacket of red satin, with tight short sleeves. They wore caps, the usual gold coins in their hair, and a chain on their waists described as "a silver girdle with high bosses, and dependent from it in loops was a very curious and massive ornament or chain, made of eight or ten triangular silver boxes, and many large silver beads" (ibid., 134). A decade later Andreievsky saw more or less the same costume. He (quoted in Volkoff 1972, 296) describes the dancers as appearing in wide skirts of gaudy striped silk, embroidered jacket, and flowing shirt. They also wore caps decorated with coins. Contemporary with Andreievsky, Montbard's (fig. 26) illustration of public entertainers at Isna show similar outfits. The stationary dancer wears several skirts; the one in action has removed her overskirt and wears only a filmy one. Above, they wear tight skimpy jackets exposing the stomach area completely, although there is some kind of brief shirt underneath. They wear quantities of gold ornaments at the breast area and scarves on their heads.

Flaubert (1991, 195, 236–37) gives detailed descriptions of the outfits worn by the male dancer Hasan al-Bilbeissi when he saw him on two occasions in December of 1849. Basic was a black transparent chemise tucked (in the "modern" fashion) into his voluminous shintiyan, an embroidered vest coming just to the stomach, and a belt.[15] Hasan seems to have adopted the female shintiyan rather than the petticoat common to male dancers, thus rendering his costume even more "female" than normal. Distinctive to Hasan, and seemingly for the first time (or at least the first description in the travel literature) he is wearing the shintiyan so low on the hips as to expose the entire belly area, draped almost to the crotch. The stomach could be seen clearly through the gauze that "rode upon his hips like a transparent ripple with all his movements" (ibid., 236). This style of male Egyptian costuming, exposing the stomach, and expanding semi-nudity to new areas of the body, may have had results on female dance costuming.

A number of examples of female dancers do exist dressed in this Hasan-like style of costume; most are pictorial. The Brandin (fig. 22) version, which

Fig. 22. Brandin. *Almée, danseuse au Caire* (Almée, Dancer at Cairo) (Garnier Frères Edit., Paris. Imp. Dufrénoy, Paris).

may be the first example available of a woman exposing her belly, shows a dancer in filmy tucked chemise and skimpy vest. Her shintiyan is worn so low as to expose her navel and the bones of her hips. Gérôme's *Dance of the Almeh* (fig. 25) and sword dance (fig. 15) are identical in impact. Colet's written account (less detailed than one might wish) more or less confirms Gérôme's version of Badawiyya's costume around the hip area:

> A sort of shirt in bright rose gauze came from the back of her neck, floated over the hips and escaped above the throat without hiding anything of the modelling of her body.... The large pantaloons ... held at the hips by a belt ornamented with stones, fell in drifting pleats [1879, 145].[16]

Other artists of the period (fig. 23, fig. 27) show this same Hasan-like costume.

This rather bare costume, worn by female dancers from the period 1860 to later in the century, coexisted with the other costume variations described above. It did not survive for long and later in the century seems to have disappeared. If one looks at today's female belly dance costumes, however, both in the West and in the Middle East, one cannot but be struck by how much it has reconstituted the elements seen in dance dress in the middle of the 19th century: the wide flowing skirts being the modern equivalent of the male petticoat of earlier centuries, today's spangled bra seen earlier in the tiny tight vest, the contemporary bared midriff parallels the bare belly made popular by Hasan al-Bilbeissi, the modern beaded belt seen earlier as chains around the waist. In a sense, one might argue that the aesthetic of today's belly dance costume is truly indigenous to Egypt.

States of Undress, Nudity, and Veiling

Dancers seem to have performed at times in various stages of undress, for certain authors' accounts make sense only if taken to mean dancers sometimes appeared in their chemises and not much else. Clot Bey (1840, 2:89), for example, said that the indoor costumes of female dancers of ancient Egypt, as appearing on the ancient Egyptian monuments, were identical to those of dancers in his day. Michaud remarked that "we see these almées with the attitudes and the costume of today on several antique monuments" (1833–35, 5:255). These comparisons of the dress of ancient dancers, who wore simply a transparent pleated full-length dress, to that of 19th-century performers imply the latter must have dressed in an identical manner at times. Savary, for example, describes great din-

Fig. 23. Gustav Richter. *Egyptian Dancing Women—after Gustav Richter*. c. 1861 (from *The Aldine, the Art Journal of America* 9 [1879]).

Fig. 24. Louis Forbin. *La danse de l'Almée à Beni Souëf* (Dance of the Almée at Beni Suef). c. 1818 (from Louis Forbin, *Voyage dans le Levant en 1817 et 1818* [Paris: Imprimerie royale, 1819]. Courtesy of the Thomas Fisher Rare Book Library, University of Toronto).

ners with music and dance entertainment: "At the beginning of the dance, they shed their modesty along with their veils. A long dress of very light silk falls to their heels. A rich belt holds it lightly.... A gauze-like transparent shirt hardly conceals their breasts" (1785, 1:151). A much later reference to this type of semi-nudity occurs in Blanc's description of a dinner party in 1869 at a wealthy Cairo home: "The dancer would ordinarily do this dance [*Egg Dance*] wearing only her chemise, but since there were [European] ladies present, the almée kept on her blue-green robe and showed only her legs to the knee" (1876, 52). Other examples exist.[17]

Forbin's (fig. 24) 1819 print is the only known pictorial record of this ultra-thin full-length chemise as the sole item of dance costume. The dancer's complete body shows through it, but she is, at the same time, elegantly dressed, with a costly beret on her head and long flowing salta attached, jeweled belt draped loosely around her waist, and tiny jacket closed over her breasts. She is, thus, both dressed and undressed at the same time, and does indeed have some resemblance to ancient dancers. Although Forbin chose to locate his dancer performing in the street, the chemise was most likely only an indoor costume.

The Bee, identified in the travel literature from 1830 onwards, also involved various degrees of nudity. Performers would pretend to discover an insect under their clothing, and in a vain attempt to dislodge it would remove item after item while dancing. Since dancers performed semi-nude at other times, as just discussed, the main point of *The Bee*, then, was probably not the nudity, but rather the storyline. Rather than simply an example of nudity or costume, *The Bee* should be considered as choreography, and discussion is postponed to section eight.

The degree of nudity involved in the dance seems to have been up to the whim of the dancer, and some evidently did not care for too much nakedness.[18] Duff Gordon reports that one of her Egyptian friends in Qena wanted to hold a party in her honor but, not knowing her well enough yet, had decided against it: "He feared I might have [foreign] men with me, and he had a great annoyance with two Englishmen who wanted to make the girls dance naked, which they objected to, and he had to turn them out of his house after hospitably entertaining them" (1983, 100).

While accepting some degrees of semi-nudity, dancers may have been personally inclined to the normal mores of respectable Egyptian women when possible. Normally described or pictured as performing with faces unveiled, dancers may have used veiling at times. As seen in the pictorial materials, the floating veils attached to their heads and hats could easily be used in this manner. In describing an item of normal Egyptian dress, Lane explains it thus: "To supply the place of the former [large garment completely covering the body] when necessary, a portion of the tarhah is drawn before the face, so as to conceal nearly all the countenance excepting one eye" (1978, 57). One illustration (Taschen 1994, 741) in the *Description de l'Égypte* shows a dancer drawing a veil over her lower face even while performing.

Niebuhr tells us that "when dancing, they throw up their veils, and leave them to float on their shoulders" (n.d., 139). Savary says that "at the beginning of the dance they abandon with their veils the modesty of their sex" (1785, 1:151). These instances certainly suggest that prior to the performance they were veiled.[19] Perhaps the critical element in choosing to veil or not was the concept of the off-duty situation when dancers were not actually soliciting business. They might then choose modesty and respectability. Didier describes episodes with the Egyptian dancers of Khartoum in 1854, a city where they were completely free to practice their profession. After seeing their performances the night before, Didier would invite them to a late breakfast at his residence. "In order to walk through the streets, their rich dress and sparkling hairdo were covered in a kind of white *haïk* that covered them completely in the manner of the women of Morocco. Their large black eyes alone were visible" (1858, 86).

After the dance ban in 1833, full veiling provided the perfect guise for blending into the background and maintaining anonymity while still practicing as a dancer. Didier (1860, 333) first met Ghazal as she was riding from Cairo to Old Cairo; she was indistinguishable from any other veiled well-to-do middle-class urban woman until she chose to reveal herself. There are other examples.[20]

Dress of Female Musicians

Since no travel writer took an interest in the subject of the dress of those female musicians who accompanied dancers, information here is derived entirely from illustrations. The illustrations show a remarkable consistency over the study period, though, suggesting their information is reasonably accurate. Female musicians are always shown in the common dress of the people, even when appearing with richly dressed dancers. For example, Roberts (fig. 16) shows the female drum player in the typical humble blue dress, with headscarf thrown back to expose her face. Gérôme's (Ackerman 1986, cat. no. 202) painting of two female chess players shows one wearing the Hasan-style belly dance outfit, while the second wears the simple blue dress with veil thrown back. Presumably, the first is the dancer; the second, the musician. It appears it was not an important performance norm that such musicians dress beautifully.

Veiling seems to have occurred sometimes among female musicians who accompanied the dancers. Women sometimes are depicted playing while veiled (figs. 2, 3, 8). Some of these examples clearly show outdoor settings, while others are indefinite as to location. In other illustrations (figs. 1, 16, 17), the female musicians are unveiled. Figure 1 is an indefinite setting. Figure 17 shows probably an outdoors setting. Figure 16 shows a private party. As seen in European illustrations, there seems no rule or consistency in the veiling of female musicians, but perhaps this rule shows there was such diversity in actual practice.

The Aesthetics of Textiles and Jewelry

As the dancer moves through her performance space, the qualities of the costume's textiles add enormously to the aesthetic. In Egypt during the study period, apparently only a few suitable fabrics were available, and cottons and cotton variants appeared often. Muslin, a beautifully fine cotton fabric, was used for a number of items. The chemise was probably always plain muslin, but often embroidered with gold silk, or with scattered paillettes. Colors for the chemise included white, black, rose, violet, yellow, and sky-blue. In many later European pictorial materials, the chemises are so thin as to be completely transparent.[21] That basic dress item, the shintiyan, could be of regular muslin, sometimes plain but sometimes printed or worked (Lane 1978, 49). Belts and head coverings also might be made from muslin.[22] Such fine cotton would be appreciated during hot months. For example, a muslin scarf would replace a woolen cashmere shawl during the summer (Chabrol 1822, 415). Thicker cotton might be used. Lane (1978, 54) mentions calico in connection with types of headdress. Romer (1846, 1:273) mentions printed calico shintiyan worn by the four female singers of Saphiyya's entourage. Later in the 19th century, calico of European manufacture appears in the long dresses worn by performers in Upper Egypt (Appleton 1876, 85, 240).

Silk and its variants (crêpe, damask, satin, taffeta, and velvet) served as equally important elements of dancers' costuming.[23] Plain silks appeared extensively in elegant dance outfits, in the chemise, the shintiyan, the yelek, the vest, the salta (short jacket), the shawl (in the summer), and the belt. There is also mention of silk shoes. The plain silks of yelek, vests, and shawls might be embroidered with silver or gold thread. Romer (1846, 1:274) described Safiyya's dark blue silk salta as embroidered all over with a running pattern in gold thread, and edged with gold braiding and buttons. Crimson was a popular color for silk.[24] Wearing various contrasting colors of silk in different items of clothing provided an effective costuming strategy. Hackländer (quoted in A. St. James 1845, 274) describes dancers wearing red silk jackets embroidered with silver, white silk shintiyan embroidered with gold, yellow silk vests, a crimson silk shawl, and rose silk shoes.

Silk also appears in more modest outfits. Egyptian women's tob (loose overcoat) might be made from pink, rose, or violet silk (Lane 1987, 52–53), and the lightly dressed dancer on the riverbank at Dishna (Romer 1846, 1:137) wore a crimson tob of thin silk. Fromentin (1881, 283) described two dancers at Asyût in 1869 as appearing in striped silk, and in white silk with black edging.

While ordinary silk was popular for dance costuming, its variants (crêpe, damask, satin, taffeta, and velvet) were used little, and often appearing only as accent pieces and contrasts of texture. Crêpe might rarely appear in the chemise, especially in black (Lane 1978, 49). Damask is hardly mentioned. The beautifully dressed Safiyya wore a crimson damask yelek with black braiding around the edges (Romer 1846, 1:274), while two of the four dancers at Asyût in 1869 wore damask dresses in red and in blue (Fromentin 1881, 283). Taffeta is mentioned only in Ghazal's shintiyan of yellow taffeta (Didier 1860, 339).[25] Velvet appears in Kutchuk Hanem's jacket of striped velvet and satin (Curtis 1856, 134); Ghazal's scarlet velvet cap (Didier 1860, 339); skullcaps in red, blue, and black velvet with gold embroidery and trimmed in silk (Carcy quoted in Aradoon 1979, 123); and Bida's (fig. 21a) dancer's brown velvet vest trimmed with gold ribbon. Satin is mentioned several times in connection with jackets and vests. Kutchuk Hanem wore a jacket of satin striped with velvet (Curtis 1856, 134), while Ghazal wore one of violet satin (Didier 1860, 339). Dancers in Girga, around 1870, wore red satin jackets (Leland 1874, 134), and the little vests worn in Gérôme's *Dance of the Almeh* (fig. 25) and sword dance (fig. 15) look like satin. Perhaps Prisse d'Avennes's (fig. 18) two dancers wear yeleks of satin.[26]

Wool appeared only in dancers' cashmere hip shawls, worn in the colder months and even then often removed when the dance became energetic. These fine wool shawls came from northern India, but imitations of local manufacture also existed. The imported shawls were costly prestige items, often given as presents to honor both donor and recipient.[27]

Throughout the period, plain materials, material embroidered with silk or metallic threads, or striped materials seem to have been most common, while patterned fabrics were not particularly frequent according to the written and the pictorial materials. There are a few exceptions. Prisse d'Avennes' (fig. 18) illustrates his dancers with elaborate costumes. An expert on the decorative arts of Islamic Egypt, he probably wanted to feature costumes of the utmost refinement and taste. Each dancer is dressed differently from the other. One wears a chemise with a deep border of heavy embroidery. Her long yelek is patterned with an overall widely spaced small pattern, while her shintiyan bears a light

Fig. 25. Jean-Léon Gérôme (1824–1904) French, *Dance of the Almeh*, 1863. Oil on wood panel. 19 ¾ × 32 inches (Dayton Art Institute. Gift of Robert Badenhop, 1951.15).

pattern. Her shawl has contrasting wide and narrow stripes. The second dancer wears an antari with wide stripes. Her shintiyan is patterned with enormous leaves and stems. Her shawl is plain with an elaborate wide border. The effect is luxurious.

Dancers' jewelry depended on their wealth, but every dancer aspired to appear well appointed in performance. They wore decorations of all kinds on every possible part of the body. Jewelry and ornaments came in diamonds, gold, silver, brass, pearl, coral, amber, agate, and glass, and placed upon the hair, forehead, nose, ears, neck, breast, upper arm, forearm, waist, fingers, ankles, and toes. They were sewn into hats and jackets, and they decorated heavy metal amulet belts. The nose ring (a hoop of gold or silver) was noted in the early writings, but it seems to have gone out of fashion. Bead necklaces of various lengths, and bead bracelets were always common.

Colet has given a vivid description of ornaments, those worn by Badawiyya and her four young dancers in Qena in 1869:

> Large pantaloons, in a rich cloth embroidered with silver, held up on the hips by a belt ornamented with stones, fell in flowing pleats.... Circles of gold or silver circled their fine ankles, and on the toes of their bare feet as on their fingers, shone rings with stones. Their arms were encircled near the wrists with bracelets of sequins, golden serpents and jasper beads. On their chests and breasts hung a triple strand of golden sequins which tinkled with each movement of their bodies. The same sequins mixed with diamonds shone in their long hair, cut in tresses [1879, 145–46].

Hair decoration, common to all well-to-do women up to Lane's time and particular to dancers in the later part of the century, provided a particularly dramatic feature. Lane (1978, 556–57) describes women's hair decor as consisting of an always-uneven number of plaits (11 to 25, with 15 the most common), into each of which three black silk cords were woven. Along each cord hung gold or pearl ornaments, or coral beads. Dancers would perfume their hair to cast a delicious scent as it swung while they moved, and in this manner they employed a sense not common in the Western arts, that of smell.

21

The Musicianship of Dancers

A Musical Group with Multiple Talents

Female entertainers often exhibited a high degree of musicianship, for many had talents not only as dancers, but also as singers who might vocalize or mime the words to the songs that provided the dance music. In this they showed great familiarity with the repertoire of the day.[1] They also played musical instruments, including accompanying themselves with their finger cymbals. Since dancers were also musicians they expected high standards in their accompaniment.[2] Clot Bey went so far as to say: "When the dancers perform ... a little orchestra ... accompanies them, and they are so attuned to the sentiment of the beat that I have seen them unable to dance if the music didn't mark the rhythm well (1840, 2:91). This musicianship of dancers formed a basic part too of the dance aesthetic of the period, one fully appreciated by their local audiences.[3]

An excellent account of how a small ensemble, with dancing, singing, and the playing of musical instruments, might operate at a private party occurs in Curtis's description of entertainments at Kutchuk Hanem's house in January 1850. Underneath Curtis's (1856, 138–45) pompous remarks lies a real sensitivity to the artistic interactions of the performers, where a group of female and male artists combine their talents during an entire evening. The cast of characters numbered five: Kutchuk Hanem, the dancer in training Zanuba (Curtis calls her Xenobi), a woman assistant Curtis nicknames Giraffe, the older woman he calls Hecate (obviously not her real name) described as an ex-dancer, and finally Hecate's husband, described as having played for her in her youth. Curtis set the stage with Giraffe, Kutchuk Hanem, and Zanuba already present in the house when "presently an old woman came in with a tar, a kind of tambourine, and her husband ... with a rabab, or one-stringed fiddle" (138). These two seated themselves on the carpet near the door, then the company of five began to play all together, for the three women were already playing clay drums (darabukka) and brass cymbals. The group next began to sing for "this was Egyptian Polyhymnia precluding Terpsichore" (139).

Kutchuk Hanem finally rose to dance. At this point "old Hecate beat the tar into a thunderous roar. Old husband drew sounds from his horrible rabab, sharper than the sting of remorse" (141). Zanuba and Giraffe were then on darabukka, each playing "until I thought the plaster would peel from the wall" (141). Kutchuk, who presumably was playing the finger cymbals during the prelude, used them during her dance performance. "Her hands were raised, clapping the castanets" (141). During the excitement of this dance, Hecate and her husband "threw their hands and arms excitedly about their instruments, and an occasional cry of enthusiasm and satisfaction burst from their lips" (142). After Kutchuk Hanem's solo, Zanuba danced alone, and presumably Kutchuk Hanem picked up Zanuba's darabukka, since we know from Flaubert's (1991, 283–84) account that she was a fine player. Next the two danced a duet and at this point the second darabukka would have been laid aside. Suddenly, unexpectedly, Hecate, the tar player, rose to her feet, took up the finger cymbals, and "with the pure pride of power advanced upon the floor, and danced incredibly" (144). Supposedly at that point no one would have been on tar. The evening concluded with "slow, sweet singing" (145).

In this small orchestral group one finds one string (rabab) with a mixture of percussion (tar, two darabukka, and finger cymbals) supplemented by voice. Instrumentalists serve as singers and dancers, and dancers as instrumental musicians, and singers. Obviously the five functioned as a close-knit small performance group totaling years of experience, all fully aware of the music, the texts, the rhythms, and the dance. Such a concert was possible through the multiple talents of the performers. In this group of four women and one man, the key importance of dancers to the production of professional dance music can be seen clearly.

Musicianship Shown in the Playing of Finger Cymbals and in the Miming of Songs

Although travelers of the 18th and 19th centuries often described the brass cymbals attached inevitably to dancers' fingers, most overlooked the fact these provided an extra layering of sound to the orchestra, a notable contribution to the aesthetics of the dance. Only the musicologist Villoteau devoted space to a discussion of cymbals of all sizes. In his article on dancers' instruments, Villoteau precisely names dancers' cymbals. "The names zyl, senoug, kas and saggat all equally applying to crotales ... can be used for the crotales of Egyptian dancers; but we have noted that the names senoug and saggat have been especially reserved [for them] in ordinary usage" (1809b, 981). He concluded that "this instrument ... yields a very agreeable sound, very clean and high, when nothing interferes with its vibration" (1809b, 981). There are three types of sounds made, he said. The most brilliant sound came when dancers hit them together on the edges, less sound came when they hit them with one partially covering the other, the sound is almost muffled when they hit them vertically, one exactly covering the other (1809a, 696).[4]

Villoteau (1809a, 696) found a complex relationship of saggat to choreography, and believed the instrument contributed brilliantly to the overall impact of the dance. He felt the saggat gave enormous energy of expression, and described its liquid clinking sounds as highly sensual. He observed how dancers hit the saggat one against the other, sometimes in succession, sometimes at the same time, depending on the effects they wanted to achieve. Dancers chose various sounds and suitable rhythms that they fitted perfectly to the meanings they wished to paint, and consequently were astonishingly adept at creating dance pantomimes.[5] Indeed, finger cymbals were virtuoso instruments, ones capable of making subtle sounds that could translate the dance's physical meaning into musical ones.

Singing often served as the single focus of an Egyptian evening's entertainment (as described in section three), but singing usually occurred also during an evening involving dance performances. Singing might take place prior to the dance, alternate with the dance, take place to conclude the evening, or, importantly, take place during the dance itself as the dancer often mimed or sang the text. In this manner the song texts provided an important layer of meaning for the dance.[6]

Dance performances inevitably included love songs, a popular feature of Arabic art music. Clot Bey (1840, 2:73) compared these poems to European romances, describing them as often melancholy and relating the pains of love. They were divided into couplets with a recurring refrain, often consisting of "yah leyly, yah leyly" (oh night, oh night). Villoteau described (with considerable negative bias) the mood created by the male singers through the texts:

> An accent of abandon, and a languor with which these male singers express melancholy sexual pleasure deluges most of these songs; but we would be remiss in rendering the lascivious and shameless accent which they rejoice in adding to the immoderate words, that breathe a brutal and indecent love, often beyond all reason [1809a, 679].

Combes wrote of the song Safiyya sang during her performance as "if you had heard her cry of love that penetrated to the marrow of the bone ... you would have thought you heard the neighing of an amorous mare" (1846, 1:220).

The important correlation of song text to choreography, where the dancer was said to mime the words of the poem in her dance, remains an open research question for there exists scant information in the travel literature to illustrate this important aspect of the relationship of the two arts. Jomard described a Napoleonic song that expressed the sentiment: "Oh you who wish pleasure: come, my friend, untie the knot of your belt and approach" (1822, 732). To this line of poetry the dancer ties and unties the belt of her costume. This particular dance motif and its poetic line had a long life, for Didier (1860, 240) heard the same verse in 1854 and suggested it was "put into action," but this time boy dancers carried out the performance.

Leland (1874, 136) wrote in detail of a dance where the dancer five times approached an actual cup as if tempted, fled as if afraid, finally succumbing, and drinking from it. This choreography finds a close correlation in the Arabic poetic repertoire where various lines can involve wine and passing the cup. The lover begs his beloved to pass the cup, wine takes away all sorrows, the lover takes the cup and becomes intoxicated with the beloved's eyes, they lie under the jasmine for half the night, both enraptured. The erotic symbolism here is evident. Villoteau (1809a, 680n) had described wine as the metaphor of sexual passion, and Leland here astutely identified the cup of this dance as "symbolic of temptation" (1874, 136). This dance with a cup appears to be the choreographic equivalent of the poetry. That the dancer was a successful mime can be judged by Leland's choice of words. With "thirsty lips just dallying with the [cup's] edge ... she thrilled and shivered.... No longer able to resist, she approached the cup with throbs and pauses." After taking the cup, she "merrily danced about the room in quick step with her head thrown back" (ibid., 136).

Flaubert records the song to which Hasan al–Bilbeissi and his male companion danced in a hotel, and with this song he also identifies a number of choreographed movements, although he does not tie any to an individual poetic line. He gives a translation of the poetry of the Arabic text as

> a Turkish object with a slim body possesses keen and penetrating eyes; the lovers, on their account, have passed a night in slavery; I sacrifice my soul for love of a fawn who can tame lions; my God, the nectar of this mouth is sweet, is sweet to suck; is not this nectar the cause of my languor and my despair; oh full moon, enough of these torments; it is time to keep your promise to the suffering lover [1991, 236–37].

He describes a number of dance movements, speaking of their "femininity" as he saw it. The two men moved forward and backward, with completely impassive faces (caked with makeup and dripping with sweat). When they walked they shook their pelvises with a short and convulsive movement compared to a fluttering of the muscles. When the pelvis moved the rest of the body was still. When the chest moved, nothing else moved. They advanced with arms outstretched all the time playing the saggat. Sometimes they fell onto the ground on their backs, (presumably onto the front of the lower leg, with bent knees) then, with a movement of the thighs, rose again with a bound. During the salutes and bows they made frequent stops when then their red pantaloons would bellow out then collapse on themselves. From time to time the buffoon with them would make ribald jokes and place his lips on Hasan's stomach, buttocks, and thighs. During the entire dance Hasan never stopped looking in the mirror.[7]

The two men danced for two hours, so obviously there is not enough choreographic material provided to fill the entire performance. It is difficult in this instance, as a result, to match the song text to any of the choreographic movements. Unfortunately, Flaubert's account is the only one located in the travel literature with both an attempt to describe extensive choreographic movements along with their specific song text, leaving an enormous void where one would hope to answer more precisely how dancers normally mimed the text of sung poems.

22

The Aesthetic of Dance Movements

Body Parts in Motion

Even if their remarks were usually brief, individual European observers frequently singled out various body parts in motion, and, taken as a whole, the travel literature does reveal reasonably well how dancers articulated a wide range of movements. Since the small subtle movements of Middle Eastern dances are hard to capture, however, the illustrations have been less helpful except in giving impressions of poses of heads, arms, and legs. Overall there is not much material dealing with each aspect of dancers' bodies, therefore no attempt has been made here to examine any possible changes in movement repertoire over the study period.

Dancers' heads appear to have been active in performance, operating independently, and the illustrations and texts reveal relationships with the neck and shoulders in a variety of positions. Seven of these are identified. The first four may belong with the slower parts of the dance, and the next three with the faster. First, heads may tilt slightly sideways on the neck, with chin slightly bent downward, and eyes looking down (figs. 16, 17, 18). Second, heads may be held straight forward on the neck, with chin up or down (figs. 2, 8, 18, second figure from the left in fig. 19). Third, heads may be held perpendicular, and looking directly forward (figs. 10, 16, 19).

The fourth, and a common position, shows the head looking over one shoulder (figs. 8, 10, 15, 17, 21a, 22, 24, 26). Fifth, heads may roll from side to side across the chest or roll in a complete circle, even bending well back. "Her face voluptuously bent backwards, rolled to one side then to the other" (Goupil-Fesquet 1843, 74). "The dancer dropped her head back while pressing her arms to her chest" (J. St. John 1834, 1:112). Mayer (fig. 3) shows the head of the dancer to the far left apparently in the process of such rolling, while the dancer second to the left in Mayer (fig. 3) drops her head violently far back. Gérôme (fig. 25) shows a similar, if much softer, head movement.

Sixth, dancers might make jerking movements of the head, expressed as "making their heads move in a feverish gesture expressing abandonment to folly" (Blanc 1876, 113). "Her head stayed perpendicular except for some jerks back and forth to the music" (Carcy quoted in Aradoon 1979, 123). Finally, in a seventh movement, both Aziza and Kutchuk Hanem performed neck movements that astonished Flaubert. "Aziza's neck slid on her spine from back to front and often from side to side" (1991, 295).[1]

European writers remarked favorably on the intense beauty of dancers' eyes, and certainly dancers used their eyes to communicate directly and effectively with their audiences.[2] Eyes might provide a dramatic beginning. "Her brilliant eyes darted lightning and at an agreed signal the dance began" (Lenoir 1872, 105). They might engage in "exchanging speaking glances" with the men (Bartlett 1849, 114). During the performance, dancers might withdraw into themselves then reach out to the audience by means of their eyes. "Her eyes, which, as is the custom, she generally kept half-closed in dancing, the lashes sometimes even resting on the cheeks, seemed, when they opened and beamed around the room, to fill it with redoubled light" (B. St. John 1973, 2:70).

Expressions might be lively, fiery, or solemn, depending on the phase of the dance. "Her eyes wandered and flashed" (B. St. John 1850, 150). Gérôme's (fig. 25) *Dance of the Almeh*, for example, captures the mood of the dancer when she draws into herself. Carcy noted how the performer he saw maintained a remote manner during performance. "They have, in fact, two distinct characteristics—for one, the pose of the head, solemn and set, the facial expression remaining serious throughout, the mouth just barely smiling" (quoted in Aradoon 1979, 124).

Arms played an important role in the dance, with a number of varied positions. Here the pictures have been invaluable for it is reasonably easy to capture arm positions, and many are available for analysis. For the most part dance illustrations indicate that arms provide a soft effect in the choreography. "They spread, lower or softly raise them [arms] while rounding them as if they were seeking or expecting a kiss; then they bring them close to the body and almost over their lowered eyes" (Villoteau 1809a, 696–97). Hands almost invariably hold small metal cymbals attached to the fingers of each hand. "The movement they displayed in striking them against each other gave infinite grace to their fingers and wrists" (Denon 1973, 232). Generally arms are not raised high as in ballet, nor fully extended with locked elbows. One finds arms that extend wide open and down; make interesting framings of the head, and lift together in front of the head. They involve only the front plane, the space in front of the dancer. Usually held at waist level or above, they may sometimes fall.

Artists show three general arm positions. The most common emerges from the many available combinations and articulations of bent elbows with each arm independent of the other. Arms rise usually above shoulder level and spread wide, with elbows bent to right angles or more. Held in this position, the arms make many different frames for the head and chest (figs. 8, 10, 17, 18). A continuation of this position downward may result in one with arms held tight to the body at the waist. One can see such a movement made by the dancer second to the right in Figure 19.

A second position involves arms held close together and operating as a single unit. They extend directly forward, jutting diagonally upward, or close in front of the face (figs. 2—far right dancer, 19—extreme left dancer, 21a, 22). A continuation of this movement may result in a downward thrusting gesture, as shown by the dancer second from the left in Figure 19. The dancer on the extreme right in the same illustration holds a position intermediate between arms thrust outwards diagonally, and fully down to the ground. In this second position Aziza of Aswan "held out her two long arms ... shaking them from shoulder to wrist with an imperceptible quivering, moving them apart with soft and quick motions like those of the wings of a hovering eagle" (Du Camp quoted in Buonaventura 1990, 72).

A third position shows arms spread wide and fully extended, though with slightly softened elbows. This dramatic pose appears in Gérôme's (fig. 25) *Dance of the Almeh*, but the pose has a long history ranging from the left-hand dancer in Figure 2, the central dominating figure of Figure 6, through Richter's Figure 23.

Dancers' chests are hardly mentioned except when exertion of the performance might cause the chest to heave. She "writhe[d] in an agony of joy; her broad bosom ... heaved and panted with passion" (B. St. John 1850, 150). "As the dance proceeded ... their bosoms heaved and panted" (Hackländer quoted in J. St. James 1845, 275). Even descriptions of shimmies of the shoulders and bust are few. "After the prelude, came a singular trepidation of the shoulders and hips with the legs and feet in place" (Blanc 1876, 51).[3] Andreievsky (quoted in Volkoff 1972, 296) describes how the dancers alternated shoulder and hip shimmies, while the rest of the body was stationary.

The hip area came in for much attention in the travel literature, and some writers identified hip movements as even central to the dance aesthetic. "One knows that the principal and even unique characteristic of their dances consists of constant and supple movement of the hips" (Jomard 1822, 733). Minutoli too spoke eloquently of the hips. "The principal talent of these dancers consists not in nimbleness of the feet, in the lightness and equilibrium of the body, and in the gracefulness of the attitudes and motions, but in an extreme mobility of the hips" (1827, 200).

A movement known today as the hip shimmy caused comment[4]: "They turn and stop in an amorous position. There, with stilled body, knees half bent, arms outstretched and head hanging, only the thighs execute the most passionate and secret movements. The eyes take on a languid air, and shut" (Prisse d'Avennes 1930, 53). Dancers often did this movement in pairs, facing each other and standing still. Redouté saw a performance when "two women, in the interval of light and quick jumps, approached one another and remained in place, with lively movements in the hips, without moving the rest of the body; they agitated their thighs rhythmically with extreme suppleness" (quoted in Hermant 1798, 51).[5] The hip shimmy might just as often be executed while dancers moved around the performance space (Flaubert 1965, 184–85).

Only Flaubert describes a movement often known today as the hip drop. Kutchuk Hanem's servant Bamba danced in a straight line and "goes with a lowering and raising of the thigh on one side only—a sort of rhythmic limping of great character" (1991, 283). Brandin's (fig. 22) dancer, with the tight concentration required, may be performing this movement.

Soft full-body movements or "undulations" also formed part of the movement repertoire. Leland said that "the first dancing of all Ghawazi is simply moving about to the music and undulating the body" (1874, 135). Both Hackländer and Andreievsky used the metaphor of the snake to describe this movement in the dance. "They twined round each other snake-like, with a suppleness and a grace such as I had never seen before" (Hackländer quoted in J. St. James 1845, 275). "Sometimes she folded her supple body with the movements of an amorous serpent" (Andreievsky quoted in Volkoff 1972, 296). Perhaps the far left dancer in Figure 19, with her torso curved forward in relation to the pelvis, is performing a body wave or undulation.

Vibrations across the entire body are also described.[6] The dancer Goupil-Fesquet hired to dance on his boat inspired him to write:

> Her thighs and hips trembling imperceptibly soon moved with an unbelievable rapidity that disturbed the body's contours. I cannot find a comparison more appropriate to the effect of this movement, on our eyes, than an immobile object that seems to move from across the undulating emanations rising from hot water [1843, 74].

Vibrations might progress, and develop into more violent movements, those comparable to contractions. Kutchuk Hanem developed her choreography in this manner. "When she had completed the circuit of the spot on which she stood, she advanced slowly, all the muscles jerking in time to the music, with solid substantial spasms" (Curtis 1856, 141). Leland, too, describes the same progression, of a dance that involved "moving the lower part of her body forward more and more with a vigorous quivering, and once in ten seconds starting a convulsion, which gradually becomes more frequent" (1874, 136).

Dancers also used a crouching position, with bent knees, at an intense moment of the choreography. "There, with immobile body, the knees bent, arms extended, head bent, the thighs only execute the most passionate movements" (Prisse d'Avennes 1930, 53). "The head, shoulders and arms eagerly bent forward, waist in, and haunches advanced on the bent knees—the posture of a cobra about to spring" (Duff Gordon 1983, 100). Leland describes a dancer who "sinks slowly almost to her knees ... moving the lower part of her body forward more and more with a vigorous quivering" (1874, 135).

Movements of the legs in Middle Eastern dance are hardly comparable to those of many other dance forms, yet dancers used small walking steps effectively. Of Badawiyya's troupe, Colet wrote that "their delightful feet lifted and moved in unison with the sculptural feet of their mistress" (1879, 147). Describing Safiyya, Romer wrote that "she shuffled about upon a very small space of ground without executing anything like a step; in short she put every part of her body into movement except her feet" (1846, 1:276). Such footwork can be seen in Gérôme's (fig. 25) *Dance of the Almeh*. She has moved across her rug with small shuffling steps and the rug is twisted and rumpled. Small steps also constituted the important basis of some elaborate hip work. Gérôme's (fig. 15) sword dancer walks forward on demi-pointe in a series of dainty steps.

Dancers might also stamp their feet or drop them percussively. In Asyût in 1869, Blanc described four dancers who "advanced ... drew back ... stamped their feet in unison, then advanced once more" (1876, 113). Aziza of Aswan "stood on one foot, raised the other, her knee making a right angle, then falling" (Flaubert 1991, 295).

Kutchuk Hanem, Safiyya of Isna, and Aziza of Aswan, seem to have executed a specialty combination lower leg and footwork step, found in Combes, Flaubert, and Curtis.[7] Flaubert's description is the most evocative. "She [Kutchuk Hanem] raised herself sometimes on one leg, sometimes on the other, a marvellous thing: one leg resting on the ground, the other passes in front of the tibia of the first, all in a light leap. I have seen this dance on old Greek vases" (1991, 283).

Larger stepping out movements, using the full leg extended from the thigh, also formed part of the repertoire. In the illustrations, Roberts' (fig. 16) dancers move with a slight step, while dancers depicted by Baurenseind (fig. 2), and von Mayr (fig. 8) move more vigorously. Writers also identified leaping steps, and

Fig. 26. George Montbard. *Ghâwazi dansant la danse de "la guêpe"* (Ghâwazi Dancing the Dance of *The Bee*). c. 1880 (from Georges Montbard [Charles A. Loyes], *En Egypte: notes et croquis d'un artiste* [Paris: Monde illustrée, [18—]).

these, too, can be seen in the illustrations. Sonnini (1799, 2:322) described how the dancers alternated "quick light leaps" in their choreography. "They leap while shaking their tambourines, and the disorder, the vivacity of their steps recall the madness of bacchantes" (Du Bois-Aymé and Jollois 1812, 110n). Large leaping steps provide the energy of the tambourine dance depicted in Forbin's (fig. 24) print. In Montbard's (fig. 26) depiction of the dancer she also leaps. Rising high on one leg, she kicks the other behind, and raises her right arm high and forward in a strong movement.

Male performers, who traditionally had danced with bared belly, probably made popular those movements specific to the abdomen. In connection with Hasan in 1849, Flaubert says that "he made his belly roll like a wave" (1991, 195). Bayle St. John described the way a male buffoon in Alexandria in 1846 performed his mimicry of female dancers, but noting his "powers of ... moving the muscles of his abdomen in a very droll way whilst all the rest of his body remained quiescent" (1850, 57). Significantly, there are absolutely no references to female dancers carrying out this body movement recorded over the entire century of the study. This indeed is ironic, considering the name eventually ascribed to female performances—Danse du Ventre and belly dance.

Male clowns involved in the dance alongside female dancers cried out, laughed, imitated their movements, and made phallic gestures (discussed fully in section eight). Only Marmont speaks specifically on the latter topic. While discussing the use of the phallus as an object displayed during public festivities he says: "One sees often, in the dances, gross imitations" (1837–38, 3:315–16).[8]

Section Eight
Choreography and Performance

23

Six Choreographic Elements Basic to the Dance

The travel literature describes six choreographic elements that seem to have appeared consistently from 1760 to 1870, these six features being: dancers used a small performance space; they moved continuously; they repeated the same movements over and over; they were adept at isolating the various parts of their bodies; their choreography relied on pairs of dancers, or combinations of pairs, rather than solo performances; dances involved considerable eroticism. Unlike the first four, the last two features generated considerable comment in the travel literature.

Of the first element, Volney (1959, 392), among a few others, pointed out that dancers used a small performance ground, and much of the illustrative material shows this building block, with pairs of dancers performing close together.[1] The second element, constant motion, also received some limited attention. "With the two almés ... everything was in motion throughout their persons" (Combes 1846, 1:219). "The dances of the almées ... consist always of a constant light oscillation of the muscles of the body" (Blanc 1876, 112). Of the third, often writers complained of what they perceived as tedium in the repetitive nature of the dance. "But the dances of the almées, at least those performed in public, are quite monotonous and soon tire one's attention" (Blanc 1876, 112).[2] Others, however, found such repetition stimulating. "It is wonderful how they will continue to agitate every muscle in the most violent and rapid manner for hours, quivering from head to foot as if electrified" (Leland 1874, 132–33). Of the fourth, Savary perceptively identified the characteristic of body isolations in Middle Eastern dance, and expressed it well: "When they start to move, their forms and contours of the body separate in succession" (1785, 1:151). Other authors throughout the period noted the same element.³ Carcy comments, "When one isolates ... the upper half of the almée's body, one finds in her ... severe poses ... in complete contrast with the rest of the body, which is very loose, [and] contorts itself with incredible mobility and suppleness" (quoted in Aradoon 1979, 124). In representing the body as a succession of parts attached independently, most illustrations capture this aspect of the dance well. Heads are usually off-center from necks, torsos from pelvises, and pelvises from legs.

The fifth element noted by travel writers, pairs of dancers together, is of considerable interest to dance historians and merits a full discussion. Professional female belly dancing today in Egypt (as elsewhere) most often consists of solo performances, but this practice was not the norm during the study period. Although some dancers are mentioned as dancing solo, more routinely within the Egyptian fantasia and even during street performances women danced only briefly in solo moments or solo episodes, and performed at length in pairs and in various combinations, depending on the total number of dancers present in the company. For example, six dancers and two male musicians provided the command performance for General Menou in 1798. Here two women began the dance while the others sang (Denon 1973, 232). Dauzat's (Dumas [and Dauzats] 1846, 222–25) entertainment at Clot Bey's establishment included four dancers who performed together, plus a buffoon, and four male musicians. A representative group appears in Mayer's *An Egyptian Ball at Ned Sili* (fig. 3); here six dancers perform in two groups of three. A dwarf in costume appears at the right. In *Danse d'Almées, à Sihout* (fig. 19), four women dance together as a group, another dancer sits on a visitor's knees, and male musicians are in evidence.⁴

Since it might seem difficult to pair vastly unequal talents, one wonders whether the presence of a star (someone of stature in the dance world) affected the performance. In both Flaubert's and Curtis's accounts of their evenings with Kutchuk Hanem, it is clear that she danced with a female partner, as well as in solo episodes. The famous Safiyya of Isna also danced with a female partner (Combes 1846, 1:219). Her complete troupe seems to have consisted of two dancers including her, and an unspecified number of female singers, and male musicians.

There are examples of solo dancers as today, but usually within unusual circumstances. Hasna, accompanied by three male musicians, danced alone for Gérôme's party in the Faiyûm. On the other hand, the performance lasted only one hour, after which she left, the event not being the normal full evening's entertainment (Lenoir 1872, 103–07). When Bayle St. John's landlords wished to hold a clandestine family celebration they had to make do with two performers, Kala and Aisha, since most of the local dancers of Alexandria were terrified of the police. Kala danced while Aisha played the drum (1850, 147–50). Goupil-

Fesquet (1843, 73–74) hired this same stripped-down troupe, a single dancer and one female singer-musician, to ride on his boat up to Cairo. Again, this type of performance was dictated by problems created after the edict of 1833, for such women were routinely obliged to leave the boat before reaching the police post just outside the capital. There were 15 other dancers present in Qena in 1869 when Badawiyya executed her famous solo sword dance, but she was alone on the stage. This seems one clear example of a star performing entirely without other dance support. Didier (1850, 50–51) also talks of a solo sword dance in Khartoum. It is likely that since this dance required great skill and suppleness, and since it did not seem to be part of the normal repertoire of Egyptian dancers, only a few women had the training and talent to execute it.

It was the erotic, the sixth element noted, that universally captured the imagination and frequent censure of European observers. A level of sexuality appropriate to Egyptian dance performance did not conform to European tastes, and, not able to incorporate what they saw into their range of expected behaviors, travelers reacted uneasily:

> The points of more salient expression were warmly applauded, both by old and young [Egyptians]; none were here ashamed openly to evince, what it is considered more decent to veil, in our own *refined* community, where the accomplished art of the opera figurante is skilled in throwing a still more dangerous charm of mingled grace and piquancy over the same idea, which in all its *unveiled grossness*, forms the characteristic expression of the Egyptian dance [Bartlett 1849, 114].

While the eroticism of Egyptian dance was important to the aesthetic, it might often be subtle, and even negotiable between dancer and audience. At a Cairo party he attended, Michaud describes how the young dancer was forced to respond to the Egyptian audience's demands:

> Mothers who accompany their daughters put themselves beyond maternal feelings, and greediness alone motivates them. In a Cairo house I saw a very beautiful almée, pressured by several young men to take certain more or less licentious positions; the young dancer hesitated, and her mother approached her, saying in a loud voice: "Do what they ask you or I'll kill you" [1833–35, 5:257].[5]

Performers themselves might define the level of sexuality of the dance, choosing to maintain and even increase it, perhaps in the hopes of more monetary reward. At times the dancer might single out an honored guest for special attention and these attentions might be symbolically sexual in nature (Bartlett 1849, 114).

On the other hand, dancers might choose to lay aside sexuality during the performance intervals and be "offstage" in their manner, and there is self-confidence and professional maturity implied in such shedding of their stage persona. In 1798, Denon first compared two dancers to two French entertainers, then remarked, "Josephina and Hanka ... when the dance was ended, possessed all the delicacy of manners of the women whom they resembled" (1973, 233–34). Duff Gordon, too, describes such an instance:

> Seleem Effendi ... during the pause in the dancing called "el Maghribeeyeh," the best dancer, to come and talk. She kissed my hand, sat on her heels before us, and at once laid aside the professional galliardise of manner, and talked very nicely in very good Arabic and with perfect propriety ... she seemed very intelligent [1983, 136].[6]

Some perceptive Europeans grasped that the quality of eroticism lay as much in the dancer as in the dance. Probably Didier captures this idea most clearly when he describes the talented Chama of Khartoum: "What was most charming in her was the chaste grace of her dance; not a movement, not a gesture, overstepped the limits of the most reserved decency, yet still she managed to be utterly seductive" (1858, 103). Bayle St. John (1850, 150) contrasted the powerful dancing of the strong-willed Kala with the "pretty tripping and graceful licentiousness" of her timid companion Aisha.[7] Class of performer might also affect quality of sexuality. Combes (1846, 1:22n) defended his unqualified admiration for the great Safiyya's artistry by claiming those who found Egyptian dance sexually offensive had seen only dancers of a lesser class.[8] Finally, it appears that sexuality was a learned quality, instilled in dancers along with dance technique. Bayle St. John describes children in training, competent but still lacking this skill. They "were quite a credit to the establishment, and though barely ten years old, had little to learn, except passion. Like two lovely automata, they went through every manoeuvre of their elder sisters" (1973, 1:23).

As a body of work, the illustrative materials fail to convey the quality of eroticism, for many of them stress the pretty, the decorative and the innocuous.[9] The notable exception, Gérôme's *Dance of the Almeh* (fig. 25), has been criticized today as an Orientalized view of Egyptian women, a depiction of them as unthinking beings, possessed of unlimited sensuality, the subject of male fantasies. Certainly the painting can be read in this manner if one chooses to do so, yet one admires Gérôme for tackling the elusive quality of this dance's sensuality. One might argue, also, that any perceived offensive quality to his painting lies not in the depiction of the dancer but rather more in the absence of an exuberant native Egyptian response. Only the African soldier is happily engaged in the performance. The other soldiers, foreigners to Egypt in fact, are taking it dourly indeed.

24

Extending the Definition of Choreography

Any discussion of Middle Eastern choreography needs to address points usually not found in typical modern Western theories. Since there were no theaters, dance took place within a wide variety of settings such as private homes, coffee houses, streets, boats, the banks of the Nile, and public squares. Dancers usually were in public view or "onstage" in these situations so entrances and exits, intermissions, and even the intervals for collecting money from the audience may usefully be regarded as part of the complete choreographed dance event.

Instead of making a dramatic entrance it was common for dancers and musicians first to greet guests personally, to provide a lengthy musical overture, and participate in refreshments with their audience. Romer (1846, 1:273–74) provides a good description of the pre-dance phase of an event at Safiyya's house in Isna. The guests were first offered pipes, with an attendant attempting to pour perfumed oil over Romer's face and throat. Four female musicians entered, sat on the floor and began to sing and play. Twenty minutes later Safiyya herself entered grandly enough but then only to welcome her guests. She "gracefully saluted me by touching my hand, and then kissing her own and carrying it to her forehead." Combes's 1834 evening in Isna serves as a second example. After dinner the guests rose from the table and went to sit on divans. At eight o'clock the male musicians, dancers, and female singers arrived at the house, with "all the noise of their brilliant jewellery." The dancers then socialized with their audience-to-be, sitting for a while beside the guests, the musicians crouched in a corner against the wall. Pipes, coffee, and brandy circulated among all the entertainers and guests; finally tea arrived. Only then did the dancing begin (1846, 1:218–19). Even in a humble outdoor setting traditional social niceties might be observed. Forbin (1819, 87–88) describes watching the dance among the ruins in Qûs in 1818 where the young performers also brought him coffee.

Later in the century, shaking hands was deemed a polite gesture. "Four almées entered ... they came forward solemnly to greet each of us with a handshake, in the English custom" (Carcy, quoted in Aradoon 1979, 122). Andreievsky writes that at his late-night impromptu outdoor performance the dancers "approached the tourists and shook their hands as if they were old friends" (quoted in Volkoff 1972, 296).

When dancers were already "on-stage" there needed to be several cues for the start of the performance. This would be particularly important when dancers were outdoors—in the streets, before coffee houses, or along the Nile. James St. John (1834, 1:109) writes an attractive description of the dancer in a coffee house rearranging her costume, then tying on her heavy belt, and removing her shoes in preparation for the performance, all this in front of the spectators. Bayle St. John describes the same actions that constituted a formal signaling of dance readiness, as such part of an extended meaning of choreography:

> When the first song was over we requested Kala to dance.... Rising to her feet, she threw aside her mantle, and bound a long shawl firmly round her hips; then taking a pair of castanets, she stepped into the middle of the carpet, threw her arms aloft like a Bacchante, assumed a graceful pose for a moment, then began [1850, 149–50].

There also existed a possible prelude with arm movements and then salutations to mark the beginning of the performance. Clot Bey (1840, 2:92) described such a salutation to the four quarters of the room as the dancers entered onto the dance space. Goupil-Fesquet's single dancer also carried out this traditional gesture. She "lowered her eyes to the ground ... raised her bare arms to the sky, and beating small brass cymbals ... made several steps in a circle, turned her head to right, left, in front and behind as a prelude" (1843, 73–74). The formal entrance might also include singing, especially when a troupe was involved. Dauzat's (Dumas [and Dauzats] 1846, 1:225) four dancers sang as they paraded in a line before the guests. Leland also described such a beginning: "Before the regular dancing commences, yet while undulating about the room, the Ghawazi generally sing with constant repetition one or two verses" (1874, 133).

Breaks or intermissions during the evening also expand the definition of Middle Eastern choreography. Dancers did not necessarily leave the performance space after each act but might involve themselves with their audiences in two ways. First, they used these opportunities to solicit money from the guests. Second, as evening's entertainment might be long they needed some less physically demanding alternatives to dancing.

Performers often made the collection of money a highly ritualized part of their act, with a set patter of call and response between the person collecting the money (often a servant of the performers) and the dancers. "Such a one has given many mahboobs or kheyreeyehs, turning a few piasters into a much larger number of gold coins of considerably greater value. His mistress or another of the awalim replies ... 'May he have the like [rejoicing]' or 'May he have a recompense'" (Lane 1978, 495).

Dancers often used assertive methods of collecting fees. Clot Bey (1840, 2:93–94) described the collection of money as an assault on the persons of the male guests. Bayle St. John (1973, 2:71) explained it was the custom to make presents to the dancers at the end of each applauded dance, or at any rate toward the close of the evening. Clot Bey suggested an alternative strategy, that of pausing at the climax of a performance: "When the dance reaches its more libidinous moment, there are some moments of repose, during which the almées come and bother the spectators" (1840, 2:93). In particular, dancers' solicitations were addressed to the principal guest and to those they felt might be generous. Burckhardt explains his proverb, "The fly knows the face of the milk seller," as "this proverb chiefly refers to the dancing girls, who, when they are brought for the amusement of company, pay attention particularly to those whom they soon discover to be the most inclined towards them" (1984, 21–22).

Spectators sometimes made compensation directly onto dancers' bodies—on the forehead, cheeks, and chin. Dauzats (Dumas [and Dauzats] 1846, 227) gives a graphic description of coins adhering by the sweat of dancers' bodies, the performers then shaking until the coins dropped into a silver jar. Dancers attempted to keep the coins from falling off as they continued moving. "The most adroit are those who can keep on the greatest number for the longest period without touching them. This often leads to some very original wagers" (Clot Bey 1840, 2:75).

Besides serving as breaks for the collection of money, pauses in the performance stretch the definition of choreography in a second way. An evening's entertainment might often last several hours and dancers could not keep in motion indefinitely. During non-dancing intervals dancers might play musical instruments and sing, informally mingle with the guests, or carry out other activities. Hackländer describes such playing and singing by the two dancers he saw: "In the intervals between the dances, they played on their tambourines, and sang a melancholy air" (quoted in J. St. James 1845, 276). Kutchuk Hanem rounded off her evening for Curtis with music, "Slow, sweet, singing followed" (1856, 145). After the dancing concluded, performers might also engage in conversation with the guests (Denon 1973, 233; Duff Gordon 1983, 136).

Another type of intermission and respite for the dancers took place when members of the audience rose to join in with them. At this point their dancing would have been considerably more relaxed. Carne reports on the consul's daughter's wedding he attended in Damietta around 1823.[10] While the performers danced, "many of the guests of both sexes joined in dancing, while others formed in groups to enjoy their chibouque [pipe] and coffee" (1826, 73). Hackländer describes another such incident: "The company too, were not altogether idle; now and then, one of the ladies jumped up from the divan, and mingled in the dance; and we, too, were once obliged to take part in it" (quoted in J. St. John 1845, 276).

Dancers often sat on the laps of male guests in the intervals, in a manner that made Europeans uncomfortable. L'Hôte describes dancers at Girga with Champollion's party:

> There you are, Fathmé, pretty coquette, stretched out on illustrious knees. Was it through a premonition to feed your vanity that you would have chosen him? Head on his shoulder, face against his face, you look at him and smile, and your dear fingers coloured in henna seem to search, under the black mane of his thick beard, a smile that matches your own [1993, 130].

All these instances of the second type of intermission can usefully be considered as "choreography" in the Middle Eastern context.

25

Three Identifiable Dances

Identifying Separate Dances

As described in section seven, the travel writing contains a surprising amount of excellent first-hand observations of body parts in motion, but descriptions of actual dances do not appear until after the Napoleonic period. During the research process I found it instinctive to sort these (usually short and fragmentary) descriptions of performances into three major groupings, and I eventually concluded the groupings had captured three identifiable dances. This typology appeared all the more relevant during a final review of Clot Bey's material when I suddenly realized he, too, had identified three types of dance in Egypt (but without giving adequate clues as to their nature). "They have several types of dance. One, the most bold and brutal, is exclusively imprinted with the Egyptian character; another seems to be combined with Greek dance; the third is known under the name of dance of the bees" (Clot Bey 1840, 2:93). I decided to name two of "my" newly found dances the *Love Duet,* and the *Pure Dance,* and of course, I kept the name of *The Bee.* Clot Bey's "bold and brutal" dance, then, would be equated to my *Love Duet,* the dance "with Greek character"[1] to the *Pure Dance,* and, of course, *The Bee* is common.

Some pertinent observations by Galland, dating from the Napoleonic occupation, also confirmed part of my conclusions and subsequent decisions. Here he differentiates between two types of dance—"lascivious dances" (perhaps the *Pure Dance*) and "shameful scenes" (perhaps the *Love Duet*). "Not only do the almehs play, change and execute lascivious dances that are really unsavoury, but they often represent shameful scenes, even the most contrary to nature, and it isn't uncommon in these scandalous farces that little boys copy these representations to the letter" (1804, 2:24).

Pure Dance

Unlike the other two identified dances, *Pure Dance* had no storyline with mimed sequences, and consisted of movements only, hence my name for it (with emphasis on the second word). With this name I make no commentary on the dance's moral intent—I might equally have called it *Abstract Dance*.

Some authors described this dance as having neither sections nor complex choreography. Others did make mention of clearly marked divisions and describe these as having associated movements and tempos. Probably these variation in complexity depended on the dancers and the occasions. Lane describes the dance as its "chief peculiarity being a very rapid vibrating motion of the hips from side to side" (1973, 377). Watching dancers at Asyût, Blanc (1876, 113) described the movements as consisting of a constant shaking; the dancers in a group advanced and retreated, beat their feet in a rhythm, and shook their heads. They then repeated these same steps endlessly. Carcy describes a similar simple performance consisting of on-the-spot hip shimmies increasingly moving faster and faster, some vibrations and some arm work. Dancers performed these movements stepping forward and backward. Then "each one did her dance, first alone, then in twos, threes, and finally all four together" (quoted in Aradoon 1979, 124).

Most authors, however, identified at least two phases in performances, but in describing these used heavily value-laden, rather than neutral, words. For example, terms used for the progress of the dance through various sections consisted of "from voluptuous" to "lasciviousness" (Denon 1973, 232); "from slow and only voluptuous" to "drunkenness and delirium" (Taylor 1856, 265); "first modestly coquettish" then "wanton frenzy" (Bartlett 1849, 114).[2] The comte de Marcellus identified three sections for he claimed the dance was at first "languor and melancholy" followed by an "awakening of the senses with pronounced and lively movements," and finally an ending that was "disorder and drunkenness" (quoted in Carré 1956, 1:210). Despite the evaluative nature of these expressions, they do show the pace and phasing of the dance. Obviously, there were usually two distinctive parts, slow and fast (and sometimes medium).[3]

Such evaluative words hardly help with a precise understanding, so what *did* the dancers actually do when they performed? Fortunately, authors could also describe parts of the choreography in detail and with some objectivity. Clot Bey wrote that the dance proper first consisted of standing immobile, with the upper part of the body still. The arms carried the dance as the dancers expressed various emotions with them. Then, little by little, much hip work was added. "Agitated by an unending trembling, that by and by they accelerate with an audacious energy, or slow with languor, their thighs and hips ... feign the most sensual physical emotions" (1840, 2:92–93). Blanc (1876, 51–52) described two sections of the piece he saw at a Cairo party in 1869, a dance beginning with much arm work, and the body in a stationary position. He wrote of unspecified body movements (probably much shaking) accompanied by many and varied arm movements that conveyed emotions and, in some sense, ideas. Then the dancers, in a second phase, "intoxicated" by their music and the earlier shaking of their bodies, moved off the spot, and took up other and "lascivious" poses.

Hackländer and Lenoir wrote of somewhat more complex choreographies. Hackländer (quoted in J. St. James 1845, 275) described a dance with movements first performed by the body and arms in an "easy and regular" manner (rather similar to Clot Bey above); then the dance took on a more fiery character, the two performers using their bodies in many more attitudes, including entwining themselves around each other. Their chests moved greatly in deep breaths with the effort of the dance at this point. Then began an important sequence of alternation between fast dancing and slow dancing, with arms and bodies drooping to express the slow parts. In the Faiyûm, Lenoir (1872, 105) describes Hasna's solo dance beginning in a slow and cadenced manner, while she "scarcely moved from the spot to which she seemed bound by her feet." At this point she was making "incredible inflexions." Next, when the music accelerated, "imperceptible and hasty steps succeeded" with "almost convulsive movements" and a "dislocation of the hips." Lenoir saw these latter as the bedrock of the dance. The music increased again and Hasna responded with "contortions" of her head and arms of a "feverish and savage character." She then sank to her knees to make "new figures, more strange and picturesque" than before. Hasna danced for an hour, so this description covers an extended performance. Here she has added floor work of some complexity to the so-called two-part choreography.

Other writers are more forthcoming than Lenoir with details of the floor work, a part of the dance first described in Napoleonic times and which might be executed sitting, kneeling, or lying bent back onto the ground. "Sometimes she sat on the ground and executed the same movements [as standing] with a suppleness and ease that was astonishing" (Jomard 1822, 733). In describing Safiyya, Combes says, "Then she fell to her knees as if to try to seduce you, and her look was plaintive, her song passionate ... she danced in all her body" (1846, 1:221). Andreievsky watched a dancer who "knelt, and bending with suppleness or leaning backwards ... seemed to be imploring grace from the goddess of love, and these slow movements revealed all the soft voluptuousness of the Orient" (quoted in Volkoff 1972, 296). Kutchuk Hanem favored dramatic floor work: "Suddenly stooping, still muscularly moving, Kuchuk fell upon her knees, and writhed, with body, arms, and head upon the floor, still in measure—still clanking the castanets, and arose in the same manner" (Curtis 1856, 142).[4]

Leland (1874, 135–36) contributes a remarkable description, although here the choreography reverses, with the immobile section second. The dancer first moved about, with undulations. She then ran "waves of motion ... from head to foot" and, over these, other tiny waves. She then stopped, became stationary below the waist, and wove her upper body in rocking and swaying movements of "intense passion." She sent convulsive movements along the waist, arms, and head. She then became still, but, "the movement, passion and exertion are not less intense." She moved her breasts, at times only one breast, as if "vitality remained in them alone." At this point the dance changed again into a third section. She sank slowly almost to her knees, moved the lower part of the body "forward more and more with a vigorous quivering" and once every ten seconds starting a convulsion that became more and more frequent. She then "expired." Leland's account suggests that the traditional stationary-then-moving sequences might be reversed if the dancer chose a more personal take on the dance. She also ended by dying, a seldom noted choreographic touch.[5]

The dance did not progress from slow to fast only once in reaching its conclusion. Hackländer said it beautifully: "Now, they let their arms drop, and their whole frames seemed to collapse in utter exhaustion; then might you see how a new thought arose within them, and strove to express itself in impassioned gestures" (quoted in J. St. James 1845, 275). Clot Bey (1840, 2:92–93) wrote that the hip-work sections of the dance might alternate innumerable times between fast and slow without stopping. Prisse d'Avennes also noted the same recurrences, but did not identify if the different phases alternated between fast and slow. "Then they kneel as if overcome by the weight of these sensual pleasures, then rise to begin again new tricks and new pantomimes" (1930, 54).

Dauzats (Dumas [and Dauzats] 1846, 1:222–26) describes a lavish performance that included two additional choreographic features, floor patterns,[6] and the inclusion of a male clown. The clown entered, leading a line of four dancers singing as they approached the audience. The group then turned quickly on the spot, retreated from the audience with their backs to them, and formed two wings that advanced and crossed over each other in "ingenious figures" while they moved. "During this time they keep in their movements the simplest and most noble poses like ancient statues." At this point, the start of the dance proper, Dauzats becomes far less objective and his description less precise. Little by little the dance became more animated, movements became more "voluptuous." The male singers raised their voices and the dancers' gestures took on a "lascivious" character. The clown now mingled with the dancers, making obscene gestures. Finally, in keeping with the singing and the music, the clown and dancers arrived "at a paroxysm of the most vehement and unlicensed passion." Now the voices rose above the music, and dancers and clown engaged in a "bacchanalian struggle." Finally, panting and with their hair in disorder, dancers threw themselves into the laps of the (male) audience members. One can identify two sections to the choreography, the part before the clown joins the action, and after.

The clown figure was not unique to this party at Clot Bey's house, for other travelers noted his presence. Michaud described a performance in a humble setting where "a sort of fool who mingled with their dances, had shells on his head that he made follow the beat, and whose noise accompanied the orchestra" (1833–35, 5:87). Estourmel (1844, 2:453–54) writes of a private party in 1833, with four dancers, and a male clown who carried a candle in each hand and laughed and cried out during the dance. When a male performer would not be appropriate, a female might take over his role. At the royal wedding of 1845 the choreography one day involved five female dancers and the clown character played by a female dancer wearing a fool's cap who "cleverly enough imitated and ridiculed their gestures" (Lane-Poole 1846, 108). The number of examples of the clown figure overall indicate it an important choreographic element of the *Pure Dance*.[7] These male figures, with their comic gestures and sardonic commentary on the dancer, speak probably of non–Islamic roots in the *Pure Dance*. Indeed, as already mentioned, Clot Bey (1840, 2:93) spoke of this particular dance as "combined with Greek dance."

Love Duet

The *Love Duet* (and also *The Bee*) belongs within a widespread tradition of pantomime and play-acting where female dancers were not the sole practitioners. The travel literature contains incidental references to these activities. In the streets actors might be casual beggars or members of the Banu Sasan, while at weddings professional male actors would perform. Section three outlined scenarios of farces seen at royal weddings and the majority of plots seem to have been silly, chaotic, scurrilous, and totally appreciated by local Egyptian audiences of both sexes at all levels of society.[8]

Among early writers a few praise female performers for their skills of play-acting and pantomime, a special talent in addition to their dancing. Speaking of their "pantomime ballets" (1785, 1:150), Savary goes on to comment that "one is astonished at the mobility of the features where they easily assume expressions suitable to the roles they are playing.... The looks, the gestures, everything speaks, but in a manner so expressive that it is not possible to misunderstand" (1785, 1:151).

Speaking of female entertainers performing early in the 19th century at events in the great houses, de Montulé comments more explicitly, "Like the Italian *improvisatori*, they repeat extempore tales and songs which they accompany with the drum and the flute" (1821, 88). Taylor, too, writing of his trips in the

1820s, says, "Sometimes they play among themselves sorts of comedies, that, without being brilliantly inventive, have nevertheless the ability to charm" (1856, 265). There is some faint suggestion of this aspect of dancers' earlier repertoire in Hackländer's account of the private party he attended around 1840. At the end of the evening the entire party, dancers and guests, enacted tableaux from *The Thousand and One Nights* "which were frequently changed with prompt and orderly facility ... an old Copt recited passages from them, accompanied by music, in explanation of each scene" (quoted in J. St. John 1845, 276). This aspect of dancers' repertoire seems to have faded in importance as the 19th century progressed, or at least there is no available evidence to suggest they continued as actresses as well as dancers and musicians. These acting talents, however, lived on in the two dances called the *Love Duet* and *The Bee,* where they were essential.

Usually performed by two women, the *Love Duet* and its plot were first described in detail by Napoleon's Savants. On a tour of the Delta, Du Bois-Aymé and Jollois were invited to a wedding at the home of a leading citizen of Mahalla el-Kubra, and recorded their impressions:

> Those songs [of female entertainers in the upstairs apartments], accompanied by the tambourine and other Egyptian instruments, lasted for an hour and a half, when two a'lmeh came down into the court, where they performed the most lascivious dances: one of them imitated the man, the other the woman; and they enacted by overly expressive movements—to the eyes of Europeans—the attack of the lover, the resistance and the fall of the young girl; but the Orientals take a great pleasure in these faithful representations, and young people of both sexes watch them freely [1812, 109].

Villoteau (1809a, 694–97) was present at a performance of this dance and gives not only a detailed description but also his personal interpretation of meanings.[9] As explained in section seven, he also gives a unique record of how dancers used their finger cymbals in combination with the movements. Villoteau portrays what he calls both the "soul" and the "body" responding to the steady growth of amorous feelings as portrayed in the dance. The soul, depicted by the dancer's acting, goes through various stages, first simple joy followed by "uneasiness, then melancholy; worry and discontent came next; soon unrest spread through all the senses showing an impatient need to acquiesce." Finally, Villoteau says he saw "satisfaction ... one judges that desire was satiated." The dance did not end there, however. Satisfaction soon became shame; this feeling also faded. "Confidence was born again, and passion arose with even more strength than before." Movements in the dance were at first too slight ("innocent") to offend Villoteau. Gradually, however, movements became more sexually explicit, the body beginning to assume what Villoteau felt were highly immodest positions. "Drunkenness" and "spasms" marked the first climax of the performance. The dance would then continue as cycles of the same pantomime, he says, until the audience was satisfied, or perhaps the dancer was exhausted. He sums up his description of the dance as, "In a word, all the movements of that dance tend to express the combat of modesty against love, the triumph of the latter and the defeat of the former."

Chabrol (1822, 463) describes the same dance and adds important information—the use of a belt and the fact that the dance might be acted out by one dancer alone. He describes the dancer's lightly tied belt as the only defense she can offer against love. "She touches it lightly, seems to obey an irresistible force in dancing to the sound of the [musical] instruments." The belt is shaken loose by the dance movements and gradually becomes untied. "Then modesty, one moment overcome by passion, arises again; the protective scarf is knotted once more; the dance taken on again a more serious character, that then gives way to vivacious feelings which prey on the dancer." The same cycle repeats itself, with the "feeble band" coming loose again. Love conquers, however. The dancer "succumbs to her emotions; her movements slow, and she seems plunged into a delicious bliss." Jomard also describes similar movements, adding that a particular song with words accompanies the dance, "You who wish to enjoy pleasure: come, my friend, untie the fringes of your belt, and approach" (1822, 733).[10]

The same explicit choreography continued for a quarter of a century or more, for Prisse d'Avennes (1930, 54) describes much the same movements: "Often two women dance together; one imitates the pursuit of the man, the other the gentle resistance of the woman." The dance simulated "all the positions, all the movements, all the convulsions of pleasure." Prisse d'Avennes says one might see "sweet words, tender sighs, ardent kisses, rapport of their tongues, and swooning at the supreme moment." Other authors wrote similar accounts.[11]

The *Love Duet* seems to have developed less sexually explicit interpretations as the century progressed. The earlier version resolved sexual tension by simulated physical satisfaction. Later examples include a female and a "male" in situations of tension, but the newer choreography provides for an eventual dissipation of the built-up energy by other devices. They may be separated and waiting to meet, they may quarrel and reconcile, alone she may repent her actions, one may even "die" and have to be revived. The dance may finally only mime the words of a sung love text.

James St. John (1834, 110–13) describes in detail a version of the *Love Duet* he saw at a great coffee house in 1833. The dancer stands in the twilight at the door of her tent, waiting for her lover. She is "pensive, restless, tortured by doubts, by suspicion, by jealousy." The moon rises as she waits, and she begins to sing.

Finally, the lover (another female dancer) arrives, and now the dancer, despite her earlier eagerness, becomes coy and pushes him away. She "plays the coquette; retires while he pursues." Her eyes betray her, however, for her "feet and heart are running different ways." The dance continues to become more impassioned, her body manifests her feelings, she closes her eyes, she drops her head backward, she presses her arms against her chest. The dance reaches its climax in a "paroxysm of passion" but then the dancer repents. She becomes "melancholy, dejected, humiliated." St. John then indulges himself in some Victorian moralizing, in suggesting that she repents her sin and her lost home, and recalls her innocence, "when her soul was untainted." St. John's (1851, 3–4) later version of the same dance incident contains other details, particularly dealing with the eventual meeting of the two lovers. Musicians sound out the lover's arrival by horse. "Powerful emotions of delight, expressed by both her countenance and gestures, now shook her frame, and prepared you for the raptures of meeting." She now reproaches him, they quarrel, simulate a separation with indifference, but finally reconcile.

In Hackländer's (quoted in J. St. John 1845, 275) account around 1840, one sees another blander version of the *Love Duet* danced by two women at a private party, the third piece of the evening. The first dancer sinks slowly to the ground; as she descends her movements become faint, dying, and gentle. She suddenly falls on the carpet and lies in a graceful and attractive position. The second dancer grasps her around the waist, caresses her and tries to bring her to life, her face showing anguish and distraction. Slowly, the first dancer gains consciousness, raises herself slowly, becomes more and more vigorous with gestures increasing in definition. Both dancers then show their joy with lively dance movements that conclude the duet. Other travelers saw what is probably the *Love Duet* and were not offended by the version they witnessed—perhaps these, too, were a watered-down version. "The perfection consists of reproducing in dance all the gradations of love" (Taylor 1856, 264). "The two almés [Safiyya and her companion] ... pretended to be provoking each other to combats of love. Everything about them was in motion; their faces were animated and their attractive looks full of expression" (Combes 1846, 1:219).

Finally the *Love Duet* might consist only of miming the words to a love song, sung by the musician. "How I did long to transport the whole scene before your eyes—Ramadan warbling intense love songs, and beating on a tiny tambourine, while Zeyneb danced before him and gave the pantomime to his song" (Duff Gordon 1983, 380). In such versions, the old tension that gave the *Love Duet* its edge is long gone.

Even prior to the banning of female public street performances, the *Love Duet* seems to have been a dance performed also by young men, but examples of this version in the travel literature are few. Exceptionally, Denon (1973, 205) described Greek boys in Rosetta. He speaks disapprovingly of this dance, saying it progressed from "hedonistic pleasure" to "lasciviousness," augmented by the fact that the performers, being males, showed scenes that "love has reserved for the two sexes in the silence and mystery of the night." Around 1870, Leland saw a young man with a boy dressed as a girl, on the road to Cairo's river port. The performance, he says, was "immoral to a degree unknown, undreamed of anywhere in Europe for a thousand years or more in dramatic show" (1874, 66). This may have been a remnant of the *Love Duet* still alive.

The Bee

Clot Bey (1840, 2:93) singled out a disrobing dance called *The Bee* as one of three distinctive dances found in Egypt in his day, and his analysis suggests this dance had a longstanding local tradition. Prisse d'Avennes also had his opinion: "The civilization introduced by Méhémet-Ali has already made its influence felt in Egypt in repudiating this national dance that people of good manner no longer dare see" (1930, 57). Late in the century Montbard (18—, 8) was to judge *The Bee,* as performed in coffee houses of Upper Egypt in the 1880s, as a decadent dance—also implying it was an older dance on a decline. Some modern arguments support this point of view. The Egyptian writer Saad el-Khadem (1972, 60–68) sees *The Bee* of the 19th century as ancient, the descendant of a dance of Coptic Egypt and associated with the motif of death. He identifies both Egyptian and Greek elements in it. It is very tempting to cobble this information into a quasi-history, to ignore the intervening research-empty two thousand years, and declare *The Bee* to be the true and direct descendant of an ancient dance done on Egyptian soil, as does el-Khadem.

There are serious problems surrounding systematic study of this dance. First, no eye-witness account or any mention of this dance by name exists in the extant travel literature until the spring of 1830 when Dauzats attended a party in Abu Za'bal, near Cairo. This void is surprising if the dance had a long and established tradition. Second, all, but one, first-hand descriptions and references located to date are by authors writing in French. English travelers, even Lane, seem generally unaware of this dance.[12] This French connection is also a curious phenomenon for a dance supposedly of major and long-standing importance.

One might attempt a reverse argument, based on eye-witness and other French evidence, suggesting that this dance had been imported into Egypt at the time of greatly increased tourism just prior to 1830 as a tourist entertainment device.[13] It might even be possible to argue that the dance arrived in 19th-century Egypt from Iran, for a curious cousin of the dance still existed recently in 20th-century Iran as a game for women and executed by women in private. "*Murcheh dareh* (having ants) is an extremely erotic performance that involves a striptease and the seductive pretence of ants crawling over one's naked body" (Haery 1982, 154).

This "tourist" interpretation seems to lack a certain validity since one first-hand account provides reasonably strong evidence against it. *The Bee* was performed simultaneously before both Egyptian males and secluded females at a Muslim wedding in Cairo in 1836, to much approval by both sexes (Voilquin 1978, 377). Here the groom, a well-to-do middle-aged Turkish merchant, had recently set aside his first and obstreperous wife to marry a teenage girl. I find it improbable that such a man would be interested in the "latest foreign craze" for his wedding. This episode argues for the long establishment of the dance, but, unfortunately, is the only first-hand example involving the preferences of local Egyptian audiences identified thus far for this study.

The existence of male performers of *The Bee* also argues against this dance as titillating entertainment for male heterosexual European tourists. The Coptic cloths of the early Christian period show both boys and girls in action dancing and disrobing, and el–Khadem (1972, 60–68) concludes both young men and young women performed this dance at that time. There is some evidence from the 19th century, too, of a male presence. In Cairo, after seeing Hasan al–Bilbeissi's first performance, Flaubert (1965, 185) confidently says he will next arrange for the star to dance *The Bee* for him, although nothing apparently came of this wish. Later, in Aswan, Flaubert's guide Joseph[14] said his single previous viewing featured a male performer (1991, 353). Sailors seem to have been associated with this dance. Romer made some curious comments about one of her sailor's performance. With a long stick in his hand, he did "one of those extraordinary dances (in this country called *the wasp dance*) which used to be peculiar to the (now banished) Ghawazees, or dancing-girls of Cairo—evidently of the same origin as the Mosca, or Fly Dance, which I saw performed by the Gitanas of Granada" (1846, 1:117). She gives no other details, and it is unclear what the choreography might have included.

Although the history of this dance remains ambiguous there are good descriptions of the choreography in several fully developed variations. The pantomime-dance of *The Bee* begins with the drama of a dancer stung by this insect underneath her clothing. The choreography develops out of this first moment of pain, movements progressing from slow and peaceful to more and more frenzied. The dancer wants to make the insect stop its attack, so systematically removes one piece of clothing after another in search of the bee and its stinger. Usually the dancer reaches a final stage of nudity or near nudity, to the applause of the audience. Within this concept there might be many variations.

The Bee might be a solo, paired, or group dance. There might be a prelude setting the stage for the attack in a garden, or one with a flower featured as the home of the bee. There were various ways of acting out the pain of the sting, and the dancer might even seek solace from members of the audience. As well as disrobing, there might be re-robing, all carried out continuously with the music. Finally, the degrees of nudity varied.

Kutchuk Hanem danced *The Bee* as a solo (Flaubert 1991, 285). Dauzats (Dumas [and Dauzats] 1846, 1:227), Voilquin (1978, 377), Didier (1858, 52), and Blanc (1876, 139) also describe or imply solos. Marmont (1837–38, 3:314), however, writes of two dancers stung by bees, and Clot Bey (1840, 2:93) suggests that more than one dancer was involved in the choreography he saw. Prisse d'Avennes (1930, 55) and Colet (1879, 148–49) write of the dance involving a group, with one member stung and the others helping her to find the bee. Michaud implies the same for he writes that the distressed young woman "calls her companions" (1833–35, 5:257). Montbard (fig. 26) provides the only illustration of *The Bee;* his solo dancer performs with the energy and tension one might expect, but otherwise his illustration gives no confirmation of the written records.

From Dauzats's (Dumas [and Dauzats] 1846, 1:227–28) detailed eye-witness account one can see a fully developed concept of the peaceful garden in which the dancer "walks" (i.e., dances) prior to the arrival of the bee. She promenades to a calm musical accompaniment, picking flowers to make a bouquet. The words of the song describe butterflies, a nightingale, and a bright sun, images that she mimes word for word. Suddenly, she picks the fatal rose; the insect chases her. She shoos it away and continues with her plucking. It returns, this time on the attack. At this point in the dance, in her version, Voilquin (1978, 377) adds some details and describes a gentle approach of the bee towards the dancer, mistaking her for a flower, fanning her with its wings then stinging her. A separate dancer may have pantomimed the bee itself in this performance, though it is not clear. Colet (1879, 148) describes how the dancer imitates the humming of the bee at the point of being stung. After the sting the dancer would usually cry out, announcing the presence of the insect. "They cry and repeat constantly 'ah, the bee, ah, the bee'" (Marmont 1837–38, 3:314); others report the same.[15] When Kutchuk Hanem danced, however, it was Flaubert's guide Joseph who called out, while beating his hands (Flaubert 1991, 285).

Other versions showed considerable drama. Dauzats (Dumas [and Dauzats] 1846, 1:227–28) describes how the dancer has not been able to drive away the bee with her belt; she crosses her arms over her breast but the bee enters the front of her costume and is lost among the folds of the fabric. She tears off her clothes; she is nude, but the bee still attacks. She rolls on the ground in a frenzy of cries.

Colet (1879, 149–50) describes how Badawiyya of Isna and her four acolytes performed a tragedy, one that she compares to the story of Niobe with her dying children. Badawiyya believes her four children to be menaced by the bee; they dance about her, holding out their arms and tearfully crying for her help. They half open their shirts. She takes each of them in turn into her arms and sucks what she believes to be the sting on their breasts. The real bee, now furious, flies over Badawiyya's head, finally entering her clothes. She utters loud groans. The youngest of her children rushes to her, tears open her shirt, but too late. Badawiyya crosses her arms over her bared chest, turns her back on the audience, and drops dead.

Instead of concentrating on the drama of pain, the dance might emphasize other aspects of performance. Marmont (1837–38, 3:314–15) describes an impressive episode wherein two dancers disrobed under their large black silk coats that they opened and closed continuously, waving them "across the vision of the spectators." The dancers then dress under the silk coat, all the while dancing in unison. Blanc (1876, 139) also tells of a performance in which the dancer disrobed then dressed again in time to the music. In these two examples *The Bee* has more dance-like qualities. Prisse d'Avennes writes of another version that here emphasizes sexuality. The dancer remained more or less stationary while her companions removed her clothing, piece by piece, in search of the insect. The victim took "the most voluptuous poses, the most tantalizing attitudes" (1930, 55).

Male singers or musicians might enter the drama at critical moments. Dauzats (Dumas [and Dauzats] 1846, 1:228) writes that at the moment the chased bee returned, the musicians tried to rally the dancer, but when the bee attacked in a fury they laughed as the dancer tried to flee. Colet describes how Badawiyya's male singer and the musicians "enlivened the feet of the dancers" (1879, 149). Audience members, too, might become directly involved. Dauzats (Dumas [and Dauzats] 1846, 1:228) writes that suddenly, as if seeking a refuge, the dancer bounded onto the knees of one man, hiding her head and shoulders in his hair, and her body in his cloak. In Colet's (1879, 148) second version of this dance, the nude dancer approached the man who had thrown the most money at her so far, then flung herself into his arms.[16] The angry bee continued to buzz in her hair. Only her new savior could rescue her, and then only by pressing more pieces of money onto her forehead.

The final degree of nudity in *The Bee* might vary. Dauzats (Dumas [and Dauzats] 1846, 1:228) is most specific about the end point of the dance and the total nudity of the dancer. Voilquin is equally specific: "The last veil goes" (1978, 377). Prisse d'Avennes says, "Finally the last garment falls, to universal applause, and the completely nude dancer shows off her body to an assembly that ceaselessly demonstrates its admiration" (1930, 55). Flaubert makes it clear that, while dancing, Kutchuk Hanem disrobed down to a small scarf with which she hid herself, then throwing it away at the end (1991, 285). Other versions have only partial nudity. Marmont (1837–38, 3:314–15) describes undressed performers dancing under a large coat that they opened and closed while waving it in the faces of the audience. Other authors tell that dancers ended in a thin chemise. Clot Bey says dancers undressed to a light veil that they opened and closed, having "on their body only a light veil ... they dress again in time to the music" (1840, 2:93).

Ultimately, nudity may have depended on audience demand. Discussing *The Bee* generally, Michaud says, "In the end she will find herself quite undressed, if the spectators do not let up their demands" (1833–35, 5:257). The extent of nudity might have depended, too, on the dancer. Flaubert (1991, 285) suggests that Kutchuk Hanem did not care to do this dance, and, in fact, she seems to have done it without any spirit. Colet (1879, 148) says that, as a great artist, Badawiyya chose her own highly dramatic rendering of this dance, rather than the traditional nude version.

One may conjecture a good deal about *The Bee* as Egyptian entertainment at the time of the study. It was most likely true that it was judged suitable for private space only, unlike even the *Love Duet* that did take place in public venues. Didier (1858, 52) described the dance as popular with the Turks, but as somewhat "raw" was not one performed outdoors in public spaces, and all eye-witness examples in the literature discuss private indoor performances. This dance, however, seems to have been judged suitable for local audiences of all classes, a conclusion suggested by the example of the mixed audience at the wedding attended by Voilquin in 1836 (1978, 377).[17] Dauzats (Dumas [and Dauzats] 1846, 1:218–229) describes at length a party given by Clot Bey, Egypt's chief medical officer, for his French compatriots. At this society event the choreographic offerings included a particularly vivid rendition of *The Bee*.[18] The distinguished French diplomat Marmont (1837–38, 3:314–15) also saw this dance as a guest of Clot Bey.

26

Accessory Dances

Dances with Tambourine, Sword, Stick, Glass, Cup, and Pot

As the 19th century progressed, writers mention the *Love Duet* less and less in its explicit versions, and increase their descriptions of dances featuring some accessory. The large influx of talented young male Turkish performers, the ginks, could easily have brought these new dance techniques and stunts from Istanbul to Cairo around the 1830s, to be copied by both local khawals and female entertainers.[1]

An exception, a dance with a tambourine, was noted early in the travel literature, one described as having large leaping movements (Du Bois-Aymé and Jollois 1812, 110n). There exist two illustrations of this dance, one from the *Description de l'Égypte* (Taschen 1994, 741) and one by Forbin (fig. 24). In both, the dancer bounds with tambourine held high, and in these examples the tambourine appears more a dance accessory than a musical instrument. There are no known examples of this dance later than Forbin's 1819 illustration, and perhaps the dance went out of style.[2]

The sword dance, or dance with dagger or curved sword, seems to have been a men and women's folk dance of the Bedouin and Africans, later taken up by some professional female Egyptian dancers. Jean Marie Coutelle provides the first description of it from a festival he witnessed on his trip through Sinai during the Napoleonic campaigns. "The Arabs, on their feast day, don't seem more gay than normal. The young men only, with a sword or poignard in their hands, make movements, gestures, that roughly imitate combat" (1812, 301).[3]

Belzoni writes of an evening's feast he happened upon in a town south of Cairo. Here he witnessed a Bedouin dance with 30 men in a row singing, and, with one foot in front of the other, in perpetual motion on the spot. Two women with daggers ran towards the men and retreated, waving their daggers and fluttering their garments (1821, 143).[4] Both these early examples appear to be communal dances, not professional ones. Another non-professional version of the sword dance might be more realistic and less of a metaphor. Duff Gordon describes an after-dinner entertainment with local Egyptian dignitaries and visitors in Luxor. Two of the male guests demonstrated the sword dance with large straight swords and round shields. "One dances a *pas seul* of challenge and defiance with prodigious leaps and pirouettes and Hah! Hahs! Then the other comes and a grand fight ensues.... It really was heroic.... Attitudes were alike grand and graceful" (1983, 224).

The literature of the 1850s and later begin to describe professional female dancers engaged in a sword dance. Gerard de Nerval (1929, 1:11) writes of a Nubian troupe outdoors in a courtyard at a Cairo wedding. Male Nubian dancers moved backward and forward, led by a veiled woman with a curved saber in her hand, "threatening" the dancers and running away from them in turn. Nerval does not indicate whether the female dancer was Nubian or not.

A fully developed sword dance may have presented too many challenges to be widely popular among professional Egyptian dancers. While in Khartoum, however, Didier witnessed an extraordinary performance. The circle of spectators sat so dangerously close to the dancer as to feel her costume as she whirled. Sometimes she swung the sword over her head, while sometimes she stabbed it into the ground. The dancer "exerted much agility and even more suppleness: for the movements of the feet, arms, the whole body, had to combine, to work together ... so to speak, to harmonize without effort, without being strained" (Didier 1858, 51). The dancer had to be both flamboyant and careful of her audience. Didier describes how he receives a cut on his finger from the sword coming too close. After the dance the frantic dancer was officially pardoned for her serious transgression, one that might have caused her considerable retribution had Didier not passed off the incident as trivial.

The talented Badawiyya chose a sword dance for her signature piece at the official performance in Qena in 1869. Both Blanc and Colet saw and described her dance, though each chose to stress different aspects of the choreography. In Blanc's (1876, 137–39) version, she entered with two bare swords held against her hips like the handles of a moving vase. She crossed the swords behind her back and performed a hip shimmy. She then put one of the swords on her head and danced with it suspended there. Finally, she placed the swords near her eyes, and held them there while still dancing.[5] Next, a Bedouin youth lay on the carpet, his arms tight to his side. She moved around him menacingly, with her flying robes in erotic gestures. The young man bent his knees as a seat for her, and putting the swords against her cheeks, she circled about, dragging the young man with her.[6]

Colet's (1879, 150–51) version, supposedly of the same performance, varies from Blanc's account in her choice of details, for example she omits any mention of the male colleague. In Colet's version Badawiyya took two curved swords, raised them crossed above her head, thus framing it with steel. She rose on her feet and shot out a fiery glance. Meanwhile, a musician played a military march, and the vocalist sang of combat. She leaped, shaking the spears in time to the music and "their vibrant clicking sounds like the defiance of a duel to the death" (151). Her arms came down and she put aside one of the sabers. Next, she performed a warlike dance step: "She mimes the drunkenness of war and the joy of triumph" (ibid.). As she waved the saber its flashing light echoed the sparkling of her jewels. She placed the sword on her hip, in a gesture that Colet found reminiscent of the Amazons. Gérôme (fig. 15) chose to paint a moment where Badawiyya, sword on her head, rises to a half-toe and moves forwards in a hip shimmy. She extends one sword point down to the ground; her left arm rests on her hip, making a right angle. The illustration shows some of the details described by both Blanc and Colet. The sword dance did continue after Badawiyya's time as a choreographic offering in Upper Egypt, for Montbard (18—, 8) mentioned it briefly in his later description of Isna. He, however, complained of the low standards of performance.

It is "common knowledge" among modern Western belly dance lovers that contemporary use of a hooked wooden cane by professional Egyptian female dancers began in imitation of an ancient male tradition of a combat dance with staves. Such a dance still exists in the male folk repertoire (Salah 1979, 240). Perhaps there had been a longstanding female folk dance tradition using a stick or cane, but evidence does not exist in the travel literature or elsewhere (for example, in Saleh). Late in the century, an 1880 illustration by Montbard (18—, 257) does show a veiled Egyptian peasant woman and unveiled young girl holding short sticks in front of them in a kind of stationary dance. The woman bends forwards slightly; the girl thrusts her stick to the ground.

Some accounts show that, in the later 19th century, professional dancers did use a stick to create an accessory dance. At Enani Bey's dinner party in 1869, Blanc wrote of a *Dance of the Egg*[7] that featured not an egg but a rod, a dance he described as graceful, artistic, and daring. The dancer "performed, kneeling on a carpet and leaning on a baton, a type of dance, 'the dance of the egg.' ... There is a part of the dance in which the dancer, leaning languorously upon the baton, which she holds in front of her, suddenly sinks down and covers her face with her kerchief" (1876, 52). Gérôme, who most likely would have been present at this party, has among the corpus of his works one of a standing dancer leaning on a five-foot stick (Ackerman 1986, cat. no. 336). Another, a later 19th-century picture, also shows a dance with a cane. One of the two lively dancers holds a three-foot stick in both hands, with arms high over her head (Buonaventura 1990, 39). Writing at the end of the study period, Leland makes the passing comment that "sometimes a stick is used in these performances" (1874, 137).

Toward the middle of the 19th century, travelers began to describe dances with a glass, cup, or pot as a featured accessory. Hackländer's (quoted in J. St. James 1845, 275) evening with its series of dances included one with a glass full of rosewater. The dancer placed the glass between her teeth and moved about rapidly (in a repetition of the *Pure Dance* she had done just previously) without spilling a drop. She then grasped one of the men in the audience around the waist, bent backward still dancing, and finally rose to pour the rosewater over his clothes. She then dropped the glass, kissed her damp partner, and bounded back into the center of the room. Kutchuk Hanem, too, performed such a dance. She placed a cup of coffee (this would have been the small local kind, one without handles) on the floor, danced before it, sank onto her knees before it while play-

Fig. 27. Alfred-Henri Darjou. *La Danse de la Gargoulette* (Pot Dance). 1869 (from Florian Pharaon, *Le Caire et la Haute Egypte* [Paris: E. Dentu, 1872]. Princeton University Library).

ing the finger cymbals, bent her head lower and lower, then, grasping the edge of the cup in her teeth, rose suddenly with a bound (Flaubert, 1991 286).

Leland gives two different versions of cup dancing in the Girga area, around 1870. The choreography of the first is highly suggestive of the *Love Duet* in a representative version. Mentioned briefly in section seven, Leland's vivid account is worth repeating here in full:

> Placing a cup, symbolic of temptation, on the ground, she danced around it ... turning the body and sinking low with great grace and exquisite art. The cup appeared to exercise a terrible fascination, but she seemed afraid to drain it. Five times, without aid from her arms, she almost lay on the ground with her thirsty lips just dallying with the edge, and then rising, swept in dance, and thrilled, and shivered, and turned, and sank again. The sixth time she had completed a circle, and no longer able to resist, she approached the cup with throbs and pauses, and then, without using her hand, lifted it from the ground with her lips alone, draining it as she rose, and the tragedy of temptation being over, merrily danced about the room in quick step, with her head thrown back, holding the cup all the time in her mouth [1874, 136].

Leland reports on a second version (that he did not see, but a companion did) in which dancers made cups run from the head down the side of the face, along the arms and back (ibid., 136).

Leland (ibid., 136) also describes a pot dance in which two performers placed a vase on their heads and danced alternately for long periods without letting it drop. Such an event appears in a representation by the French artist Alfred-Henri Darjou (fig. 27). A sole female dances on a rug in what appears to be a rural coffee shop with sides wide open to greenery and views of the Nile. The artist included the usual onlookers, such as smokers, chess players, a coffee attendant, and musicians. The dancer is well captured with her downward gaze, her graceful swaying body nonetheless deeply concentrated on keeping the pot aloft. The Egyptian author el-Khadem (1972, fig. 81) considered this image suitable to reproduce in his book on Egyptian folk dance, and it is indeed attractive with its air of authenticity.

Epilogue

General Comments

Western dance enthusiasts would find it inconceivable that early ballet had fallen into total oblivion, that the names and works of dance greats of past centuries were now unknown. Western enthusiasts expect to find on library shelves such works as Cyril W. Beaumont's *Complete Book of Ballets* describing choreographers and dancers who made these works come alive on the European stage for over 100 years. It is in this same spirit that this project adds to the wider process of locating Egypt's past professional entertainment scene as a testament to its vitality, and a salute to those who maintained its traditions. While attempting to keep something of the flavor of the original travel accounts, this book has made an effort to downplay their romantic and derogatory aspects, with the goal of revealing accurate aspects of an entertainment culture previously buried or obscured under the weight of the travel report. Above all, this book tries to acknowledge those distant Egyptian female entertainers as professionals in the performance arts. The book has not glossed over nor minimized the difficulties of their life situations, situations that often led to them using their bodies in ways other than in the performance of their arts. The book does not glorify their performances, but tries to depict them accurately. It does not see entertainers as victims, however, though financial conditions were certainly hard enough. Female entertainers are not presented as anomalies, but as part of a larger group of women of the working class going about their lives as active agents, doing their best, and then retiring to another kind of life. In a sense, such accounts presage faintly the vivid stories of modest performers in Nieuwkerk's modern accounts.

There are aspects of the dance not addressed in the travel literature, and therefore not possible to include in this book. Missing almost completely are the voices of the dancers themselves and their native Egyptian audiences. They could have supplied considerable data about the guilds, could have resolved confusion of terms for dancers discussed in section two, could have explained the subtleties of the ban on public dancing, added information about training and recruitment, about how dancers lived day to day, would have had interesting things to say about the meanings of the choreographies as presented in different settings. They certainly would have talked about issues not even suspected by foreign travelers. But we do not have their voices, except (occasionally) indirectly speaking through the words of outsiders.

It is important to remember that regardless of whether the Middle Eastern dance form studied here was subject to some forms of cultural misinterpretation and manipulation through the texts and illustrations of foreign viewers between 1760 and 1870, the actual dance itself as it existed in Egypt retained its own character and agenda. There has been no information to suggest that foreign influences had any significant impact whatsoever on dance performances, that travelers had changed the actual dance into their own image of it. The real dance remained in Egypt, living, and growing, and eventually evolving within its own criteria.

Changes to the Dance Tradition and the Guilds

In the Egypt of the study period, professional female dancers kept their arts alive often under great difficulties, able to hand down a dancing tradition that has survived until the present. This book has shown them bending (for example, under the bans of the 14th and 17th centuries) and then flourishing when times were more generous, for example after the Ottoman occupation of 1517 when these new rulers took a completely different approach to supervising guilds of female performers. At that time female public dancers successfully found the vitality to capture an excellent new type of performance opportunity in the new coffee houses. On the other hand, one senses, although it is impossible at this time to prove, that the late–18th century was the final hurrah for a long performance tradition in Egypt, that the 19th century was only a holding period in the arts out of which a newer tradition reemerged in 20th-century Egypt.

Some of the evidence presented suggests these 19th-century changes. The literature hinted that upper-class entertainers had served as actresses as well as dancers and musicians, but that this part of their repertoire was fading even by the end of the 18th century. The *Love Duet* was undergoing some self-censorship, as shown in later versions of the choreography, and perhaps it melded with the *Pure Dance,* eventually to become one single piece. Certainly one cannot see this dance today. One cannot see *The Bee* today, either. Further research on the late–19th century will certainly locate the most recent instances before these dances disappeared completely from the Egyptian scene. The *Pure Dance* continued without substantial modifications, but the figure of the buffoon did not survive. While the tambourine dance was an 18th-century offering not evident later, other accessory dances, with cups, sticks, and swords, seem to have appeared around the middle of the 19th century in professional dance. The trend continued into the 20th century, and dances included even candelabra and chairs. On the other hand, the corpus of body movements underlying the various dances seem to have continued intact over this period, leaving one to wonder just how old they may have been. These movements, probably identical to those of modern times, appear always to have defined the female Egyptian dancer. In this sense, the dance has come down intact for generations, for dancers were always free to repackage these movements into new offerings that pleased their clientele more.

There is no coherent suggestion in the travel literature that the tripartite guild structure, so clearly identified in the Napoleonic period, continued as such into the later 19th century. Under Muhammad Ali, the stability and function of all the guilds gradually declined, and those of female entertainers seem to have undergone the same kind of changes. On the other hand, it is interesting to see some female entertainers (not really classifiable as to a particular guild) singled out in the tax records of the 1820s and 1830s. Obviously at this point in time they possessed some kind of officially recognized group identity, although the implications remain obscure.

One can usually locate clearly the guild of female singers of the 1801 list in the later travel literature as a separate group if not necessarily as a designated formal corporation. It is clear that great singers continued to enjoy much of the same renown and reward they had for centuries, but one senses (with no large body of evidence) a steady decline in the standards of earlier centuries in the entry requirements for this profession. It has been difficult to identify later examples of the raqqâsîn at work with total assurance, but it is obvious that certain female dancers still retained their professional standing in Cairo long after a ban applied forcefully onto street dancers, and prostitutes. Whether or not Corporation 200 continued to exist in any version of its Napoleonic form, it evidently continued to impact on certain female dancers who could claim membership in a more approved professional grouping, even up to 1869, the end of the study period. During the reign of Muhammad Ali, the guild of ghawâzî evolved otherwise, exemplified significantly by the life of Badawiyya. Despite her outstanding professional reputation she had not been called to Cairo during the Suez celebrations of 1869, but was obliged to await the foreign guests in her hometown. Such cavalier treatment of a fine artist highlights the shadow cast over this corporation by Muhammad Ali's dynasty.

The Concept of "Meaning" in Professional Egyptian Dance

As pointed out in the introduction, one can usually access insider knowledge when dealing with present practices, but in the case of the past, one often works with limited materials. Dance is not a universal language, its text easily explained, and when dealing with the dance traditions of another culture one needs local interpreters. It is here, at the level of meaning that the travel literature has fallen short. Western observers may have watched with a keen eye and recorded accurately but have not left a significant body of information about how Egyptians themselves felt about the professional dance, what place the dance had in their personal lives, and how the dance fitted into their culture. It is possible, however, to try to access meaning indirectly, through an examination of the numerous contexts in which this dance took place, and for that the travel record includes some data.

What This Dance Is Not

At the risk of seeming simplistic, before looking at possible meanings for this professional dance tradition, it is important to look at what the dance is *not*, to see what cultural practices this dance was not associated with, what situations it did not take meaning from during the study period. First, this dance did not take place at funerals, nor at activities associated with death. It was not a dance of group solidarity, nor one associated with cultural mourning for past nationalistic glories. It was neither a dance celebrating harvests or planting, nor one demonstrating feats of strength and martial abilities. It certainly was not a dance connected to spiritual practices. Although dancers, as did other public entertainers, took advantage of certain recurring Islamic religious events to perform in public spaces, the dance itself had no impact on the religious ceremonies, and drew no meaning from them, but rather serving the secular side of these events.

Contexts Giving Meaning to This Dance: Occasions of Joy

All examples from the travel literature show that this dance took place within situations of joyful celebration, that pleasure and happiness were its basic connotations, its *raison d'être*. Yet there were limits to its applicability. As related, Duff Gordon provides a short but telling anecdote in this respect on her dinner and day's visit spent with a Muslim friend and his family. She reports that the planned dance component of the visit had been canceled, for "he had meant to make a dance-fantasia, but as I had not good news it was countermanded" (1983, 48). Bayle St. John, too, provides the information that his landlady's planned fantasia had to wait out her year of mourning for her husband. Obviously, this Egyptian dance was meant to be part of an already-happy celebration, not meant to reverse a sad one.

As we have seen, travelers often wrote about the public side of dance, since before the ban these occasions were easily accessed. Major communal events, such as the days-long celebrations of the birth of the Prophet Muhammad, the Tanta fair during the festival of Saint Badawi, the cutting of the dike during the Nile flood celebrations, the departure of the official pilgrimage to Mecca—all were situations involving, for ordinary people, a release from mundane activities and a time simply to enjoy life. Dance was seen as one factor contributing to the success of such events, and, as Lane even pointed out, the absence of the dancers would make a festival "less merry than it used to be" (1978, 449). The concept of associating dance legitimately with hospitality seems to have been stretched to include the coffee house performance, for numerous descriptions exist in the literature. Again, these would be situations of the enjoyment of leisure time with one's companions, in a sense the public face of private sociability. Finally, the Egyptian custom of welcome for the traveler manifested itself in dance performances in Nile-side towns where boat traffic brought both many local Egyptians and foreign visitors passing from one place to another.

Professional dance accompanied private dance events, organized within major life milestones of a celebratory nature, particularly weddings, and the occasion of a birth. Even simpler situations, such as release from a problem (for example, St. John's description of exemption from military service), might justify a private party with dance. Hospitable welcome for traveling acquaintances also served as an important context, for hospitality often included dance, a situation where other local friends and dignitaries might be invited to take advantage of the circumstances.

Contexts Giving Meaning to the Dance: Public Space Versus Private Space

Modern discussions have made much of the separation of the sexes while watching dance in Egypt, men watching in public space and women in private space, suggesting this dichotomy provides meaning though which one can understand the dance better. Evidence from the travel literature shows a more complex reality for the late–18th and early–19th centuries, and while men and women had certain distinctive viewing patterns (men composed the clientele at coffee houses; some classes of women held entertainments in the harem), these did not necessarily translate into such a clear ideal pattern as public and private dance spaces. Ordinary Egyptian women had access, alongside men, to watch dance in public spaces during the secular aspects of great religious observances and saints' days (e.g., examples given by Champollion, Lane, Bartlett, Duff Gordon). Certain instances of Muslim weddings have shown that both men and women together sometimes watched the same performances (examples given by Belzoni, Michaud). Non-Muslim groups in particular did not separate the sexes for entertainments in private households (examples given by Estourmel, Hackländer in James St. John, Bayle St. John). One cannot, then, use the variable "space" to provide a meaning for this dance; the dance did not define itself through its performance locale in that different spaces indicated a separate kind of dance.

Contexts Giving Meaning to the Dance: Gender-Specific Performances or Class-Specific Performances?

Can the idea of gender provide meaning, for example an assignment of certain dancers to perform for women exclusively and others for men? While such arguments have been cogently argued for this custom at the beginning of the 20th century in Egypt (for example, Zuhur 1998), evidence from the travel literature suggests otherwise for the late 18th and early 19th centuries. Two compelling incidents, described previously in this book, show the same dancers performing for both men and women in separated quarters. Voilquin describes women at a wedding, watching from the harem grill the dancer below performing for the male guests. Didier describes dancers performing for men outdoors, then passing into the harem to dance for women. It appears that in the Egypt of this period professional dance had significance for both sexes equally, not deriving meaning as a woman's dance performed by a woman's dancer, and a man's dance performed by another type of performer.

If the gender-specific audience is of less relevance in the context of the study period, do other types of audience add to an understanding of meaning? Chapter 1 argued for the existence of two identifiable types of dancers, the ghawâzî and the raqqâsîn, with the latter clearly more privileged. I argued that it was the variable of class that differentiated these two types of dancers, with the raqqâsîn performing for the wealthy, and the ghawâzî for more ordinary viewers. The type of audience, then, gave meaning to the dancer and to her performance, with more esteem and social approval accorded to those with more respectable audiences, in a sense leading almost to the concept of two types of dance, one more of an art form than the other.

Contexts Giving Meaning: Men Dancing, Dressed as Women

Lane made the point that even pre-ban devout Egyptians often hired males in preference to females when seeking dance entertainments. One needs to ask, then, if the two sexes were totally congruent in meaning and function at all times in the Egypt of this period. Could men and boy dancers carry out completely all the meanings and functions of this dance? Unfortunately, the travel literature maintains a total silence on this question and one is constrained to limited eye-witness evidence. Certainly the ginks and khawals performed in identical situations, such as at coffee houses, in public festivals, at weddings, and even at private parties. They also seem to have danced the same dances. Here there appear to be no differences, and it seems Egyptians in general were prepared to consider male dancers equivalent to female.

The modern dance theorist, however, might wish to probe more deeply. Significantly, the ginks and khawals "pretended" to be women; that is, they dressed as females, and affected feminine mannerisms. Men and boys danced, but only through disguising their bodies as the other. In this regard, male dancers paid indirect homage to the key importance of female performance to the underlying meaning of this dance. It is impossible to know how Egyptians of the time would explain the custom of the male transvestite; however, a modern dance theorist would conclude that, in this Islamic context, at this period in Egypt, in this particular dance, male dancers and female dancers did not really convey the same meanings as they performed. The hiring of males by devout Egyptians might be taken as an indication that they wished to remove the stain of actual femaleness from the dance itself while still maintaining its essential illusion.

Contexts Giving Meaning to the Dance: The Broader Cultural Context

The dance ban of 1833 discussed shows vividly the relationship of this dance and its practitioners to Egyptian society; that is, the meaning accorded it within the context of cultural practices. The ban proved that while female public dancers provided a much-appreciated element in the secular side of public events, certain elements among them were dispensable. The question remains whether it was the dance itself or women judged disposable. Was dance itself too important in the popular imagination to do away with entirely? The Egyptian authorities were quite prepared to allow public dance to continue after the ban in the persons of male practitioners, so it appears they accepted the necessity of dance performance itself, not wishing to alienate the common people who expected these entertainments as a matter of course. This dance obviously had meaning as a popular Egyptian cultural practice among the masses.

After the 1833 ban, female professional dance was particularly vulnerable among the wealthy, who had never been compelled either to hire female dancers, or maintain a dance culture for their own pleasure. The continuing presence of professional dance among them, as attested by examples in the travel literature, indicates a general acceptance of the dancers' art by those who set societal standards. In other words, professional female dance enjoyed continuing widespread acceptance as part of Egypt's cultural landscape. Those who could, continued to avail themselves of such entertainments.

The 1869 Suez Canal official celebrations, calculated to impress visiting foreign dignitaries with Egypt's modernity and links to Europe, provide a particularly telling view on the status of dance and dancers within the later Egyptian context of the day. Egyptian authorities resurrected female public dance and promoted it as worthy of foreign eyes, providing no less than three official performances during the Nile tour in Upper Egypt. Still, it appears that the ban on public dancers continued in force, implying a callous disregard for the dancers themselves. Considering the importance of the engineering triumph of the Suez Canal to Egypt's reputation, one marvels that professional female dance was associated with it at all. In an indirect manner, Egyptian officials seem to have acknowledged that this dance performed by these artists was not an inappropriate means of manifesting Egyptian culture, while at the same time inadvertently demonstrating dance's lowly place within it.

Meanings East and West: Sexuality, Costume, Dance Myths

Meanings can change and grow over time, and the adoption of this dance form, by the West and beyond, in the 20th century has resulted in a reassessment of certain aspects of it by its new practitioners. Meanings have been reconfigured from their Egyptian past into new searches for underlying messages—in the areas of sexuality, dress, and explanatory myths—largely in a search for respect and respectability.

From my reconstructions of the *Love Duet* and *The Bee* presented in this book, one understands that these dances manifested a high degree of explicit eroticism. As discussed at length in Chapter 8, it was this quality that particularly offended Western observers, while, as shown in the eye-witness reports, Egyptian audiences of both sexes seem to have appreciated the quality and applauded its expression. As a result, certain European travel writers could deplore the "depravity" of Egyptian viewers, and suggest that Egyptian women should be barred from watching at all. Times change and, as discussed above, Egyptian performances seem to have expressed the quality of sexuality in more muted forms as the 19th century progressed. Explicit expressions can hardly be found today, as, in both East and West, belly dance performances clearly avoid extremes of this earlier meaning, implying it is deemed inappropriate to a modern aesthetic.

Ironically, in the West, theorists are giving greater room to the implications of how sexuality and dance may intersect. Jane C. Desmond believes that dance provides a particularly fertile ground for the study of the sexuality of the body, and equally the opposite, that sexuality might become a topic at the center of legitimate dance theory. She writes:

> With its linkage to sex, sexiness, and sexuality, dance provides a dense and fecund field for investigating how sexualities are inscribed, learned, rendered, and continually resignified through bodily actions. Analyzing dance can help us understand how sexuality is literally inhabited, embodied, and experienced. It can open the way to the new area of investigation ... a kinesthetics of sexuality [2001, 7].

Suddenly, belly dancing's past sexiness becomes not so shocking, no longer a subject for ridicule and dismissal, but offers a window into some interesting analyses. In particular, this avenue may shed some light on why such a dance, both in the past, and today, ruffled the feathers of many European viewers but remained a subject for their constant attention and comment. In this regard, Karayanni's recent writings on foreigners' attitudes to Egyptian male and female dancing bodies (in the past and in recent times), and their resulting anxieties, are a particularly welcome new theoretical contribution. Perhaps as a result of such work, eventually the practice of modern belly dance may reclaim tones of this aspect of its earlier meanings.

Meaning of the Dance Costume

For Egyptians of the 18th and early–19th centuries, the female dancer's costume simply identified her as an entertainer. Further, a rich, elaborate dress meant she was successful at her trade, possessing money enough to attire herself in silks, and adorn herself with gold ornaments. Now, new meanings have been read backward into the dance costume. Modern opinion tends to credit the present (almost universal) belly dance costume as originating in Hollywood's imagination then reimported to the Middle East, and into Egypt specifically, one more example of successful cultural imperialism. Modern feminists point out the important concept that imperial and religious ideological battles are often fought over the idea and control of women's bodies. In this context, the Eastern dancer is deemed to wear a Western-derived costume, one invented as a parody of Eastern opulence and decadence, one now imposed by the powerful cultural imperialism of the West on the less-powerful East. In this paradigm, the Eastern dancer's modern costume can be seen as one more of so many defeats. But is it?

As I described it, in the bare costume worn for approximately 20 years around 1850, all the elements of 20th-century costume exist. In artists' renditions of that period, one finds: a heavy waist belt as a major feature, with metal ornaments that swing with the movements; bareness of the top of the body; semibared breasts; the costume covering legs but not necessarily waist; a swinging skirt revealing parts of the legs; bare feet; a profusion of gold and silver ornaments, long hair, and well-defined eyes. Finally, it is only a short step from dancers' 19th-century vest to the modern brassiere concept. Bareness seems to have been curtailed in later decades of 19th-century Egypt, and more modest dance outfits appeared. When dress norms allowed more visible flesh, however, the bare style was ready to reassert itself in the 20th century.

This costume history shows most elements of the present-day costume were originally innately Egyptian, not imported concepts. Rather, the reverse is true, the idea of such a costume probably went from East to West, before returning home in a true example of the cross-fertilization of ideas. What underlies the present discussion of origins is, again, the concept of women's bodies. At the time of this study, Western opinion (particularly in the 19th century) deemed women of the East as decadent and amoral (seen particularly in female dancers), while their own women were modest and seemly. Now, Eastern opinion often casts Western women as decadent, and insists on the modesty of their own. Within this continuing (often bitter) exchange, it is difficult to deal with topics of such sensitivity in an impartial manner, and my suggestions as to the indigenous origins of the belly dance costume may not be welcomed by either East or West.

Meanings of the Dance Today: A Question of Perspectives and Methodology

Section six took on an important task: to identify Western myths about Egyptian dancers (as written in the travel literature), to evaluate these stories as sources of history, and, to a certain extent, to see if these Western perspectives endure in modern discourses about Egyptian dancers of the 18th and 19th centuries. During this examination, it became clear that past notions continue to adulterate Western writings of the present. Specifically, there remain lingering traces of 19th-century visions of "The Orient," as three examples show. First, modern writers seem far more intrigued than the travel literature with myths such as the "massacre of the four hundred." This story is in the process of becoming one more almost-unstoppable misinterpretation of Egyptian dance history as lurid happenings. Second, while attention has been showered on Kutchuk Hanem as the prototype of the Oriental dancer, very little attention has been paid to her contemporaries, the other dancers of Egypt, unique individuals with real professional careers. This deficiency, this "one dancer is all dancers," stems directly from the familiar and unfortunate Orientalist approach. Third, in modern popular beliefs in the Roma (gypsy) domination of Egyptian dance in the 18th and 19th centuries, contrary to negative evidence, one finds another intractable dance myth in the making. Here dance cannot simply be itself, but must have some element of mystery, an esoteric cachet.

Two new agendas have also made their mark, from the critics of cultural imperialism and the modern demands of certain feminist discourses. The story of the "missing 'awâlim," for example, appeared only once in the travel literature (during the Napoleonic period) and never reappeared there. Modern attention gives the story far more importance and credibility than it originally had as a travel piece. One suspects that the story fits well with the idea of female empowerment, the idea that certain women with personal presence were able to withstand the might of the French invaders. This idea of specialness may also lie in modern efforts to clearly differentiate two types of dancers and elevate one, one with a less reprehensible and more acceptable lifestyle to today's belly dance enthusiasts.

Within modern discussions of cultural imperialism, the 1833 ban on public dancers often becomes yet one more example of unfortunate foreign influence on indigenous culture. Yet this conclusion has been based on only the one example of a dance ban, ignoring the fact that there were other instances in earlier centuries. Further, this particular ban on dance also has meaning within the wider context of official disapproval of other sorts of popular entertainments. While foreigners tended to see the ban only from their own perspectives, then and today, evidence shows the 1833 ban, like those before it, arose from purely internal Egyptian motives. While cultural imperialism was, and continues to be, pernicious, one needs to be careful in the use of the concept as an explanatory device.

The developing field of dance history in the Middle East, then, needs to be mindful of its methodologies. In researching the past, one must pay particular attention to what is likely myth and what is likely fact (or approximate fact). This is not to say that dance myths are not important; they are, but they are unsatisfactory history, revealing more about those writing them than about their subject matter. Myths need to be untwined from history, honored as likely stories, and laid aside when appropriate. Further, since researchers continue to come from the West in numbers, the imposing of Western agendas on the data becomes all the more likely. The two approaches identified here, a Western feminist perspective and the deploring of cultural imperialism, will not ultimately end in a rich and complex body of knowledge about dance across the Middle East. One waits impatiently for new topics by emerging researchers, particularly those from the countries in question.

Appendix One: Biographical Facts About Selected 18th- and Early 19th-Century Travel Writers and Artists

Appleton, Thomas Gold. American. Traveled to Egypt in 1874–75 and produced a mundane travel account interspersed with useful comments on dance. He illustrated his own work.

Bartlett, William Henry. British. Traveled to Egypt in 1845. A topographical artist and world traveler, known in North America for his illustrations of Canadian cities and landscapes.

Baurenseind, Georg Wilhelm. German. Artist. (See Niebuhr.)

Belliard. (See Napoleonic expedition.)

Belzoni, Giovanni Battista. Italian/British. Lived in Egypt 1815–19. Came to Egypt to interest Muhammad Ali in a hydraulics project, but remained to work as a collector of antiquities, some eventually destined for the British Museum. His best-selling book and his exhibit in Piccadilly inspired an early wave of Egyptomania across Britain.

Bida, Alexandre. French. An artist famous for his black-and-white illustrations for Shakespeare, Molière, the Gospels and the poetry of de Musset. Bida made four trips to the Middle East and included visits to Egypt in two of them, in 1850 and 1861. He published *Souvenirs d'Egypte* (around 1855) with E. Barbot, from which the two lithographs (figs. 21a, 21b) in this book are taken.

Blanc, Charles. French. Traveled to Egypt in late 1869 as a delegate to the Suez Canal opening ceremonies. An art critic, he remarked on dancers and dance with a practiced eye, particularly on Badawiyya of Qena.

Browne, William George. British. Traveled to Central Africa, Egypt and Syria from 1792 to 1798.

Burkhardt, John Lewis. Swiss. Traveled to many areas of the Middle East and Africa (with extensive travel in Egypt) from 1812 to 1817. Burkhardt is the first known European to visit Mecca. He died in Egypt in 1817, and is buried in Cairo under an Arabic name.

Chabrol. (See Napoleonic expedition.)

Champollion, Jean-François. French. Traveled to Egypt in 1828. Famous for his brilliant decipherment of the Rosetta stone, an important key to ancient Egyptian writing and history, Champollion took this first trip to Egypt both for business and pleasure. He participated in three dance parties, two with female performers and one with male performers. The young artist Nestor L'Hôte accompanied him.

Clot, Antoine-Barthélemy. French. As Muhammad Ali's surgeon in chief, Clot-Bey (as he was known in Egypt) lived in Egypt from 1823 to 1860. His two-volume work on Egypt, published in 1840, covers extensive topics about this country, and is probably reliable in most respects when it deals with dance and dancers, a subject he covered in some detail.

Colet, Louise. French. Traveled to Egypt in 1869 as a member of the French delegation to the Suez Canal opening ceremonies. A journalist, she is best remembered today as the mistress of Gustave Flaubert, the famous novelist. Colet provides an excellent description of Badawiyya of Qena.

Combes, Edmond. French. He traveled to Egypt, Nubia, and the Red Sea from 1833 to 1835. Perhaps he later served as France's vice-consul in Egypt. His account is important for its eye-witness description of the renowned Safiyya's performance in Isna in early 1834, but the book is not widely remembered today.

Coutelle. (See Napoleonic expedition.)

Curtis, George William. American. Traveled to Egypt in 1849–50. Editor at *Harper's* magazine and Harper and Brothers publishing house. His eye-witness description of his visit to the famous dancer Kutchuk Hanem has continued to keep his rather extravagant writing in the public eye (among belly dance enthusiasts anyway) to this day.

Darjou, Alfred-Henri. French. Artist who specialized in genre and cartoons. He made one trip to Egypt for the Suez Canal ceremonies in 1869, when *La Danse de la Gargoulette* (fig. 27) was done. The image exists both as a black-and-white book illustration, and as an oil painting held in a private collection.

Dauzats, Adrien. French. Traveled to Egypt in 1830. An artist, he was a member of the company of the diplomat Baron Taylor on his second visit to Egypt. Dauzats included an excellent account of dance witnessed as a guest of Clot Bey in his book describing his visit (also see Dumas, Alexandre).

Denon, Vivant-Dominique. French. An interesting figure with a career as scholar, courtier, collector, and adventurer, who managed to survive and thrive politically before, during, and after the French Revolution. He took part in the Napoleonic expedition to Egypt of 1798 to 1801. After returning to France, he rushed into print, in 1802, his own beautiful book on the Napoleonic campaign with many of his drawings of modern and ancient Egypt, preempting the later publications by the Savants. He included a costume image of a dancer of Alexandria (fig. 5), but gives credit to "Citizen Rigo" for the original sketch.

Didier, Charles. Swiss. Traveled to Egypt, the Red Sea area, and Nubia in the fall, winter, and spring of 1853–54. Didier created three books from his one trip. A mediocre travel writer on the whole, but genuinely interested in people, Didier describes entertainers, and actual music and dance performances, with meticulous care and thoughtful insights.

Du Bois-Aymé. (See Napoleonic expedition.)

Duff Gordon, Lady Lucie. British. Lived in Egypt from 1862 to 1869. Already famous for her *Letters from the Cape,* Duff Gordon settled in Luxor for her health. She learned Arabic, immersed herself in the local community, and took a caring interest in the people of Egypt at all levels. She died there. Her books still generate interest and have been reprinted today.

Dumas, Alexandre *père*. (See also Adrien Dauzats.) French. The famous novelist never set foot in Egypt, but somehow managed to have later editions of Adrien Dauzats' journal of his trip there published under his own name.

Dutertre, André. French. This artist took part in Napoleon's Egypt campaign of 1798 and became a member of the Institut d'Égypte. His skill lay in portraiture, and he drew 184 portraits of the officers and scholars of the expedition, which are still appreciated today. Most likely, therefore, the image *Almés ou danseuses publiques* (fig. 9) represents actual women. He is also the source for the dancers of Plates C, Plate LL (1; 5) and Plate MM (3) of the great *Description de l'Égypte*.

Flaubert, Gustave. French. Traveled to Egypt in the fall, winter, and spring of 1849–50. Several years prior to his fame as a novelist, Flaubert accompanied his friend Maxime Du Camp, who was traveling on behalf of the French government (copying paintings and inscriptions, and taking photographs). Flaubert is noted and discussed today in belly dance circles for his details on two visits to the famous dancer Kutchuk Hanem in Isna. The information, however, remained unpublished during his lifetime.

Forbin, Louis Nicolas Phillippe Auguste, comte de. French. Traveled to Egypt in 1818. His book includes a magnificent illustration (fig. 24) of a leaping dancer with a tambourine.

Fromentin, Eugène. French. A highly respected artist, he traveled to Egypt in 1869 as an accredited member of the French delegation for the Suez Canal opening ceremonies. He turned his artist's eye on the three official dance performances he saw. His reactions are recorded as short but insightful travel notes. He is the probable source for Figure 19.

Galland. (See Napoleonic expedition.)

Gérôme, Jean Léon. French. An artist famous and respected during the 19th century for his Oriental images, he traveled to Egypt in 1856, 1862, 1868, 1869, and 1881. Gérôme produced 17 paintings of Egyptian dancers (mostly at rest), with two of these well known today in dance circles, the *Dance of the Almeh* (fig. 25) and a sword dancer (fig. 15), the latter in two versions.

Hackländer, S. W. German. Traveled to the Middle East in 1840–41. His full account of a dance evening is reprinted in James St. John's 1845 volume. The description is important for its detail of an entire evening, and a complete set of four choreographies making up a dance program.

Hamont, P.N. French. Lived in Egypt from 1828 to 1842. A veterinary surgeon, Hamont not only reported directly to Muhammad Ali, but also traveled throughout Egypt dealing with problems in the field. His two-volume description of Egypt of his day is often unflattering to the administration. He had things to say about dancers and their relations to society, and these statements seem reasonably accurate.

al-Jabarti, Shaikh 'Abd al–Rahman. Renowned Egyptian chronicler who witnessed the Napoleonic invasions and, as a respected local notable, served on Napoleon's advisory council. He died early in Muhammad Ali's reign.

Jollois. (See Napoleonic expedition.)

Jomard. (See Napoleonic expedition.)

Lane, Edward William. British. A major figure, Lane lived in Egypt during three periods, from 1825 to 1828, from 1833 to 1835, and from 1842 to 1849. He first went to Egypt for his health, but soon found his life's direction there. His famous *Manners and Customs of the Modern Egyptians* appeared first in 1836—its focus on "modern" Egypt rather than its antiquities was unusual at the time. Lane's translation of *The Thousand and One Nights* next appeared in 1839–41. He then embarked on his major work, his classical *Arabic-English Lexicon,* for which he returned to Egypt in 1842. He died in 1876 before completing this work. His *Manners and Customs* continued to be reprinted, the classic edition being the fifth, printed in 1860. It was widely read (and heavily plagiarized) by his European contemporaries.

Lane-Poole, Sophia. British. The sister of Edward Lane, she and her children traveled with him to Egypt in 1842 and remained there during his stay. She worked directly with her brother in the preparation of her own book of letters from Cairo (he edited and approved the contents). Her chapter on wedding festivities in the royal harem in 1845 is extraordinary for its details.

Larrey. (See Napoleonic expedition.)

Leland, Charles. British. Traveled to Egypt in the early 1870s. His book reflects throughout his notion of European superiority but he was a keen observer and outstanding recorder of the dances he witnessed.

Lenoir, Paul. French. Traveled to Egypt in 1868 (and 1881). As a young artist, Lenoir accompanied Gérôme on the 1868 trip that included a stop in the Faiyûm area. Here Lenoir saw and described Hasna in a fine performance. His book contains sketches by Gérôme (fig. 13), including two female portraits.

L'Hôte. (See Champollion.)

Marmont, Auguste Frédéric Louis Viesse de, Duc de Raguse. French. A member of the French Napoleonic expedition (1798–1801), Marmont had a distinguished career, later serving as governor of Dalmatia. He returned to Egypt on a diplomatic mission in the fall of 1834 and was entertained by Clot Bey with an evening of dance.

Mayer, Luigi (Ludwig). Italian. Traveled throughout the Ottoman Empire from 1792 to 1796 with Robert Ainslie, British ambassador to Constantinople. He illustrated about a hundred scenes in Egypt, including two of dancers and their dance troupe (fig. 3). Mayer appears to have been an artist careful with details, and love of Egypt's people and countryside.

Mayr, Heinrich von. Bavarian? Served as court painter to Herzogs Maximilian, Duke of Bavaria. He accompanied the duke when his entourage toured Egypt in 1838. He recorded Egypt in almost cartoon-like paintings, including the scene of a troupe of dancers at Asyût (fig. 8).

Michaud, Joseph F. French. Traveled to Egypt in 1830–31. Rather than travel exclusively on the Nile, Michaud wandered in other areas, asking thoughtful questions along the way, and behaving more as a journalist than a tourist. He wrote his book as a series of sequential letters to a friend.

Minutoli, Wolfradine (von der Schulenburg) von Watzdorf, freiherrn von. German. Visited Egypt from 1820 to 1822. She and her husband traveled extensively, meeting with all the intelligensia. Her account of a dance entertainment in a harem is one of a few such eye-witness accounts.

Montbard, Georges (Charles Auguste Loyes) French. An illustrator and caricaturist who lived in exile in England, he wrote and extensively illustrated a book on his trip to Egypt of around 1880 (see Figure 26).

Napoleonic expedition. French. Napoleon arrived in Egypt with both an army and a group of scientists. The occupation (1798 to 1801) generated an enormous amount of literature on Egypt, both from the military men (e.g., Belliard, Denon, Larrey) and the scholars (e.g., Chabrol, Coutelle, du Bois-Aymé, Galland, Jollois, Jomard, Redouté, Villoteau). In particular, this group of scholars contributed separate essays to the great *Description de l'Égypte*, published by the French government over 15 years. This publication contained engravings showing dancers at rest and in performance, including two reproduced here, figures 6 and 9.

Nerval, Gérard de. French. Traveled to Egypt in 1843. The famous writer is reliable for only three witnessed performances, one with dancing boys, one a wedding procession at night, and one of a Sufi religious celebration. All three are outstanding for detail and quality of observation. The rest of his dance information he most certainly borrowed from Lane.

Niebuhr, Carsten. German. Sent by Frederick V of Denmark, Niebuhr headed a scientific voyage across Egypt to the Red Sea, with Bombay, India, as its final destination. He spent some months in Cairo in 1761, where he saw female public dancers. The artist of the expedition, Georg Wilhelm Baurenseind, drew them in performance (fig. 2). Baurenseind died during the voyage and cannot be the source for the final version of his original sketch.

Pococke, Richard. English (later Bishop of Meath). Having traveled in Egypt from 1737 to 1738, he produced an outstanding source for information of all types on the country of that period. His line illustration (fig. 1) of the public dancer and her female drummer is the oldest known illustration of female dancers by a European artist.

Prisse d'Avennes, Émile. French. Lived in Egypt from 1829 to 1844, and 1858 to 1860 (dates estimated). A draughtsman, he served in the Egyptian army. He then embarked on a career as an archaeologist, and popularizer of Middle Eastern culture in Europe. His drawings and publications described five thousand years of Egyptian arts. He never received adequate public recognition in France for his work. His short essay on Egyptian dancers seems overblown, but surely he was in a position to understand his subject. His lithograph of dancers (fig. 18) is well known today and still available to collectors.

Rifaud, Jean-Jaques. French. Artist. The young Rifaud was seized by the spirit of Egyptomania that was growing in Paris by 1805, but his army career kept him from visiting the country until 1814. He worked under the French consul Drovetti, collecting antiquities to be sent to the Louvre. In Egypt, he made extensive drawings in the fields of botany, zoology, and mineralogy. He returned to France in 1827 and spent much of his later life trying to get his material published. A 1998 retrospective in Belgium recognized him as an important figure. His dancers appear in Figures 4 and 11.

Roberts, David. Scottish. Artist. Traveled to Egypt in 1838–39. Roberts's lithographs of all aspects of the Egyptian scene have continued to be popular with collectors, but today he is receiving renewed acknowledgment for his artistic talents. His well-known illustration (fig. 16) of a Cairo dance performance came about by accident; Roberts was invited to a party by a casual acquaintance who was staying briefly in the city. Roberts kept a travel diary, which remains unpublished.

Romer, Isabella Frances. British. Traveled to Egypt in 1845–46. A popular writer of her day, Romer carried much cultural baggage with her on her visit, but did manage to include some important dance information, such as a description of Safiyya of Isna and one of a displaced ghawâzî, in private employment.

St. John, Bayle. British. Son of James St. John. He lived two years in Alexandria, Egypt (1846 and 1847), and later traveled on the Nile from 1850–51. During his first stay, St. John learned Arabic and mixed mostly with young local Egyptians. His amusing stories contain rich social commentaries. His later trip also generated good dance material, including an account of the popular Hasna of Qena.

St. John, James. British. Father of Bayle St. John. He traveled in the fall, winter, and spring of 1832 and 1833. St. John's major encounter with public dancers took place at a large coffee house just outside Cairo, and there are three versions of this event. He rehashed his first book in a later edition that included material from other authors. He also wrote the plate captions for Prisse d'Avennes' lithographs in the *Oriental Album* that included the latter's well-known dance image (fig. 18).

Savary, Claude Étienne. French. He lived in Egypt from 1775(?) to 1779. Savary produced his material on Egypt as a series of letters commissioned by the French court. His is often described as the romantic view of Egypt, compared to the more rationalist one of Constantin Volney. When writing about female singing and dancing, Savary lists and praises the talents of those who performed for the wealthy. He is the first known European to speak of a dancer as an individual by providing a name (Badawiyya of Samannûd) and some biographical information.

Stanhope, Hester Lucy. British (sister of William Pitt). She dashed in and out of Cairo and Alexandria in 1812. Her book is actually narrated by her physician (Charles Meryon), who formed part of her entourage. Stanhope went on to an almost-unbelievable expatriate career in Lebanon.

Sonnini de Manoncourt, Charles Nicolas Sigisbert. French. He traveled from 1777 to 1778 throughout Egypt, south to Aswan. His interests lay in the fauna and flora. He despised the street dancers, yet wrote a considerable amount of useful information about them; he also managed to record a few accurate comments about dance steps. His scientific skills made him a good observer.

Testas, Willem de Famars. Dutch. The only Dutch Orientalist painter, Testas was distantly related to the French artist Émile Prisse d'Avennes and traveled with him in Egypt from 1858 to 1860. He helped the latter in the preparation of his published works. He later went to Egypt in 1868 with the Gérôme expedition. Presumably, it was then that he produced his *Egyptische danseres in een tent* (fig. 14).

Villoteau, Guillaume. French. He went to Egypt as one of Napoleon's scholars (1798 to 1801). A talented musicologist, Villoteau produced a long treatise in the *Description de l'Égypte* on Egyptian music, song texts, and musical instruments, as well as a chapter on dance and its practitioners. (See also Napoleonic expedition.)

Voilquin, Suzanne. French. She lived in Egypt (mainly Cairo) for two years, from 1834 to 1836, as a member of a St. Simoneon group. She eventually went to Russia. She witnessed a wedding's dance entertainment for male guests from the window of a harem, providing a unique account. Reprinted today, her memoir is often part of women's studies.

Volney, Constantin François Chassboeuf. French. He traveled to Egypt briefly in 1783 and was confined to Cairo because of warfare among the Mamluks; he left shortly for Syria. His few unflattering remarks about the dancing girls and his invaluable definition are found in the Syrian section of his book. He is often contrasted as the French rationalist, compared to Savary's romanticism.

Wilkinson, John Gardner. British. He spent 12 consecutive years in Egypt, from 1821 to 1833. He left for health reasons but visited many times subsequently. He is known as one of the first and greatest archaeologists of Egypt. His *Modern Egypt* (1843), basically a guidebook of essential facts for travelers, was once widely quoted.

Appendix Two: Travelers' Terms for Female Entertainers: Selected Passages by Date of Travel

1743–45 Pococke, Richard. "Other women who go barefaced about the streets, dancing, singing and playing on some instrument" (1743–45, 1:192, margin note); "Dancing women of Egypt" (caption to pl. 59).

1761 Niebuhr, Carsten. "Dancing women." (n. d., 134); "Public dancing girls" (ibid., 136); "Dancing girls ... dance for hire either in places of public resort, or in private houses upon festive occasions. Those dancers are called ... at Cairo, Ghasie" (ibid., 139).

1777–79 Savary, Claude Étienne. [At Fuwa] "Women of pleasure ... execute songs and dances of the country" (1785, 1:67); [in Cairo] "[Female] singers [at the public baths] ... dance and sing voluptuous songs" (ibid., 131); [in Cairo] "Egypt ... has its improvizers. They are called almé savantes.... They dance in a manner completely different from ours" (ibid., 149/50); [in Cairo] "The ordinary people have their almé. These are girls of the second class" (ibid., 155); [at Tanta] "The most famous courtesans of Egypt ... display their talents for dance, song and galantry" (ibid., 282); [in Lower Egypt] "A [female] dancer who was amusing the assembly, bounded before us" (ibid., 297).

1779 Sonnini, Charles Sigisbert. "Dancing girls ... come to tender their services [at the coffee house]" (1779, 1:248); "There were dancing girls [performing in the canal bed at Cairo]" (ibid., 2:322); "We were entertained with poets and [female] dancers equally devoted to the worship of Venus [at a coffee house]" (ibid., 3:282).

1783–85 Volney, Constantin François. "Those who carry out this profession [dance] are called *raouâzi*, and those who excel take the title *almé*, or expert in the art" (1959, 392).

1792–98 Browne, William George. "The dancing girls form a distinct class" (1806, 90); "Female singers who frequently accompany their voices with an instrument" (ibid., 92); "The last [to perform] are the female dancers or ghawasie" (ibid., 92).

1798 Mayer, Luigi. "Foua ... celebrated for the female singers and dancers educated there, who made it their profession to travel about, and exhibit their skill at public festivals" (1801, 45).

1798–1801 Villoteau, Guillaume. "The a'ouâlem are the professional [female] singers and dancers. It appears there are two sorts: one group who behave decently ... the other appears at all the festivals" (1809a, 1:694); "The second type of a'ouâlem ... are the public dancers ... one distinguishes these by the name of ghaouâzy" (ibid., 695).

1798–1801 Galland, Antoine. "We have here the 'alméhs' or wise women, who ... go into homes to entertain with songs and lascivious dances and other like activities: these are the 'alméhs' of the first class.... But there are others, of an inferior class ... who frequent the streets" (1804, 2:24).

1803 (?) Hume, Dr. "At Alexandria there were very few dancing girls" (1818, 400).

1812 Stanhope, Hester Lucy. "Not knowing how to pass the evening we resolved to send for the dancing women" (1983, 1:163).

1812–17 Burkhardt, John Lewis. "When the singing women perform in Egypt they collect money from all the persons present" (1984, 155); In Egypt, "Individuals are found belonging to a tribe of prostitutes called Ghazye ... or in the plural Ghowázy" (ibid., 173); "They are generally, but not always, dancers and singers" (ibid., 175).

1815–19 Belzoni, Giovanni Battista. "Lights I frequently saw through the windows of the seraglio ... the ladies were at such times amusing themselves in some way or other.... Dancing women are often brought to divert them" (1821, 14); [At an outdoor wedding] "The entertainment began with dancing, by two well-known and distinguished performers" (ibid., 18).

1817–18 Forbin, Louis Nicolas. "*Almeh* ... executing dances of a lively nature" (1819, 82) [A footnote explains that almeh means "public female dancers."]; "I watched the Arab Ghaouâzy dance. The *almeh* of that wandering tribe are the most supple and the most delightful" (ibid., 94).

1818–19 Montulé, Éduard de. "I have frequently met the Almeks in the course of my journey; these women wander about Egypt and for money perform lascivious dances.... These singers are but of the second order, whereas there some at Cairo and other great cities, who only appear in the palaces, and upon festivals on solemn occasions" (1821, 88).

1821 Minutoli, Wolfradine. "A dance, executed in this country only by a privileged caste of females, called gavanaki in Egypt, and halme among the Turks" (1827, 198); "Those who sing are called halme, in the plural, halvalem. They enjoy a better reputation, and are more esteemed than dancers" (ibid., 199n).

1823 Carne, John. [at a society wedding in Damietta] "A number of Almeh girls commenced their voluptuous dance to the noise of the tambour and castanets" (1826, 73); "There are at Cairo a superior sort of Almeh girls, who are sent for by the ladies, and amuse them with dancing, singing and music" (ibid., 165).

1828 Champollion, Jean-François. "The captain of the *Athyr*, who profited from our stay in town to spend his time with the Alméh" (c. 1986, 54); [on the riverbank at the village of Nadir] "Three clowns or farce players, followed by two Alméh (or 'filles savantes')" (ibid., 67); "The principal [female] singer, named Nefisséh.... Some of the passages of these Alméh resembled very much our old French airs" (ibid., 78); "I had six Alméh or *wise girls* (and very wise) come, who danced and sang from six until two in the morning" (ibid., 89).

1828 Taylor, Isidore Justin. "Most travellers confound the ghawazy with the almées; according to others, the almées were uniquely singers. We who have visited the Orient twice, we are convinced that the almées both sing and dance" (1856, 264–65).

1830 Michaud, Joseph F. [in a coffee house at Nadir] "Several young women were dancing" (1833–35, 5:87); [referring to the fair at Tanta] "Reed tents filled with courtesans and almés" (ibid., 5:89); [near the pyramids] "Troops of almées from the village of Abousir" (ibid., 5:307); [in Cairo] "There is a café where almées and jugglers usually gather" (ibid., 5:251); [at Clot Bey's dinner] "Next several companies of almées came, for there is hardly a fête without almées in this country" (ibid., 6:84); "Song writers who write songs for the almées for solemn occasions" (ibid., 6:301); "Damietta also has its almées, but they do not appear in public places; often the rich give concerts to which they call the female singers ['cantatrices']" (ibid., 6:358).

1832–33 St. John, James. "Among the most interesting and remarkable spectacles in the modern capital of Egypt, are the performances of the almé ... the 'dance of the almé,' is the opera of the Orientals" (1834, 1:105); [at a coffee house just outside Cairo] "The principal almé now prepared to dance" (ibid., 1:108). Of the same performance he later writes: "The principal Ghazeeyeh now prepared to dance" (1845, 269). Again, later, he writes: "During my first residence in Cairo, I paid a visit to the village of Shaarah, inhabited chiefly by Ghawazi and Awalim, or singing girls" (1851, 4).

1833 Estourmel, Joseph. "He proposed to me that I accompany him to the home of the drogoman of the Austrian consul to see dance the preeminent Almées of Cairo" (1844, 2:453).

1834–36 Voilquin, Suzanne. [at a wedding] "It was in these circumstances and in that place I was given the chance to see for the first time the almées, or wise girls ['filles savantes']; the most elegant among these priestesses of debauchery, able to go, so they told me, into the harems of Turkish women, whom they taught passionate songs and romantic stories; they also recounted marvellous Persian and Arab tales" (1978, 376).

1840 Clot Bey [Clot, Antoine Barthélemy]. (Note: Clot Bey lived in Egypt from around 1823 to 1860; I have dated his information here with the publication date of his book.); [with respect to the fair at Tanta] "Clowns, 'filles de joie,' [female] dancers, wandering [male] musicians, come" (1840, 1:200); "Women arrange to have visits by female singers [chanteuses] and almées" (ibid., 1:333); "The dancers of the country, the almées" (ibid., 2:42); "These romances are sung by the almées at public and private festivities" (ibid., 2:74); "Egyptians have their [female] singers named *aoualem* and in the singular *almée;* a word that Europeans apply improperly to all the dancers" (ibid., 2:86); "The *gaouasys* (this is the name of the public dancers)" (ibid., 2:90n); "The almées are generally young and pretty women.... They dance in groups of two or four" (ibid., 2:91–92).

1843 Wilkinson, Sir Gardner. "Here [Qena] many of the *Almeh* women reside, who have been forbidden to dance at Cairo" (1843, 2:128); "Esné has become the place of exile for all the *Almehs* and other women of Cairo, who offend against the rules of the police, or shock the prejudices of the *Ulemas*. The learning of these *'learned women'* has long ceased; their poetry has sunk into absurd songs; their dancing would degrade even the *motus Ionicos* of antiquity; and their title *Almeh* has been changed to the less respectable name of *Ghowázee,* or women of the Memlooks" (ibid., 2:268).

1846 St. John, Bayle. "She announced her readiness to give a regular Levantine soirée—of which 'the Awalim' were to form the principal attractions. One of the most authoritative writers on Egyptian manners particularly insists on the fact that the Awalim (Sing. Almeh) are not dancers, but singers, and points out that most Egyptian travellers have fallen into a mistake by confounding them with the Ghawazee, or regular tribe of dancers. It is true that an Almeh depends principally on her voice; but her feet, or rather her hips, form also a part of her stock in trade. Possibly, since the banishment of the Ghawazee, their unpersecuted sisters have inherited their accomplishments. At any rate, when I asked to see the dancing girls, Sitt Madoula instantly referred me to 'the Awalim'" (1850, 146).

1850 Flaubert, Gustave. "That evening we returned to Kutchuk-Hanem's—there were four danseuses and chanteuses/Almées/ (the word almée means wise, blue-stocking. As one would say whore which goes to prove Monsieur that in all countries women of education !!!....)" (1965, 244).

1850 Curtis, George William. "The Howadji entered the bower of the Ghazeeyah" (1856, 130); "Kushuk Hanem entered her bower" (ibid., 132).

1851 St. John, Bayle. [in the Delta] "A colony of Ghawazees, or dancing-girls, was here established" (1973, 1:23); "Kalah, the Jewish Almeh, whom I knew in Alexandria, once told me a curious story" (ibid., 1:27) "We returned, therefore, towards the boat, despairing of seeing.... Hosneh-et-Taweelee ... the principal Ghawazees had all been pressed that night into the service of the Bouluk" (1973, 2:69).

1853–54 Didier, Charles. [in Cairo] "The almées, in Arabic *a'ouâlem*, that is *wise*, had been included in the ban, the dancers that is, for the singers as one will see later had found favour with the son [Abbas] and the mother" (1860, 331); [with reference to Ghazal] "One will realize that I had discovered an almée, and one of the most well-rounded almée, singing well, dancing better, and superior to those one calls Ghâwazi, an Arabic word of which the two Greek terms Laïs or Phryné would be the most exact translation" (ibid., 336); [in Khartoum] "The almées, *a'ouâlem*, or dancers, in Egypt form a separate caste" (1858, 48); "We had also several times in the morning visits from the almées we had seen dance the night before.... they shared our bachelor luncheon" (ibid., 86); "From morning to evening, and almost from evening to morning, the celebrations of which the almées were the key. Sometimes, it is true, but rarely, they exhibited in the interior of the harem, and for the women exclusively" (ibid., 101).

1862–68 Duff Gordon, Lady Lucie. [at a concert with Sakna in Cairo] "The eight younger Halmeh (i.e., learned women, which the English call Almeh and think is an improper word) were ugly and screeched" (1983, 20); [in 1864, in Qena] "I was glad to see the dancing-girls" (ibid., 99); [in 1866] "I saw one of the poor dancing girls the other day (there are three in Luxor), and she told me how cruel the new tax on them is" (ibid., 322); [in 1868] "On Christmas day I was at Esneh ... I made fantasia and had the girls to dance. Zeneb and Hillaleah claim to be my own special *Ghazawee*.... Nothing is so antique as the *Ghazawee*—the real dancing girls" (ibid., 380) [Note: This is the only time Duff Gordon uses this term—she consistently uses "dancing girls"—and here she transposes the z and the w].

1869 Blanc, Charles. [in Cairo] "Little by little, made bold by the music ... the almées moved, they took more lascivious positions" (1876, 32); [at Asyût] "The almées had been requisitioned to amuse us with their dances by torchlight" (ibid., 112); "The *ghawasies*, the dancers of popular festivals, were sent to Qéneh, which has become, par excellence, the city for dancers of this type, who are not at all of the same status as those almées received in the harems. But it happens that the *ghawasies* have more talent than the dancers of Cairo" (ibid., 137); "Isna, like Qéneh, is a place assigned to the almées, or rather the *ghawasies*" (ibid., 239); [with respect to the ancient murals at Beni Hassan] "The same, absolutely the same [movements] of the spectacle given by the almées of Cairo and by the *ghawasies* of Qéneh" (ibid., 276).

Chapter Notes

Chapter 1

1. Fraser 1991. This was my master's research at York University, Toronto, Canada.
2. Deagon is talking about an Egyptian dance history of the far more distant past than I deal with; however, the principles are the same.
3. The field of women's studies has accepted that since women are so seldom included in texts, whatever exists must at least be given serious consideration as allowable evidence.

> The roles of women in agriculture, health, crafts, religion, politics, the arts, and other areas have often been regarded as negligible, exceptional, and infrequent or irretrievable for other than the very recent period. However, far more is available than one may think; much of it lies hidden in non-obvious sources: oral testimony, mythology, life histories, genealogies, religious records, *missionary and explorer accounts* [emphasis mine], archaeological excavations, language, legal codes, land tenure arrangements, oral and written literature, or cultural lore and fables [Johnson-Odim and Strobel 1999, xxxi].

4. Saleh (1979, 128) considers belly dance as an ethnic dance of Egypt. She lists four contemporary local names for this dance: *raqs misri, raqs baladi, raqs sharqi, raqs arabi.*
5. Brooks's article includes seven useful questions for historians:

> How can I approach a document to "let it read itself" to me? How can I hear what a document is telling me? What sorts of questions yield which sorts of answers? How critical is the role of language in penetrating meanings of documents we encounter? What is the role of visual imagery (iconography) in understanding verbal documentation? How does the researcher determine the contextualization necessary for bringing the document to life? How can the historian translate the document's meaning into a perspective understandable to the contemporary reader? [2001, 5].

6. The following example (intentionally chosen from a different period of study) points out that even scorn, error, and misconception can offer much to dance history. The Christian rhetorician Arnobius, writing about the Greek and Roman pagans of his day, asks if God had sent human beings into the world so that they should

> swell out their cheeks in blowing the flute; that they should take the lead in singing impure songs, and raising the loud din of the castanets, by which another crowd should be led in their wantonness to abandon themselves to clumsy motions, to dance and sing, form rings of dancers, and finally raising their haunches and hips, float along with a tremulous motion of the loins? [Davies 1984, 20].

This virulent criticism gives good information about dance in Numidia (roughly modern Tunisia/North Africa) in the 4th century—the instruments accompanying singing, choreography of the rings, and, finally, an exceptionally vivid movement description.

7. I do not imply there has been no portrayal of female entertainers in Arab literature. For example, in her *Arab Social Life in the Middle Ages*, Shirley Guthrie describes a female professional singer from the 13th century,

along with her manuscript picture (1995, 171–77; pl. 18).

8. Henni-Chebra's article discusses Egypt from the late–19th century to the present.

Chapter 2

1. "Man of religion whose function as scholar, teacher and doctor of the law of Islam conferred considerable prestige and authority" (al–Sayyid Marsot 1994, 285).

2. These children came from outside the Islamic regions, usually from the Euro-Asian steppes to the north, or from the Caucasus area. Young female slaves had similar origins; they often married into the same Mamluk households. These young Mamluks would not normally know either Arabic or Turkish on arriving in Egypt. Turkish had been a widespread language of the military across the Middle East for many centuries and continued to be the preferred first language in Egypt. The young slaves did learn enough Arabic to enable them to perform their religious duties, for they became Muslim upon entering a household.

3. Often, promising young men would marry the master's daughter and inherit his money and military power.

4. Napoleon's secret and sudden departure from Egypt in the summer of 1799 raises many unanswered questions. He gave several cogent reasons for his returning to France, virtually alone, but he did, in effect, abandon his troops.

5. Muhammad Ali's dynasty did not end until the overthrow of King Farouk in 1952.

Chapter 3

1. All translations from French sources are my own.

2. As one base line for examining foreign presence in Egypt, Clot Bey gives the numbers of foreigners residing there in the 1830s and 1840s: Italians, 2,000; Maltese, 1,000; French, 700 to 800; English, 80 to 100; Austrian, 60 to 100; Russian, 20 to 30; Spanish, 15 to 20; Swiss, Belgian, Dutch, Prussian, Swedish and Danish, 100. Obviously, the French were not the most numerous. He gives the number of Turks at 12,000, Egyptian Muslims at 2,600,000, and Copts at 150,000 (1840, 1:167).

3. The artist died while the expedition was in the Red Sea region. Others must have worked his sketches into their final published version, and the Baroque-like figures watching the dancers are surely added to the original record.

4. Rifaud's large collection of pictures was not published until many years after his return to Europe, and he remained obscure.

5. Lane originally trained as a draftsman in London before going to Egypt.

6. Brandin's *Almée, danseuse au Caire* (fig. 22) of the same period also manifests this feeling.

7. I have estimated these dates from various sets of information, none absolutely authoritative.

8. Gérôme traveled to Egypt in 1856, 1862, 1868, 1869, and 1881. His 1869 trip resulted in the painting of the saber dance (fig. 15). *Dance of the Almeh* (fig. 25) might have been the result of either the 1856 or 1862 trip.

9. The prolific French author Alexandre Dumas *père* is credited as a co-author of Dauzats's book, and Dumas's name alone appears on later editions. Dumas, however, never traveled to Egypt.

10. Badly sabotaged in her aspirations for a medical career in Egypt, Voilquin left Cairo for France, eventually residing in Russia. Today, her reprinted memoir is often included in women's studies.

11. Du Camp copied paintings and inscriptions and took photographs of the monuments from one end of Egypt to another during late 1849 to the spring of 1850.

12. Biographies of all dance artists mentioned by name throughout the book appear in Chapter 6.

13. Hamont appears in Auriant's 1943 bibliography; however, his material has not been utilized in more recent works.

14. Prisse d'Avennes's lithograph is entitled *Ghawazi or dancing girls (Rosetta)*.

15. For example, Karayanni (2004) concentrates on Flaubert in his exposition of Kutchuk Hanem's dance, and accords far less importance to Curtis.

16. Aradoon, Buonaventura (1989), and Nieuwkerk cite him, for example.

17. Didier is listed in both Aradoon and Auriant, but these references have not brought him much later notice. In any event, neither author cites Didier's book on his Nile trip, *Cinq cents lieues sur le Nil*, a work full of dance information.

18. Colet and Duff Gordon did not, although Duff Gordon was uneasy with the dance in her first letters.

Chapter 4

1. Section six, dealing with choreography, identifies one dance with a local name, *The Bee*. This was a specific dance with a storyline, however.

2. The Wehr dictionary (1994, 788) gives the following: sing. *ghâziya*, pl. *ghawâzin*. Wehr (1994, 745) gives: sing. *'âlima* (pronounced *'alma*). No plural form is listed. Al-Sayyid Marsot (1995, 121), however, gives the plural *awalim* for female entertainers.

3. This is based on the sample listed in appendix two. There may be other writers who have yet to be identified.

4. Among English writers, only Lane and James St. John use the term *'awâlim* as the plural form. St. James uses *awâlim* for "singing girls" in his comments (1851) on the book of plates by Prisse d'Avennes.

5. James St. John represents this change. In his 1834 work, he uses *almé* only; then, in 1845, in his chapter "Dancing Girls of Egypt" he refers to them as *ghazeeyeh* and *ghawazee*. English writers who use *ghawazee* solely include Roberts, Romer, Barlett, Duff Gordon, and the American Leland.

6. Champollion, L'Hôte, Flaubert, and Lenoir use only *almah*. Some French writers—Chabrol, Villoteau, and Clot Bey—use both terms. Blanc defines both groups in 1869.

7. An English writer also said much the same:

> One of the most authoritative writers on Egyptian manners particularly insists on the fact that the Awalim (Sing. Almeh) are not dancers, but singers, and points out that most Egyptian travellers have fallen into a mistake by confounding them with the Ghawazee, or regular tribe of dancers. It is true that an Almeh depends principally on her voice; but her feet, or rather her hips, form also a part of her stock in trade ... when I asked to see the dancing girls, Sitt Madoula instantly referred me to the Awalim [B. St. John 1850, 146].

Poché (1996, 46) points out this same discussion among early travel writers.

8. This fine screening leaves Villoteau, Prisse d'Avennes, Lane, Clot Bey, Bayle St. John, and Duff Gordon.

9. One reads less of this discussion in 19th-century literature after public dancers were banned from the streets of Cairo and Alexandria around 1834.

10. "Besides these almées of gentle company, there are other almées of low estate, bacchantes of the crossroads. Addressing themselves to the lowest sensations, having neither the grace nor instruction of the others, they seek to overcome these deficiencies with indecency" (Taylor 1856, 265).

11. According to Nieuwkerk (1995, 37), even the term *'awâlim* developed considerable negative connotations late in the 19th century.

12. "Convention does not permit the a'lmeh to be introduced often into those homes that follow etiquette and morals closely; they appear only on days of great festivals.... The dances of the ghaouâzy that one sees in the streets of Cairo, are strictly excluded" (Chabrol 1822, 418).

13. Minutoli, traveling in the early 1820s, also made an intriguing suggestion along the lines of ethnicity, that one term was used among the upper-class Turks in Egypt, while Egyptians (that is, the local people) preferred the other: "A privileged caste of females, called gavanaki in Egypt, and halme among the Turks" (1827, 198).

14. Both types of singers seem to have been valued, for 'Abd ar-Raziq (1973, 67) says the chronicles suggest the sultan may at times have called on "popular" singers of both sexes for his large-scale entertainments.

15. Speaking of the term *'alima*, al–Sayyid Marsot (1995, 121) points out that "in the singular the term can mean both learned women, the female equivalent of ulama, and women of the entertainment business, depending on the context, but the plurals differ: the plural for entertainers is awalim." She says the other plural is *alimat*. Although she does not elaborate on this, she implies that one cannot assume *'alima* is always the equivalent of a "learned woman."

16. While the word *'alima* appears in Lane's lexicon, it has no meanings remotely connected with performance, unlike in the modern Wehr work.

17. Cenghe or cenghi was the Turkish version of the word *jank* (Popescu-Judetz 1982, 53).

18. Although tied intimately to the arts of female performers in the medieval period, the Persian harp had long passed out of use by the time of this study period. Lane never saw an instrument but did have access to centuries-old manuscripts with illustrations and reproduces these in his *The Thousand and One Nights* (Lane 1865, 1:204–05).

19. Two other Persian terms listed in these dictionaries, *ghaaz* and *ghaaza*, have meanings

such as: "patch on a garment; split open; tears, rent, slit or crack; want or scarcity; rouge for the face; noise or cry; water bird or goose; money of the least value." Tellingly, Romer noted that the small gold coins on dancers' costumes were called *Gazis* (1846, 137). Through the associated meanings of these three Persian words one arrives at a picture of a group of ragged, noisy, peripatetic performers, working for poverty-level wages, and behaving rather like the wild geese in their precipitous arrival and sudden departure. "Whenever there is a religious festival or a fair ... they repair as industriously as flies and beggars" (B. St. John 1973, 1:28).

20. Some of the heads of guilds appear identified by name, names that reveal their gender and ethnicity (for example, Coptic or Turkish), but Raymond does not give such details in his published materials.

21. The word *musicien* can indicate an orchestra of all men, or men and women both.

22. Lane (1978, 373), too, stressed that the female street dancers normally appeared with their own musicians, explaining this by saying they belonged to the same tribe.

23. Villoteau does not state quite as explicitly as Chabrol the two terms and the differentiation of place of performance. He does, however, start one section of his article with the subtitle "The A'oualem, the Ghaouâzy or public dancers." He then goes on to discuss the differences of status of the two groups. It is clear he associates the term *ghawâzî* with the street dancers (1809a, 694).

24. Villoteau (1809a, 678n) and Lane (1978, 354), both of whom were knowledgeable in musical matters, used this term.

25. In Lane's classical lexicon the verb *r-q-s* means "to dance," with a female form for dancer.

26. Raymond cites al–Jabarti as saying that the raqqâsin took part as a guild at the marriage of the daughter of Isma'il Bey (Raymond 1956–57, 160n8). A footnote in Baer (1964, 33n97) also identifies this same citation from al–Jabarti.

Chapter 5

1. Burkhardt explains that this refers to dancers who pay extravagant attentions to those from whom they expect large tips.

2. Burkhardt explains that this means the wedding was not a success. The reference to the singers indicates that they suddenly repented of their lives and did not turn up for the performance.

3. "There is no party without them, no festival where they are not the ornament" (Savary 1785, 1:150). "In Cairo, there is no party in Christian households nor in Muslim ones where the almées are not called; there are [entertainers] for every class and for every price" (Michaud 1833–35, 5:256).

4. Her son's father, now deceased, had been an Austrian subject. The son would normally have provided military service in Italy.

5. Burkhardt (1984, 177) and Prisse d'Avennes (1930, 57) relate similar anecdotes.

6. Accepted Islamic teaching not found in the Qur'an but arising out of Islam's earliest contexts and based on rigorous scholarship as to its religious authenticity.

7. Hanawalt discusses European women in medieval England moving beyond their socially prescribed territory of the home.

8. The same ideas did appear in the travel literature (e.g., Villoteau 1809a, 699).

9. Hanawalt (1998, 76), for example, talks about the requirements for veils and hoods worn by "decent" English medieval women when they moved into the streets.

10. Nieuwkerk discusses this same point in her theoretical section of dishonorable professions in general, especially in Europe. Hanawalt shows that, in medieval times, European women as different as streetwalkers and the pious Beguines (nuns) were looked upon with official disapproval for stepping out of their physical space—that is, their homes.

Chapter 6

1. See also: Du Bois-Aymé and Jollois 1812, 118; Jollois 1822, 358.

2. Editorializing, Michaud (1833–35, 7:36) expressed surprise that neither the city nor the dancers' area seemed unduly noisy or unruly because of their large, permanent presence.

3. A considerable presence may have existed in Damanhûr, however, an inland Delta city just southeast of Alexandria. In the late 18th century, Sonnini (1799, 2:120) remarked that this town was "infested with courtesans" who had set up tents near the town and were working in front of the coffee houses. His remarks constitute the only information extant on this settlement.

4. Jomard (1822, 581) mentions a "Cha'ryeh

Gate" and an area in the north of Cairo called "el-Cha'ryeh." Browne (1806, 539) calls "Bab es Sharié" an "ancient, strong and low gate" and locates it on his map to the north of Cairo.

5. Luxor was also a deportation destination for Cairo dancers during Abbas's reign. In 1854, Didier (1858, 332, 858) tells of such exiles there.

6. Descriptions of Kutchuk Hanem in Isna (Flaubert 1991, 362, 383) date from the spring of 1850. Even at the time of the 1869 official Nile voyage, Isna was one of the three stops where major dance entertainments took place for European guests of the government; Fromentin (1881, 295) implies that there was still a large quarter in the town for the many entertainers who lived there. In 1872, Carcy (quoted in Aradoon 1979, 124) held an entertainment on his boat, with five dancers; he claimed that, after Cairo, Isna held the reputation as the best city for dancers.

Chapter 7

1. Suzanne Sawa (1987, 94) makes this same point about the women singers of the medieval court in Baghdad.

2. Here Savary is not distinguishing between singers and dancers, for he continues by describing their dances, but I am concentrating on the skills involved in female singing.

3. He was a guest in the home of an Armenian physician, doctor to the ruler of Egypt. The concert took place during celebrations for the birth of the Prophet Muhammad.

4. Muhammad Ali's grandson and his successor as ruler of Egypt.

5. Nieuwkerk (1995, 36) gives details on Almaz's career and retirement.

6. Auriant (1977, 14–19) gives details about Sakna (from a "traveler") that I have not been able to confirm. Originally a mud-carrier on a work site, she had been discovered by a daughter of Muhammad Ali. She was a dancer as well as a singer in her youth but later concentrated on singing. She was favored by Said, the ruler of Egypt. It was rumored that her husband was only a servant to her; it was also said that she prostituted herself; that she was a procuress among the elite; and that she owned an extremely costly hat which she lent to wealthy women when they married.

7. A direct translation from the Arabic.

8. Egyptians evidently used the term *fantasia* to describe a party with singing and dancing, and the travel literature adopted this usage.

Chapter 8

1. During Abbas's rule (1849–54) dancing may not have been allowed, even to them. Didier (1860, 331) says that although singing was permitted, dancing was forbidden.

2. Dauzat's book was published under the authorship of Dumas, and appears as such in the bibliography.

3. The golden hat pieces known as *kurs* might cost thousands of gold pieces, indicating the status of the performers.

4. Lane (1978, 22–26) describes the *mandara* as a ground-floor apartment situated off the central courtyard, intended for receiving male visitors. Grated windows separated this space from the court. Lane devotes several pages to the decorations and furnishings of this important room.

5. It seems surprising that this was a Muslim wedding as the male French visitors later were able to watch the bride appear unveiled in a series of different dresses; this despite the fact that they record that two women kept writing out "happy is he who lives under the laws of the Prophet," suggesting that it was. The French visitors were surprised, too, at the mixed company and suggested such an open wedding would probably not be found in Cairo.

6. There were actually *two* brides being married at the same wedding, one being Muhammad Ali's youngest daughter, Zaynab.

7. Not be confused with the illustrious Safiyya, who danced between 1825 and 1850, nor with "Little" Safiyya, made famous in Flaubert's accounts of his trip to Isna in 1850. All three appear in detail in section five.

8. The easiest way to access the entire series of plates of the *Description de l'Égypte* is through the modern reprint by Taschen, listed in the bibliography.

Chapter 9

1. The days after the end of Ramadan, a month-long central event in Islam.

2. Both the Bab al–Futuh and the Bab al–Nasr are located near each other in the north of Cairo. Michaud and Lane refer to the same cemetery.

3. Lane saw female dancers performing in this cemetery during 'Id and gives an account in his diary entry of February 12, 1834 (Sattin 1988, 71–72).

4. Even in Cairo, coffee houses were normally small and modest. The average one was

a small apartment ... whose front ... is towards the street.... Along the front, excepting before the door, is a mastab'ah or raised seat, of stone or brick, two or three feet in height and about the same in width, which is covered with matting; and there are similar seats in the interior on two or three sides [Lane 1978, 334].

A few urban coffee houses, however, were more substantial. One in Rosetta, described by Jollois (1822, 350), was a large building situated on the Nile. This coffee house had two rows of windows (one above the other), two interior courts, and benches running along the walls. Outside, along each face, a system of canopies, covered with vines, provided shade where patrons might sit, sheltered from the sun. Other large cafés also existed (Montulé 1821, 15; J. St. John 1851, 3–4; Michaud 1833–35, 5:251; Lane 1978, 453).

5. Inevitably, one has to deal with Gérôme's five pictures of dancers in cafés. Did the dancer of the 1863 *Dance of the Almeh*, of whom we know nothing, perform in a coffee house? Gérôme's coffee houses do not resemble any either illustrated or described elsewhere in the literature. This does not automatically render them inauthentic. I choose to believe that she *did* dance as depicted in the painting, and that the artist repeated this same setting in his later works (probably too often) as an earlier successful artistic device.

6. From Aisha Ali, one learns that

there are three tribes from which the Ghawazee of Upper Egypt originated—the Halab, the Nawar, and the Batar.... The Nawar women sometimes are courtesans as well as entertainers but the Halab people are only entertainers and the Batar are like the Halab. Khalil [her informant] thinks that some of them come from Syria, Lebanon and Iraq, while others were from Morocco. Although their families have lived in Upper Egypt for five or six generations, they are still considered "foreigners" by the Saidi families [1981, 10].

7. Blanc does not say directly that Badawiyya was a member of the ghawâzî. Based on his clear differential of the two groups, the fact that she lived in Qena, that Blanc states the ghawâzî had more talent than the Cairo dancers while claiming she was the "best dancer in Egypt," one concludes that she was a member of this guild.

8. There was considerable talent in Qena. Bicharra, the local consul, had hired the best local female dancers and male musicians (Blanc 1876, 137), and there were 15 dancers in all (Fromentin 1881, 291).

9. Here Blanc uses a European ballet term for an ethnic or specialty dance.

Chapter 10

1. Here Didier uses the usual local term for "party with entertainment" to describe a moving entertainment. It may be an atypical usage unique to him.

2. Nerval (1929, 1:63–65) gives a vivid description of dancing boys performing in public.

Chapter 11

1. Of the same performances L'Hôte (c. 1993, 125) says the dancers were "mamlouks dressed as women."

2. Warburton (1846, 1:289) suggests that these "Arnauts" consisted of men from other nationalities besides Albanian.

3. "A superior sort of Almeh girls" amused harem women with dancing, singing, and music (Carne 1826, 165). The ghawâzî entertained with dancing and taught their "voluptuous arts" (Lane 1978, 299).

4. Sonnini (1799, 2:323–24) speaks of female dancers, tumblers, jugglers, and buffoons together; Browne (1806, 91) mentions wrestlers, male singers, storytellers, female singers, female dancers, and rope dancers at a Ramadan event; Champollion (c. 1986, 67–68) says three buffoons and two female singers came onto their boat at Nadir; James St. John (1845, 217) talks of male drummers, monkey trainers, and female dancers together in Cairo.

5. Allegedly from al-Jabarti, as quoted in Stanley Lane-Poole, *Cairo—Sketches of Its History, Monuments, and Social life* (London: J. S. Virtue, 1898, 319).

6. See also Clot Bey (1840, 1:336).

7. Gérôme's biographer Gerald Ackerman says that this painting cannot be based on a real event, but gives no explanation as to why this is the case. One wonders if he would have said the same for two male musicians playing chess.

Chapter 12

1. Bartlett does not give the purpose of the entertainments. Judging from the mixed crowd

and the large platform setup, this event might have been in connection with a local saint's day celebration.

2. Lane describes the crowds thusly: "It is commonly said by the people of Cairo that no man goes to the mosque of the Hasaneyn on the day of 'A'shoora but for the sake of the women—that is to be jostled among them" (1978, 425). He relates how he became tightly wedged among four women there. Bayle St. John (1850, 57) describes how, at Ramadan, the packed crowds in an Alexandrian bazaar included men and women both, the women becoming the particular targets of extreme crowd control. James St. John (1845, 218) describes Egyptians with "their wives and children" outside the city gates at the celebration of the Mahmal, with groups of "dancing girls" and other entertainers in evidence.

3. Minutoli (1827, 198–200) writes that her Egyptian hostess invited her to a harem party with the intention of showing and "making her admire" the dance. The local women present singled out one of the dancers for their praises.

4. Voilquin does not make clear who is doing the dancing here, the women guests or the servants. They were not professional dancers as she later claimed she had not been able to watch a performance of the 'awalim until near to her departure from Egypt.

5. Lane says, "They [ghawâzî] dance ... before the men in the courts, so that they may be seen also by the women from the windows" (1978, 404).

6. This word is used often in the travel literature as a local Egyptian term to describe a party with music and dance.

7. In other Christian Egyptian families, women watched entertainments with the men of the family, even alongside male European guests, for example: Chabrol 1822, 463; Carne 1826, 73; Estourmel 1844, 2:453; Hackländer, quoted in J. St. James 1845, 273.

Chapter 13

1. Michaud makes the intriguing remark that entertainers were trained as a group, and later sorted by talent. "Those who have most profited from their education have a more distinguished rank and are admitted into the harems and houses of the rich; the others are reserved for the amusement of the people" (1833–35, 5:255).

Chapter 14

1. Such as gardeners, brokers of the camel market, saddlers, cup-makers, dyers of silks, tinsmiths, ironmongers, and sellers of small wares.

2. Mengin's (1839) edition lists the 1833 revenues of Egypt in local currency, the bourse. Clot Bey converts these 1833 figures into francs, and I have used his work here since Jomard, too, uses the franc in discussing Mengin's work on the Egyptian revenues of 1822.

3. Interestingly, revenues from entertainment seem to have remained constant against a rise in total revenues, suggesting the decade had not been good to these professions. Mengin discusses the growth of Alexandria as a center of government and commerce, and an increase in its population. Against this development, Cairo declined in importance (1839, 225–28). Possibly during the decade the capital had less wealth for the traditional arts.

4. Unfortunately, he never speaks consistently about which groups he describes, and uses the terms "almées," "female dancers," "prostitutes," and "public women" loosely and synonymously throughout his book. Since his account explains the exile of certain women from Cairo and Alexandria, along with the termination of this tax-farm, his evidence probably applies to the ghawâzî (and perhaps to the prostitutes).

5. It is hard to believe that the dancers were not paid. In any event, the point made is that dancers were not afraid to make their opinions known.

6. The value in today's currency is not known, but obviously the imported shawl was of great price.

7. Besides three annual week-long events at Tanta, one occurred in Disûq (just south of Fuwa) a week after each of the Tanta celebrations. A Christian festival on the Damietta branch of the Nile also formed part of the same circuit.

8. Auriant does not provide references for this valuable information.

9. Romer went to Safiyya's house in Isna for a performance. Flaubert and Curtis went to Kutchuk Hanem's house in Isna.

10. Lane 1865, 1:282; 1:283.
11. al–Sayyid Marsot 1995, 110.
12. Ibid., 121.
13. Ibid., 122.
14. Tucker 1985, 91.
15. Wealthy women spent much time

embroidering. They sold their work through a dallâla (Lane 1978, 191).
16. al–Sayyid Marsot 1995, 121–22.
17. Taschen 1994, 713.
18. Ibid., 700.
19. Villoteau 1809a, 700.
20. Burkhardt 1984, 214, 227, 231.
21. Lane, quoted in al–Sayyid Marsot 1995, 114.
22. al–Sayyid Marsot 1995, 110.
23. Tucker 1985, 91.
24. Nashat and Tucker 1999, 79.
25. Champollion c. 1986, 66; Lane 1978, 48. Lane says these women were generally gypsies.
26. Tucker 1985, 108.
27. Various writers commented on their modest dwellings. "Huts which they erect in the environs of the cities" (Montulé 1821, 88). "The ghowazys have in every town or considerable village a small quarter assigned to them, where they live in large huts or tents, seldom in houses" (Burkhardt 1984, 175). "Their ordinary habitations are low huts, or temporary sheds, or tents" (Lane 1978, 376). "Their quarter [in Luxor] consists of a little cluster of hovels outside the village" (Bayle St. John 1973, 2:69). Aziza's dwelling in Aswan was an "earthen shack hardly high enough for her to stand" (Flaubert 1991, 295).
28. This might be a sleeping alcove, however, since steps lead down to another area, not shown.
29. He probably means *below* the Makattam hill, under the Citadel. Al-Jabarti's (1788–96, 6:102) anecdote about a dancer tells that she lived in this district. A *hawsh* was an open courtyard where huts were erected for individual families, usually the very poor and rural immigrants (al–Sayyid Marsot 1995, 112). The name Hosh [*hawsh*?] Bardak suggests perhaps Burkhardt's khan was really such an establishment, not the substantial merchant-style building he implies. Investing in a hawsh was a popular outlet for wealthy women investors; perhaps a successful dancer had made such a purchase.
30. Some practicing dancers seem to have been already married. Burkhardt (1984, 176) suggests that public dancers who had tired of their profession might consider marriage to some local dignitary if she had lost or divorced an earlier husband. Hamont's (1845, 1:318) description suggests that some "public women" were already married and with families to support. Michaud says that some were married to the man in charge of their group, a "man in charge of several almées marries them in front of a judge, and produces them in the world as his legitimate wives" (1833–35, 5:256).

Chapter 15

1. "A new career opens when the old one has closed; and Safia, who has lately become a decent gentlewoman of Cairo, after twenty years of public life, is by no means an extraordinary instance" (B. St. John 1973, 26). St. John was writing this as a result of his 1851 trip.
2. Flaubert sees her Isna home from Kutchuk Hanem's window in March of 1850: "Two windows, one onto the mountains, another onto the city—from there Joseph shows me the large house of the famous Saphiah" (1991, 281).
3. This alleged discovery ("Égypte sous la domination de Méhémet Ali," 1848, 46) probably took place in the summer of 1832 (the major Tanta fair took place in July) as Abbas was in Syria with the army under his uncle Ibrahim from 1831 to 1832; he may have found her on his return. The liaison would have been of short duration if she were sent to Isna by late 1833, to be there early in 1834. She might have been about 17 at the time of her discovery by Abbas.
4. Hamont (1845, 1:488–89) tells, in great detail, a somewhat unbelievable story. Abbas gave a costly *nargila* (smoking pipe) to Safiyya, who later sold it in the bazaar. Abbas saw it offered for sale, and confronted her on the matter. He imprisoned her in the citadel, whipped her personally 200 times on the buttocks, and sent her to Isna. Prisse d'Avennes (1930, 56) gives another version; he says she was spared from the law against public dancing in Cairo, but "her lover" was jealous of her dancing in public, and, hence, sent her to Isna to join the women already banished there. Both stories illustrate the type of gossip about dancers at the time.
5. Warburton (1846, 1:291) arrived in Isna in 1843, just after the Arnauts (soldiers) had caused much discord in the town on finding Safiyya and other performers removed by the governor for fear of trouble. Annoyed, the troops burned her home to the ground. Safiyya was in possession of her own home when Romer (1846, 1:273) visited her in 1846, for the performance took place there. Auriant (1943, 18–20) gives a rather fanciful reading of Warburton. Also see Nieuwkerk (1995, 35).
6. "Accurate expressions are lacking in our

language for giving exact and rigorous descriptions for these astonishing dances. Thus the words writhe, convulsions, contortions, that usually express painful and disagreeable ideas, and which I must use for want of better, here don't yield gracious and attractive images" (Combes 1846, 1:219).

7. Biasi (quoted in Flaubert 1991, 195n), Flaubert's modern editor, makes this comment but does not give any supporting evidence.

8. Karayanni (2002, 89–92) discusses Flaubert's reactions to Hasan. He has a different take than mine on Flaubert's comments.

9. This name is probably Turkish, meaning "Little Lady."

10. I lean towards Flaubert's assessment rather than Curtis's overly sentimental one.

11. While recalling painful episodes of her life, Colet (1879, 208) did say she would find it curious to see one of the dancers of Flaubert's past in the state of a "living mummy," but she was only making a general comment. Perhaps she was thinking of Kutchuk Hanem, although she never mentions her by name. In her admiration for Badawiyya of Qena (discussed elsewhere), she praises this fine performer as if she had no memories of the dancers of Egypt to haunt her.

12. An alleged portrait, a woodcut of her head and shoulders, appears in Auriant (1943), supposedly taken from Curtis's account. There is no such portrait in Curtis's 1856 New York edition, which I consulted. Perhaps the portrait appeared in the 1852 London edition, but I was unable to confirm this. In any event, where would Curtis have obtained such a portrait?

13. She would have been in her early sixties at the time, not an age at which dancers continued to perform at that period in Egypt. Besides, Andreievsky states that the older female performers only sang.

14. Karayanni's (2002, 48–71) interpretations of Kutchuk Hanem's persona and her dancing are quite different from my own. She obviously continues to inspire constant and varied controversy.

15. Not to be confused with the great Safiyya of Isna.

16. Flaubert (1991, 295), however, says that she danced in a low, poor, earthen hut on the outskirts of the town, obviously her home. This may have been a second and private performance just for him, for Flaubert describes sexual relations with her afterwards.

17. Flaubert (1991, 353) uses the term "shut up," implying that they danced on the boat in their private quarters.

18. Flaubert here uses the word *savante* (learned) as if he is referring to the expression of which he was aware: "femme savante," one of the literal translations of 'awâlim.

19. Here dance generation is not equated with a lifetime, but with 15 or so years for an average career.

20. Didier (1858, 53) noted the Ethiopian dancers performed in the style of their Egyptian colleagues.

21. Not to be confused either with the renowned Safiyya of Isna of the 1830s, or with Flaubert's "Little" Safiyya of Isna of 1850.

22. The account recalls the terror described in Auriant's (1943) record of soldiers passing through Isna and burning the town, when the great Safiyya lost her home. Auriant's account also says that town officials had earlier removed the dancers from danger.

23. The Rijksmuseum of Amsterdam dates the watercolor as 1863, but the artist was not present in Egypt at that time. He traveled in 1858–60 and in 1868.

24. Colet (1879, 145) implies that the dance took place on the carpeted deck of a docked boat. The boat may have been tied up at the consul's home.

Chapter 17

1. The Belliard war material came out in 1831 and possibly Michaud read it before he published his letters. Or perhaps he heard the story directly from Belliard; the two men were contemporaries.

2. Auriant makes no specific references but, based on his wording, he must have read Belliard and la Jonquière.

3. There was widespread belief that the plague was caused by overwork, excessive consumption of wine or hard spirits, "intemperance with women," and fear (Galland 1804, 2:53).

4. Galland (1804, 1:171) says that plague was extreme in Alexandria and Damietta, but Cairo had only a few cases. Syria was also badly hit and the French army there suffered greatly. The proclamation was obviously intended as a precautionary measure.

5. Baron Larrey, chief medical officer with the French army, concerned with the high rate of syphilis among the soldiers, conceived the idea of such a hospital. Egyptian women

infected with venereal diseases were retained, treated, and released after being cured. Women impregnated by French soldiers were also retained so as to be prevented from having abortions. All French soldiers with venereal diseases were rounded up and sent to the military hospital (Larrey 1809, 510–11).

6. Galland (1804) uses the writing device of going day by day and month by month, as if he were using his diaries verbatim.

7. Galland follows his account of the drownings directly with another, dealing specifically with prostitutes and their procurers, implying that he is talking only of this group of women.

Chapter 18

1. Materials listed in the military records of the French campaign say that prior to the French invasion the custom was to punish prostitutes by whipping or banishment for (unspecified) bad behavior (la Jonquière, n.d., 5:232n).

2. The author's 1845 *Egypt and Nubia*, from which this quotation is taken, is a later pastiche based on his sole visit to Egypt in the fall of 1832 and into the spring of 1833. This early restriction on dance to which he refers obviously dates from the fall of 1832, when he first arrived in Egypt, or the spring of 1833, when he was ready to depart. Later, in the same book, he says that all ghawâzî had already been sent to Upper Egypt and married off to soldiers; he presumably means *after* the edict. St. John has not been too meticulous with his dates or his continuity.

3. Others suffered indirectly. Bayle St. John (1850, 97) tells of a certain Hanna, who worked as principal clerk in the Alexandria registry office for "public women," and who lost his position when this profession was closed down.

4. In Hamont's (1845, 1:489) narrative, Safiyya receives two hundred strokes of the whip on the buttocks, a far more severe punishment than Lane suggests was the norm. Amnesty International Canada, in its *Activist* (Dec. 2000 / Jan. 2001, 1), describes a modern whipping in Saudi Arabia, meted out to a migrant worker from the Philippines for allegedly meeting and talking to a male stranger: "I started counting and when it reached 40 I thought I could not make it.... At last it reached 60.... I could not explain the pain experienced." Obviously, even the 50 lashes described by Lane was not a light punishment, and two hundred seems almost unbelievable. Bayle St. John describes the terror of those young women who danced at an abortive clandestine performance just outside of Alexandria in 1847. "The poor women were perfectly awe-stricken; and, pale and shivering, huddled together on their carpet awaiting their doom—stripes and imprisonment at least, if not banishment" (1850, 161).

5. Combes left Marseilles on August 7, 1833, and, while in Cairo, decided to leave for a trip as far south as Dongola (in Sennar) on December 13, 1833. He says he reached "Siout" (Asyût) by January 1, 1834. After Isna, he continued south to other parts of Africa before returning, via the Red Sea and Suez, to spend three months in Cairo. He left Egypt for good in December 1834.

6. See also Combes 1846, 1:162n.

7. Estourmel (1844, 2:453) was invited to a family party featuring what he was told were "first-class almées of Cairo," on May 28, 1833. Estourmel makes no mention of a ban on public dancing at that time, but, then, his interests did not lie in this direction.

8. I did not have access to Lane's diaries, which might have resolved the dilemma of conflicting dates.

9. Buonaventura (1990, 69) states that this event occurred in 1866, but does not give a reference. Nieuwkerk (1995, 36) concludes that it most probably took place during the reign of Abbas, from 1849 to 1854; she also indicates (Ibid., 36n31) that the date is still far from exact.

10. Prisse d'Avennes (1930, 58) has a unique take on the ban on prostitution. He claims that as births were going down while prostitution was rising, closing the brothels would provide a remedy.

11. Such freedom from the infraction appears in the Bayle St. John (1850, 161) incident in Alexandria around 1847; the dancers fled out the back window while he remained to confront the police. Clot Bey says:

> One knows the severity which relations of Christian men and Muslim women are forbidden and punished in the Ottoman Empire. This crime has been regarded as so great by Muslims that infractions put men outside the protection of their consuls if they are guilty. In Egypt, tolerance in matters of morals is greater than in the rest of Turkey. If it happens that police arrest Europeans taken in the act with women of the country they are almost always released without even a punishment. I have seen some Frenchmen

who instead of appreciating this tolerance only abuse it all the more [1840, 2:166].

12. Henni-Chebra and Poché (1996, 84) identify another case of a ban that took place at the end of the 19th century. Certain Egyptian notables and intellectuals had managed to close down an establishment providing belly dance entertainments, a place owned by Greeks. The owners brought their case before a special tribunal set up to regulate affairs between foreigners and Egyptians. The tribunal ruled that professional dance was not immoral, and allowed the owners to reopen.

13. Societies everywhere often project onto their female members the onus for changes not welcomed by traditional elements in the population. It would be interesting to compare social conditions in Egypt during the four previous bans with those in 1833.

14. By the time of Muhammad Ali's death in 1849, 14 of his 17 male children had predeceased him. Three immature sons still lived (al–Sayyid Marsot 1984, 80–81). Abbas, his oldest grandson and the senior male family member, was then the legitimate successor.

15. In 1831, by the time Abbas was 18, he was sent on military training under his uncle Ibrahim, then fighting in Syria. "Complaints about his military behaviour, or lack thereof, flowed regularly from Ibrahim" (al–Sayyid Marsot 1984, 88). A year later, in 1832, Ibrahim asked that he be recalled, and Abbas returned to Egypt. As an adult family member, he was entitled to a senior post in the administration, so was appointed governor of the Western District (Ibid., 89). He was governor of Cairo around 1846. Abbas became ruler in 1849. He died in 1854.

16. J. St. John 1845, 20. This regulation must have appeared late in 1832, or very early in 1833, to fit with St. John's travel dates.

17. This association of the ban and Abbas gives a reasonable explanation for the banishment of Safiyya in 1833. As a well-known courtesan, she would hardly fit with Abbas's new posturing as a man of high moral rectitude. On the other hand, he seems later to have taken up with Kutchuk Hanem before becoming ruler in 1849. Perhaps he banned her for the same reason. Dates are consistent with this explanation.

Chapter 19

1. Now widespread in North Africa, and in certain countries of the Middle East, the zar (and its variants) originated in central Africa, probably in Ethiopia. Neither a professional performance nor a folk dance, the zar is intended to relieve women temporarily from painful psychological states caused by malign spirits.

2. Burkhardt said that some ghawâzî claimed to be of Arabian descent: "They are a race distinct from all other public women, and relate with pride that their origin is Arabian, and they are of the true Bedouin blood" (1984, 173). The public dancers of the time seemed particularly prone to want to be known as non–Egyptian.

3. Other writers acknowledge that "whenever the gypsies (Roma, Sintes, and others) settled in a given culture, they adapted the latter's folk music and dances for their own use. And so their dances kept changing under the influence of each culture they came across" (al-Rawi 1999, 42).

4. Lane-Poole (1846, 70) tells of a female Roma rope dancer at a wedding in 1834. The Persian word *ghaazi*, suggested in section two as a possible source of the term *ghawâzî*, includes the meanings rope dancer or courtesan, and ties directly with this occupation practiced by some female Roma (but, significantly, not by the ghawâzî).

5. Metin And does not use the Persian term *jank*, obviously the older root source for both the Turkish and Arabic terminology.

6. In modern Arabic, the word for *Roma* still comes from the root "*gh-j- r*" a word with mainly negative connotations: "scold, use abusive language, curse, swear" (Wehr 1979, 780).

Chapter 20

1. Many illustrations of the 18th and 19th centuries appeared originally only in black and white, with coloration added after publication.

2. The latter only within the confines of their homes.

3. Romer saw Safiyya of Isna enter the performance space in full finery in a salta, presumably emphasizing her conformity with well-to-do good taste (1846, 1:273).

4. This illustration is based on the work of a local Egyptian Christian (Coptic) artist and not on that of a European traveler.

5. He does not refer the reader to the magnificently dressed dancer (fig. 6) of the *Description de l'Égypte* just discussed. He may have been familiar only with the common street dancers in Cairo at that time.

6. Worn by well-to-do women of Lane's day (but seemingly not by dancers) the *milaya* was a long piece of material worn outdoors over all clothing, head, and hands. It was formed from two pieces of cotton sewn together, woven in a kind of plaid in blue and white, or with stripes, with red weaving at each end (Lane 1978, 55).

7. Other well-off dancers may have also been traditionalists. Curtis (1856, 133–34) described Kutchuk Hanem in 1850 as dressed in the conventional outfit of chemise, silk shintiyan, striped satin and velvet antari, and shawl belt, with her hair arranged in the usual gold coin décor.

8. In particular, the elaborate and costly kurs, or gold cap that fitted on top of a small turban, disappeared.

9. Bida's (figs. 21a and 21b) two performers of the 1860s (dancer and drummer), however, demurely wear chemise and vest covering their breasts, and tucked under the shintiyan, pulled up well above their waists.

10. Later in the century, an unattractive ankle-length dress seems to have been the norm, as worn by dancers at the Chicago World's Fair (Buonaventura 1990, 20).

11. They also may have started theme dances, such as cup dances, sword dances, and more athletic tricks common to male dancers. These ideas are explored in section eight.

12. Only Didier records the Arabic for this loose vest, "sodeyry" (1860, 339). The Wehr dictionary identifies the *sudairi* as "vest, waistcoat or bodice" (1994, 592).

13. Gérôme's figure 15 shows his version of this outfit.

14. Carcy provides a final reference to vests in his description of well-dressed dancers at a Cairo party around 1870. They wore chemises of muslin, and shintiyan with a silk sash with dangling silver chains and silver amulets. Their vests were of embroidered velvet or silk (quoted in Aradoon 1979, 123).

15. For a wedding procession (December 1, 1849), he wore a chain belt with gold square ornaments. For the hotel performance (December 29, 1849), a cashmere shawl.

16. Other than Colet's, unfortunately no written description exists for this costume innovation for female dress first identified for Hasan al–Bilbeissi.

17. Other descriptions of scanty dress: Savary 1785, 1:298; Stanhope 1983, 1:164; Lane 1978, 373.

18. Kutchuk Hanem performed *The Bee* for Flaubert, but had insisted on privacy. She sent away her sailors, blindfolded the younger musician, and covered the eyes of the older musician with his turban. Even then, her heart wasn't in it: "She danced only a short time and doesn't like to perform this dance any more" (Flaubert 1991, 285).

19. Sonnini (1799, 2:323) says dancers conclude the choreography by "letting down their veils and screaming with all their might." Redouté (quoted in Hermant 1798, 51) writes that the performers unveiled with fear and only when compelled by the French military. Of the same performance, Denon (1973, 231) says the dancers made a great deal of fuss in uncovering their mouths and eyes. At the wedding parade he saw in Cairo around 1843, Nerval (1929, 1:8) says that some of the dancers and singers were veiled.

20. Bayle St. John's clandestine party in 1846 required the four dancers to arrive discreetly and fully covered over their dance costumes. Then "the white mantles or blue wrappers were thrown aside; so were the veils; and the supple forms of the dancers were displayed" (1850, 159–60).

21. I have never seen muslin this thin, although *nainsook* comes close. *Nainsook* is originally of Indian manufacture. The name comes from Urdu: *nain* (eye) + *sukh* (pleasure). Obviously, the body forms revealed through the cloth were always part of its appeal.

22. The tarha was often made of muslin and decorated on the ends with colored silks (Lane 1978, 51). Women might wear muslin turbans (Hume 1818, 398–99).

23. Crêpe is a twisted raw silk with a crisped surface. Damask is a rich silk with woven designs and figures. Satin is a silk with glossy surface on one side. Taffeta is a kind of light thin silk. Velvet is silk with a short, dense, smooth pile surface.

24. Safiyya wore crimson silk shintiyan (Romer 1846, 1:274). Hackländer describes a crimson silk shawl (quoted in A. St. John 1845, 274).

25. Gérôme's (Ackerman 1986, 202) dancer in his painting of two female chess players wears bright yellow shintiyan that may be made of taffeta.

26. Hume described three wealthy Circassian women wearing shintiyan of red and white striped satin made in Damascus. Their "pelisses" (probably yeleks) were "light blue satin, spangled with small silk leaves, and oth-

ers of pink satin and gold" (1818, 404). Of course, these were not dancers, but the information shows that satin was present in the important shintiyan, and yelek, although satin may have been too heavy to dance in comfortably.

27. Minutoli (1827, 199) describes how the diva Nafissa insisted on a cashmere shawl prior to considering any request for her services. Lane-Poole (1846, 3:133) tells of such shawls given as gifts to senior members of the harem staff at the royal wedding in 1845.

Chapter 21

1. Villoteau (1809a, 679–94) and Lane (1978, 364–69) provide texts of love songs that likely served as dance repertoire.

2. At the 1869 Cairo party Blanc attended, he (1876, 51) says the better musicians played indoors for the dancers while the others were outside in the courtyard.

3. Other descriptions of female singers and accompanists: Redouté, quoted in Hermant 1798, 51; Marcellus, quoted in Carré 1956, 1:210; Andreievsky, quoted in Volkoff 1972, 296; Romer 1846, 1:273; Didier 1860, 338–39.

4. Villoteau (1809a, 697–98) devotes two pages to finger cymbal patterns, adding that he could have included many more. He illustrates each in musical notation. For each of the 11 patterns, he lists the tempo, the meter, and instructions on how to position the cymbals.

5. "In a word, all the movements of this dance tend to express the combat of modesty with love, the triumph of the latter and the defeat of the former. As the movements of the dance and the clicking of the castanets were either moderate, balanced and gentle, or more pronounced and more lively, or they became more intermittent and the sounds lost their sharpness and became more muffled and softened, one sensed that the combat was more or less equal, or that the stronger triumphed and enjoyed his advantage, and the more feeble succumbed to the will of the conqueror" (Villoteau 1809a, 697).

6. Dancers gave physical expression to poems with long traditions and great depths of meaning. It is tempting to believe that well into the 19th century entertainers still retained the scholarship behind this aspect of their art.

7. Amalgamated here are Flaubert's two accounts of the same performance by Hasan. One comes from the diary record of December 29, 1849 (1991, 236–37) and one from letter ten to Louis Bouilet of January 15, 1850 (1965, 184–85).

Chapter 22

1. Flaubert (1991, 263) provides the sole record for a choreographic movement performed until recently by the public dancers of Luxor and involving the head. Near Beni Suef his sailors called a "prostitute" to come aboard to dance; then followed a dance done back to back and head to head.

2. See also: J. St. John 1834, 1:112; Combes 1845, 1:219; Hackländer, quoted in J. St. James 1845, 275.

3. See also: L'Hôte c. 1993, 129; Andreievsky, quoted in Volkoff 1972, 296.

4. See also: Lane 1973, 377; Clot Bey 1840, 2:92/93; Flaubert 1991, 197; Carcy, quoted in Aradoon 1979, 123; Andreievsky, quoted in Volkoff 1972, 296.

5. See also: Sonnini 1799, 2:323.

6. "Suddenly the whole surface of her frame quivered in measure with the music" (Curtis 1856, 141). "Through their transparent shirts their limbs were seen to vibrate" (Colet 1879, 146). "Sometimes she began to shiver, arms open" (Andreievsky, quoted in Volkoff 1972, 296). "Waves of motion ... run from head to foot, and over these waves pass with incredible rapidity the ripples and thrills ... look like a smaller sea ribbed with a thousand wavelets" (Leland 1874, 135). "Safia's body trembled, shivered, vibrated" (Combes 1846, 1:220).

7. "Would that you saw her [Safiyya], throwing one of her beautiful legs backwards, in an adroit and assured manner" (Combes 1846, 1:220). "Once only there was the movement of dancing, when she [Kutchek Hanem] advanced, throwing one leg before the other as gypsies dance" (Curtis 1856, 141). "[Aziza] put the left foot in the place of the right, and the right in the place of the left alternatively, very fast" (Flaubert 1991, 295).

8. Phallic gestures were not exclusive to the dance. "If the phallus is no longer the object of any cult, it is however exposed in public as a sign of joy" (Marmont 1837–38, 3:315). "A great number of these ancient divinities were suspended on cords that crossed the road, and were put in motion constantly to amuse the people" (Ibid., 3:316). In another procession consisting of rope dancers, harlequins, and 60

richly decorated carts representing the trades, leading them was a young man sporting a two-foot phallus which he moved constantly for the crowds (Burkhardt 1984, 138). Flaubert (1991, 174) also mentioned a "mobile phallus" in connection with a circumcision parade he saw in Alexandria.

Chapter 23

1. Similar remarks can be found in: Volney 1959, 392; Villoteau 1809a, 695; Lenoir 1872, 105; Carcy, quoted in Aradoon 1979, 123. Several illustrations show legs planted firmly, suggesting little displacement across the dance space. For example: Mayer fig. 3; Lane fig. 17; Prisse d'Avennes fig. 18; Bida fig. 21a; Brandin fig. 22; Fromentin fig. 19.

2. See also: Jomard 1822, 733; Romer 1846, 1:276; Blanc 1876, 112; Andreievsky quoted in Volkoff 1972, 296.

3. See also: Sonnini 1799, 2:322; Flaubert 1965, 185; Carcy, quoted in Aradoon 1979, 124; Leland 1874, 132. "The dancing-girl I saw moved her breasts by some extraordinary muscular effort, first one and then the other" (Duff Gordon 1983, 103).

4. Champollion (c. 1986, 89) hired six dancers in Cairo to dance and sing for a party from 6 p.m. until 1 a.m. The impromptu party organized by Stanhope's (1983, 1:163) male companions raised three dancers and one male musician. At Qena, in 1869, Badawiyya, plus 15 dancers and many male musicians, entertained the guests (Fromentin 1881, 291). Andreievsky's (quoted in Volkoff 1972, 295–97) unscheduled late-night performance at Abu Tig included a troupe with six women and four men. The two older women sang, the men played, and the other four women danced all together. Four dancers graced Bayle St. John's (1850, 160) aborted clandestine bachelor party in Alexandria, with two dancing and two playing the drum. The dancer Ghazal suggested a total of four dancers and three male musicians as a minimum to provide for Didier's grand (but ultimately failed) fantasia in Cairo (Didier 1860, 338). A grouping of two dancers appears often in illustrations, for example: Baurenseind fig. 2; Rifaud fig. 4; Lane fig. 17; Prisse d'Avennes fig. 18; Roberts fig. 16; Bartlett fig. 10; von Mayr fig. 8; Richter fig. 23.

5. Bayle St. John describes the 1847 family party in Alexandria:

At one side of this was to sit Fransis, and at the other Antun, another fast young Levantine—their office being to excite and spur on the two poor women who were to degrade themselves for our amusement; for it is worthy of remark, that the better class of these unfortunate creatures retain certain lingering ideas of modesty and decorum, and would not dare, if left to themselves, to develop all the capabilities of the Arab dance [1850, 148–49].

6. The great Safiyya chose to amuse herself during the evening's interval. While the French hosts played *The Marseillaise*, waltzes, contredances, and gallops, in a light-hearted manner, she danced on to these European rhythms, stepping completely out of her stage character (Combes 1846, 1:221).

7. He made similar remarks about Hasna of Luxor, who "but slightly over passed the bounds of delicacy, and gave real pleasure by the supple elegance of her movements" (B. St. James 1973, 2:71).

8. "Besides the almées of good company, there are other almées of a low class, bacchantes of the highway ... having besides neither the grace nor instruction of the others, they seek to surpass them in indecency" (Taylor 1856, 265). Savary (1785, 1:155–56) had earlier come to the same conclusion.

9. Montbard (fig. 26) conveys some of this quality, but stresses vulgarity as well. Shay (1996, 182) points out that none of the historical Persian miniatures he has seen indicate any hint of sensuality, lewdness, or sexuality. He concludes that Iranians, members of the class and culture, looking at the miniatures would be able to read these qualities into their interpretations of the scenes.

10. Undoubtedly Basil Faker. Minutoli (1827) gives a great deal of information about him as she and her husband stayed in his home in 1821. He acted as consular agent to six different powers (Ibid., 175), and was Greek Orthodox by faith (Ibid., 179). An educated man, he seems to have been on familiar terms with passing Europeans. His wife came from Syria.

Chapter 25

1. Clot Bey is referring to ancient Greece dancing, not Greek dance of his time.

2. See also: Lane 1973, 377; Hackländer, quoted in J. St. James 1845, 275.

3. The illustrative materials show examples of both the slow and fast sections of the dance.

Gérôme's *Dance of the Almeh* (fig. 25), sword dance (fig. 15), and Bida's (fig. 21a) dancer maintain a soft inner focus. Brandin (fig. 22), Lane (fig. 17), and Bartlett (fig. 10) show quiet intensity on the part of the performers. In contrast, Baurenseind's (fig. 2) dancers, and Fromentin's dancers (fig. 19) perform in a dynamic fashion. The tambourine dancer from the *Description de l'Égypte* (Taschen 740, 1994), Forbin's (fig. 24) work, von Mayr's (fig. 8), and Montbard's (fig. 26) dancers all demonstrate even more animation.

4. This must be the movement still done today, with lower leg folded tightly under the thigh, with the buttocks resting on top of the ankles.

5. Badawiyya also died in her version of *The Bee*.

6. Clot Bey warned travelers not to expect a complex European-like choreography even when two or four dancers worked together: "Although they put a certain symmetric harmony into their movements, one must not expect to see them form regular tableaux, like those designed by able choreographers for our own theatres" (1840, 2:92).

7. Other writers who saw or note male clowns in performance with female dancers are Galland (1804, 2:24); Forbin (1819, 93–94); Flaubert (1965, 185); and Leland (1874, 137). The costumed dwarf with pointed cap in Mayer's (fig. 3) image represents this clown figure at the end of the 18th century. The crouching male figure beside the two dancers in von Mayr's (fig. 8) illustration of two dancers at Asyût represents this clown in the middle of the 19th.

8. Lane (1978, 384) calls their offerings as "low and ridiculous farces" and describes a typical plot in full detail.

9. Villoteau says that the spectators "left" when they had seen enough, implying that they were free to go. This was probably an outdoor public performance he is describing. Chabrol seems to have been describing an indoor private performance of this dance.

10. It is not clear where and when Jomard saw these performances.

11. Other accounts also suggest the explicit version of the *Love Duet*. Speaking of street dancers of the "second order," Savary says, "Decency does not permit me to say to what lengths they carry the license of their gestures and postures" (1785, 1:155–56). In a coffee house in Nadir, Michaud saw "several young women dancing, holding castanets in their hands, and playing the most obscene pantomimes ... add to this, songs that our interpreter did not dare to translate" (1833–35, 5:87). Bayle St. John's account of Kala and Aisha implies that perhaps they were performing this dance: "These two women ... went on descending step by step to a depth whither my pen and almost my memory refuse to follow them" (1850, 150). Marmont commented, "Their usual dances are accompanied by obscene gestures, gross images" (1837–38, 229). Of the Asyût performance in 1869, Fromentin said, "Their dance is stupid and abject; always the same pantomime; you know which one" (1881, 283). In 1864, Duff Gordon saw in Qena a performance of what may have been this dance:

> I could not call it voluptuous any more than Racine's *Phèdre*. It is Venus *toute entière a sa proie attachée* [Venus attached to her prey], and to me seemed tragic. It is far more realistic than the "fandango," and far less coquettish, because the thing represented is *au grand sérieux* [very serious], not travestied, *gazé*, [disguised] or played with [1983, 100].

Leland said, "Sometimes the two girls dance a *duo*; and I have seen this made quite as improper, though not so sickly sentimental, as in any opera-house in Europe" (1874, 137).

12. Warburton (1846, 1:296), who did not witness the dance personally, does mention it, so obviously he had access to accounts by other travelers, probably English. He calls it by its alternative name, *Wasp Dance*. Romer (1846, 1:117), who also calls it the *Wasp Dance*, describes only a male version that she saw.

13. *The Bee* inspired a version for the Paris stage in Théophile Gautier and Jean Coralli's 1843 ballet *La Péri*, the title role danced by the famous ballerina Carlotta Grisi.

14. Originally from Genoa, Joseph had served in the Egyptian army and afterwards acted as servant and interpreter for many travelers; he knew Egypt from end to end.

15. On this cry of "oh, the bee!" at various stages of the dance, also see: Clot Bey 1840, 2:93; Prisse d'Avennes 1930, 55; Blanc 1876, 139; Flaubert 1991, 353.

16. It is not entirely clear from her account if Colet actually saw this version. She apparently did see the version danced by Badawiyya in Qena.

17. Another example, later than the study period, appears in a modern book of readings on 19th-century Egypt. Here the dance was an

entertainment for an enthusiastic all-female audience. Since the original author was writing a novel instead of an eye-witness account I am not entirely certain that this particular event ever took place (Mabro 1991, 130).

18. Michaud describes an evening as the guest of Clot Bey:

> We took our place at a banquet prepared for us; then there arrived several companies of almées, for there is no festival without almées in this country; our evening passed alternating with this spectacle and conversations about France and Egypt. The professors of Abouzabel seemed to us as grave as the ancient doctors of Heliopolis; as learned as the priests of the sun, they possessed everything to make science quite amiable [1833–35, 6:85].

Michaud probably saw the performance of *The Bee* that he describes (Ibid., 5:257) at this evening with Clot Bey. Certainly, Dauzats had seen this dance while a dinner guest of the good doctor, as had the distinguished Marmont.

Chapter 26

1. For example, falling to the knees and bending backwards was one of their dance moves.

2. Later in the century there are, however, two illustrations of entertainers holding the tambourine. In the background of his *Pyrrhic Dance*, Gérôme (Ackerman 1986, cat. no. 335) shows a woman waving a tambourine, but not dancing. Montbard (18—, 18) illustrates a posed figure holding a tambourine.

3. He next describes a dance in a semicircle, including two women who advance and retreat. The men make a cry used to order camels to kneel.

4. El-Khadem's (1972, fig. 86) image probably comes from Belzoni's (1821) book.

5. It is difficult to imagine choreographically what Blanc is saying here.

6. The young man must not have been lying on the ground at this point, but crouching with a deep knee bend and thus making a "seat."

7. It is not clear why the author used this name for this dance; there is no mention of an egg in his account.

Bibliography

'Abd ar-Raziq, Ahmad. 1973. *La Femme au temps des mamlouks en Égypte*. Cairo: Institut français d'archéologie orientale du Caire.
Ackerman, Gerald M. 1986. *The Life and Work of Jean-Léon Gérôme: With a Catalogue*. London: Sotheby's Publications.
Ahmed, Leila. 1992. *Women and Gender in Islam: Historical Roots of a Modern Debate*. New Haven: Yale University Press.
Ali, Aisha. 1981. "Meetings in the Middle East." *Arabesque* 7 (3): 8–11.
And, Metin. 1976. *A Pictorial History of Turkish Dancing: From Folk Dancing to Whirling Dervishes, Belly Dancing to Ballet*. Ankara: Dost Yayinlari.
Appleton, Thomas Gold. 1876. *A Nile Journey*. London: Macmillan.
Aradoon, Zarifa. 1979. *The Oldest Dance*. Stanford: Dream Place Publications.
Aubade, Camille. 1997. *Le Voyage en Égypte de Gérard de Nerval*. Paris: Éditions Kimé.
Auriant [Emilienne d' Alençon, pseud.]. 1943. *Koutchouk-Hanem, l'almée de Flaubert: Suivie de onze essais sur la vie de Flaubert et son oeuvre*. Paris: Mercure de France.
———. 1977. "Almees and Ghawazees." Trans. Marianna Mustacchi. *Arabesque* 2 (6): 14–19.
Ayalon, David. 1962. "The Historian al-Jabarti." In *Historians of the Middle East*, ed. Bernard Lewis and P. M. Holt, 391–402. New York: Oxford University Press.
Baedeker, Karl. 1892. *Egypt: Handbook for Travellers*. London: Dulau.
Baer, Gabriel. 1964. *Egyptian Guilds in Modern Times*. Jerusalem: Israel Oriental Society.
Bartlett, W. H. 1849. *The Nile Boat: or, Glimpses of the Land of Egypt*. London: Arthur Hall, Virtue.
Beaumont, Cyril. 1956. *Complete Book of Ballets: A Guide to the Principal Ballets of the Nineteenth and Twentieth Centuries*. London: Putnam.
Behdad, Ali. 1994. *Belated Travelers: Orientalism in the Age of Colonial Dissolution*. Durham: Duke University Press.
Belliard, Augustin Daniel, et al. 1830–36. *Histoire scientifique et militaire de l'expédition française en Égypte*, 10 vols. Paris: A. J. Denain.
———. 1842. *Mémoires du Comte Belliard: Écrits par lui-même; Receuillis et mis en ordre par M. Vinet l'un de ses aides-de camp*, 3 vols. Paris: Berquet et Pétion.
Belzoni, Giovanni Battista. 1821. *Narrative of the Operations and Recent Discoveries Within the Pyramids, Temples, Tombs and Excavations in Egypt and Nubia, etc.* 2nd ed. London: John Murray.
Bénézit, E. 1999. *Dictionnaire critique et documentaire des peintres sculpteurs dessinateurs et graveurs*. Nouv. éd. Entièrement

refondue, reveu et corr. sous la direction des héritiers de Jacques Busse. Paris: Gründ.

Bey, Ali. (1816) 1970. *Travels of Ali Bey in Morocco, Tripoli, Cyprus, Egypt, etc.*, 2 vols. England: Gregg International.

Bida, A., and E. Barbet. 1851. *Souvenirs d'Egypte*. Paris: Impr. Lemercier.

Blanc, Charles. 1876. *Voyage de la haute Égypte: Observations sur les arts égyptien et arabe*. Paris: Librairie Renouard, H. Loones, successeur.

Bosworth, Clifford Edmund. 1976. *The Mediaeval Islamic Underworld: The Banu Sasan in Arabic Society and Literature*, 2 vols. Leiden: E. J. Brill.

Boustany, Saladin. 1971. *The Journals of Bonaparte in Egypt: 1798–1801*, 10 vols. Cairo: Al-Arab/Dar al-Maaraf. Reprints.

Brooks, Lynn Matluck. June 21–24, 2001. "Recovered Meaning: Documents and Interpretation." In the Proceedings of the Annual Society of Dance History Scholars Conference, p. 5. Baltimore: Goucher College.

Browne, William George. 1806. *Travels in Africa, Egypt, and Syria From the Year 1792 to 1798*. 2nd ed. Enlarge London: T. Cadell and W. Davis, etc.

Buonaventura, Wendy. 1983. *Belly Dancing: The Serpent and the Sphinx*. London: Virago Press.

———. 1990. *Serpent of the Nile: Women and Dance in the Arab World*. New York: Interlink Books.

Bürgel, J. C. 1979. "Love, Lust, and Longing: Eroticism as Reflected in Literary Sources." In *Society and the Sexes in Medieval Islam*, ed. Afaf Lutfi al-Sayyid Marsot, 81–117. Malibu, CA: Undena Publications.

Burkhardt, John Lewis. 1984 (reprint). *Arabic Proverbs: Or the Manners and Customs of the Modern Egyptians Illustrated From Their Proverbial Sayings Current in Cairo*. London: Curzon.

Carlton, Donna. 1994. *Looking for Little Egypt*. Bloomington, IN: IDD Books.

Carne, John. 1826. *Letters from the East*. London: H. Colburn.

Carré, Jean Marie. 1956. *Voyageurs et écrivains français en Égypte*, 2 vols. Rev. 2nd ed. Le Caire: Institut français d'archéologie orientale.

Centre Cuturel Français de Turin. 1998. *Voyage en Egypte: récits de femmes du XIXème siècle*. Turin.

Chabrol, Gilbert-Joseph Gaspard de. 1822. "Essai sur les moeurs des habitans modernes de l'Égypte." In *Description de l'Égypte (ou Recueil des observations et des recherches qui ont été faites en Égypte pendant l'expédition de l'armée française, publié Par ordre du Gouvernement)*, État Moderne, vol. 2, pt. 2, 361–524. Paris: Imprimerie royale.

Champollion, Jean-François. 1986. *Lettres et journaux écrits pendant le voyage d'Égypte: recueillis et annotés par H. Hartleben*. Paris: Christian Bourgois éditeur.

Chennells, Ellen. 1893. *Recollections of an Egyptian Princess by Her English Governess*. Edinburgh: Blackwood & Sons.

Churi, Joseph H. 1853. *Sea Nile the Desert and Nigritia: Travels in Company with Captain Peel, R. N. 1851–52*. London: The author.

Clot-Bey, A[ntoine]- B[arthélemy]. 1840. *Aperçu général sur l'Égypte*, 2 vols. Paris: Fortin, Masson.

Colet, Louise. 1879. *Les pays lumineux: voyage en orient*. Paris: Librairie de la Société des Gens de lettres, E. Dentu.

Combes, Edmond. 1846. *Voyage en Égypte, en Nubie*, 2 vols. Paris: Desessart.

Coutelle, Jean Marie Joseph. 1812. "Observations sur la Topographie de la Presqu'île de Sinaï, les moeurs, les usages, l'industrie, le commerce et la population des habitans." In *Description de l'Égypte (ou Recueil des observations et des recherches qui ont été faites en Égypte pendant l'expédition de l'armée française, publié par les orders de sa majesté l'empereur Napoléon le Grand)*, État Moderne, vol. 2, pt. 2, 277–304. Paris: Imprimerie impériale.

Cruysmans, Philippe. 1982. *Orientalist Painting/Peinture Orientaliste*. Trans. Jonathan Fryer. Brussels: Editions Laconti and P. & V. Berko.

Curtis, George William. 1856. *Nile Notes of a Howadji*. New York: Harper & Brothers.

Danielson, Virginia. 1988. "The Arab Middle East." In *Popular Musics of the Non-Western World: An Introductory Survey.* Ed. Peter Manuel. New York: Oxford University Press.

Davies, J. G. 1984. *Liturgical Dance: An Historical, Theological and Practical Handbook.* London: SCM Press.

Deagon, Andrea. 2003. "Framing the Ancient History of Oriental Dance." *Habibi* 19 (3): 32–41.

Décoret-Ahiha, Anne. 2004. *Les danses exotiques en France 1880–1940.* Paris: Centre national de la danse.

Denon, Vivant. 1973. *Travels in Upper and Lower Egypt.* New York: Arno Press, Middle East Collection. Reprint and translation of 1802–03 edition.

Desmond, Jane C., ed. 2001. "Making the Invisible Visible: Staging Sexualities through Dance." In *Dancing Desires: Choreographing Sexualities on and off the Stage*, 3–32. Madison: University of Wisconsin Press.

Didier, Charles. 1858. *Cinq cents lieues sur le Nil.* Paris: Hachette.

———. 1860. *Les nuits du Caire.* Paris: Hachette.

Doubleday, Veronica. 1999. "The Frame Drum in the Middle East: Women, Musical Instruments, and Power." *Ethnomusicology* 43 (1): 101–34.

Du Bois-Aymé, Jean-Marie. 1809. "Mémoire sur la ville de Qoçeyr et ses environs et sur les peoples nomads qui habitent cette partie de l'ancienne troglodytique." In *Description de l'Égypte (ou Recueil des observations et des recherches qui ont été faites en Égypte pendant l'expédition de l'armée française, publié par les orders de sa majesté l'empereur Napoléon le Grand)*, État Moderne, vol. 1, 193–202. Paris: Imprimerie impériale.

Du Bois-Aymé, Jean-Marie, and Jean-Baptiste Prosper Jollois. 1812. "Voyage dans l'intérieur de Delta, Contenant des Recherches géographiques sur quelques villes anciennes, et des Observations sur les moeurs et les usages des Égyptiens modernes." In *Description de l'Égypte (ou Recueil des observations et des recherches qui ont été faites en Égypte pendant l'expédition de l'armée française, publié par les orders de sa majesté l'empereur Napoléon le Grand)*, État Moderne, vol. 2, pt. 1, 91–120. Paris: Imprimerie impériale.

Duff Gordon, Lady Lucie. (1902) 1983. *Letters from Egypt.* London: Virago.

Dumas, Alexandre [and Adrien Dauzats]. 1846. *Quinze jours au Sinai*, 2 vols., 2nd ed. Paris: Recoules, Librairie Commissionaire.

———. 1848. "Égypte sous la domination de Méhémet Aly." *Égypte.* Volume in series. *L'Univers, Histoire et Description de tous les Peuples.* Paris: Firmin, Didot Freres, Editeurs.

———. 1913–36. *Encyclopædia of Islam.* 1st ed. Leiden, Netherlands: E. J. Brill.

———. 1998. *L'Égypte au regard de J.J. Rifaud (1786–1852).* Nivelles: Société Royale d'Archéologie et de Folklore de Nivelles et du Brabant Wallon.

Estourmel, Joseph. 1844. *Journal d'un voyage en orient*, 2 vols. Paris: Crapelet.

Ettinghausen, Richard. 1984. "Jean-Léon Gérôme as a Painter of Near Eastern Life." In *Islamic Art and Archaeology: Collected Papers.* Ed. Myriam Rosen Ayalon. Berlin: Gebr. Mann Verlag.

———. 1999. *Explorer Égypte et la Nubie au début du XIXe siècle.* Morlanwelz: Musée royal de Mariemont.

al-Faruqi, Lois Ibsen. 1978. "Dance as an Expression of Islamic culture." *Dance Research Journal* 10 (2): 6–14.

———. 1985. "Music, Musicians and Muslim Law." *Asian Music* XVII (Fall/Winter): 3–36.

Flaubert, Gustave. 1965. *Les lettres d'Égypte d'après les manuscrits autographes: édition critique par Antoine Youssef Namaan.* Paris: A. G. Nizet.

———. 1991. *Voyage en Égypte/Gustave Flaubert: édition intégrale du manuscrit original établie et présenté par Pierre-Marc de Biasi.* Paris: B. Grasset.

———. 1996. *Flaubert in Egypt: A Sensibility on Tour; a Narrative Drawn from Gustave Flaubert's Notes and Letters.* Trans. and ed. Francis Steegmuller. New York: Penguin.

Forbin, Louis Nicolas Phillippe Auguste. 1819. *Voyage dans le Levant en 1817 et 1818.* Paris: Imprimerie royale.

France, Commission des sciences et arts d'Égypte. 1809–22. *Description de l'Égypte: où, recueil des observations et des recherches qui ont été faites en Égypte pendant l'éxpédition de l'armée française*. État Moderne, 2 vols., 1 Atlas. Paris: Imprimerie imp.

France, Commission des sciences et arts d'Égypte. 1809–28. *Description de l'Égypte: où, recueil des observations et des recherches qui ont été faites en Égypte pendant l'éxpédition de l'armée Française*, 21 vols. Paris: Imprimerie imp.

Fraser, Kathleen W. 1991. "The Aesthetics of Belly Dance: Egyptian-Canadians Discuss the Baladi." M.F.A. Thesis, York University, Toronto.

———. 1992. Review of *Serpent of the Nile: Women and Dance in the Arab World*, by Wendy Buonaventura. *Dance Research Journal* 24 (2): 45–47.

———. 2002. "Public and Private Entertainments at a Royal Egyptian Wedding: 1845." *Habibi* 19 (1): 36–38.

———. 2004. "Learning Belly Dance in Toronto: Pyramids, Goddesses and Other Weird Stuff." In *Canadian Dance: Visions and Stories*, ed. Selma Landen Odom and Mary Jane Warner, 423–34. Toronto: Dance Collection Danse.

Gadamer, Hans-Georg. 1976. *Philosophical Hermeneutics*. Trans. and ed. David E. Linge. Berkeley: University of California Press.

Galland, A. 1804. *Tableau de l'Égypte pendant le séjour de l'armée Française*, 2 vols. Paris: Code civil officiel, Palais du tribunal/chez Galland.

Garafola, Lynn, ed. 1997. *Rethinking the Sylph: New Perspectives on the Romantic Ballet*. Hanover, NH: Wesleyan University Press.

Gautier, Théophile. 1991. *Voyage en Égypte: presentation et notes de Paolo Tortonese*. Paris: La Boîte à Documents. Reprints.

Gérôme & Goupil: Art and Enterprise. 2000. Paris: Éditions de la Réunion des musées nationaux.

Gonse, Louis. 1881. *D'un voyage en Égypte*. Paris: A. Quantin.

Goupil Fesquet, Frédéric Auguste Antoine. 1843. *Voyage d'Horace Vernet en orient, rédigé par M. Goupil Fesquet*. Paris: Challamel.

Graham-Brown, Sarah. 1988. *Images of Women: The Portrayal of Women in Photography of the Middle East—1860 to 1950*. New York: Columbia University Press.

Güell, Eduardo Toda y. 1889. *A Través del Egipto*. Madrid: El Progresso Editorial.

el-Guindi, Fadwa. 1990. *El Sebou': Egyptian Birth Ritual*. Los Angeles: El Nil Research and Office of Folklore Programs, Smithsonian Institution, 16mm, 27 min.

Guthrie, Shirley. 1995. *Arab Social Life in the Middle Ages: An Illustrated History*. London: Saqi Books.

Haery, Mahmoud M. 1982. "Ru-Howzi: The Iranian Traditional Improvisatory Theatre." PhD diss., New York University.

Haïm, S. 1969. *New Persian-English Dictionary*. Teheran: Librairie-Béroukhim.

Hamont, P. N. 1845. *L'Égypte sous Méhémet-Ali*, 2 vols. Paris: Léautey et Lecointe.

Hanawalt, Barbara A. 1998. "At the Margins of Women's Space in Medieval Europe." In *'Of Good and Ill Repute': Gender and Social Control in Medieval England*, 70–87. Oxford: Oxford University Press.

Hanna, Judith Lynne. 1988. *Dance, Sex, and Gender: Signs of Identity, Dominance, Defiance, and Desire*. Chicago: University of Chicago Press.

Hattox, Ralph S. 1985. *Coffee and Coffeehouses: The Origins of a Social Beverage in the Medieval Near East*. Seattle: University of Washington Press.

Hayyim, Sulayman. 1968–69. *The Larger Persian-English Dictionary Designed to Give the Persian Meanings of 80,000 Words, Idioms, Phrases, and Proverbs in the English Language, etc.* Tehran: Beroukhim.

Henni-Chebra, Djamila, and Christian Poché, eds. 1996. *Les danses dans le monde arabe ou l'héritage des almées*. Paris: L'Harmattan.

Hermant, M. A. 1895. "L'Égypte en 1798," *La Revue bleue*, 4th series, 3 (2): 48–52.

Herold, J. Christopher. 1963. *Bonaparte in Egypt*. London: Hamish Hamilton.

Hering, Fanny Field. 1892. *Gérôme: The Life and Works of Jean Léon Gérôme: From*

Autobiographical Notes and Letters by the Artist Himself. New York: Cassell.

Hume, Dr. 1818. "Remarks on the Manner and Customs of the Modern Inhabitants of Egypt." In *Memoirs Relating to European and Asiatic Turkey and Other Countries of the East*, by Robert Walpole, 2nd ed., 388–406. London: Longman, Hurst, Rees, Orne, Brown.

Ibn Iyas, Muhammad. 1955–60. *Journal d'un bourgeois du Caire: chronique d'Ibn Iyas/traduit et annoté par Gaston Wiet*, 2 vols. Paris: A. Colin.

al-Jabarti, 'Abd al–Rahman. 1888–96. *Merveilles biographiques et historiques; ou chroniques du cheikh Abd-el-Rahman el Djabarti; traduites de l'arabe par Chefik Mansour bey et al.*, 9 vols. Le Caire: Imprimerie nationale.

———. 1971. *Bonaparte's Proclamations as Recorded by 'Abd al–Rahman al–Jabarti.* In *Journals of Bonaparte in Egypt, 1798–1801*, vol. 10. Cairo: Dar al-Maaref.

Johnson-Odim, Cheryl, and Margaret Strobel. 1999. "Conceptualizing the History of Women in Africa, Asia, Latin America and the Caribbean, and the Middle East and North Africa." In *Women in the Middle East and North Africa*, ed. Guity Nashat and Judith E. Tucker, xxvii-lxi. Bloomington: Indiana University Press.

Jollois, Jean-Baptiste Prosper. 1822. "Notice sur la ville de Rosette, comprenant la description de la traversée par mer d'Alexandrie dans cette ville, et du voyage par le Nil de Rosette au Kaire." In *Description de l'Égypte (ou Recueil des observations et des recherches qui ont été faites en Égypte pendant l'expédition de l'armée française, publié Par ordre du Gouvernement)*, État Moderne, vol. 2, pt. 2, 333–60. Paris: Imprimerie royale.

Jomard, Edmé François. 1822. "Description abrégée de la ville, et du voyage par le Nil de Rosette au Kaire. In *Description de l'Égypte (ou Recueil des observations et des recherches qui ont été faites en Égypte pendant l'expédition de l'armée française, publié Par ordre du Gouvernement)*, État Moderne, vol. 2, pt. 2, 579–786. Paris: Imprimerie royale.

Jomard, M. [Edmé François]. 1836. *Coup d'oeil impartial sur l'état présent de l'Égypte, comparé à sa situation antérieure.* Paris: Béthune et Plon.

Julien, Philippe. 1977. *Les Orientalistes.* Fribourg: Office du Livre.

Kaeppler, Adrienne. 2000. "Dance Ethnology and the Anthropology of Dance." *Dance Research Journal* 32 (1): 116–21.

Kalfatovic, Martin R. 1992. *Nile Notes of a Howadji: A Bibliography of Travelers' Tales from Egypt, from the Earliest Time to 1918.* Metuchen, NJ: Scarecrow Press.

Karayanni, Stavros Stavrou. 2002. "The Ghaziya and the Khawaja: Kuchuk Hanem and Flaubert's Sexual Homelessness." *Habibi* 19 (1): 18–21.

———. 2004. *Dancing Fear and Desire: Race, Sexuality & Imperial Politics in Middle Eastern Dance.* Waterloo, Canada: Wilfred Laurier Press.

el-Khadem, Saad. 1972. *Al-Raqs al-shabi fi Misr (Folk Dance in Egypt).* Cairo: Cultural Library Series, Egyptian General Book Organization.

La Jonquière, Clémont Étienne Lucien Marie de Taffanel. n.d. *L'Expédition d'Egypte: 1798–1801*, 5 vols. Paris: Henri Charles-Lavanzelle.

Lane, Edward William. (1860) 1973. *An Account of the Manners and Customs of the Modern Egyptians.* New York: Dover.

———. (1863) 1984. *Arabic-English Lexicon.* Cambridge: Islamic Texts Society.

———. 1865. *The Thousand and One Nights.* Ed. Edward Stanley Poole, 3 vols. London: Routledge, Warne, and Routledge.

———. (1895) 1978. *An Account of the Manners and Customs of the Modern Egyptians.* The Hague and New York: East-West Publications.

———. 2000. *Description of Egypt: Note and Views in Egypt and Nubia Made During the Years 1825, 26, 27, and 28, etc.* Ed. Jason Thompson. Cairo: American University in Cairo Press.

Lane-Poole, Sophia. 1846. *An Englishwoman in Egypt: Letters from Cairo Written During a Residence There in 1845–6, with E. W. Lane Esq., by his Sister.* Second Series. London: Charles Knight.

———. 1851. *An Englishwoman in Egypt:*

Letters from Cairo Written During a Residence There in 1842–4, with E. W. Lane Esq., by his Sister, 2 vols. London: C. Cox.

Larrey, Dominique le Baron. 1809. "Mémoire et observations sur plusieurs maladies, Qui ont affecté les troupes de l'armée Française pendant l'expédition d'Égypte et de Syrie, et qui sont endémiques dans ces deux contrées." In *Description de l'Égypte (ou Recueil des observations et des recherches qui ont été faites en Égypte pendant l'expédition de l'armée française, publié par les orders de sa majesté l'empereur Napoléon le Grand)*, État Moderne vol. 1, 427–524. Paris: Imprimerie impériale.

Lelland, Charles. G. 1874. *The Egyptian Sketch Book*. New York: Hurd and Houghton.

Lenoir, Paul. 1872. *Le Fayoum, le Sinaï et Pétra.: expédition dans la moyenne Égypte et l'Arabie pétrée, sous la direction de J. L. Gérôme*. Paris: H. Plon.

Lexová, Irena. (1935) 2000. *Ancient Egyptian Dances*. Mineola, NY: Dover.

L'Hôte, Nestor. 1993. *Sur le Nil avec Champollion: lettres, journaux et dessins inédits de Nestor L'Hôte: premier voyage en Égypte, 1828–1830/Recuellis par Diane Harlé et Jean Lefebvre*. Orléans-Caen: Éditions Paradigme.

Lièvre, Viviane. 1987. *Danses du Maghreb: d'une rive à l'autre*. Paris: Éditions Karthala.

Mabro, Judy, ed. 1991. *Veiled Half-Truths: Western Travellers' Perceptions of Middle-Eastern Women*. London: I. B. Tauris.

Marcel, J. J., Amédée Ryme, et al. 1848. *Egypte*. Volume in Series *L'Univers, Histoire et Description de tous les Peuples*. Paris: Firmin, Didot Frères, Éditeurs.

Marmont, Auguste Frédéric Louis Viesse de, duc de Raguse. 1837–38. *Voyage du maréchal, duc de Raguse: en Hongrie, en Transylvanie, dans la Russie méridionale ... en Syrie, en Palestine, et en Égypte, 1834–35*, 5 vols. Paris: Ladvocat.

Maximilian, Herzoge. 1978. *Wanderung nach dem Orient im Jahre 1838/unternommen u. skizziert von d. Herzoge Maximilian in Bayern*. Munich: Verlag W. Ludwig.

Mayer, Luigi. 1801. *Views in Egypt from the Original Drawings in the Possession of Sir Robert Ainslie Taken During his Embassy to Constantinople*. London: Printed by Thomas Bensley for R. Bower.

McPherson, J. W. 1941. *The Moulids of Egypt*. Cairo: N. M. Press.

Mengin, Felix. 1839. *Histoire sommaire de l'Egypte sous le gouvernement de Mohammed-Aly ... précedée d'une introduction et suivie d'études géographiques et historiques sur l'Arabie par M. Jomard*. Paris: Fermin Didot.

Meriwether, Margaret L., and Judith E. Tucker, eds. 1999. *A Social History of Women and Gender in the Modern Middle East*. Boulder: Westview Press.

Michaud, J. *Correspondance d'orient, 1830–1831*. 1833–35 (seven volumes). Paris: Ducollet.

Milleliri, Jean-Marie. 1993. *Médecins et soldats pendant l'expédition d'Égypte:1798–1799*. Nice: B. Giovanangeli.

Minutoli, Wolfradine (von der Schulenburg) von Watzdorf, freiherrn von. 1827. *Recollections of Egypt: by the Baroness von Minutoli*. London: Treuttel & Würtz, Treuttel, Jun. & Richter.

Montbard, Georges [Charles A. Loyes, pseud.]. 18—. *En Égypte: notes et croquis d'un artiste*. Paris: Monde illustrée.

Montulé, Édouard de. 1821. *Travels in Egypt During 1818 and 1819*. London: Printer G. Sidney, for Sir Richard Phillips.

Nashat, Guity, and Judith E. Tucker. 1999. *Women in the Middle East and North Africa: Restoring Women to History*. Bloomington: Indiana University Press.

Nerval, Gérard de. 1929. *The Women of Cairo: Scenes of Life in the Orient*, 2 vols. London: Routledge.

Niebuhr, Carsten. (1792) n.d. *Travels Through Arabia and Other Countries in the East*. Trans. Robert Heron. Beirut: Librairie du Liban.

———. 1968. *Reise beschreibung nach Arabien und den umliegenden ländern*, 3 vols. Graz: Akademische Druck—u. Verlagsanstalt.

Nieuwkerk, Karin van. 1995. *A Trade Like Any Other: Female Singers and Dancers in Egypt*. Austin: University of Texas Press.

Pharaon, Florian. 1872. *Le Caire et la Haute*

Egypte: dessins de A. Darjou. Paris: E. Dentu.

Poché, Christian. 1996. "La danse arabe: quelques repères." In *Les danses dans le monde arabe ou l'héritage des almées,* ed. Djamila Henni-Chebra and Christian Poché. Paris: L'Harmattan.

Pococke, Richard, Bp. of Meath. 1743–45. *Observations on Egypt: Description of the East and Some Other Countries,* vol. 1. 3 pts. in 2 vols. London: printed for the author by W. Bowyer.

Popescu-Judetz, Eugenia. 1982. "Köçek and Çengi in Turkish Culture." *Dance Studies* 6: 46–58.

Prisse d'Avennes [Émile]. 1930. *Petits Mémoires secrets sur la Cour d'Égypte suivis d'une Étude sur les Almées.* Paris: Jacques Bernard la Centaine.

Racy, Ali Jihad. 1983. "Music." In *The Genius of Arab Civilization: Source of the Renaissance,* ed. J. R. Hayes. 2nd ed. Cambridge: MIT Press.

al-Rawi, Rosina-Fawzia. 1999. *Grandmother's Secrets: The Ancient Rituals and Healing Power of Belly Dancing.* Trans. Monique Arav. New York: Interlink.

Raymond, André. 1973–74. *Artisans et commerçants au Caire au XVIIIe siècle,* 2 vols. Damas: Institut Français de Damas.

———. 1956–57. "Une Liste des corporations de métiers au Caire en 1801." *Arabica* 3 (4): 150–63.

Redouane, Aïcha, and the Al-Adwar Ensemble. 1993. *Egypte: art vocal et instrumental du XIX siècle.* Paris: Ocora, Radio France, CD-C560020.

Roberts, David. 1846–49. *Egypt and Nubia: From Drawings Made on the Spot by David Roberts,* 3 vols. in 2 pts. London: F. G. Moon.

———. 1996. *Egypt: Yesterday and Today.* Shrewsbury: Swan Hill.

Romer, Mrs. [Isabella F.]. 1846. *A Pilgrimage to the Temples and Tombs of Egypt, Nubia, and Palestine in 1845-6,* 2 vols. London: Richard Bentley.

Rosenthal, Franz. 1979. "Fiction and Reality: Sources for the Role of Sex in Medieval Muslim Society." In *Society and the Sexes in Medieval Islam,* ed. Afaf Lutfi al Sayyid Marsot, 3–22. Malibu, CA: Undena Publications.

Said, Edward W. 1979. *Orientalism.* New York: Vintage Books.

———. 2001. "Farewell to Tahia." In *Colors of Enchantment: Theater, Dance, Music and the Visual Arts of the Middle East,* ed. Sherifa Zuhur, 228–32. Cairo: American University in Cairo Press.

St. John, Bayle. 1850. *Two Years in a Levantine Family.* London: Chapman and Hall.

———. (1852) 1973. *Village Life in Egypt,* 2 vols. New York: Arno Press, Middle East Collection.

St. John, James Augustus. 1834. *Egypt and Muhammad Ali; Or, Travels in the Valley of the Nile,* 2 vols. London: Longman, Rees, Orme, Brown, Green & Longman.

———. 1845. *Egypt and Nubia: Their Scenery and Their People, Being Incidents of History and Travel from the Best and Most Recent Authorities Including J. L. Burckhardt and Lord Lindsay.* London: Chapman and Hall.

———. 1851. *Oriental Album: Characters, Costumes and Modes of Life in the Valley of the Nile: Illustrated from Designs Taken on the Spot by E. Prisse: With Descriptive Letterpress by James Augustus St. John.* London: J. Madden.

Saleh, Magda Ahmed Abdel. 1979. "A Documentation of the Ethnic Dance Tradition of the Arab Republic of Egypt." PhD diss., New York University.

Sattin, Anthony. 1988. *Lifting the Veil: British Society in Egypt, 1768–1956.* London: J. M. Dent.

Savary, [Claude Étienne]. 1785. *Lettres sur l'Égypte: où l'on offre le parallèle des moeurs anciennes & moderne de ses habitans; etc.,* 3 vols. Paris: Onfroi.

Sawa, Suzanne Meyers. 1987. "The Role of Women in Musical Life: The Medieval Arabo-Islamic Courts." *Canadian Women's Studies* 8 (2): 93–95.

al-Sayyid Marsot, Afaf Lutfi. 1984. *Egypt in the Reign of Muhammad Ali.* Cambridge: Cambridge University Press.

———. 1995. *Women and Men in Late Eighteenth-Century Egypt.* Austin: University of Texas Press.

Shay, Anthony. June 13–16, 1996.

"Limitations of Iranian Iconographic Sources for the Development of Historical Evidence of Iranian Dancing." In the Proceedings of the Society of Dance History Scholars Nineteenth Annual Conference. Minneapolis: University of Minnesota.

———. 1999. *Choreophobia: Solo Improvised Dance in the Iranian World*. Costa Mesa, CA: Mazda Publishers.

———. September 2002. "Dance and Jurisprudence in the Islamic Middle East." *Habibi* 19 (2): 26–39.

———. 2002. "Is a Picture Worth a Thousand Words?: Iconographic Sources of Middle East Dancing." *Habibi* 19 (1): 22–35.

Shay, Anthony, and Barbara Sellers-Young, eds. 2005. *Belly Dance: Orientalism, Transnationalism and Harem Fantasy*. Costa Mesa, CA: Mazda Publishers.

el-Shayyal, Gamal el–Din. 1962. "Historiography in Egypt in the Nineteenth Century." In *Historians of the Middle East*, ed. Bernard Lewis and P. M. Holt, 403–21. Oxford: Oxford University Press.

Shiloah, Amnon. 1962. "Réflexions sur la danse artistique musulmane au moyen âge." *Cahiers de civilization médiévale* 5 (4): 463–74.

Shoshan, Boaz. 1993. *Popular Culture in Medieval Cairo*. Cambridge: Cambridge University Press.

Siliotti, Alberto. 1998. *Egypt Lost and Found: Explorers and Travellers on the Nile*. London: Thames and Hudson.

Sonnini, Charles Sigisbert [de Manoncourt]. 1799. *Travels in Upper and Lower Egypt: Undertaken by Order of the Old Government of France ... translated from the French by Henry Hunter D.D.*, 3 vols. London: J. Stockdale.

Stanhope, Hester Lucy. 1983. *Travels of Lady Hester Stanhope*, 3 vols. Salzburg: Institut fur Anglistik und Americanistik, Universität Salzburg.

Starkey, Peter, and Janet Starkey, eds. 1998. *Travellers in Egypt*. London: I. B. Tauris.

Steingass, Francis. J. 1984. *A Comprehensive Persian-English Dictionary, Including the Arabic Words and Phrases to be Met with in Persian Literature, Etc.* 7th impression. Enlarged. Rev. ed. London: Iran University Press, Routledge & Kegan Paul.

Taschen, Benedikt. 1994. *Description de l'Égypte: publiée par les ordres de Napoléon Buonaparte*. Köln: Benedikt Taschen.

Taylor, Isidore Justin Séverin. 1856. *L'Égypte, par le R. P. Laorty-Hadji*. [pseud.] Paris: Bolle-Lasalle.

Thompson, James. 1988. *Orientalist Nineteenth Century Painting*. Dublin: National Gallery of Ireland.

Thompson, William Irwin. 1989. *Imaginary Landscape: Making Worlds of Myth and Science*. New York: St. Martin's Press.

Tucker, Judith E. 1985. *Women in Nineteenth-Century Egypt*. Cambridge: Cambridge University Press.

Villoteau, Guillaume. 1809a. "De l'état actuel de l'art musical en Égypte, ou Relation historique et descriptive des Recherches et Observations faites sur la Musique en ce pays." In *Description de l'Égypte (ou Recueil des observations et des recherches qui ont été faites en Égypte pendant l'expédition de l'armée française, publié par les orders de sa majesté l'empereur Napoléon le Grand)*, État Moderne vol. 1, 605–847. Paris: Imprimerie impériale.

———. 1809b. "Description historique, technique et littéraire, des instrumens de musique des Orienteaux." In *Description de l'Égypte (ou Recueil des observations et des recherches qui ont été faites en Égypte pendant l'expédition de l'armée française, publié par les orders de sa majesté l'empereur Napoléon le Grand)*, État Moderne 1: 847–1016. Paris: Imprimerie impériale.

Voilquin, Suzanne. 1978. *Souvenirs d'une fille du peuple: ou, la saint-simonienne en Égypte, 1834 à 1836*. Paris: F. Maspero.

Volkoff, Oleg V. 1972. *Voyageurs russes en Égypte*. [Le Caire]: Institut français d'archéologie orientale du Caire.

Volney, C. F. [Constantin François]. 1959. *Voyage en Égypte et en Syrie [pendant les années 1783, 1784 et 1785]: publié avec une introd. et des notes de Jean Gaulmier*. Paris: The Hague, Mouton.

Walther, Wiebke. 1993. *Women in Islam: From Medieval to Modern Times*. Rev. ed. Princeton: Markus Wiener Publishing.

Warburton, Eliot. 1846. *The Crescent and*

the Cross; or, Romance and Realities of Eastern Travel, 2 vols. 4th ed. London: Henry Colburn.

Wehr, Hans. (1979) 1994. *Arabic-English Dictionary: The Hans Wehr Dictionary of Modern Written Arabic*. 4th ed. Ed. J. Milton Cowan. Ithaca, NY: Spoken Languages Services.

Wiet, Gaston. 1964. *Cairo, City of Art and Commerce*. Norman: University of Oklahoma Press.

Wilkinson, Sir Gardner. 1843. *Modern Egypt and Thebes: Being a Description of Egypt*, 2 vols., 2nd ed. London: John Murray.

Wilson, Kax. 1979. *A History of Textiles*. Boulder: Westview Press.

Winter, Michael. 1992. *Egyptian Society Under Ottoman Rule, 1517–1798*. London and New York: Routledge.

Wood, Leona, and Anthony Shay. 1976. "Danse du ventre: a Fresh Appraisal." *Dance Research Journal* 8 (2): 18–30.

Yeazell, Ruth Bernard. 2000. *Harems of the Mind: Passages of Western Art and Literature*. New Haven: Yale University Press.

Zuhur, Sherifa, ed. 1998. *Images of Enchantment: Visual and Performing Arts of the Middle East*. Cairo: American University in Cairo Press.

———. 2001. *Colors of Enchantment: Theater, Dance, Music and the Visual Arts of the Middle East*. Cairo: American University in Cairo Press.

Index

Numbers in ***bold italics*** indicate pages with photographs.

Abbas 54, 61, 62, 127, 129, 130, 131, 132, 133, 135, 160, 161, 164–65
'Abd ar–Raziq 36, 37, 59, 72, 90, 95, 106, 110, 172
Abu Tig 53, 78
Abu Za'bal 66, 231
Aisha of Alexandria 129, 216, 218
Alexandria 9, 16, 49, 72, 82, 115, 130, 210; restrictions on dance in 50, 65, 70, 75, 90, 159, 160, 161, 164, 165; Bayle St. John in 26, 44, 216
alma ('awâlim) 34, 35, 37, 39
Almaz (singer) 63
And, Metin 83, 170
Andreievsky, V. 53, 132, 190, 207, 208, 220, 225
Appleton, Thomas Gold 21, 53, 54, 91, 186–87, ***186***; biography 253
Arabic-English Dictionary (Wehr) 37
Arabic-English Lexicon (Lane) 27
Arabic music *see* music
Aradoon, Zarifa 10, 38, 137, 140
Aswan 27, 55, 115, 121, 150, 232; Aziza of 79, 96, 132, 135, 185, 207, 209; Safiyya of 29, 71, 138–39
Asyût 1, 40, 53, 72, 80, 132; and Badawiyya of Qena 144; performances in ***185***, 186, 190, 197, 209, 224
audience 35, 36, 64, 67, 68, 100, 101, 226, 242, 246, 247, 249; dancers' relations with 61, 65, 113, 126, 130, 131, 163, 206, 217, 219, 220, 227, 233, 234, 235, 237, 239; response to dance 4, 22, 27, 29, 72, 99, 200, 222, 229, 232
Auriant [pseud.] 115, 132, 151, 152, 153, 154, 157
Aziza bint Sathi 60
Aziza of Aswan 79, 96, 132, 133, 135–36, 185, 206, 207, 209

Badawiyya of Qena 25, 53, 80, 143, 144, 209, 217, 243; *Bee Dance* 234, 235; costume 187, 193, 199; sword dance ***142***, 237–38

Badawiyya of Samannûd 78, 125
Baer, Gabriel 108, 109, 110, 111
Baghdad 168, 172, 173
Balkh 168
Bamba of Isna 133–34, 208
banishment of female entertainers 52, 54, 55, 67, 68, 70, 71, 76, 78, 90, 93, 98, 121, 129, 196, 242, 248; and Abbas 164–65; in context 164, 166, 251; date 160–63; and government 72, 80, 115, 136, 148, 158–59; punishments during 159–60; target group 65; and transvestites 81, 82, 130, 187, 230, 247
Banu Sasan 94, 95, 169, 227
Barmacides ("Barāmikeh") 168, 169, 172
Bartlett, William Henry 99–100, ***100***, 161, 185, 217; biography 21, 253
Battle of the Pyramids 16, 149
Baurenseind, Georg Wilhelm 19, ***19***, 183, 210
Beaumont, Cyril W. 241
The Bee ***210***, 223, 227, 228, 249; Badawiyya of Isna and 234; basic choreography 232–33; history 231; male performers 232; nudity in 195, 234–35
Belliard, Gen. Augustin Daniel 39, 151, 152, 154, 155–56
Belzoni, Giovanni Battista 62, 101, 237; biography 253
Beni Suef 55, 74, 75, 92, 160, 170, ***194***
Bicharra (consul) 80
Bida, Alexandre 23, ***188***, ***189***, 197; biography 22, 253
Bilbeis 110, 130
Black dancers 55, 79, 135
Blanc, Charles 55, 80, 143, 144, 161, 185–86, 194, 209, 224, 233, 234, 237; biography 25, 253
body movements 4, 45, 101; arms 179, 206; belly 190, 210; chest 207; full body 208;

291

heads 205; hips 181, 207; legs 185, 209; phallic gesture 211; and song text 203–204
Bosworth, Clifford Edmund 94, 156, 168, 169
boy dancer *see* gink; khawal
Brandin 190, *191*, 193, 208
Brooks, Lyn Matluck 12
Browne, William George 34, 60, 89; biography 253
Buktor, Jesus (consul) 104, 142
Bulaq 149, 154, 163
Buonaventura, Wendy 3, 10, 46, 63, 131–32, 149, 152, 153, 161, 170, 239
Burkhardt, John Lewis 48, 52, 53, 75, 78, 79, 91, 96, 109, 118; biography 26, 253; on gypsies 171; proverbs 43

Cairo 15, *19*, 39, 46, 64, 81, 96, 110, 117, *162*, *191*, 232; and coffee houses 94, 98, 107; costumes in 184, 185, 187; and dance ban 54, 65, 90, 93, 135, 137, 138, 159–62, 165; dancers' settlements in 48, 52, 92, 109, 116, 118, 131, 132; female performances in 22, 60–61, 62–63, 66–67, 68, 74, 75, 77, 94, 98, 101, 107, 130, 163, 194; guild list 39, 64, 81; gypsies 170; male performances in 82–85, 231, 236; Napoleon Bonaparte and 16, 148, 149–50, 152, 153
Carcy, Frédéric de 67, 216, 224
cane (stick) dance 232, 238–39, 243
Carne, John 46, 50, 53, 67, 222
çengi 171
Chabrol, Gilbert-Joseph Gaspard de 24, 75, 76, 100, 182, 229
Chama of Khartoum 137, 218
Champollion, Jean-François 46, 49, 50, 61, 75, 83, 90, 113, 114, 126, 222; biography 27, 253
choreography *see The Bee*; cane (stick) dance; cup (pot) dance; "dance of Alexandria"; "dance of the egg"; *Love Duet*; *Pure Dance*; sword dance; tambourine dance; zar
Clot, Antoine-Barthélemy *see* Clot Bey
Clot Bey 36, 109, 171, 179, 184, 193, 221; biography 25, 254; and dance ban 95, 96, 158, 159, 163; on dancing 200, 220, 223, 224, 226, 231, 235; as host 65, 66, 113, 216; on singing 61, 202
clown (in dance) *20*, *21*, 66, 69, *77*, 211, 226–27
coffee house performance 28, 45, 49, 50, 53, 59, 74, 77, 78, 94, 98, 114, 116, 138, 219, 229, 242, *239*, 247; and Badawiyya of Sammanûd 125; and *The Bee* 231; and dance training 107; origin 76; and tax farms 111; and transvestites 65, 82, 83, 247
Colet, Louise 80, 131–32, 143, 144, 187, 193, 199; on *The Bee* 233, 234, 235; biography 25, 254; on saber dance 237, 238
Combes, Edmond 35, 40, 53, 121, 127, 128, 129, 202, 209, 218, 219, 225; biography 254; on dance ban 158, 159, 160–61
consuls 49, 50, 91

Corporation 137 39, 59, 112
Corporation 139 39, 81–84
Corporation 192 39, 40, 41, 65, 72–74; ethnic diversity in 79; social status 78
Corporation 200 39, 40–42, 64, 70, 112, 135, 243
costume (for performing) 4, 23, 85, 118, 136, 184, 193–96; in Edward Lane's day 177, *178*, 179, 181; in 1840s and beyond 77, *100*, 185; and European style 186, *186*; of female musicians 196; influence of transvestites on 187, *188*, 190; Napoleonic elegant forms 20, *51*, *70*; 182–83; simple outfits pre–Edward Lane *13*, *19*, 183; in style of Hasan al-Bilbeiss 190, *191*, 192, *192*, 193; textiles and jewelry 196–99
Coutelle, Jean Marie Joseph 24, 236
cup (pot) dance 203, 239–40
Curtis, George William 35, 96, 107, 134, 161, 165; biography 28, 254; on Kutchuk Hanem 131, 132, 133, 200–201, 216, 221
Cypris of Khartoum 137

Damascus 131
Damietta 49, 50, 67, 91, 93, 126, 222
dâmina al-maghânî 110, 112, 172
"dance of Alexandria" 130
Dance of the Almeh 23, 140, 144, 187, 193, 198, *198*, 206, 207, 209; criticized as sexist 218
"dance of the egg" 185, 194, 238
Danse d'Almées, à Sihout **185**, 216
danse du ventre 10, 33, 210
Darjou, Alfred-Henri 5; *239*; 240; biography 254
Dauzats, Adrien 66, 113, 220, 221, 226; on *The Bee* 231, 233, 234, 235; biography 24, 254
Deagon, Andrea 10
Décoret-Ahiha, Anne 33
Delta (region) 48, 49, 50, 67, 72, 89, 90, 94, 109, 125, 130, 150, 162, 163, 228
Denon, Vivant 50, *51*, 62, 83, 126, 182, 218, 231; biography 24, 254
Description de l'Égypte 20, 24, 70, 71, 86, 97, 117, 181, 182, 195, 236
Desmond, Jane C. 249
Didier, Charles 38, 82, 96, 116, 130, 132, 136–37, 165, 235; biography 28, 254; on performers in Upper Egypt 55, 71, 79, 106, 115, 131, 138, 160, 217, 238, 246; on singing 61–62, 63, 203
Dishna 53, 182, 197
Disûq 114
djenk (genk) 38, 107
Doubleday, Veronica 153
Drovetti, Bernardino 22
Du Bois-Aymé, Jean-Marie 24, 49, 67, 103, 228
Du Camp, Maxine 79, 96, 135
Duff Gordon, Lady Lucie 44, 54, 61, 62, 63, 90, 93, 98, 103–104, 113, 142–43, 166, 195, 218, 244–45; biography 26, 254–55
Dugua, Gen. Charles 151, 152, 154–55

Dumas, Alexandre 255
Dutertre, André 20, *97*, 255

An Egyptian Ball at Ned Sili **20**, 120, 216
Egyptian Canadian 4, 167, 172
Enani Bey 67
Esna *see* Isna
Estourmel, Joseph 29, 68, 101, 227
Ethiopia 55, 79, 133, 137, 138, 140
Ezbekiyya 75, 84

Faiyûm 55, 75, 76, 139, 140, 185, 216, 225
Faker, Basil (consul) 67, 91
fantasia 63, 65, 71, 82, 103, 104, 136, 162, 187, 216, 245
Fathma of Girga 126
Fathma of Khartoum 137
festivals 59, 65, 72, 81, 99, *100*, 101, 114, 166, 245, 247; *see also* Said 'Abd al-Râchim; Tanta
finger cymbals *see* musical instruments
Flaubert, Gustave 121, 130, 134, 165, 208; on Aziza of Aswan 79, 96, 135, 185, 206; biography 24, 255; on Hasan al-Bilbeissi 82–83, 190, 203–204, 210, 232; on Hasna of Isna 53, 54; on Kutchuk Hanem 35, 107, 131, 132, 133, 201, 216, 233, 235, 240
Forbin, Louis Nicolas Phillippe Auguste, comte de 53, 54, 74, 92, 120, 121, 170, 183, *194*, 195, 220, 236; biography 21, 255
Frederick V (of Denmark) 19
Fregia of Khartoum 137
Fromentin, Eugène 55, 80, 143, 144, *185*, 186; biography 25, 255
Fuwa 46, 48, 49, 50, 78, 107, 113, 118

Galland, Antoine 24, 36, 152, 154, 156, 223
Gautier, Théophile 140
Gérôme, Jean-Léon 76, 98, 139, *139*, 140, *142*, 144, 196, 216, 238, 239; biography 255; *Dance of the Almeh* 23, 140, 187, 193, 198, 206, 207, 209, 218
ghawâzî 39, 41, 70, 78–79, 80, 84, 95, 111, 112, 120, 129, 148, 158, 159, 160, 161, 162, 177, *178*, *180*, 243, 246; and gypsies 121, 170, 172, 173; and Kutchuk Hanem 132; and massacre 151, 153; and (associated) musicians 40, 85, 105, 144; and performance locale 47, 72, 74–77, 93; and Persian origin 71, 168, 169, 172, 173; as term for female entertainers 34, 35, 38; *see also* Corporation 192
Ghazal of Cairo 71, 136–37, 160, 187, 196, 197, 198
gink 39, 65, 81, 82, 163, 203, 236, 247; arrival in Egypt 83; attitudes to 81–82; influence on costuming 187, 190; at royal wedding 84–85; *see also* Corporation 139; khawal
Girga 53, 54, 113, 126, 190, 198, 222, 240
Giza 52, 131
guilds 37–42, 48, 106, 107, 108–109, 111, 120, 159, 242, 243; *see also* Corporation 137; Corporation 139; Corporation 192; Corporation 200; shaikha al-maghani

gypsies (Roma) 79, 85, 121, 148, 153, 168, 169, 170, 173, 251; and Egyptian dancers 171–72; etymology of name 171

Hackländer, S.W. 28, 66–67, 187, 221, 222, 225, 226, 228, 230, 239; biography 255
Hadely of Cairo 130
Hamont, P.N. 43–44, 65, 82; biography 25–26, 255; and dance ban 90, 112, 158, 159, 160, 162, 163
Hanka of Mutûbis 126, 127, 218
harem 3, 24, 25, 29, 41, 67, 68, 72, 93, 103, 117, 246; eye-witness descriptions 93–94, 101; royal harem 68–70, 85, 106, 114, 183; and Sakna in 62–63; singing in 61–62, 64
Harun al-Rachid 168
Hasan al-Bilbeissi 82–83, 130, 203, 204, 210; costume style 190, 193, 196
Hasna of Luxor and Qena 53, 54, 91, 129, 132, 134–35
Hasna of the Faiyûm 76, 98, 139–40, 185, 216, 225; depiction *139*, *141*
Hayyim, Sulayman 38
Heliopolis 52, 92, 109
Henni-Chabra, Djamila 2, 10, 185
Herold, Christopher J. 151–52, 154, 157
Hillaliyya of Luxor 140, 143
Hollywood 3, 250
housing (of female entertainers) *97*, 116, 117–18
Hume, Doctor 49

Ibn Ayas 60
Ibrahim (son of Muhammad Ali) 165
income (of female entertainers) 55, 75, 77, 92, 110, 113–15, 116, 118, 121, 219, 220, 234, 250; cashmere shawls as 61, 69, 114; *see also* tipping
Iraq 105, 168, 172
Islam and dance 45, 59, 163, 245
Ismail (descendant of Muhammad Ali) 18, 25, 80
Isna 29, 54, 80, 91, 96, 116, 128, 131–32, 133, 186, *186*, 190; and dance ban 55, 115, 159, 160, 161, 165; sword dance in 238
Istanbul 15, 19, 54, 83, 108, 187, 236

al-Jabarti, 'Abd al-Rahman 43, 46, 96, 149, 150, 156; biography 255; use of raqqâsin 38, 40, 64
Jammala (singer) 63
jankiyya 37, 38, 169, 171, 172
jewelry 66, 117, 118, 179, 199
Jews 36, 38, 44, 61, 74, 81, 107, 129, 168
Jollois, Jean Baptiste 49, 67, 103, 228; biography 24
Jomard, Edmé François 46, 95, 111, 183, 203, 229; biography 24
Jonquière, Clément Étienne la 152, 154, 155
Joseph (Flaubert's guide) 130, 232, 233
Josephina of Mutûbis 126, 127, 218

Kafr Raiak 52
Kala of Alexandria 68, 71, 129–30, 143, 168, 169, 172, 216, 218, 220
Karayanni, Stavros Stavrou 11, 249
Khadem, Saad el- 231, 232, 240
Khartoum 28, 55, 103, 106, 137, 195, 217, 218, 237
khawal 19, 65, 81, 82, 130, 163, 203, 236, 247; attitude to 81–82; influence on costume 190, 187, 190; at royal wedding 84, 85; *see also* Corporation 139; gink
Kutchuk Hanem 24, 28, 35, 52, 96, 134, 251; biography 55, 79, 116, 117, 121, 127, 129, 131–33, 162, 165; costume 197, 198; performances 107, 200–201, 206, 209, 216, 221, 225, 233, 235, 239

Lane, Edward 46, 60, 61, 76, 93, 95, 106, 112, 116, 168, 221, 224, 245; biography 22, 26–27, 29; on dance ban 159, 160, 161; on dance costumes 177, *178*, 179, 181, 182, 195, 199; on guilds 40–41, 78–79; on gypsies 171, 172; on male performers 81, 83, 85–86, 247
Lane-Poole, Sophia 65, 68–70, 84–85, 93, 114, 115, 183; biography 29, 256
Larrey, Baron Dominique Jean 24
Latifa of Qena 140–43
Leland, Charles 53, 54, 65, 190, 231, 239; biography 28, 256; on choreography 203, 208, 209, 220, 225–26, 240; on dance ban 162
Lenoir, Paul 55, 76, 98, 139, 140, 225, 256
L'Hôte, Nestor 54, 83, 113, 126, 222; biography 27, 256
literacy (of female entertainers) 60, 105, 106, 137
Love Duet 223, 227–31, 235, 236, 240, 242, 249; less sexually explicit 229
Lower Egypt 13, 19, 48–52, 65, 72, 78, 89, 91, 107, 114, 127, 150, 163, 165
Luxor 24, 54, 75, 91, 102, 112, 113, 134, 140

Maghibiyya of Luxor 79, 140, 143
Mahalla el-Kubra 49, 67, 89, 150, 228
Mamluks 15–17, 54, 150
mandara 67
Manfalut 53
The Manners and Customs of the Modern Egyptians 22, 27, 29, 37, 177
Marcellus, comte de 120, 224
Marmont, Auguste Frédéric Louis Viesse de 52, 211, 233, 234, 235; biography 24, 256
marriage (of female entertainers) 40, 44, 47, 72, 85, 102, 121, 127
Matarieh 52
mawâlid 59, 114; *see also* festivals
Maximillian, Herzoge, Duke of Bavaria 25, 34, 50, 53, *77*, 78
Mayer, Luigi (Ludwig) 5, *20*, 99, 107, 120, 181, 182, 205, 206, 216; biography 19–20, 256
Mayr, Heinrich von *77*, 185, 209; biography 25, 256
Mecca 57, 75, 105, 106, 172, 245

Medina 52, 105, 106, 172
Mediterranean Sea 9, 19, 49
Mengin, Felix 111
Menou, Gen. Jacques François 49, 62, 126, 151, 216
Michaud, Joseph F. 48, 64, 74, 77, 99, 153, 184, 193; biography 256; on dance locations 49, 50, 52, 75, 78, 94, 109, 114; on performance 60, 66, 106, 217, 227, 233, 235
military 15, 44, 91, 92, 100, 112, 138, 245; *see also* Mamluk
Milleliri, Jean-Marie 152, 154, 157
Minutoli, Wolfradine von Watzdorf freiherrn von 43, 50, 53, 54, 67, 93, 94, 207; biography 25, 256; on Nafissa 61, 62, 114
Minya 53, 78
modernization 16, 25, 26, 193, 248; of Egyptian dress 184
Montbard, Georges 55, 190, 210, *210*, 231, 233, 238; biography 21, 256–57
Montulé, Edouard de 60, 227
Morocco 105, 143, 196
mughaniyya 37
Muhammad Ali 27, 28, 49, 69, 84, 85, 92, 95, 245; biography 16; and dance ban 17, 65, 121, 148, 158–66; and employment of expatriates 25–26, 64; and guilds 109, 243; and taxation 111, 112
Mukattam Hills 52
music 24, 29, 35, 59, 62, 90, 94, 130, 149, 172, 173, 201, 202
musical instruments 24, 46, 70, 86, 105, 106, 120, 200, 221, 229; finger cymbals 23, 24, 85, 200, 201, 202, 206, 228, 240
musicians *19*, *20*, *21*, 39, 50, 67, 69, 78, 82, 83, 85, 90, 92, 95, 113, *162*, 163, 193; with dancers 22, 39, 40, 41, 53, 66, 74, 120, 128, 135, 136, 143, 163, 216, 219, 230, 234, 240; ensemble 200–201, 216; literacy 105; taxation 111; and Villoteau 62, 86, 149
Mutûbis 48, 49, 62, 126, 127

Nadir 50, 78, 114
Nafissa of Cairo 61, 62, 114
Napoleon Bonaparte 21, 49, 91, 151, 152, 156; era 2, 17, 43, 46, 50, 53, 71, 72, 83, 96, 182, 183, 223, 225; guild list 39, 85, 95, 109; invasion of Egypt 16, 149–50, 154, 155; and Savants 20, 24, 40, 67, 75, 86, 100, 107, 203, 228, 236
Ned Sili *20*, 99, 120, 216
Niebuhr, Carsten 19, 38, 74, 120, 170, 195; biography 13, 257
Nieuwkerk, Karin van 2, 3, 4, 10, 41, 45, 153, 161, 241
Nile River 1, 25, 48, 50, 52, 53, 75, 80, 84, 98, 113, 133, 144, 161, 166, 219, 248; drowning in 148, 151, 152, 155
Nora of Girga 126–27
nudity (in dance) 190, 193, *194*, 195, 232, 233, 234–35

occupation (of Egyptian women) 110, 117; of gypsies 170
Orientalism 3, 4, 18, 27
Ottoman empire 15, 16, 20, 25, 37, 46, 83, 92, 108, 109, 110, 113, 242

partnering in dance *13*, ***100***, 208, 215, 216
party 44, 58, 66–66, 112, 196, 200, 245; Appleton at 91; Bayle St. John at 90, 134; Blanc at 185, 194, 238, 224–25; Champollion at 27, 61, 83, 222; Curtis at 28; Dauzats at 24, 113, 226–27, 231; Didier at 63, 103; Duff Gordon at 62, 142, 195; Estourmel at 29, 227; Gérôme at 216, 239; Hackländer at 66–67, 228, 230; James St. John at 91; Michaud at 217; Voilquin at 67, 101; *see also* fantasia
Persian harp 38, 81, 171
plague 16, 24, 154, 156, 157
Poché, Christian 2, 10, 33, 45
Pococke, Richard *13*, 14, 34, 78, 183; biography 21, 257
police 89, 90, 93, 110, 111, 112, 129, 130, 136, 158, 159, 163, 164, 217
Popescu-Judetz, Eugenia 171
Prisse d'Avennes, Émile 28, 50, 52, 92, 109, 115, 121, 160, ***180***, 198, 209, 226, 229; on *The Bee* 231, 233, 234; biography 22–23, 257
prostitutes 26, 52, 78, 112, 115, 116, 153, 155, 161, 181, 243
prostitution 95–96, 111, 121, 154, 159, 160, 163, 165
proverbs 26, 43
punishment (of entertainers) 159–60; *see also* banishment
Pure Dance 223, 224–227, 239, 242, 243

Qena 45, 48, 52, 53, 54, 64, 76, 79, 103, 134–35, 140, 141, 143, 160, 195; and Badawiyya of 80, 144, 199, 217, 237
Qûs 52, 53, 74, 120, 220

raqqâsîn 38, 41, 70, 79, 159; defined 39, 40; at official functions 67; possible members 71, 135, 136, 138; at royal wedding 68–70
raqs Arabi 33
raqs baladi 1, 11, 33
raqs masri 33
raqs sharki 1, 33
Raymond, André 37, 38–39, 90, 108, 109, 110–11
Redouté, H.J. 24, 126, 208
research on Middle Eastern dance 2, 10, 12, 28, 37, 167, 242
retirement (of female entertainers) 115, 118, 120–21, 129
Rifaud, Jean Jacques *21*, 102, *102*, 257; biography 22, 257
Roberts, David *162*, 163, 181, 196, 209; biography 22, 257
Roma *see* gypsies
Romer, Isabella Frances 29, 53, 54, 115, 182, 197, 232; biography 258

Rosetta 48, 49, 50, 76, 88, 114, 231; Rosetta stone 27

Saffiya ("Little" Safiyya) 133, 134
Safiyya of Aswan 71, 138–39
Safiyya of Isna 34–35, 55, 116, 117, 144, 160; biography 127–29, 164; costume 184, 197; in performance 202, 209, 216, 218, 219, 225, 230
Said 'Abd al-Rachîm 53, 76
Said, Edward 27, 33
Saida (singer) 61
St. John, Bayle 44, 78, 82, 103, 107, 114, 116, 121, 163, 168, 170, 210, 221, 245; biography 26, 258; on Hasna of Qena 54, 91, 134; on Kala of Alexandria 71, 90, 129, 148, 216, 218, 220; on Kutchuk Hanem 52, 131, 132; on Safiyya of Isna 127, 128
St. John, James 50, 52, 55, 75, 92, 112, 114, 118, 121, 220, 221; biography 28, 258; on coffee houses 53, 78, 98; on early dance ban 159; on *Love Duet* 229–30
Sakna of Cairo (singer) 62–63, 120
Saleh, Magda Ahmed Abdel 5, 11, 33, 181, 238
Salt, Henry (consul) 26
Samannûd 78, 125
Sattin, Anthony 161
Saudi Arabia 3
Savant 20, 24, 38, 40, 67, 73, 86, 100, 107, 152, 228; *see also* Napoleon Bonaparte
Savary, Claude Étienne 34, 35, 48, 49, 60, 74, 94, 106, 118, 193–94, 195, 215, 227; on Badawiyya of Samannûd 78, 79, 125; biography 23, 258
Sawa, George 6
Sayyid Marsot, Afaf Lutfi Al 46, 47, 89, 92, 106, 165; terms for entertainers 37, 38; on women and economics 108, 110, 115, 116, 118
schools (for dancers) 50, 107
Sellers-Young, Barbara 3
sentimentality 22, 23
sexuality in dance 11, 22, 23, 215, 217, 218, 234, 248, 249
shaikha al-maghani 108, 109, 117, 120; Safiyya of Isna as 128
Shay, Anthony 3, 10
Shoshan, Boaz 116
singing 34, 35, 39, 41, 60, 61, 67, 68, 75, 76, 78, 100, 202, 220, 221, 226; in harem 94; and Islam 45; singing boys 83, 90; skill set in 106, 200, 201; *see also* Aziza bint Sathi; Sakna
Sinnûris 98, 139, ***139***, 140, ***141***
Sitt Madoula (landlady) 44, 103
slaves 15, 36, 59, 60, 116, 133, 172, 173; cost 66, 113; at royal wedding 69; training 105–106
Sonnini, Charles Nicolas Sigisbert 34, 50, 53, 54, 76, 78, 89, 90; biography 27, 258
Stanhope, Hester Lucy 258
status (of entertainers) 35, 37, 40, 43, 46, 47, 60, 62, 74, 78, 85, 94, 153, 248
Steingass, Francis Joseph 38
Sudan 3, 55, 79, 92, 115, 137, 138

Suez Canal 13, 18, 25, 53, 67, 80, 81, 131, 161, 187, 243, 248
sword dance 80, *142*, 143, 193, 209, 236–38, 243; at royal wedding 69, 85
Syria 26, 79, 103, 112, 131, 155, 156, 165, 171

tambourine dance 183, *194*, 210, 236, 243
Tanta 48, 72, *73*, 113, 114–15, 127, 163, 164, 166, 245
taxation 39, 47, 90, 91, 94, 95, 108, 110–12, 118, 158, 163, 165, 243
Taylor, Isidore Justin Severin 24, 35, 224, 228, 230
Testas, Willem de Famars 140, *141*, 258
textiles 196–99
Thompson, William Irwin 147
tipping 113–14, 221
Tonino Bey 80, 143
transvestite *see* gink; khawal
Tucker, Judith 45, 109, 110, 116
Turkey 46, 83, 167, 170, 171, 184

Upper Egypt 48, 53, 55, 74, 76, *77*, 78, 83, 89, 93, 248; costumes in 186, 197; and dance ban 50, 52, 72, 75, 80, 113, 136, 159, 160, 162; and Ethiopian dancers 79; and invasion of Egypt 16, 150, 155; police 90; tax farm in 112

veiling 46, 47, 69, 100, 126, 136, 194, 195, 196, 234, 235, 237, 238; of female musicians 120; hat with 183; of singers 62, 63, 85

venereal disease 152, 155, 156
Villoteau, Guillaume 60, 107, 114, 120, 206, 228–29; biography 24, 258; on definitions 35, 38, 40; on finger cymbals 201, 202; on male musicians 74, 85, 86, 105; on "missing 'awâlim" 62, 149, 150
Voilquin, Suzanne 67–68, 83, 94, 101, 102, 232, 234, 235; biography 24, 258
Volney, Constantin François 34, 35, 215, 259

Walther, Wiebke 105–106, 172
Warburton, Eliot 127
wedding 2, 45, 59, 61, 74, 82, 89, 94, *102*, 232, 237, 245, 246, 247; at Asyût 53, 186; at Damietta 222; ginks and khawals at 84–85; at Mahalla el-Kubra 49, 67–68, 103, 228; procession 38, 82, 130; proverb 43; and raqqâsin 40, 70; rope dancing at 65; tax on 110
Wehr, Hans 37
Wilkinson, Sir Gardner 160, 161, 259
Winter, Michael 108
women writers 29

Xenobi *see* Zanuba of Isna

Zanuba of Isna 107, 133, 134, 200, 201
Zanuba of Mutûbis 126, 127
zar 167
Zaynab of Luxor 140, 143
Zuhur, Sherifa 2, 3, 33